The War in the Air
Volume 3

The War in the Air
Volume 3

A History of the RFC & RNAS in Africa, the Air Raids on Britain & on the Western Front 1916-17 including the Battles of Arras

ILLUSTRATED

H. A. Jones

LEONAUR

The War in the Air
Volume 3
A History of the RFC & RNAS in Africa, the Air Raids on Britain & on the Western Front 1916-17 including the Battles of Arras
by H. A. Jones

ILLUSTRATED

First published under the title
The War in the Air Volume 3

Leonaur is an imprint of Oakpast Ltd

Copyright in this form © 2018 Oakpast Ltd

ISBN: 978-1-78282-782-5 (hardcover)
ISBN: 978-1-78282-783-2 (softcover)

http://www.leonaur.com

Publisher's Notes

The views expressed in this book are not necessarily those of the publisher.

Contents

ADDENDA AND CORRIGENDA FOR VOLUME 1

Entered by H. A. Jones in Volume 3

p. 96. Statements relative to first flight over England. Note. A report of a Committee of the Royal Aero Club, published in January 1929, records the opinion that Lieutenant-Colonel J. T. C. Moore-Brabazon, M.C., made the first free flight in England, during the week-end 30th of April—2nd of May 1909, free flight being defined as occurring 'when the machine, having left the ground, is maintained in the air by its own power on a level or upward path for a distance beyond that over which gravity and air resistance would sustain it'.

p. 189, top line. For August 1913 read July 1913.

p. 227, 'A' and 'B' Flights of No. 4 Squadron flew from Eastchurch direct to Amiens on the 13th of August 1914. 'C Flight went to Dover from Netheravon on the same day.

p. 240, line 10. For Lieutenant Corballis read Lieutenant Rabagliati

p. 246, line 9. For 4.0 a.m., read 4.0 p.m.

p. 253, line 8. For left wing read right wing

p. 313, line 2 from bottom. For Pierse read Peirse

Preface

This third volume tells of the part played by aircraft in the destruction of the *Königsberg*, and in the campaigns against German East Africa and German South-West Africa; gives an account of the air attacks on Great Britain, 1914-16; reviews the problems of supply, administration, recruitment, and training, 1914-16; and outlines the air developments and operations on the Western Front in the winter of 1916-17, and during the Battle of Arras, 1917.

In the compilation of the account of the airship raids on Great Britain, the author has been helped by the official air-raid reports, produced during the war under the direction of Lieutenant-Colonel H. G. de Watteville. To check his account, the author visited Berlin where, through the courtesy of the President of the *Marinearchiv*, he studied the original reports of the naval airship commanders for the period not yet covered by the published German official naval history. The President also placed at the author's disposal the services of a former Zeppelin commander. The records of the military airships are in the care of the President of the *Reichsarchiv*, Potsdam, who gave the author unrestricted access to the reports from the outbreak of war. For the willing and frank help given by these officers he expresses his gratitude.

The author had conversations with surviving war-time Zeppelin commanders, and he also took the opportunity to compare notes with *Reichsarchiv* officials who are concerned with research into military air operations in France and other theatres of war.

The German airship reports confirm in general, but not in detail, the British air-raid reports. The Zeppelin commanders had to face many difficulties. They set out on their long journeys with no reliable knowledge of the weather conditions over the British Isles. Slight miscalculations of the changes of wind strength and direction led to errors of navigation which are reflected in the places named as bombing targets in the commanders' reports. Nor was there much opportunity to check navigation by direct observation. It is clear that the airship crews were continuously baffled by the darkening of English cities. The German directional wireless stations were not of much help. The angle subtended by the bearings obtained when an airship made a wireless call for her position was, of necessity, narrow, and the resultant calculation was, at best approximate, and, sometimes, definitely inaccurate.

The British air-raid reports were compiled from information obtained through wireless stations, from intelligence sources, and from direct observation, supplemented by the check afforded by the dropping of bombs.

The air-raid maps which accompany the volume are printed as they were compiled during the war, with the exception that the author has been able to identify all the military airships, about which we were often uncertain, and to confirm the identity, in a very few doubtful instances, of naval airships. Where a study of the German records has indicated a possible minor inaccuracy in the maps, a note has been added.

In this volume the author is concerned with the activities of the airships in their attacks on Great Britain. He was, however, impressed by the records of the great amount of reconnaissance and other work accomplished by naval airships over the North Sea. The reader should remember that the air raids were a part only of the operations of the German naval airship fleet.

The author has, once again, to thank those officers who have commented on his narrative, and to record his indebtedness to Professor D. Nichol Smith who read the volume in proof.

Above all, he testifies to the courteous and continuous help he has received from the Director and Staff of the Air Historical Branch.

H. A. Jones.

CHAPTER 1

Flying Operations in German East and South-West Africa

Germany emerged from the scramble for Africa towards the end of the nineteenth, and the beginning of the twentieth century, with two considerable and two minor territories. The first colony to be founded, and the best suited to European settlement, was in South-West Africa, where, in 1883, a Bremen merchant had established a trading station at Angra Pequeña. In the following year the district which had been assigned to this adventurer by local treaty was taken under the direct protection of the German emperor. In this same year, 1884, Germany got a footing in Togoland and in the Cameroons, and, on the other side of the continent, three enterprising young Germans pushed inland from the Swahili coast and made a treaty with a Usambara chieftain which proved to be the modest beginning of a German sphere of influence that was to extend inland to the great lakes of Victoria, Tanganyika, and Nyanza over an area nearly double the size of Germany.

The most comprehensive of the many agreements about German territory in Africa was that concluded between Great Britain and Germany on the 1st of July 1890. By this time German South-West Africa embraced an area two and a half times as large as the United Kingdom, or more than half as large again as Germany. Articles of this agreement ceded Heligoland to Germany in return for her recognition of a British protectorate over Witu and the islands of Zanzibar and Pemba.

THE *KÖNIGSBERG* OPERATIONS

On the eve of war, the light cruiser *Königsberg* was lying in the

THE RUF

KÖNIGSBERG

July

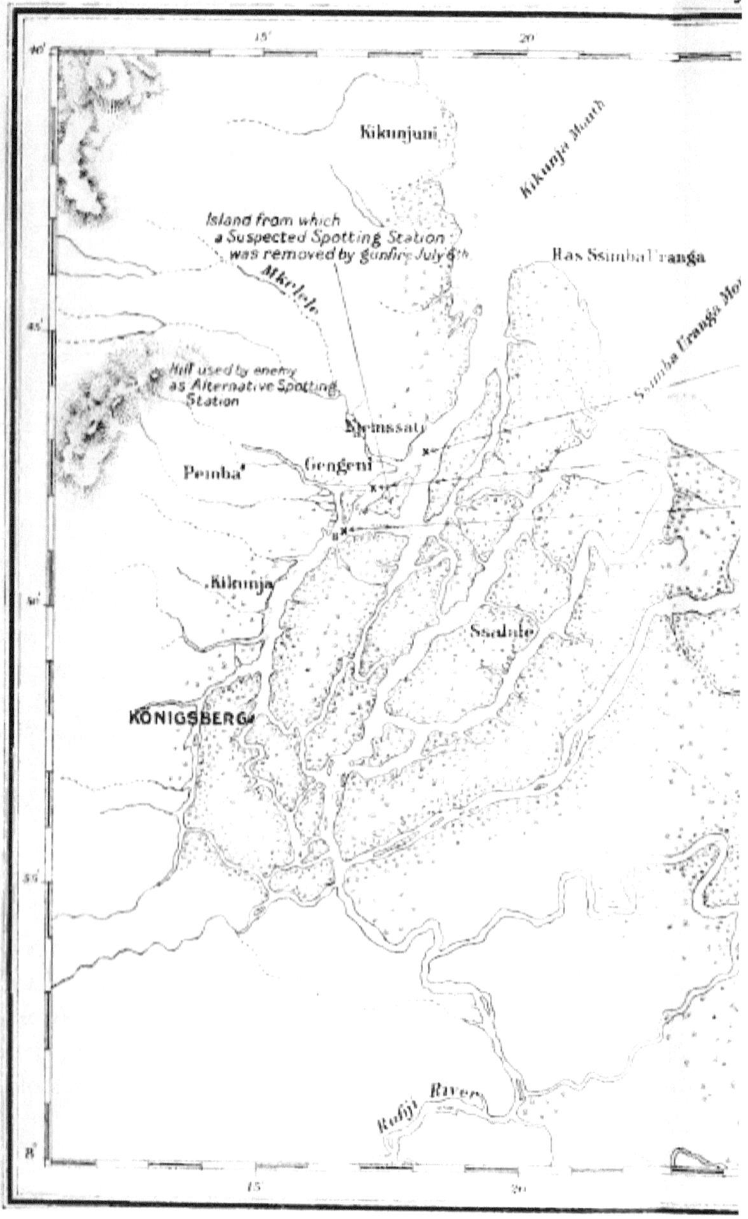

IJI DELTA.
OPERATIONS.
1915.

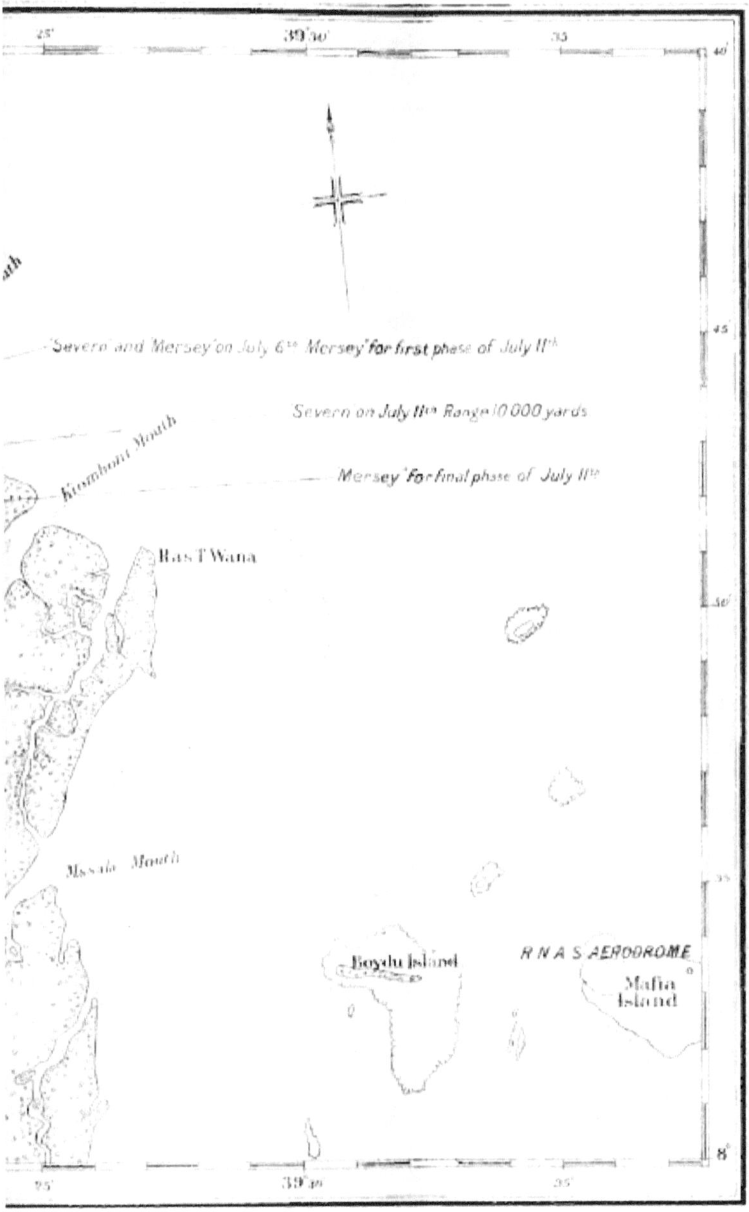

harbour of Dar-es-Salaam, the capital of the German East African Protectorate, and it was against this ship that the first flying operations of the war, in this territory, were made. The German cruiser did not await the rupture of peace. On the 31st of July 1914 she put to sea in readiness for a raiding cruise in the Indian Ocean, and at the beginning of August she was operating in the Gulf of Aden. For a spell she disappeared, but on the 20th of September she was back, unexpectedly, off Zanzibar, where she surprised and sank the British light cruiser *Pegasus*. The raider was then lost again until the end of October 1914, when she was reliably reported to be lying up the Rufiji delta.

Her commander could not have chosen a more inaccessible spot. The delta forms some two hundred square miles of swamp, a maze of channels dotted with mangrove-tangled islands and treacherous with shifting sand and mud banks. It was impossible to say in which of the five fairly-well-defined main tideways the *Königsberg* was. Nothing of her was visible from the sea, nor was surface reconnaissance easy as the coastal flats between the mouths were manned by the enemy. The collier *Newbridge* was sunk by the British cruiser *Chatham* in the likeliest of the channels, but the blockading of all the tideways would have immobilised a fleet. Nothing effective, indeed, could be done until the exact location of the German cruiser was known.

Just before the outbreak of war a civilian pilot, Mr. H. D. Cutler, had been giving exhibition flights, off the beach at Durban, in two ninety horse-power Curtiss flying-boats, the property of Mr. Gerard Hudson, a South African mining engineer. Before the war was many days old one of the flying-boats had been taken over by the Commander-in-Chief of the Cape Station, Vice-Admiral H. G. King-Hall, and Mr. Cutler had been given a commission in the Naval Air Service. Here, then, was a means for finding out the position of the *Königsberg*, and the *Kinfauns Castle*, which had been converted as an auxiliary cruiser, was sent round to the Cape to fetch the flying-boat and her pilot. They were embarked at Simonstown on the 6th of November 1914, but soon after the auxiliary cruiser left port she ran into stormy weather, and the ailerons on the flying-boat were smashed by the heavy seas. A wireless message was sent to Mr. Hudson asking him to strip the ailerons from the second flying-boat and have them packed ready for the *Kinfauns Castle* to take on board as she passed Durban. This was done.

A midshipman, A. N. Gallehawk, was appointed to be Flight Sub-Lieutenant Cutler's observer, and on the journey up the coast he helped to get the flying-boat ready for use. When the party disembarked at the proposed base, the tiny island of Niororo, eighteen miles off the Rufiji coast south of Zanzibar, it was found that the hull of the flying-boat was leaking and that the sun's heat upset the carburation. For two days the officers worked on repairs, and on the 22nd of November Cutler, flying alone, was just able to get the craft into the air.

This month brings the north-east monsoon to the Swahili coast, with high temperatures and tropical rains. The sky was lowering as Cutler rose above the water, but he headed for the Rufiji in his first reconnaissance attempt. The flying-boat was not fitted with a compass, and the pilot made the coast too far south. Almost at once the storm broke, but Cutler flew up and down the coast vainly searching for the delta until his petrol was nearly finished, when he turned out to sea again. He could now find no trace of the *Kinfauns Castle*, and he was compelled at last to alight on the beach of an uninhabited island. Thence he was rescued by the merest chance.

The crew of a captured enemy *dhow* reported they had seen the aircraft well south of the Rufiji, and this slender clue put the auxiliary cruiser on his track. A hole had been knocked in the hull of the flying-boat on the rough foreshore: it took two days before this was repaired, and then Cutler tried again. This time he had better luck. He made a wide search of the delta and discovered the *Königsberg* about twelve miles up one of the main tideways. She was close to the bank, well hidden by the trees, but headed downstream with fires alight and all guns in position, evidently alert to take her chances of a sortie. When the pilot returned with his news he was not readily believed, as captured German charts showed no water for a ship of the *Königsberg's* displacement beyond four miles from the mouth. It was considered desirable that another reconnaissance should be made at low water, and that Cutler should be given, if the flying-boat would respond, the help of a trained naval observer.

But the flying-boat, hull leaking, would not respond, and the hull of the fellow boat at Durban was sent for. Ten days passed before this arrived and was fitted, with the help of the ship's blacksmith, and then Cutler flew over the delta for the second time carrying Captain D. B. Crampton, R.N., of the *Kinfauns Castle* in the observer's seat. The reconnaissance was successful, and the truth of the original observation was confirmed. It had been hoped that once the German cruiser was located, the *Chatham* would be able, with the help of observation from the flying-boat, to tackle her at once, but the air report made it clear that she was well out of range of the British cruiser's guns.

Another reconnaissance, a few days later, made at low tide to see how far sandbanks might impede the raider from coming out, disclosed that she had shifted her berth about a mile and a half into the next tideway. Meanwhile the *Chatham*, the only ship in these waters that could effectively tackle the *Königsberg* if she came out, had gone off temporarily to Mombasa. If the German raider was indeed making her way down the river, there was every likelihood she would escape. For a few anxious days it was impossible to get the flying-boat off the sea, made turbulent by the monsoon, but on the 10th of December Cutler took a chance offered by a lull in the weather and went off alone. The hull of the flying-boat was now in such poor condition that leaking could not be prevented and no observer could be carried.

Cutler had got no farther than a mile down the tideway when his engine failed and he was forced down in the mouth of the river, where his seaplane went aground about fifty yards from the shore. The pilot pumped petrol into the top tank with the hand-pressure pump, and he was about to crank the engine when rifle fire was opened from the bank and the engine was hit and put out of action. Cutler's descent was seen from the tug *Helmouth*, which was lying about ten miles off the entrance to the Rufiji, and Midshipman Gallehawk was sent off in a motor-boat to rescue his pilot, although there was little hope he could arrive in time.

Cutler, meanwhile, unable to set fire to the flying-boat, threw overboard everything he could detach, and it was not long before three Germans and about fifteen *askari* (native soldiers; not a distinct tribe), were wading out to him. Within a few minutes he was a prisoner and the *askari*, under the guidance of the Germans, were dragging the flying-boat ashore. They succeeded in getting it about thirty yards up the beach, and some of them hurried inland with their prisoner, who reports that as they penetrated into the bush they passed several Germans moving down to reinforce the small post on the river.

A little later Cutler heard the tug's guns in action, and he learned afterwards from a German officer what happened. The motor-boat, supported by the tug's fire, dashed in and Midshipman Gallehawk, wading through the mud, made fast a line to the flying-boat. With difficulty, under continuous rifle fire, the rescuing party got the flying-boat off, and it was delivered, in a sinking condition, to the *Kinfauns Castle*. It had been wrecked beyond repair, and it was eventually given an honoured place in the Durban Museum. So, ended the first attempts to keep watch on the *Königsberg*. There may be more striking incidents in the history of naval aircraft in the war; there are few which, for quiet gallantry, can beat this story of an under-powered flying-boat, patched and repatched, made fit for service first with the ailerons and then with the hull of its fellow, operating in monsoon weather, from the beach of a tropical island, over jungle swamp.

******

> Flight Sub-Lieutenant Cutler remained a prisoner of war until November 1917, when, with other prisoners, he was left behind by the retreating enemy. During the rapid war of movement which began in the spring of 1916 the prisoners lived a nomadic life in the bush. They suffered much from fever and from lack of food, and their privations in the rainy season were extreme. 'Though we had a pretty hard time,' says Cutler, 'we could not complain much at our treatment as the Germans themselves had to live under almost similar conditions.'

******

The admiral now knew what he must ask for from home before he could tackle the destruction of the *Königsberg*. He suggested, besides seaplanes for bombing, a ship of light draught and heavy armament. The Admiralty had, at the moment, no monitors ready and to spare, but they at once set about the formation of a small flight of bombing aircraft. The intention was to send out Short folder seaplanes, with Canton Unné engines, but these could not be got ready in time, and in their stead two Sopwith seaplanes, with 100 horse-power Monosoupape-Gnome engines, were loaded in the *Persia* and sent by the Red Sea route under the command of Flight Lieutenant J. T. Cull. The party included a second pilot, Flight Lieutenant H. E. M. Watkins, and eighteen ratings, some of them specially skilled men from the Lang propeller works and from Sopwiths, graded as petty officers or leading mechanics.

The *Persia* left Tilbury on the 16th of January 1915 and arrived at Bombay on the 8th of February. There the Sopwiths were erected and tested, and the air detachment was then transferred to the *Kinfauns Castle* for Niororo island, where it arrived on the 21st of February. One of the Sopwiths was got out at once and loaded with bombs. The capabilities of these seaplanes, which were of a new type, were as yet vaguely understood, and the first attempt to get off the water was made with a load of two 50-lb. and four 16-lb. bombs, full petrol, and an observer. This proved hopeless. By a process of elimination, spread over four days, not unattended by mishaps, one of the seaplanes at last got away with only the pilot, without bombs, and with but one hour's supply of petrol. Even then the seaplane would not go above 1,500 feet, and all hopes of the immediate destruction of the *Königsberg* by bombing vanished.

There was little prospect, however, of getting other seaplanes for some time, and many devices were tried to improve the performance of the two Sopwiths. But before the first week had passed one of them had been wrecked beyond repair, and by that time it was clear that the Monosoupape engine, dependent for its air-supply on the opening of the exhaust valve and the passage of air through the nosepiece, was unsuited to the rarefied atmosphere of a tropical climate. Further, in the scorching air, propellers warped and burst, glue melted, rubber tubing shrivelled, and the bottoms of the floats peeled off. Nor did the personnel escape. Some of the mechanics, misled by the impunity with which the old island chief and his wives squatted for hours on the beach, paddled between the beach and the seaplane with the minimum of clothing, and many of them, for days afterwards, were laid aside in picric acid bandages.

The method of getting the seaplane off the water may be mentioned. It was hoisted out, wings folded. The pilot and observer would then unfold the wings while an attendant whaler stood by ready to tow the seaplane clear. When it was clear, the observer would start up the engine, and as the seaplane could not be induced to rise if he remained he would take a header over the side and swim to the whaler. This procedure worked for a time, but an incident towards the end of April made it unpopular. One of the pilots, as he was about to take off, caught sight of a shark's fin breaking surface ahead of his swimming comrade. His urgent signals attracted the swimmer, who was able to get back to the safety of the floats.

Meanwhile, in March 1915, news had arrived that other aircraft and personnel were on their way from home, and at the beginning of April they reached Durban in the armed liner *Laconia*. The naval air detachment went south from Niororo to bring up the new reinforcements. When the cases were unpacked the aircraft proved to be three Short seaplanes, at once recognised as old friends long since left behind at the Isle of Grain air station. These, the only seaplanes that could be spared, were in poor condition, and much work would be necessary before they could be made fit for flying. The detachment went back to Niororo, where they arrived on the 23rd of April.

It was soon clear that the Shorts, although middle-aged, would be good enough for reconnaissance work, and on the first flight over the Rufiji, made on the 25th of April, the *Königsberg* was successfully located a dozen miles up the north or Kikunja channel. She made good shooting at the Short while the observer, Air Mechanic E. H. A. Boggis, was taking photographs. (The original detachment had brought out from England a 7x5 Goerz Anschutz camera.) On the way back the seaplane, which refused to go much above 600 feet, came under rifle fire from the banks, and a chance bullet tore away the air intakes and closed the main oil pipe. The pilot, Flight Commander Cull, was forced down, but the seaplane was towed safely home, and when the photographic plates were developed they gave clear views of the cruiser.

Other successful reconnaissances followed from time to time, the observer's seat often being occupied by the Flag-Commander, the Hon. R. O. B. Bridgeman. During one of these coastal reconnaissances a Short, flown by Flight Lieutenant H. E. M. Watkins, was brought down by a shot from the beach and was wrecked when it hit the water. When the Short became overdue, Flight Commander Cull took up another seaplane in search and came upon the wreckage with the pilot and observer clinging to one of the floats. There were no ships in sight, and as there was danger from sharks and from enemy craft Cull alighted, picked up the pilot and his passenger, and taxied with them out to sea for some miles until he fell in with a patrolling whaler.

It was as much as the Shorts could do to get to the Rufiji, and there was still no prospect of attacking the German cruiser with bombs. Unwilling to accept a period of threatened stagnation, Commander Bridgeman planned to torpedo the *Königsberg* with the help of the air service personnel and a motor-boat which had recently arrived for their use. The motor-boat was fitted with a super-silencer and torpedo-dropping gear, and it was proposed that it should be navigated, at night, within striking distance of the *Königsberg*, when a torpedo would be released. The attack was rehearsed, but just when everything was ready for the attempt news came of the impending arrival of two monitors and of further reinforcements of aeroplanes and seaplanes.

At the beginning of June 1915, the two six-inch monitors, *Severn* (Captain E. J. A. Fullerton, R.N.) and *Mersey* (Commander R. A. Wilson, R.N.) reached Mafia after an adventurous voyage from Malta. Meanwhile steps had been taken to provide a landing-ground for the aeroplanes on Mafia island. (A German island, it had been occupied by troops from Mombasa in January 1915.) The site was not very desirable, but it was the only possible one. In its original state it was covered with, short trees and scrub which spread into a swamp at one end. The inhabitants of the island were organised to clear the ground, and attempts, which proved useless, were made to drain the swamp. The Public Works Department at Zanzibar, pressed into the scheme, had erected a serviceable corrugated iron hangar by the 20th of June and had also built grass and corrugated iron huts for the personnel.

On the 18th of June the *Laurentic* had arrived bringing the Naval Air Service reinforcements under Squadron Commander R. Gordon. The aeroplanes were two Henri Farmans of steel construction, fitted with 140 horse-power Canton Unné engines, and two Caudrons (80 horse-power Gnome engines). The packing cases which contained the aeroplanes and spares, weighing two tons apiece, were floated shorewards on two naval cutters lashed together, dragged, pulled, and lifted through the surf by the natives and laboriously trundled up the mile and a half of jungle path to the aerodrome.

The ships and the aircraft were now on the spot, but the task before them was a novel one. To destroy a ship of war, concealed twelve miles up a defended tropical estuary, by the combined action of shallow-draught vessels and aeroplanes required organisation and rehearsal. Consultations between the captains of the monitors, the gunnery experts of the fleet, and the flying officers took place, and a simple spotting system, based on the clock-code, was evolved, and experimental dummy attacks were made. During the exercises two of the aeroplanes, one of each type, were wrecked.

The admiral decided to open his attack without further loss of time, before the coming of the monsoon, and all was ready for the operation on the morning of the 6th of July, which dawned fine. Reconnaissances made from time to time during the period of preparation showed that the *Königsberg* was still in position, trim, and alert as ever. The two monitors entered the Kikunja mouth of the Rufiji at 5.20 a.m. on the 6th of July and began to work their way up river under desultory fire from both banks. To cover the ships while they were taking up their firing positions, the Caudron aeroplane, piloted by Flight Lieutenant Watkins, aimed bombs at the German cruiser from 6,000 feet, but no hits were scored. At 6.5 a.m., before the Caudron left to return to Mafia, the Henri Farman (Flight Commander Cull and Flight Sub-Lieutenant H. J. Arnold) arrived over the monitors ready to spot the fire. There was, however, an initial delay.

A strong current, running towards the entrance, swung the anchored *Severn* out of position, and it was not until 6.48 a.m. that she opened fire, at a range of 11,000 yards, the *Mersey* following almost at once. Nothing of the enemy cruiser could be seen from the British ships. The *Severn's* first salvo was reported from the aeroplane to be 200 yards short and to the left. For the next twelve minutes a steady fire was kept up, but no direct hits were reported. Then the *Königsberg* began to reply with rapid four and five gun salvos. Thanks to a German observation post, concealed in a tree of a nearby island, that went undetected for the first hour, her fire was accurate and the monitors were several times straddled. After three-quarters of an hour a shell struck the forward 6-inch gun of the *Mersey*, killing four of her crew, knocking out the remainder, and all but exploding the magazine; another shell sank a motor-boat alongside. The *Mersey* then shifted her berth and had only just got clear when a salvo burst on the spot where she had been anchored.

The *Severn*, meanwhile, kept up her fire and, at 7.51 a.m., was rewarded with a wireless message from the aeroplane that she had made her first direct hit. For the next twenty minutes her fire was consistently good. News of five or six further direct hits came down from the observer, the remaining shots being reported mostly just over. At 8.10 a.m. the *Mersey* joined in once more, but the fire of both monitors was now reported off the target. From the time that the *Mersey* reopened fire the spotting was taken over by the Caudron (Flight Lieutenant V. G. Blackburn and Assistant Paymaster H. G. Badger), which had left Mafia again at 7.37 a.m. The *Königsberg's* salvos were now falling so close to the *Severn* that Captain Fullerton decided to shift his position and open the range. This decision to move came just in time, as a similar one had done for the *Mersey*,

As the *Severn* got under way, a closely-grouped salvo burst in her wake. Soon after she moved, a platform and khaki figures were seen from the monitor in the mangroves about 400 yards from the ship. Three three-pounder shells brought the platform down and three 6-inch lyddite shells, dropped into the position from point-blank range, made a quick end of the observation post that had given the *Königsberg* her accuracy. The fire from the German cruiser, from now onwards, fell away, although it was clear there was an alternative spotting post, probably on Pemba Hill, but certainly some distance off. The *Severn* again anchored, and firing at the longer range was reopened at 9.50 a.m. At the same time the Caudron was relieved by the Henri

Farman, flown by Squadron Commander R. Gordon, with Flight Sub-Lieutenant Arnold as his observer. Unfortunately, the wireless communication between the aeroplane and the monitors now broke down, and the ships thereupon shifted closer in to get direct observation from the foretop, but this also failed.

The Caudron reappeared at 11.45 a.m. but had to go back almost at once with a failing engine. At 1.40 p.m. the Henri Farman arrived on the scene once more and took up the spotting on fire being re-opened at 2.30 p.m., but the results were now disappointing. All the shots were reported well short of their target, but, as was subsequently discovered, the air observer was deceived. It was not at the time realised that the mud and mangrove swamp in the neighbourhood of the *Königsberg* was so soft that the fuse in the lyddite shells fired by the monitors was often not detonated. The shells so falling were difficult or impossible to observe, and some of them reported as short were well over. Nothing further of note was achieved and the monitors retired about 4.0 p.m. The two aeroplanes, which had been fired at throughout the day by the German cruiser, had totalled fifteen hours in the air, and one of the observers had been up for nine hours. The *Königsberg* had been hit and damaged, but she had not been destroyed, and air, reconnaissances during the next few days left no doubt that the operation must be repeated.

Time was pressing. If the monsoon broke, the co-operation of the aeroplanes might prove impossible. The enemy daily expected a renewal of the attack, but at dawn, and they were therefore taken by surprise when, at midday on the 11th of July, the monitors re-entered the tideway. Once again, however, the *Königsberg* was well served by her forward observation posts, and she soon began to drop salvo after salvo close enough to the *Severn* to cover her with Rufiji slime before she had a chance to fire a shot.

★★★★★

> Prisoners stated that a German officer was within thirty yards of the *Severn*, in a tub buried in the mud, with only his head showing. He was connected by telephone with the *Königsberg*, but the line was cut at the cruiser's end by one of the early shots fired by the monitor.

★★★★★

Flight Commander Cull with Flight Sub-Lieutenant Arnold had left Mafia Island about 11.50 a.m. Only the anchored *Severn* was to be spotted for as the *Mersey* was to keep moving in an attempt to draw the enemy's fire. The gunners on the *Königsberg*, however, were not deceived, and they concentrated on the *Severn*, which fired her first salvo at 12.30 p.m. at a range of 10,000 yards.

The observer in the aeroplane, which was flying about 3,000 feet, reported that he saw nothing of the monitor's first and second salvos. The sights were thereupon brought down 400 yards, but the next three salvos were likewise unobserved. The sights were brought down again, and the eighth salvo fell in the river close to the *Königsberg*: the next salvo scored a hit. The aeroplane observer continued to report hits from 12.42 p.m. A few minutes later an enemy shell exploded near the aeroplane, almost putting her out of control, and splinters carried away two of the cylinders. The engine stopped and the pilot had no choice but to alight in the river. Flight Commander Cull said:

> We started planing down towards the *Mersey* as, though the *Severn* was much nearer, I did not want to interfere with her fire just now though all the shots were falling before the forebridge of the *Königsberg*,
>
> On our way down, Flight Sub-Lieutenant Arnold continued very coolly sending corrections, and gave one very important one ("H.T. All 'forward"), bringing the *Severn* shots from forward to amidships, and we had the satisfaction of seeing shells falling on the middle of the *Königsberg* before we lost sight of her. He also informed the *Mersey* we were hit and asked them to send a boat.'

The aeroplane touched the water about a hundred yards from the *Mersey* and turned over: the observer was thrown clear, but the pilot went under entangled in his belt and the wreckage. He got clear after a struggle, and both officers were eventually picked up by the boat from the *Mersey*,

Meanwhile, as the aeroplane was going down, the *Severn*, profiting by the observer's last message, trained her guns farther aft, and almost at once an explosion rent the German cruiser. Although observation from the air was now cut off, the *Königsberg* was burning fiercely and columns of black and yellow smoke made her position clear to the monitor. Unobserved fire continued and was rewarded from time to time by the distant boom of further explosions.

At 1.40 p.m. the *Mersey* was ordered to pass ahead of the *Severn* and close to 7,000 yards from the *Königsberg*. Four minutes later the Caudron (Flight Lieutenant Watkins, pilot, Lieutenant A. G. Bishop, observer) was over the *Mersey* ready to take up the spotting again. The German cruiser now offered a sorry spectacle to the airmen. Her middle funnel had been blown away and she was enveloped in flames aft. The *Mersey*, with the help of the aeroplane, got a direct hit with her third salvo, and after twenty-five further salvos had been poured into the battered cruiser she was blazing so fiercely from stem to stern that further firing seemed unnecessary. At 2.20 p.m. the monitors retired, firing at both banks as they passed out of the tideway.

Next day the fleet returned to Zanzibar. From there the *Laconia* went to Mombasa to put ashore the Naval Air Service personnel for service up country in the land campaign against German East Africa. At Mombasa they found, awaiting them, two Caudron aeroplanes and three Short seaplanes which had recently arrived from England. The airmen had not seen the last of the Rufiji. The admiral was anxious for a final reconnaissance of the *Königsberg*, and one of the Caudrons was sent back from Mombasa to Mafia. The reconnaissance was made in the beginning of August, and the report and photographs showed that the cruiser had a list of about fifteen degrees, with her starboard battery under water. Her quarterdeck was red with rust, which meant it was submerged at high tide, the top masts were gone, her centre funnel was heaped across the ship, and the observers could state definitely that she would never take the sea again.

There was, however, one disturbing feature. A lighter, lying alongside the vessel, seemed to be taking off her guns.

★★★★★★

The salved guns were ten 4.1 inch and a number of lighter calibre as well as machine-guns. They did good service in the ensuing land campaign. (See *Kreuzerfahrt und Buschkampf*, by Vice-Admiral Max Looff, which gives a first-hand account of the destruction of the *Königsberg* and the subsequent adventures of her survivors.)

★★★★★★

That this would probably happen had been expected, but it was not considered possible to do anything to prevent it at the time. As soon as the air report was received, bombing of the lighter was ordered, but before this could be done the Naval Air Service had to be diverted for urgent work up-country.

German South-West Africa

On the 6th of July 1915, the day on which the monitors dealt their first blow against the *Königsberg*, the campaign against the German colony in South-West Africa came to an end. It was only in the final stage of the operations that aircraft and Naval Air Service armoured cars played a part, but their co-operation derives interest from the climatic and topographical difficulties of the country.

German South-West Africa was naturally fortified against invasion. The thousand miles of fog-bound coastline is flanked by a wide belt of waterless sand dunes considered by the German colonists to constitute an impassable barrier. Another 'thirst belt' on the south and the Kalahari Desert on the east contributed to the equanimity of the defenders. The colony was well prepared for war. The small but highly-trained force of German regulars and reservists was abundantly supplied with munitions, and had, in addition, the help of two aeroplanes which had arrived in the country before the war. Had the troops been led with the same skill and determination as their comrades in East Africa the campaign would, possibly, have been greatly prolonged.

When the Union Expeditionary Force began operations against German South-West Africa at the beginning of September 1914 no aircraft were immediately available. The nucleus of a South African Aviation Corps had been formed before the war, and in August 1914 a small group of South African officers was in training at Farnborough in England. These officers went into action in France with the original squadrons of the Royal Flying Corps, but in November 1914 Captain G. P. Wallace, the senior of the South African officers, had been recalled from France to England to form a flying unit for service in German South-West Africa.

At this time Henri Farman in Paris was building an aeroplane, constructed mainly of steel-tubing, which, fitted with the Canton Unné engine, seemed suitable for tropical flying, and an order for twelve was given by the Admiralty, delivery of the aeroplanes being promised for the end of February 1915. The remaining South African officers returned from France meanwhile, and two of them were sent to South Africa to recruit men and to prepare a base aerodrome.

There were delays in the production of the Henri Farmans. The first was delivered in January 1915, but only two more had been received by the end of March. On the 15th of March twenty-six mechanics, directly enlisted or transferred from the Naval Air Service, left, with transport and other material, for South Africa, and on the 3rd of April Captain Wallace, two other officers, and eight mechanics followed with the balance of the material and with the aeroplanes. These

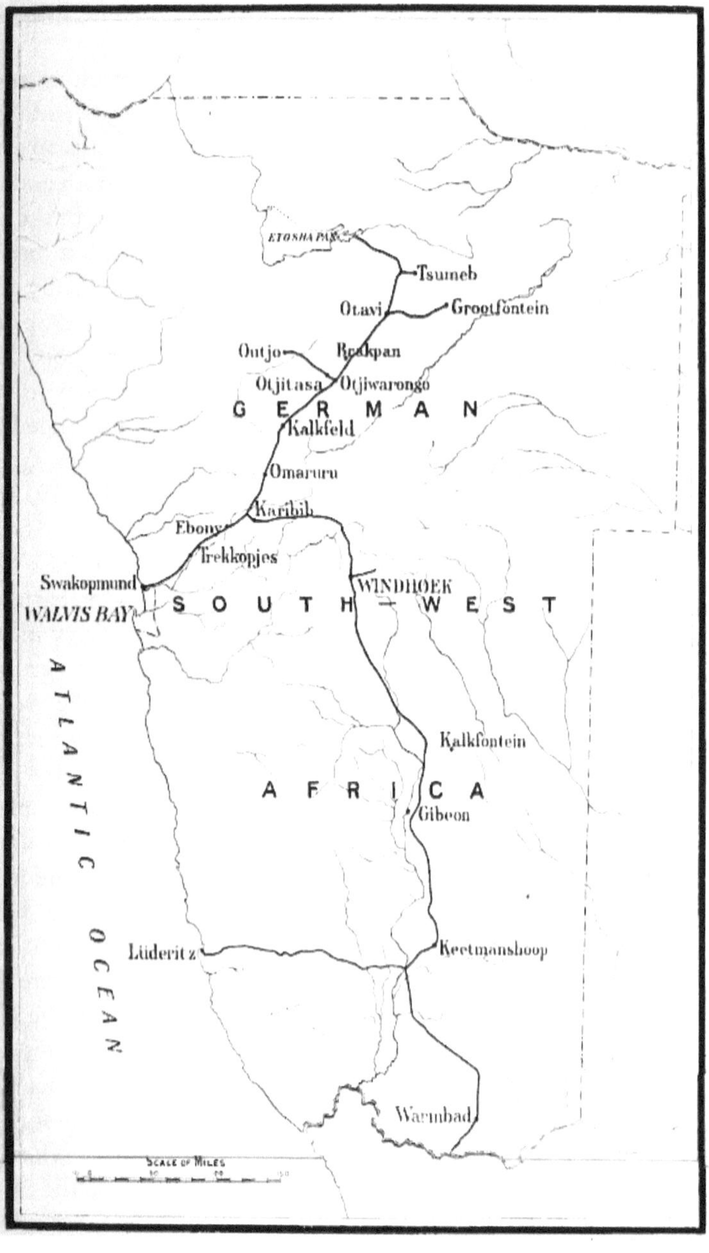

ETOSHA PAN
Tsumeb
Otavi
Grootfontein
Outjo
Otjitasa
Otjiwarongo
G E R M A N
Kalkfeld
Omaruru
Karibib
Ebony
Trekkopjes
Swakopmund
WALVIS BAY
WINDHOEK
S O U T H - W E S T
A T L A N T I C
O C E A N
Kalkfontein
A F R I C A
Gibeon
Lüderitz
Keetmanshoop
Warmbad
SCALE OF MILES

were the three all-steel Henri Farmans and two B.E.2c aeroplanes which had been handed over to the detachment by the Admiralty. Walvis Bay was reached on the 30th of April 1915. Owing to heavy seas, and to the inadequacy of the arrangements for the housing of the aeroplanes on board, two of the Henri Farmans were seriously damaged on the voyage out.

The situation when the aeroplanes arrived on the scene was as follows. The campaign had opened in the south in September 1914, and by April 1915 three main columns had penetrated into German territory. On the 14th of April Lieutenant-General J. C. Smuts arrived at Kalkfontein to co-ordinate the further advance of these three forces, and two days later they were all on the move. The advance, energetically pushed over difficult country, culminated in a sharp action at Gibeon on the 27th of April 1915, in which the enemy troops were routed. This success brought the southern campaign to a close, and the Union columns were dispersed, some of the units being sent to reinforce General Louis Botha's northern force.

This northern force had landed at Walvis Bay on Christmas Day 1914. General Louis Botha took command early in February 1915, and at once the force moved forward. In the middle of April, No. 1 Armoured Car Squadron of the Royal Naval Air Service arrived with twelve cars to co-operate in the advance, and they were sent by rail to Trekkopjes and placed at the disposal of Colonel P. C. B. Skinner, the commander of the 3rd Brigade. Before dawn on the 26th of April Colonel Skinner moved forward to make a reconnaissance in force towards Ebony, but he encountered strong enemy columns advancing against his camp, and he retired on Trekkopjes, where he was attacked later in the morning. In the repulse of the attack, nine of the armoured cars, whose presence came as a surprise to the enemy, did conspicuous work.

A German pilot had flown over the camp and had seen the cars, but he mistook them for field kitchens and so reported them. The cars, under the direction of Lieutenant-Commander W. Whittall, took up a position in advance of the infantry and were in the forefront of the action from 7.0 a.m., when the enemy fire opened, until 12.30 p.m., when the German columns retired. During all this time they drew much of the enemy's gun fire, and, in their turn, they raked the German infantry from almost point-blank range with their machine-guns. The cars were hit by shrapnel or splinters, but none was put out of action, and the only casualty was one man wounded.

******

'Colonel Skinner informed me', says Lieutenant-Commander Whittall in his report of the action, 'that he considered it was the heavy and accurate 'fire from the cars which decided the enemy to draw off. The opinion of 'the Staff generally is that had our cars not been present, the enemy would, 'in all probability, have been able to push home his attack and to capture 'the camp, which would unquestionably have set back the whole campaign 'for a considerable time.'

******

There were few other opportunities for bringing the cars into action, and their work during the remainder of the campaign was chiefly patrol and reconnaissance. The condition of the country which the cars overcame was at times of extreme difficulty. A burning red shingle that ripped the tyres alternated with deep sand *sluits* through which the cars had often to be manhandled. Nevertheless, the squadron kept up with the advancing troops.

On the 6th of May 1915 General Botha successfully advanced to the capture of Karibib, and a week later he entered Windhoek, the capital, where the last of the German wireless stations outside Europe was taken intact. On the 20th of May a forty-eight-hour armistice was granted, during which terms of peace were discussed, but the enemy made impossible stipulations and the negotiations were broken off.

As a result of his rapid advance on Karibib and Windhoek, General Botha had outstripped his supplies, and before he could begin the final operations against the remainder of the enemy in the northern part of the territory he was compelled to wait at Karibib until the railway should be repaired. Not until June could the advance north be resumed, and it was in this final phase that the aeroplanes co-operated.

Soon after the occupation of Karibib, in the beginning of May, an aerodrome previously used by the Germans was made serviceable by an advanced party of the air detachment, and the first reconnaissance against the enemy was made by Lieutenant K. R. van der Spuy, in one of the Henri Farmans, on the 28th of May. His report stated that few of the enemy were left in Omaruru and that there was evidence that full arrangements had been made to abandon the place. At the beginning of June two new Henri Farmans arrived from England, and, as the B.E.2c's had suffered damage in trial flights, work on the Farmans went on day and night.

General Botha's move forward was begun on the 19th of June

1915. Omaruru was occupied without opposition and thence the advance developed into a pursuit. An aeroplane detachment, under Major Wallace, arrived at Omaruru with the advanced guard of the army and at once set about the completion of an aerodrome which had been roughly laid out by the enemy. From this place five reconnaissances, made in the three Henri Farmans, revealed the gradual evacuation of Kalkfeld.

On the 24th of June the aeroplane detachment was ordered to bomb the enemy remaining in Kalkfeld, as a preliminary to an infantry attack on the camp, but before sending out his bombers Major Wallace made a reconnaissance of the place. He could find no trace of the Germans in the camp nor was anything to be seen of them within a radius of thirty miles in the surrounding hills. As he was returning over Kalkfeld, he saw mounted troops galloping into the centre of the settlement, and they laid out for his information a white strip from which he identified them as Brigadier-General Manie Botha's column. He flew back at once with the news, and the flying detachment then left for Kalkfeld by road, the aeroplanes following next day.

On the 26th of June an advanced detachment moved on to Otjitasa, where was found a suitable landing-ground. Here two Henri Farmans arrived on the 28th. On the following day these two left to reconnoitre and bomb the enemy camp at Otavi. Each pilot dropped eight 16-lb. bombs and then flew back to Brakpan whither the detachment had meanwhile moved. Further reconnaissances during the next few days reported the progress of the enemy retreat; one of the flights, made by Captain G. S. Creed, covered a total distance of 270 miles,

It had now become clear to the enemy that further resistance was useless. A conference between the opposing commands took place, and, as a result, an armistice was proclaimed on the 6th of July, and was followed three days later by an unconditional surrender.

The opportunities open to the air service in these rapid operations were few. The Henri Farman aeroplanes came well out of the ordeal of flying in a hot atmosphere, their steel structure standing up to the climate where wood, no matter how well seasoned, must have warped badly. The only wood parts of the aeroplanes, the struts between the tail outriggers, did warp, and a number of men were employed almost continuously in making new struts. The Canton Unné engines proved reliable and there was only one instance of a forced landing caused by engine failure.

Now that the campaign was ended, a section of four of the armoured cars, under Lieutenant H. G. Nalder, left for German East Africa direct, and the remainder of the armoured car squadron returned to England. The flying unit went to Capetown, where it was demobilized, the majority of the officers leaving at once for England. The South African Aviation Corps was then remobilized (119 N.C.O.s and men) and it also followed to England at the beginning of October 1915, going direct to Farnborough, where the men joined their former officers and became No. 26 (South African) Squadron of the Royal Flying Corps. After some additional training the squadron left for service in German East Africa.

THE ADVANCE INTO GERMAN EAST AFRICA.

When Flight Commander Cull returned to Mombasa after his final reconnaissance of the derelict *Königsberg*, he found Squadron Commander Gordon already under orders to take the seaplanes to Mesopotamia. He himself and the majority of the original party that had come out from England with him were to go up country, with their two Caudron aeroplanes, to help the army in the Kilimanjaro area. The seaplane detachment left for Mesopotamia in the Laconia on the 12th of August 1915. On the 8th of September the aeroplane party left Mombasa for Maktau in a special train that housed, among other impedimenta, two Bessonneau hangars and the two Caudrons, and looked, according to an eye-witness, like a travelling circus. The train arrived at Maktau on the following morning.

Maktau, thirty miles from the German boundary was, at this time, the most advanced British armed camp. The enemy forces in this area had, from the outbreak of war, shown initiative and enterprise. They were fortunate in their commander, Colonel von Lettow-Vorbeck, a realist with no illusions, who had arrived in German East Africa in January 1914. He knew that a war was possible and he knew also, as he says, that the fate of the German colonies would be decided on the battlefields of Europe. Although the forces at his disposal were small and could play only a minor part in the war, it was his opinion that, skilfully handled, they could prevent considerable numbers of the enemy from intervening in Europe or in other important theatres.

Lettow-Vorbeck assembled his main forces on the frontier between German and British East Africa, parallel to which ran the Uganda railway, the main artery of British territory. If he could effectively threaten the 440 miles of this line the British must, he calculated, use up the greater part of their forces for its defence and would have no surplus energy for the invasion of German territory. Soon after the outbreak of war his troops had seized important positions in British East Africa.

In the middle of August 1914, they took the weakly held Taveta, the key to the gateway into German territory, and there established a strongly entrenched camp. A little later, German detachments were pushed out to Salaita Hill, Serengeti, and Mbuyuni, whence they directed guerrilla attacks against the Uganda railway, laying mines that were exploded by the engines of passing trains. The ensuing damage to the track was easily repaired, but the depletion of the engine stock in the country became serious. The strength of the German Protective Force at the beginning of the war was 216 Europeans and 2,540 *askari*. There were further, in the Police Force, 45 Europeans and 2,154 *askari*. In all, during the war, 3,000 Europeans and 11,000 *askari* were enrolled. (See General von Lettow-Vorbeck, *My Reminiscences of East Africa*, also republished by Leonaur). At no time during the campaign did the German commander have the help of aircraft.

When war began the only regular forces in British East Africa and in Uganda were two battalions of the King's African Rifles, intended primarily for police work and inadequate for the defensive role they were at once called upon to play. All the early reinforcements came from India, the first contingent reaching Mombasa at the beginning of September 1914 just in time to save the town from seizure by a German force which had worked along the coast. An abortive and costly British attack on Tanga, in November 1914, threw the British forces back on the defensive. In April 1915 Brigadier-General M. J. Tighe took over command of the British East African Forces, but during the remainder of the year there were only minor local activities. The Germans were not strong enough to take the offensive in force, and Brigadier-General Tighe had all he could do to keep his lines intact and to strengthen the numerous weak points along his extended front.

Such was the position when the Naval Air Service detachment arrived at Maktau in September 1915. Space inside the camp was scarce and a landing-ground was made outside, explosives being freely used to blow up obstructing trees and ant-hills. The hangars, however, were erected inside the camp as the aeroplanes would otherwise be at the mercy of marauding enemy patrols. Before each flight the aeroplane was wheeled out of the camp down the main road to the landing-ground while an armed party beat through the surrounding bush to dislodge hostile snipers. The first flight over the enemy was made on the 12th of October, but Taveta, the objective of the reconnaissance, was shrouded in mist and nothing of the enemy's strength could be discovered.

It will be well here to say a word or two on the country and on the conditions which the airmen had to face. The dominating feature of the area is the mass of Kilimanjaro, but a more formidable obstacle to the low-powered aeroplanes were the red-cliffed Paré Mountains, which barred the way to the important valley in German territory along which ran the Tanga-Moshi railway. The climatic conditions were peculiar. At dawn there was usually a widespread ground mist, and when this cleared low clouds often obstructed the view, especially in the mountain area.

After about 9.0 a.m., when the clouds were dispersed by the hot sun, heat bumps and a white glare made observation fatiguing. The ubiquitous dense bush offered good cover to dismounted troops, who might only be revealed through their own carelessness. Dust clouds which were a clue to moving enemy columns were sometimes misleading. Followed to their origin they were often seen to be caused by moving game. On one occasion a pilot, when he came up at last with what had appeared from a distance as a suspicious-looking cloud of dust, was only just able to escape entanglement with migrating locusts.

For a short time after the arrival of the naval air detachment, the breaking of the monsoon and a lack of spare parts held up flying. At the end of October 1915 an extra Caudron and spare parts arrived at Mombasa. The new equipment included also a workshop lorry, which was to play a useful part in the air campaign, and a Ford van that was to do service as an improvised sweeper of land mines. The weather was now better and routine air reconnaissances gradually pieced together the disposition of the enemy entrenchments. Towards the end of December three pilots arrived and, about the same time, Lieutenant Cherry Kearton, known for his photographic studies of wild animal life, was transferred from the army to the Naval Air Service as a photographic officer. A portable darkroom was constructed from Caudron packing cases, and air pictures of the German positions were soon being delivered to the army staff.

The native troops with the enemy forces now began to suffer their first experiences of aircraft bombing. On the 8th of January 1916 a pilot dropped bombs of 65-lb. weight on the camps at Serengeti and Taveta: one of the two bombs aimed at the latter camp was seen to explode in the centre of the entrenchment. This raid called forth an illuminative essay on the susceptibility of native troops to attack from the air. It was written by a German officer at Taveta and is quoted in Colonel von Lettow-Vorbeck's personal diary. It reads:

> The appearance of the aeroplane above Taveta on the morning of the 8th of January has not failed to make a considerable impression on the natives. Seized with fear and terror, they ran away from their fields and concealed themselves in the huts and in the forest. Natives who were on the road to Taveta to work there for the Government, threw away their tools and did not return for many days. Women who were on their way to the market left their produce on the road, ran home and, by exaggerating what they had seen, spread terror in places far distant. Also, the natives who had more common sense, as the Manki and Akiden, were perplexed.
>
> They considered the aeroplane as a supernatural being—*Muungu*. This *Muungu* was endowed with great power. The route which he followed had now become spirited and the land was unproductive. The natives over whom he flew were now possessed of evil spirits. . . . It is quite comprehensible that the natives, seeing the aeroplane, were shaken in their belief in the power of the Germans. According to their belief, the War-Lord is with the conqueror and not with the vanquished. The War-Lord (aeroplane) has now come from the English side and has visited the Germans by sending the evil spirit (bombs). Fate has consequently turned in favour of the English. . . .

Meanwhile preparations were going ahead for an offensive movement into German territory. Now that the operations in German South-West Africa had been successfully completed, Union forces were available for service in East Africa. On the withdrawal of the Indian Corps from France, too, Indian regiments were sent out to this new theatre of war. On the 12th of February 1916 Lieutenant-General the Hon. J. C. Smuts took over the command of the British forces in East Africa. (General Sir H. L. Smith-Dorrien, who had originally been appointed to command in East Africa, fell sick at Capetown on his way out.) He arrived at Mombasa a week later and at once went up country to make a personal reconnaissance of the position at the front. He approved and adopted, with minor modifications, Major-General Tighe's initial plans for the opening of operations in the Kilimanjaro area and, on the 25th of February 1916, he received

Government sanction to go ahead before the rainy season set in about the end of March.

The Royal Flying Corps Squadron—No. 26 (South African)—made up from a nucleus of the officers and men who had taken part in the German South-West campaign, had arrived at Mombasa from England on the 31st of January 1916 under Major G. P. Wallace. The squadron, a section of which formed a reserve aircraft park, was equipped with eight B.E.2c's, Leyland lorries and workshops, Crossley light tenders, and stores and spares. When the squadron began to unpack, it was found that the propellers of the aeroplanes had not, by some oversight, been packed at Farnborough. There were six spare propellers of a different and less suitable type, but one of these had been broken in transit, leaving only five for the eight aeroplanes.

The spare propellers had to be specially bored before they would fit the B.E.2c's, and there was delay before the squadron could get to work. By the morning of the 9th of February, the first aeroplane was ready at the Mbuyuni aerodrome, and a reconnaissance was made next evening by Captain G. S. Creed with Second Lieutenant Leo Walmsley as his observer. The officers had been sent up to search for an enemy column reported marching on Mbuyuni. Mounted troops and Naval Air Service armoured cars were already on their way to engage the enemy. The airmen had no difficulty in locating our own men, but they could find no trace of any German forces. (See *Flying and Sport in East Africa*, by Leo Walmsley, in which this flight and much of the subsequent work of the squadron is described.)

The plan for the British offensive was, in outline, as follows. The 1st Division, to which there was no allocation of aircraft, was to strike south from Longido, across thirty-five miles of waterless bush on the western side of Kilimanjaro, to the Nanjuki River and then push on between Meru and Kilimanjaro in an endeavour to cut the enemy's line of retreat at Kahe, on the Tanga-Moshi railway. The 2nd Division and the 1st South African Mounted Brigade were to strike at the enemy's main force by way of the gap between Kilimanjaro and the Paré Mountains, while a column, under Brigadier-General J. L. van Deventer, the commander of the South African Mounted Brigade, including the 3rd South African Infantry Brigade, was to turn the flank of the main enemy position at Salaita by making a wide sweep to the north by way of Chala.

In co-operation with the turning movement, air reconnaissances were made along the Lumi River and over the enemy outpost positions at Lake Chala, which were photographed. It is of interest that the attention paid by the flying officers to this stretch of country, north of the enemy's main positions, made the German command alert. General von Lettow-Vorbeck, *My Reminiscences of East Africa* says:

'The direction taken by the enemy's airmen, showed his evident interest in the country one or two hours north of Taveta. One was bound to hit on the idea that the enemy encamped east of El Oldorobo (Salaita Hill) did not intend to get his head broken a second time on that mountain but meant to work round the position by the north, and so reach the Lumi River, one hour north of Taveta.'

The 1st Division moved off from Longido after dark on the 5th of March 1916 and Brigadier-General van Deventer started for Chala in the evening of the 7th. By the 8th of March, when the bombardment of Salaita Hill began, the 1st Division had reached Geraragua, and Brigadier-General van Deventer had turned south after securing the Chala position, and was on his way towards Taveta, his progress being watched and reported from the air. Next day the advance made by van Deventer's force was such that the German positions on Salaita Hill had become untenable. The enemy had foreseen what would happen and had evacuated the position before dawn. The hill, together with Taveta, which had also been evacuated, was occupied by the British infantry in the afternoon.

The enemy troops fell back on the Latema neck, in the gap between Kilimanjaro and the North Paré Mountains. Here they offered stubborn resistance, but they were compelled by frontal attacks and by the threat, once again, of envelopment by van Deventer's force, to retire further. By the 13th of March van Deventer had occupied Moshi unopposed, the enemy retreating rapidly on Kahe; their departure from Moshi was speeded by aeroplane bombing attacks. On the 14th the 1st Division from Longido, whose advance had been impeded by the difficulties of the country, joined Brigadier-General van Deventer in Moshi, arriving too late to play a decisive part in the opening phase of the operations.

The next few days, to the 18th of March, were used in improving the road from Taveta to Moshi, in bringing up supplies, and in air reconnaissances towards Kahe and the Pangani River, the bordering country of the latter being a malarial belt of dense forest.

To understand the operations, once the armies got on the move, reference to the map is essential. The direction of the campaign was influenced by the two German lines of railway communication. The

Tanga-Moshi line ran inland from the Indian Ocean along the feet of the Usambara and Paré Mountains almost to the southern slopes of Kilimanjaro. (During the campaign this line was linked with the Voi-Taveta branch of the Uganda railway.) Following the railway, at varying distances, is the Pangani, or Ruvu, River which has its source in a multitude of streams fed by the glaciers of Kilimanjaro. The second line in the territory, the Central Railway, connected the capital, Dar-es-Salaam, with the important inland trade-route centre at Tabora, the most populous town in the Protectorate, and continued to Kigoma on Lake Tanganyika.

The rivers in the territory, of which the two most considerable are the Ruvuma and the Rufiji, are everywhere lined with jungle. Many of the slopes of the vast inland plateau, facing the rain-bringing monsoon, are covered with primeval forest. Elsewhere the plateau is part grass with bush and forest, and part *steppe*, often made impenetrable by thickly growing mimosa. The beasts of the jungle abound. The malaria-carrying anopheles and the tsetse fly render large areas scarcely habitable. A land, in other words, to make the pursuit of a few columns of determined fighters difficult and costly, and one hardly suited to the operations of aeroplanes equipped with the not too reliable engines of the early time of the war.

On the 18th of March the general advance towards the Pangani River was resumed, and by the 21st the enemy, unable to withstand the pressure, and threatened once again by a turning movement, evacuated Kahe and blew up the railway bridge over the Pangani. The information that the enemy had blown up the bridge and was on the move was brought back by an air observer in the afternoon. Pilots and observers of No. 26 Squadron had previously kept watch on the enemy movements and had also made attacks with 20-lb. and occasionally with 100-lb. bombs on the bridge, camp, and station at Kahe.

There is evidence of minor casualties at both places, but of no appreciable material damage. By dawn of the morning of the 22nd the enemy troops had slipped away across the Pangani to the fortified camps in the fertile Lembeni country. They had successfully escaped from the pincers just as they were about to close. So, ended the first phase of the operations, resulting in the complete capture of the rich Kilimanjaro-Meru area.

There followed a pause in the campaign. The rainy season now set in with violence and Lieutenant-General Smuts had to dispose his main forces where they could best weather the extremities of the climate and where he could carry out a reorganisation for the next phase. He regrouped his troops into three divisions, keeping the South Africans together in two divisions under MajorGeneral van Deventer and Major-General C. J. Brits, and forming the East African and Indian troops into another division under Major-General A. R. Hoskins. He decided that van Deventer should push into the interior from the Kilimanjaro area while the remaining divisions stayed on high and dry ground in the neighbourhood of Moshi, Himo, and Mbuyuni, with advance guards along the Pangani to watch Lettow-Vorbeck's main forces.

★★★★★★

At this time, also, a force under Brigadier-General E. Northey was operating eastwards and northwards from Lake Nyasa; a Belgian column was launched eastwards from Lake Kivu; and, in April, another Belgian column and a British column were set in motion in a southerly direction from the Uganda border near Lake Victoria Nyanza.

★★★★★★

Van Deventer's March into the Interior.

Van Deventer's march into the heart of German East Africa was a fine feat of arms. He had concentrated his division at Arusha by the 1st of April 1916, and two days later his mounted troops began to move south. They surrounded and captured an enemy detachment at Lol Kissale, a mountain in the Masai desert, pushed rapidly on to Ufiome and thence to Kondoa Irangi, which was occupied, after a sharp action, on the 19th of April. Here the division was concentrated along a dominant position. Further advance was, for the moment, out of the question as the condition of the country, under the floods of the tropical rains, held up transport.

Meanwhile it became known from captured documents that the German garrison at Kondoa had been instructed to hold out as long as possible pending the arrival of strong reinforcements. Colonel von Lettow-Vorbeck had, in fact, decided to move part of his main forces from the Lembeni front to meet the threat to the interior created by van Deventer's advance. After a series of well-executed road marches and quick rail movements, the main German body reached Kondoa early in May. On the 9th of May the enemy launched an attack, which was repulsed, and then took up strong positions surrounding Kondoa.

The rainy season had abated in the middle of May and the ground began quickly to dry. Until this time, MajorGeneral van Deventer had been compelled to operate without the help of aircraft, but it now became possible and necessary to bring up aeroplanes for reconnaissance of the enemy positions and, in particular, to keep watch for signs of movement back to the eastern sector of the territory where Lieutenant-General Smuts was about to begin the next stage of his advance.

The aeroplanes for Kondoa were supplied by the Naval Air Service detachment at Mbuyuni, which, early in May, had been reinforced. In March 1916, a detachment—afterwards known as No. 8 Squadron—had arrived at Zanzibar from England with four Voisin aeroplanes (150 horse-power Canton Unné engines) and four Short seaplanes (150 horse-power Sunbeam engines), for reconnaissance and spotting work along the coast. The arrival of this unit afforded an opportunity to relieve the original naval air personnel at Mbuyuni who had suffered much from fever, and a detachment, under Squadron Commander E. R. C. Nanson, had been sent on from Zanzibar to Mbuyuni where it arrived on the 2nd of May. A few days later the original naval air unit, except five officers, left East Africa for Zanzibar.

******

> On arrival at Chukwani, where the seaplane detachment was already established, the party was absorbed into No. 8 (Naval) Squadron the command of which was taken over by Squadron Commander J. T. Cull.

******

All the naval air personnel on the mainland were grouped under Squadron Commander Nanson whose unit became known as No. 7 (Naval) Squadron.

On taking over, he at once made arrangements to send petrol and spares to Kondoa Irangi. Flight Sub-Lieutenant Gallehawk set out for Kondoa with four mechanics and one thousand porters. The party paused at Lol Kissale for four days to make the beginnings of an aerodrome and then pushed on to Kondoa, where, after a hazardous journey during which three porters were eaten by lions, they arrived on the 28th of May. Flight Sub-Lieutenant Gallehawk directed his men in the cutting and burning of mealie fields until a passable aerodrome resulted.

Two pilots, Flight Lieutenant W. G. Moore and Flight Sub-Lieutenant N. G. Stewart Dawson, left Mbuyuni in Voisins to fly to Kondoa on the 30th of May. They were misled by their faulty maps, lost their way, and landed on the Masai plateau whence they trekked to

Ufiome. The two aeroplanes, which were undamaged, were ultimately flown to Kondoa on the 6th of June, one of them by Squadron Commander Nanson who had arrived at Kondoa with the light transport a few days previously.

No time was lost in getting to work over the enemy. Before the aeroplanes arrived, nothing was known of the country behind the German entrenched positions, but daily air reconnaissances soon gave Major-General van Deventer's staff a picture of the enemy territory. These reconnaissance flights and intermittent bombing attacks induced the enemy to stop all movements by day. The native porters attached to the German troops, still convinced that aircraft were of supernatural origin, dispersed into the bush in panic each time an aeroplane appeared. There is evidence that two bombs dropped on the 12th of June killed three and wounded eight porters and *askari*. In an endeavour to stop the threat from the air, the enemy, with great difficulty, moved forward one of the guns salved from the *Königsberg* and opened fire on the aerodrome at Kondoa. The two Voisins were moved back to a landing-ground at Salim whence the work continued.

The plans for Major-General van Deventer's further advance were largely dependent on knowledge of the enemy's possible and probable lines of retreat. The general was anxious to discover whether Lettow-Vorbeck intended to maintain his position at Kondoa or to move his main force back again to the eastern sector where Lieutenant-General Smuts was now making a rapid advance. Air reconnaissances told him what he wanted to know. They made it clear that the German line of communications ran from Kondoa to Dodoma and thence eastwards along the Central Railway.

Up to the 24th of June, there were minor indications that the enemy intended to withdraw, but on that day, pilots came back with news that the withdrawal was in full progress along the road to Dodoma. Bombs were loaded on the Voisins and attacks made on the retreating columns; one bomb was seen to hit the head of a transport column and cause a stampede. Major-General van Deventer's division, with the naval air unit in co-operation, now began a forward move on a wide front, towards the Central Railway, in pursuit of the enemy.

The Advance to the Nguru Mountains.

We must go back to the operations in the eastern sector of the territory. In the middle of March 1916, No. 26 Squadron had moved forward to temporary quarters at Taveta, and, before the rainy season set in, the officers of the squadron had continued their reconnaissances of the new enemy positions and had made bombing attacks, particularly along the railway line as far as Lembeni. When the rains came, at the end of March, the squadron moved back again to Mbuyuni, and the next few weeks were spent in the overhaul of the aeroplanes and transport. New propellers, magnetos, and other stores arrived from England and, on the 4th of May, there came a consignment of eight Henri Farman aeroplanes (140 horse-power Canton Unné engines). Meanwhile, to ensure the continuance of reconnaissance in bright intervals of weather, one aeroplane was stationed at a rough landing-ground at Kahe.

Lieutenant-General Smuts was ready to resume his advance when the rains abated in the middle of May. The direction of his initial movements was settled by the necessity of clearing the enemy troops from their strong outpost positions in the Paré and Usambara Mountains. Other enemy outposts were along the Pangani River, but the main German body in this sector was in position along the Tanga railway. Lieutenant-General Smuts decided not to move his main column down the fortified railway line, where he was expected, but to advance instead down the inner, or left, bank of the Pangani somewhat ahead of a smaller column working along the Tanga line. A third column was to push through the Ngulu gap in the Paré Mountains and join hands with the railway column. When the advance had progressed as far as Handeni, the Commander-in-Chief proposed to swing south towards the Central Railway in a concerted movement parallel with van Deventer.

The air reconnaissances preliminary to, and during, the forward movement told more than the locality and strength of the enemy positions. A rough survey of the ground ahead of the troops was made, particularly along the left bank of the Pangani; native tracks were searched out and sketched from the air, and the types of vegetation and the valleys in which the bush was broken or thin were noted.

The move forward began on the 21st of May 1916 when the Mbuyuni column left for the Ngulu gap. The other two columns concentrated at Kahe, from which they advanced on the 22nd and 23rd of May. Meanwhile No. 26 Squadron had moved to the landing-ground at Kahe in the middle of May, leaving the aerodrome at Mbuyuni to the Aircraft Park and to the Naval Air Service. The first important information of the enemy retreat came on the 24th of May, when an air observer returned with the news that there was no movement in the defensive position at Lembeni: this place was shortly afterwards occupied by the railway column.

Next day the air observers reported that open and closed trains were moving south near Same station and that there were explosions north of the station, from which it was clear that the enemy troops were retreating farther and blowing up the line as they went. Later in the day the mountain and railway columns joined forces at Same station. On the 26th of May the retreat was seen from the air to be in full progress. Part of the line towards Makanya was already destroyed and trains were on the move southward. The observers followed the direction of the enemy movements and discovered a large camp at Mikotscheni, where the Pangani and the railway meet at the feet of the mountains: The Imperial troops pressed forward in pursuit.

The squadron was hard put to it to keep up with the advance. On the 27th of May it moved to an aerodrome at Marago-Opuni on the Pangani, only the four B.E.2c's being taken as the Henri Farmans, which were being assembled, were considered too slow. But the personnel were not to be on their new landing-ground long: on the 29th they were away again another thirty miles to Old Lassiti. Great difficulties were experienced on these forward moves. The squadron was short of transport, so that what it did have was overloaded; the tyres were worn or wearing out and there were no spares, and the fine dust choked the engines. Rations were hard to find as the squadron moved in the rear of the advancing divisions, and, furthermore, as there was no doctor with the squadron, men who went sick—and in the pestilential air of the Pangani many went sick—had to rely on what attention the flying officers could give them.

When the forward troops came up to the Mikotscheni position on the 29th of May they met with opposition, but on the 30th the camp was attacked in force and, after dark, it was evacuated by the enemy. That the evacuation was imminent was clear in the evening of the 30th from an air report which stated that culverts south of Mikotscheni were being blown up by a demolition train.

Meanwhile the mountain and railway columns, after joining forces at Same station on the 25th of May, had turned off into the mountains again through the Same pass to Gonja, which they reached on the 29th. Thence the combined column had pushed forward, through the Gonja gap, to Mkomazi bridge, where the railway crosses the Pangani's tributary that gives the bridge its name. This point was reached on the 31st of May, and it was, in fact, the threat of envelopment created by the advance of this flanking column that precipitated the enemy evacuation of Mikotscheni.

On this same day Lieutenant-General Smuts's main column reached Bwiko, the station above Mkomazi, where it was necessary to make a brief halt to bring up supplies. The commander-in-chief intended to follow the enemy troops, as soon as he could, down the river direct to Mkalamo whither they had retreated by way of Mombo and the trolley line from that station. Meanwhile he was anxious to know the type of country along the new line of his advance, and the majority of the air reconnaissances were directed to obtaining this information. Extracts from a typical reconnaissance report made on the 31st of May will illustrate this phase of the air work. The observer followed the line of the river southwards from Bwiko to Mkalamo, he says:

> The area is covered with thick bush, except along the banks of the river. A passage can be found for troops and transport along the right bank, keeping close to the edge of the bush to avoid soft ground .... thence thick bush down to the river bank for four miles ... the river flats then appear again ... there are pathways on the left bank here but they run through thick bush .. ... The passage along the right bank appears to be the easier... .. no bridges ... the river changes from fast-running stream to slow-running stream.

On the 2nd of June the squadron took up a new aerodrome at Kwa-Lokua, a natural clearing in the bush which, because of the large numbers of lions in the vicinity, was renamed by the flying officers *Daniel's Den*. Two days later a reconnaissance was made beyond the entrenched enemy positions at Mkalamo, as far as Handeni, this being the first time that Handeni was visited by aeroplanes. The squadron was now beginning to have difficulty in drawing supplies of petrol and rations, for the transport of which it had to rely on its own lorries. The hundred-mile track back to Kahe, from which supplies had to be fetched, had, for the most part, been hurriedly cut through the bush, and, following the passage of the division, it was in a state of bad repair. From Kwa-Lokua, on the 5th of June, four aeroplanes flew over Mkalamo and dropped 20-lb. bombs on the German camp: at the same time air photographs of the enemy entrenchments were taken. Mkalamo was bombed again two days later when, it is known, some native porters were wounded.

It was necessary that the squadron should move on again in preparation for the further advance, and an officer was sent forward with petrol, oil, stores, and two hangars to a point about thirty miles south of Kwa-Lokua, known as Palms, where, with the help of native labour, he made a rough landing-ground, to which the squadron moved on the 8th of June. The four aeroplanes before making their landing on the new ground were flown first over the German camp at Mkalamo, on which two 100-lb. and sixteen 20-lb. bombs were dropped. An officer of the intelligence department was flown over Mkalamo again in the afternoon to make a further reconnaissance. While the squadron was at Palms its wireless section took over the field telegraph station, receiving and sending messages for all units stationed there. During the stay at Palms the weather was bad, low clouds and gales being usual, but air reconnaissances to Handeni were maintained.

On the 9th of June the British forces moved forward across the Pangani and next day, after a sharp engagement, occupied Mkalamo; the enemy retreating to Handeni. Pilots and observers had, during the previous few days, on orders from headquarters, surveyed the area between Mkalamo and Handeni for water, and had given particulars of all they could see of the conditions of water-holes, pools, and so forth.

The commander-in-chief now marched on Handeni direct but sent a second column along the railway line from Mombo with orders to turn south at Korogwe to rejoin the main body. On the evening of the 14th of June, while the advance was in progress, three pilots from Palms bombed Kwa-Mdoe, a German camp east of Handeni, with two 100-lb. and sixteen 20-lb. bombs and wounded four men in the camp. One of the bombing officers, Lieutenant W. W. Carey-Thomas, who went on to reconnoitre Korogwe, did not arrive back at the aerodrome, and a pilot who went out at dawn next morning to search for him discovered his aeroplane on the old landing-ground at *Daniel's Den*. Lieutenant Carey-Thomas, after searching vainly for the aerodrome at Palms at dusk on the previous evening had gone on and had made a good landing, but he had spent a disturbed night surrounded by lions. Mechanics were sent out to repair the aeroplane, which had been slightly damaged, and it was flown next day to Palms.

On the 18th the squadron left Palms, where it had made a comparatively long stay, for a place called Mbagui, forty miles farther south. Most of the natives attached to the squadron were now sick, and there was insufficient labour to improve the ridge and furrow of the Mbagui landing-ground which had sometime been under cultivation. Consequently, the undercarriages of two of the B.E.2c's were slightly damaged when they made their initial landings. One of the others, for some unknown reason, crashed in thick bush soon after it left Palms and both its occupants were later found dead.

Handeni was entered on the 19th of June, but Lieutenant-General Smuts pressed on without delay to Kangata. Here, in dense bush, the British forces came upon the German troops whom they attacked and defeated on the 24th. At Kangata the main body reached the Handeni-Morogoro road and, for the first time in the long advance, had the advantage of moving along a made road. They had hitherto, for two hundred miles, marched along tracks mostly cut by themselves through the bush.

Once again it was necessary to halt. The troops, weakened by sickness, needed rest, the long lines of communication had to be improved, and plans had to be concerted with Major-General van Deventer. A large camp, therefore, was established on the Msiha River at the foot of the eastern slope of Mount Kanga in the formidable Nguru Mountains. At this time, it became clear from air reports that the main enemy forces, hitherto opposed to van Deventer at Kondoa, were being withdrawn, and there was soon no doubt that they were about to be concentrated at favourable positions in the Nguru Mountains to oppose the further advance of Lieutenant General Smuts.

The halt on the Msiha River lasted until the beginning of August 1916. In July 1916, No. 26 Squadron had, for administrative purposes, been incorporated in the Middle East Brigade formed, under the command of Brigadier-General W. G. H. Salmond, to group all R.F.C. units in Egypt, Salonika, Mesopotamia, and East Africa. While Lieutenant-General Smuts was reorganising his troops, No. 26 Squadron, still using the landing-ground at Mbagui, reconnoitred and bombed the enemy camps at Kanga, and the headquarters at Turiani. The work of the pilots and observers, who had sixty miles of flying over dense bush and wood *kopjes* before they came to the enemy positions, was made difficult by the low clouds and rains of the south-westerly monsoon.

No sufficiently clear space could be found in the intervening country to give an aerodrome nearer the Nguru entrenchments. On the 6th of July the air detachment at Mbagui was reinforced by 'A' Flight of the squadron from Mbuyuni with three Henri Farmans (140 horse-power Canton Unné engines). Eight of these aeroplanes had arrived in the beginning of May, but, owing to faulty material, they had to be reconstructed before they could be trusted to fly over jungle country. One was crashed soon after arrival and there was only enough sound material for the complete reconstruction of three aeroplanes, but these were to bear the brunt of the work during the months of the long advance to the Rufiji, and the Canton Unné engines were once again, as in the German South-West Africa campaign, to prove their reliability. One of the four B.E.2c's, which had done continuous service during the long trek down the Pangani, was wrecked on the day the Henri Farmans reached Mbagui. There were now six serviceable aeroplanes, and, during July, twenty-seven bombing attacks were made on the positions in the Nguru Mountains; three and a half tons of bombs were dropped.

The material damage was not great and the casualties were confined to one European and a few *askari* and native porters. The raids, however, affected the enemy sufficiently to induce him, on the 26th of July, to send out a special patrol to attack the aerodrome. News of the intention reached headquarters and the squadron was warned. The aerodrome was put in a state of defence and the air personnel stood to arms, but the expected attack never took place. By this time an advanced Aircraft Park had been established at the railhead at Korogwe.

The Fight for the Central Railway.

While preparations were going forward in the Msiha Camp for the attack on the Nguru position, Major-General van Deventer, in the west, was rapidly closing in to co-operate. Following the withdrawal of the main enemy columns from Kondoa to the Nguru Mountains at the end of June, van Deventer had moved forward to the Central Railway on a wide front, his objective being Mpwapwa, from which place he would be in a position to co-operate with the force at Msiha. On arrival at Aneti, on the 19th of July, van Deventer divided his main force into two columns, one of which, the mounted brigade, moved on Kikombo station, while the other, a mixed column, advanced on Dodoma. The latter station was reached on the 29th of July and the former on the following day.

Meanwhile two smaller columns had been sent westward to secure van Deventer's right flank. One went to Singida, which was reached on the 2nd of August, and then moved on to Kilimatinde, on the Central Railway, to rejoin the second of the smaller columns which had occupied the station on the 30th of July. Thus, at the beginning of August, one hundred miles of the Central Railway were in our possession. Van Deventer now proceeded to concentrate his forces at Nyangalo, from which his march on Mpwapwa was resumed on the 9th of August. In the south-eastward sweep from Kondoa the Voisins of the Naval Air Service reconnoitred ahead of van Deventer's columns, reporting on the enemy camps, on which the pilots made occasional bombing attacks.

The time had now come for the opening of the attack on the Nguru Mountains which barred the way to Lieutenant General Smuts's next objective, Morogoro, a former capital of the colony about fifty miles to the south on the Central Railway. On the 3rd of August an extended air reconnaissance of the country on the British left flank, east of the Handeni-Turiani road, was made with the idea of deceiving the enemy as to the direction of the advance, but it is doubtful whether the ruse succeeded. The flight was reported to the enemy command and caused speculation, but other reconnaissance flights made over the Nguru positions told the enemy of our keen interest in this area also. The three main columns moved off on the 5th of August and by the 12th, after sharp fighting, Turiani was occupied and the enemy was in retreat. While the British columns were advancing, there were many air reconnaissances, but the thick bush offered ideal concealment for the enemy's withdrawal, and, except the removal south of German red cross encampments which indicated the retirement, nothing of importance was seen.

The British columns as they moved forward were separated by blocks of mountains, and an important task of the pilots and observers was to keep head-quarters informed of the progress of the brigades through the passes. This often meant prolonged searching. An example may be quoted. On the 9th of August all efforts, by air and on the ground, to find Major-General Brits's mounted troops failed. Captain van der Spuy set out with Second Lieutenant G. St. V. Pawson on a Henri Farman early next morning and, after a two-and-a-half-hour search through the mountain passes, finally located the column at Mediombo.

The British columns had now pushed so far ahead that further useful flying was temporarily impossible owing to the long distance back of the Mbagui aerodrome, and not until the 18th of August, when suitable ground became available at Dakawa, to which the squadron moved, could further reconnaissances be made. A landing-ground had previously been prepared at Komssanga, near a bridge across the Wami, and Leyland lorries had been sent forward with stores, but the bridge was attacked by the enemy the morning after the lorries arrived and, as three companies of enemy infantry were reported still at large in the vicinity and the aerodrome had no protection, it was abandoned and the lorries moved back to Turiani.

The first reconnaissance from Dakawa was made on the 19th of August over Kilosa and the Central Railway, when the main enemy camps were located and the roads and watercourses along the further line of advance were surveyed. During the remaining days of the lull in the operations these reconnaissance and survey flights were continued, a further flying objective being Morogoro, which received its baptism of bombs on the 21st of August.

Meanwhile van Deventer was pushing along the Central Railway towards Kilosa. On the 7th of August No. 7 (Naval) Squadron, now consisting of four Voisins, moved from Aneti, from which place it had worked since the 23rd of July, to Dodoma. From here, on the 8th of August, a long reconnaissance was made down the railway to Kongoa and back along the Tschunjo-Kikombo road. The enemy was discovered concentrated in the Tschunjo Nek, with ample rolling stock in the local sidings to ensure his speedy retreat.

On the 9th of August van Deventer moved forward from Nyangalo, across a waterless desert, and came into action with the enemy at the Tschunjo Nek position on the nth. Fighting went on throughout the night, but next morning it was discovered that the enemy had retired. He was vigorously followed and offered resistance again, later in the day, at Mpwapwa before falling back towards Kidete. On the 14th an air reconnaissance reported that the enemy had taken up a strong position west of Kidete station and that he had two heavy guns in support. The Third South African Infantry Brigade was ordered forward at once and was in contact with the Kidete position on the 15th. From here, after twelve hours' fighting, the enemy was again forced to retire on the 16th.

His retirement was watched and reported by the aeroplanes which had, on the previous day, made an eighty-five mile move to a new landing-ground at Mpwapwa. An observer came back with the news that trains were waiting in the station at Kirassa, ten miles east of Kidete. The mounted brigade was at once sent forward and, after capturing eight trucks of stores near the station, made contact with the enemy at Kirassa. The important centre of Kilosa was now within bombing reach and, on the 18th of August, a raid was made on the station and on a camp to the west: some natives were wounded. Early the following morning, Msagara station, where the enemy made a stand after being forced out of Kirassa, was bombed as a prelude to an attack by our advanced forces. Successful flanking movements over the hills, north and south of the railway, induced the enemy to evacuate Msagara and retreat on Kilosa, but he first suffered severe casualties. Touch was maintained and fighting continued, but on the 22nd, when van Deventer advanced to attack the Kilosa positions, he found the enemy gone, and he thereupon occupied Kilosa and Kimamba, farther east, without opposition.

At Kilosa, a rough aerodrome was prepared and the first Voisin flew up from Mpwapwa on the 24th of August. Next morning a large enemy camp was located and bombed at Uleia, and, farther south, at Mhange and Msegenso, retreating mounted troops, with transport and cattle, were discovered, and another large camp was found at Matengala. The air reports made it clear that the troops under Kraut, opposed to van Deventer, were making for Kidatu, where they would be able to cross the Ruaha River.

By this time the main body of the German forces, retreating before Lieutenant-General Smuts, was covering Morogoro, where air reconnaissances by No. 26 Squadron, made on the 22nd of August, had disclosed a strong enemy position at Ssimbo on the Morogoro road. Barring the way to the enemy retreat south of Morogoro stood the difficult mass of the Uluguru Mountains, and at last, it seemed, there was an opportunity to accomplish what had so often been aimed at—the complete encirclement of the bulk of the enemy troops. Lieutenant-General Smuts thereupon moved Enslin's brigade south to the Central Railway. They were in Mkata station on the 23rd and pushed southwest to Mlali next day, so blocking one important road of retreat from Morogoro.

This brigade was reinforced at Mlali by the I Mounted Brigade specially detached from van Deventer. To block the road on the eastern slopes of the mountains by way of Kiroka, Lieutenant-General Smuts after crossing the Wami turned back along that river and crossed a waterless belt to the Ngerengere River at Msungulu until east of Morogoro, which was reached on the 24th. The following day an air reconnaissance of the Uluguru Mountains discovered new camps at Uponda and Matombo which foreshadowed a southerly retreat through the mountains. This is, in fact, what happened. When the advance on Morogoro was resumed on the 26th it was found that the enemy had gone. He had taken a hitherto unsuspected track to Kisaki and so slipped once again from the enveloping pincers. He was pursued south, fighting rear-guard actions on the way.

Meanwhile van Deventer advanced against the enemy western column, under Kraut, towards Kidodi and Kidatu. Van Deventer occupied Uleia on the 26th and learned from his air reconnaissances next day that large enemy camps were along the Ruaha River and that pontoons and boats were near Kidatu, indicating that Kraut's preparations for crossing the river were well in hand. Van Deventer pressed forward, but Kraut contested the ground as he fell back towards the river from one entrenched position to another. An air report on the 8th of September indicated that Kidodi had been evacuated and that the enemy forces were south of the village near the river, the bridge across which was intact. Kidodi was occupied by van Deventer on the 10th, the enemy falling back farther to a line along the river.

While van Deventer was pursuing Kraut's detachment, the main enemy body, in retreat from Morogoro, had taken up a strong position covering Kisaki. This position was vigorously attacked on the 7th and 8th of September, but the enemy stood his ground; and it was not until the 15th, when the occupation of Dutumi, eighteen miles farther east, and a flanking movement to Dakawa, the second town of that name in the line of advance, threatened to cut the enemy's retreat to the Rufiji that he gave up the Kisaki position and retired to a defensive line along the Mgeta. It was impossible to press the attack at once. The long pursuit under primitive conditions had sorely tried the men and the transport, and rest and reorganisation were necessary once again, so that the attack against the Mgeta positions did not take place until December.

Northey's Advance from Nyasaland.

We must turn to the operations carried out in the south-west of the territory, where columns under the command of Brigadier-General E. Northey, from Nyasaland, had occupied Lupembe and Iringa in the middle of August 1916. On the night of the 22nd of October 1916, a large part of the enemy force, coming from Tabora, broke through between Alt Iringa and Ngominji and cut Brigadier-General Northey's communications with Iringa. There followed considerable local fighting in October and November, but on the 24th of November a mobile column under Lieutenant-Colonel R. E. Murray surrounded an enemy detachment north-west of Ubena and forced it to surrender two days later: seven officers, forty-seven other Europeans, 249 *askari*, a howitzer, and three machineguns were captured.

Early in December van Deventer moved his headquarters to Iringa whither No. 7 (Naval) Squadron was transferred on the 7th of December from Kilosa. Arrangements were made to send one aeroplane to co-operate with Brigadier-General Northey's troops, whose headquarters had been moved, on the 4th of December, to Ubena, preparatory to the general resumption of the offensive. The 130 miles of road from Iringa to Ubena were impassable for cars, and Air Mechanic E. W. Nelson was sent, by motor-cycle, to prepare an aerodrome. With the help of Brigadier-General Northey's engineers he had made a passably good aerodrome by the 20th of December and, on this day, Flight Lieutenant W. G. Moore flew a B.E.2c to the new landing-ground, where a hangar had been constructed of long poles, roofed with tarpaulin and having sides of grass. The enemy position on this front was at Mfrika, five miles south-east of Lupembe, and it had been carefully reconnoitred and sketched by Brigadier-General Northey's scouts. Flight Lieutenant Moore's early flights therefore were made to familiarize himself with the ground with a view to bombing the enemy camps as soon as the advance began.

Both van Deventer and Northey were ready to advance on the 24th of December in a combined offensive. Next day Northey's columns were closing in on Mfrika, and Flight Lieutenant Moore was flying over them, reporting their progress; he was able easily to locate the columns, the positions of which were marked by white calico laid out on the ground. On the 26th Flight Lieutenant Moore was able to state that the enemy troops were about to evacuate their positions as the tents had already been packed up, and he made two attacks with hand grenades dropped from a low height. The enemy slipped away that same night and was located from the air next day in entrenchments dug on the hill-tops at Msala six miles farther east. Daily bomb and grenade attacks were made on the Msala positions until the 3rd of January 1917 when the enemy troops were forced to retire eastwards with Brigadier-General Northey's troops in pursuit. On the 5th of January the B.E.2C, which had been kept serviceable by the pilot and his one mechanic, was flown back to Alt Iringa for overhaul.

Coastal Operations.

While these rapid forward movements were taking place in the interior, operations had also been successfully carried on in the coastal area, where Tanga had been occupied on the 7th of July 1916 and Bagamoyo on the 15th of August. At the latter seaport, a small force (1,800 rifles) was assembled for an attack on Dar-es-Salaam. This force which moved off in two columns, one along the coast, the other along the Ruvu and the Central Railway, met with little opposition, and when naval vessels appeared off Dar-es-Salaam on the 3rd of September 1916 the port surrendered. Lieutenant-General Smuts was now anxious that the whole coast of German East Africa should be effectively occupied, and he accordingly arranged with Rear-Admiral E. F. B. Charlton to co-operate in the seizure of all important points south of Dar-es-Salaam.

In these coastal operations No. 8 (Naval) Squadron, based at Zanzibar, took part. The squadron, it will be recalled, had arrived from England in March 1916, equipped with four Short seaplanes and four Voisin aeroplanes. These operated from Chukwani Bay, where a Bessonneau hangar had been erected and where a former palace of the Sultan of Zanzibar was put at the disposal of the Naval Air Service personnel.

Mobility for the seaplanes, essential in the coastal operations, was procured by disposing the aircraft in three ships. The *Laconia* took some of the seaplanes to Tanga in April 1916. The *Manica*, refitted after her service at the Dardanelles, had been sent to East African waters, where, early in May, she was fitted with a rough bamboo and canvas hangar and took on board a seaplane and a small party including three officers. The *Manica* went away, on the 17th of May, and made a series of photographic reconnaissances in the neighbourhood of Kilwa. These accomplished, she rejoined the Fleet on the 13th of June for a bombardment of Tanga. About this time the *Himalaya* joined the station and she also was fitted with a temporary hangar aft and took on board a seaplane, and personnel for coastal reconnaissance and spotting work. These three ships, which returned to harbour from time to time to change seaplanes and crews, dropped into something like a routine, the *Manica* usually working off the southern part of the coastline and the *Himalaya* and *Laconia* in the north.

On the 8th of August 1916 Squadron Commander F. W. Bowhill and a party of officers and men arrived, after service in Mesopotamia, as reliefs for Squadron Commander Cull's unit, which embarked for England four days later. This unit, in composition, went back almost as it had arrived at Zanzibar for the *Königsberg* operations in February 1915.

In the operations at Dar-es-Salaam and Bagamoyo in August and September 1916 the seaplanes played a part, the plans for the Bagamoyo attack being based on air photographs taken by the *Manica's* seaplane. After Dar-es-Salaam had been occupied, the *Himalaya* and her seaplane co-operated in landings at Lindi and Sudi Bay, and the *Manica* in a landing at Kilwa. When these operations were successfully concluded both ships returned to Zanzibar. At the end of November, the *Manica* co-operated again in a landing at Kisiju, but otherwise there was little air work in the coastal area down to the end of the year.

There were, however, interesting movements from Kilwa, which had been occupied on the 7th of September 1916. In October some 2,000 rifles, under Brigadier-General J. A. Hannyngton, had been taken by sea from Dar-es-Salaam to Kilwa as a nucleus of the 1st Division. On the 15th of November Major-General A. R. Hoskins took command at Kilwa, and, in the following month, there was considerable local fighting, especially in the neighbourhood of Kibata.

The Rufiji.

While the forces were being reorganised in the interior, the pilots and observers of No. 26 Squadron reconnoitred and bombed the enemy positions on the Mgeta River. On the 31st of August 1916 the squadron had moved to a new aerodrome at Morogoro, south of the station, but on this date, there were no more than three serviceable aeroplanes, all Henri Farmans.

******

> At Morogoro were 'A' and 'C' Flights, but two of the B.E.2c's of the latter Flight had been wrecked and one was being overhauled. 'B' Flight was at Mbuyuni and was being made up to strength with reinforcements newly arriving from England and from South Africa.

******

At Morogoro the squadron was two hundred miles from the advanced Aircraft Park at the rail-head of Korogwe, and the convoys which transported the supplies from Korogwe had many adventures, the personnel having at times to reconstruct bridges washed away by the floods, rebuild culverts, cut alternative paths through the bush, and corduroy long stretches of old track.

On the 18th of September 'B' Flight of the squadron was transferred to Morogoro from Korogwe and took over the B.E.2c's of 'C' Flight. This Flight went to Dar-es-Salaam, where it arrived on the 25th. (In December 'C Flight moved to Kilwa to provide air co-operation for Major-General Hoskins's force.) To this port, also, the main Aircraft Park from Mbuyuni moved on the 6th of December 1916.

Meanwhile, at the beginning of October, half of 'B' Flight had been transferred from Morogoro to Tulo, seventy miles farther south. The transport took five days to complete the move, but on the 5th of October two B.E.2c's flew to the new aerodrome in just over the hour. From the Tulo aerodrome the bulk of the squadron's air work, made up of reconnaissances with occasional bomb-dropping and artillery observation, was done during the next two or three months.

The natural cover afforded by the bush made concealment easy for the enemy, and movements were hard to discover. In their survey work, however, the airmen were more successful. The locality and state of the roads and tracks, the condition of the bridges, the presence of water-supplies, the general topographical features likely to be of military importance in the forthcoming advance—all these, formed essential basic material, in the making of the plans by the Staff. Distances were measured from the air by means of a stop watch, the aeroplane maintaining a constant air speed and allowance being made for the wind.

Hills that commanded roads received particular attention: their heights and their distances from the roads were plotted with care, the relative lengths of the shadows cast by the sun helping the observers to estimate the heights. The late autumn rains turned whole areas into impassable swamp, so that immediately before the offensive was resumed at the end of December more survey work was done to check and correct former observations.

The bombing, which could only be sporadic, did no great material damage, although petrol bombs sometimes started a blaze in the enemy positions which, with a little more luck, might have had disastrous effect. Trouble was experienced about this time with the bombs, many of them failing to explode, and the cause was ultimately traced to the primers, which had deteriorated in the excessive heat.

It was stated, on the 11th of December 1916, that of 1,600 bombs stored at the Aircraft Park, only 200 were serviceable. There was small prospect of obtaining new primers, but an air mechanic, E. R. d'Ade, had experimented with chemicals and had discovered a treatment whereby the affected primers were again made serviceable. For four months this mechanic had pursued his self-imposed task and put in all 500 bombs into working order. On the 25th of January 1917 Air Mechanic d'Ade was working in his isolated shed on the aerodrome when there was an explosion and he was killed.

To turn now to the operations on the Rufiji. The commander-in-chief intended to hold the main enemy forces to the Mgeta front while he sent a flanking column to make a wide turning movement to the west. This column was to cross the Rufiji at Mkalinzo, where it is joined by the Ruaha, and then move south-west to join the Kilwa division coming from the direction of the Matumbi Mountains. These movements were designed to cut all connexion between the enemy forces on the Rufiji and those at Mahenge, and also to surround the Rufiji forces or else deal them a final blow as they retreated south.

Rain on the Mgeta front delayed the opening of the operations from the 26th to the 31st of December 1916. A holding attack was delivered on the 1st of January 1917 from the forward positions on the Dutumi front, while two columns worked their way round the flanks. The Tulo detachment ('B' Flight) of No. 26 Squadron, which had been reinforced by two Henri Farmans from 'A' Flight at Morogoro, co-operated in the operations in this sector. Two aeroplanes, fitted with wireless, were placed under the orders of the C.R.A. to co-operate with the artillery and to report to ground stations enemy movements in their areas of operations.

The remaining aeroplanes of the detachment were to patrol continuously from 5.30 a.m. over the area Tulo-Kiruru-Kinyanguru-Behobeho Wiransi-Kisaki-Dakawa-Dutumi-Tulo. The patrolling airmen were to report urgently any sign of the evacuation of Dutumi or Dakawa and also suitable bombing targets. Message bags were carried in each aeroplane, the dropping centre being the advanced head-quarters on the Dutumi ridge. Only three officer observers were available, and eight air mechanics were impressed to do duty as observers.

The airmen flew to programme throughout the 1st of January 1917, the first day of the forward move. Soon after 4.0 p.m. the evacuation of Kiderengwa was reported, and an aeroplane was at once sent out to bomb the retreating columns. The pilot discovered a large enemy detachment in the open bush and dropped one 100-lb. and five 20-lb. bombs, upon which the enemy scattered. He returned for a second load and, when he got back over the front, found the enemy had taken up a position at Tshimbe, parallel to trenches occupied by the British easterly flanking column. The pilot dropped one 100-lb. and eight 20-lb. bombs on the enemy. The bombing was taken up later by another aeroplane and continued intermittently till dusk. Meanwhile the patrolling observers were able to keep the headquarters informed of the progress of the local enveloping columns.

An early air reconnaissance next morning, the 2nd of January, revealed no sign of the enemy troops in the positions they had held the night before, and it soon became clear that the whole force had slipped away from the Mgeta front. Finding his retreat blocked by the enveloping columns, the enemy had in fact broken up his own columns and had taken to the bush: he eventually took up a new position on the Tshogowali River south of Behobeho. Attempts to encircle this position on the 3rd and 4th of January failed, the enemy again slipping away east.

Meanwhile, on the 3rd of January, Beves's Brigade, which was making the wide turning movement, crossed the Rufiji a few miles south of Mkalinzo and secured and entrenched the bridge-head. There was, however, another crossing at Kibambawe lower down the Rufiji, but here the bridge had been damaged by floods. All the aeroplanes were concentrated on the bombing of this bridge on the 3rd and 4th of January while the enemy engineers were making desperate efforts to put it in rough repair. The bombing failed to destroy the bridge, and the repairs proved good enough for the whole enemy force to get safely across on the night of the 4th and establish themselves on the right bank of the river.

When the British forces reached the river, they found the roadway of the bridge removed, but they succeeded in making a crossing and took up a position facing the enemy. The aeroplane pilots of 'B' Flight now began the bombing of the new enemy position. On the 8th of January Lieutenant L. J. Riordan found an enemy store camp in a clearing near the Luhembero road. He dropped six petrol bombs from a low height, and one of the large *bandas*, or grass huts, went up in flames, with about a hundred loads of food.

Enemy detachments north of the Rufiji at Kisangire and Mkamba fell back south, some of them getting across the river about fifteen miles west of Utete. The gap between the westerly troops of the Kilwa division at Ngarambi and Beves's Brigade at Mkalinzo was still too big for any effective blocking of the enemy's southward retreat, and, to contract the gap, a column was ordered from Mkalinzo to Luhembero on the 17th of January and, at the same time, other troops were sent to clear the enemy from the positions south of the Rufiji at Kibambawe. These movements were successful. The south bank of the river as well as Mkindu and Luhembero were occupied on the 18th and the enemy retreated south-east.

On the 17th of January Kisegese had been occupied, following which the British troops moved on Koge. The operations between the Mgeta and the Rufiji Rivers, the crossing of the latter at Kibambawe, and the subsequent advance to Mkindu, weakened the enemy resistance in the Kibata area. The withdrawal of the enemy from his strong positions in the Kichi and Matumbi Mountains north of Kibata followed, and this made it possible for the British troops to occupy Mohoro on the south Rufiji delta on the 16th of January. In these coastal operations 'C' Flight of No. 26 Squadron at Kilwa and the seaplanes of No. 8 (R.N.A.S.) Squadron at Zanzibar co-operated with reconnaissance and bombing.

A reconnaissance, by naval aircraft, of the Rufiji delta at this time resulted in the death of the Flag Commander, the Honourable R. O. B. Bridgeman. The *Himalaya* had arrived off the Rufiji on her way down to Zanzibar to change her seaplane. Commander Bridgeman was anxious that the delta should be reconnoitred to ascertain the whereabouts of a reported enemy steamer, and, as the *Manica's* seaplane, which would ordinarily have done the reconnaissance, needed overhaul and would not carry an observer, Flight Lieutenant E. R. Moon, the flying officer in the *Himalaya*, undertook the duty, and Commander Bridgeman went up in the observer's seat, a position he had often before occupied.

The flight began at 7.30 a.m. on the 6th of January 1917, but an hour later, when the seaplane was over the delta, the engine revolutions dropped, and the pilot was forced to alight at the inland end of a creek north of the main channel. Commander Bridgeman took the pilot's seat and taxied the seaplane while the pilot tried to repair the engine. The pilot discovered that the drive for the after magneto had gone, but while he was locating the damage, the pressure in the petrol tank dropped and the engine stopped. All attempts to restart the engine were in vain, and Commander Bridgeman decided there was nothing to do but destroy the seaplane and attempt an escape on foot.

The descent of the seaplane had been watched by a German coastal patrol nearby. This patrol had, hitherto, had the use of a steamboat, but this had been dismantled on the previous day because the engines were wanted to grind corn, and the patrol therefore set out on foot. They, however, misjudged the position of the seaplane and searched the wrong end of the creek.

Meanwhile the seaplane had been flooded with petrol and fired by a Very light, and the pilot and his passenger had started off in the direction of the mouth of the river. To divert pursuit, they first swam the creek, but when they came to the opposite shore they found the bush impenetrable and were compelled to pick their way slowly through the soft mud along the bank. They were, at times, up to their necks in water and could only get relief from mosquitoes by dipping their heads.

When they became overdue, Flight Sub-Lieutenant E. E. Deans, in the *Manica's* seaplane, set off to search for them, and ultimately found the charred wreckage of their seaplane near which he landed. He fired Very lights in the hope that he would attract the attention of the officers, but as the wreckage of the seaplane was upside down, he feared it had fallen out of control and that the occupants had been killed. He waited for ten minutes and then took off again and returned to his ship. He was seen on his way home by the two escaping officers lower down the creek, but they had no means of attracting his attention and they watched him disappear into the eastern sky. The *Thistle* and the *Echo*, which were attending off the delta, were informed of the position of the wrecked seaplane and tried to reach it, but they could not get closer in than two miles owing to lack of water.

By about 6.0 p.m. the two officers had travelled some miles down the creek when they were brought to a halt by deep water at the shore's edge. Later, in the darkness, the pilot saw what looked like the outline of a boat on the far shore near where a former blockade ship, the *Somali*, was beached.

Commander Bridgeman was too exhausted to make the swim, and Moon plunged in alone and reached the far shore to find he had been deceived by a curious bush formation. He continued his swim to the *Somali* and climbed on board but found no water or biscuits. Five times during the night he attempted the return swim to the spot where he had left his companion and each time he was forced back by the tide.

At daybreak next day, the 7th of January, he got across, but could then find no trace of his companion. He swam on downstream and shortly came upon a derelict house at the water's edge, and there caught sight of Commander Bridgeman, whom he rejoined. The two now went off in search of food and were rewarded with a find of coconuts. From the latticed window frames of the house they were able to construct a raft, lashing the spars with sisal. A search of their temporary habitation yielded a broken canoe paddle and two bottles. The latter were filled with coconut milk and, when the tide turned, the raft was launched and a start made towards the mouth of the river, the broken paddle helping the officers to keep direction.

Progress was slow owing to the restricted buoyancy of the raft,

Commander Bridgeman, who sat amidships, being submerged to his neck. Into the evening and through the night, the officers struggled on. At dawn next morning they sighted the *Newbridge*, which had been sunk to block the entrance to the channel, but the tide was now on the flood and they could not get near her.

They therefore ran their raft ashore and searched inland for food and drink but found nothing. At slack water they set off again and got up with the *Newbridge* but, once again, when they clambered aboard, found nothing. They did, however, far down along the eastern bank near the mouth of the channel, get a glimpse of a boat, and they decided to make for this next morning. Meanwhile they discovered that one of their coconuts had been lost and that salt water had got into one of the milk bottles, and, for fear of losing what remained, they drank the contents of the other bottle. Before dawn on the 9th of January they pushed off once again for the eastern bank, but their raft was carried upstream on the flood tide and then, when the tide turned, was rushed down the channel and out to sea. Here new difficulties came to try them. The wind was blowing against the tide and in the lop the raft repeatedly capsized.

The two officers, worn by their three days' exposure and bitten by mosquitoes and by garfish, had scarce strength enough to scramble back each time they were thrown from their frail platform. By midday they were tossing on the open sea almost out of sight of land, and Commander Bridgeman was semi-conscious. The pilot, who was in little better condition, took the commander in his arms to keep his head above water. Then the pilot himself fell into a stupor and when he opened his eyes again in the afternoon his companion had disappeared. Flight Lieutenant Moon clung to the raft on the turning tide and about 5.0 p.m. was washed ashore. He had, from before dawn, spent thirteen hours on the raft, most of them in the open sea. Nor was his ordeal at an end.

Before he finally got clear of the water his face, hands, and feet, were lacerated by the rocks. He lay on the beach for some time, and then began to struggle inland. Shortly he met a native in a canoe and tried to bribe the man to give him a passage, but a second native appeared and he was dragged into their hut. There he was given drink and food, and as he ate noticed that the men were donning *askari* uniform.

Anxious to appear with their prisoner without loss of time, the *askari* moved off after dark and handed Moon to the commander of a German observation post about an hour and a half farther south, whence he was conveyed to hospital where he made a complete recovery. The body of Commander Bridgeman was washed ashore at Kiomboni and was buried by the enemy. In this officer the navy lost a leader of great promise and the air service a keen supporter. He never hesitated to share the risks of the flying officers, asking nothing of them he was not ready and eager to do himself.

★★★★★★

Flight Lieutenant Edwin Rowland Moon was released by the enemy in November 1917. He survived the war and became a permanent officer in the Royal Air Force. He was drowned at Felixstowe on the 29th of April 1920 as a result of an accident to a flying-boat in which he was giving instruction.

★★★★★★

On the 12th of January 1917 Admiralty orders were received for the withdrawal of No. 7 Squadron from the interior, and arrangements were made for No. 26 Squadron to take over their aeroplanes, transport, and stores. The aeroplanes were two B.E.2c's at Dar-es-Salaam, and three at Alt Iringa, and there were seven spare engines as well as transport and hangars, and the depots at Dodoma and Dar-es-Salaam.

★★★★★★

The strength and disposition of No. 26 Squadron, on the 23rd of January 1917, following the transfer, was as follows: three aeroplanes and three pilots at Kilwa, four aeroplanes and three pilots at Tulo, one pilot and five aeroplanes (of which four were to be sent to Egypt) at Morogoro, and three aeroplanes at Dar-es-Salaam. Of the last, two had been allotted to Iringa as soon as pilots were available. Four pilots were already on their way to Iringa to take over the three R.N.A.S. aeroplanes there. Eight aeroplanes were unpacked. Six pilots were down sick, but six pilots were on their way to join the squadron from England.

★★★★★★

'A' Flight of No. 26 Squadron left Morogoro for Alt Iringa on the 18th of January 1917. The Flight, after taking over the R.N.A.S. stores at Dodoma, accepted transfer of the three B.E.2c's at Iringa on the 30th of January. All the B.E.2c's were fitted with ninety horse-power Royal Aircraft Factory engines.

During the time No. 7 (Naval) Squadron had been operating in the interior, six pilots had covered a total distance in the air of 85,000 miles, and the ground personnel had overcome their transport and store difficulties so well that the aeroplanes had operated without loss or serious breakdown.

On the 20th of January 1917 Lieutenant-General Smuts sailed from Dar-es-Salaam to represent South Africa at the Imperial Conference in London, and the command in East Africa was taken over by Lieutenant-General A. R. Hoskins. It will be convenient to summarize the position when this change in command took place. The greater part of the main enemy forces, under Lettow-Vorbeck, was near Utete or east of the Lugonya River, while a strong enemy detachment was contesting the advance of a British column moving from Kisegese through Koge towards the Rufiji.

The south bank of the Rufiji was in the hands of the enemy from Utete to Nyakisiki, and another German force was four miles south of Mkindu, which was held by British troops. Such was the position in the main theatre. In the western area Brigadier-General Northey had driven the enemy east of the Ruhuje. A German detachment under Kraut was near Iringa, and other columns, under Wahle and Wintgens, near Kitanda, and two companies under Grawert at Likuju. With all these detachments, Brigadier-General Northey was in touch. At Mahenge, and along the line of the Kilombero River west and north, was another enemy detachment, while others were widely located at Lindi and westwards.

Lieutenant-General Hoskins, who was anxious to use the Rufiji for transport purposes, decided to push the enemy as far south of the river as possible, but the necessary operations were made difficult by unexpectedly severe rains that set in on the 25th of January 1917 and washed away bridges and flooded the roads along the lines of communication. By the end of February, the north bank of the Rufiji had been cleared and a column was ferried across the river near Utete, after which supplies to Utete by water became regular. By the middle of May, the Rufiji, from Utete to Kibambawe, and the country twenty miles south of the river were clear and the enemy was still retreating. Flying from the waterlogged aerodromes in the eastern sector proved impossible during these forward movements. In the Kilwa district conditions were so bad that the personnel of 'C' Flight were withdrawn to Morogoro on the 20th of February, leaving their aeroplanes behind in the care of a small detachment.

In the south-west the weather was less severe, but the flooded roads made communication with 'A' Flight, which moved south from Iringa to Ubena (Njombe) at the end of February 1917, difficult. On the

12th of February Lieutenant Leo Walmsley set out from Dodoma with a convoy for Alt Iringa. He was compelled to do the 150mile journey on foot and arrived at his destination within ten days. Eventually Dodoma had to be given up as a depot and all stores for the Flight sent by Chinde and the Zambesi River. For four months between February and June 1917 'A' Flight at Ubena received no supplies of petrol, bombs, or spares. Bombs were improvised on the spot by filling paraffin tins with dynamite, nuts, bolts, nails, and other scrap; and these, together with rifle grenades, were dropped on the enemy positions.

The petrol for the Flight had to be transported by native porters from Lake Nyasa, across the Livingstone Mountains. This meant laborious climbing to the top of the Pass, which was 6,000 feet high. The porters, for a time, found a means of easing their burden. They unscrewed the stoppers of the eight-gallon drums as soon as they conveniently could after starting, and poured part of the petrol away, refilling the drums with water when they got near Ubena. Even after this practice was discovered, it could not be efficiently checked, and it meant that all petrol had to be filtered through chamois leathers before the pilots could use it. Such air work as could be done between January and May was confined to urgent reconnaissance and bombing.

An adventure of a flying officer on the 26th of February 1917 will illustrate the risks inseparable from flying in jungle country. Lieutenant G. W. T. Garrood left Tulo on a B.E.2c with a load of bombs to reconnoitre the Utete area and did not return. A reconnaissance next morning discovered his aeroplane on its nose about twenty miles south of the aerodrome, but the pilot was nowhere to be seen. Search parties and native hunters were sent out, and the latter found Lieutenant Garrood on the 1st of March. He had been forced down in a marsh with engine trouble and had spent four foodless days trekking through the jungle and, when found, was suffering from fever, shock, and exhaustion. He was wearing only his helmet, vest, and boots. His revolver, food, and part of his clothing had been lost while he was swimming the rivers, but the bulk of his clothing had been stolen by baboons when it was drying. The pilot's experiences included a narrow escape from a crocodile while swimming a river, and a night of enforced imprisonment up a tree with a leopard beneath him.

On the day that Lieutenant Garrood was found, another aeroplane, containing Lieutenants A. H. Bottrell and W. P. Brown, failed to reach Tulo from Morogoro. The officers had missed the aerodrome and had landed forty-five miles south-east of Tulo, where their aeroplane was located on the 4th of March. The officers were nowhere to be seen, but the search for them went on from the air, and they were discovered, two days later, having progressed about fifteen miles towards Tulo. Food and quinine and instructions about the route to be followed were dropped on them, and food was dropped again on the following day. All further trace of the two officers was then lost until the 11th when they were found by native scouts and conveyed to hospital.

Considerable difficulty was experienced in keeping the widely scattered detachments of the squadron up to sufficient strength in men for even the minimum efficiency, as the climate took heavy toll.

******

> Between April 1916 and April 1917 346 N.C.O.'s and men (of whom 216 constituted the original unit from England) were on the strength of the squadron. On the 30th of April 1917 the effective strength in other ranks was 125. Of the rest, 8 had died, 33 were in hospital, and 180 had been discharged for medical reasons or invalided to South Africa.

******

On the 29th of May 1917 Lieutenant-General J. L. van Deventer took over the command from Lieutenant-General Hoskins. At this time the enemy forces were in two main bodies. The western force, based on Mahenge under Tafel, held the country for about seventy miles to the north, east, and west of that centre, and had an outlying detachment at Likuju. The main force, under Lettow-Vorbeck, was in the coastal area facing the British troops at Kilwa and Lindi. In addition, there were small enemy columns which broke back northwards, and one party, under Stuemer, that penetrated into Portuguese East Africa. (Following the declaration of war on Germany by Portugal, on the 9th of March 1916, Portuguese troops crossed the Ruvuma and occupied posts inside German territory.)

In the final phase of the operations Major-General van Deventer led the main army against Lettow-Vorbeck, while Brigadier-General Northey, with Belgian assistance, closed in on Tafel's force in the Mahenge area.

Northey's Final Advance.

To protect his communications Brigadier-General Northey sent a detachment south into Portuguese territory to deal with Stuemer's column which was making for Portuguese Nyasaland. To co-operate in this movement the headquarters of 'A' Flight of No. 26 Squadron, under Captain G. W. Hodgkinson, and one aeroplane were ordered south to Fort Johnston, where they arrived in the gunboat *Gwendoline* on the 20th of May and moved to a roughly prepared aerodrome, the surface of which was loose sand. Captain Hodgkinson organised a party of two hundred porters and directed them in the making of a narrow strip of runway down the aerodrome from beaten ant-heap. From this aerodrome with his observer, Lieutenant Leo Walmsley, he made many extended reconnaissances to find the enemy columns.

To give the B.E.2c an endurance of about five hours, the observer carried extra tins of petrol to replenish the service petrol tank of the aeroplane in the air. The arrangements for doing this were crude, but they sufficed. A piece of inner tyre rubber tubing was fixed to each can and secured with string, and when the engine had consumed the fuel in the tank, the observer was required to remove the cap from the tank, undo the string from the rubber tubing on the can, insert the tubing into the tank, and so fill up again.

A minor difficulty when this device was first tried arose from the expansion of the petrol gas in the can, due to the decrease in the atmospheric pressure when the aeroplane reached its height, and a consequent blowing out of the cycle tubing into a balloon shape. The device, however, proved successful and enabled many long flights to be made. In doing their reconnaissances the airmen were confronted with the difficulty, present throughout the whole campaign, that the maps with which they were supplied were always vague and often inaccurate, and so made navigation hazardous and the acquisition of useful information a difficult task.

By the end of June 1917 Brigadier-General Northey's column was nearing Mwembe, and by this time a new aerodrome had been taken up at Mtonia, seventy miles north-east of Fort Johnston. A reconnaissance made over Mwembe on the 29th of June reported the enemy holding a strongly entrenched position with several machine-guns in support. A sketch of the enemy positions was made from the air and handed to the officer commanding the column advancing against the village. Mwembe was taken on the 6th of July and the enemy fell back northwards. Five days later the aeroplane detachment moved from Mtonia to Mwembe and, on the 12th, the enemy position to the north was discovered and bombed, a large *banda* being set on fire.

Next day a column was found and bombed on the Maziwas-Mwembe road. On the 18th of July it was decided to withdraw the air detachment from this column to Songea, and the move was completed by way of Lake Nyasa and Wiedhafen by the end of July. But the old B.E.2c, which had responded so well to the demands made on her during her stay in Portuguese territory, did not survive the journey. Her engine failed as the pilot was taking off from the Mwembe landing-ground and she crashed into a mango tree and broke up, the occupants escaping with minor injuries.

★★★★★★

> The pilot, Captain Hodgkinson, procured a mule for his mechanic who was the more shaken, and walked back with him to Fort Johnston, the 180-mile journey taking six and a half days to complete.

★★★★★★

The operations of Northey's main columns against Tafel may be briefly summarized. His Songea column had completed its concentration at Likuju on the 30th of June 1917. From this place one B.E.2c of 'A' Flight made many reconnaissance and bombing flights over the enemy positions preliminary to the move forward, which began on the 3rd of July. Once the advance began, and the enemy vacated his prepared positions and took to the bush, air reconnaissance became of doubtful value as the bush and forest concealed all movements. By the end of July Northey had reached Mponda in his pursuit of the enemy, and as a halt was necessary preparatory to a wide forward movement in the middle of September, the aeroplanes of 'A' Flight (now two B.E.2c's) were able to resume their reconnaissance of the enemy positions in the Mponda area.

To keep the Flight supplied, great transport difficulties had to be overcome. Dodoma, the nearest point on the railway to which stores could be sent, was five hundred miles by road from the aerodrome at Likuju, and Dodoma itself was three hundred miles along the railway from the aircraft base at Dar-es-Salaam. Furthermore, only light stores could be sent by this route. Heavier material had to go by sea to Portuguese East Africa and thence overland by Nyasaland and, on this route, three months were consumed between the time of dispatch and the time of receipt. But, up to October 1917, the Flight was able to meet Brigadier-General Northey's demands with fair success. By that time, however, the two aeroplanes could no longer be kept serviceable, and this Flight took no further part in the operations.

The end of Tafel's detachment can be briefly told. Early in October 1917 Belgian troops occupied the Mahenge plateau and thence moved southwards in touch with Brigadier-General Northey's columns advancing from the west. By the 11th of November 1917 it became apparent that Tafel intended to break south in an endeavour to join Lettow-Vorbeck. In this he failed, and on the 28th of November he surrendered unconditionally with 19 officers, 92 other Europeans, and 3,300 natives. In addition, part of his command, numbering 37 Germans and 1,278 natives, had surrendered on the previous day.

KILWA AND LINDI: THE LAST PHASE.

Meanwhile some of the fiercest fighting of the campaign had taken place between the Kilwa and Lindi columns and Lettow-Vorbeck's main forces, and in these operations aircraft played a more notable part.

******

In June 1917 the War Office agreed to increase the establishment of No. 26 Squadron to 33 officers and 286 other ranks and to increase the Aircraft Park to 5 officers and 65 other ranks. This increase was made necessary by sickness and by the extra work thrown on the personnel by reason of the squadron being split up into detachments. During June 120 N.C.O.'s and men were drafted to the squadron. On the 4th of August 11 flying officers arrived at Dar-es-Salaam and four more on the 28th. This brought the squadron and the Aircraft Park up to the new establishment.

******

On the 10th of May 1917 'C' Flight of No. 26 Squadron had returned to its aerodrome at Kilwa, where the pilots found their three B.E.2c's had been kept serviceable through the rainy season by the few men who had been left in charge of them. A fourth aeroplane arrived, and throughout the remainder of the month, and in June, reconnaissance and bombing flights were made over the enemy positions preparatory to the move forward. Staff officers from the various army commands, were flown as passengers to study the ground over which their columns would be required to advance.

At Lindi an aerodrome was prepared for two Voisin aeroplanes (150 horse-power Canton Unné engines) from No. 8 (Naval) Squadron at Zanzibar. While the aerodrome was being got ready a Short seaplane (150 horse-power Sunbeam engine), first operating from the *Manica* and afterwards from a base in Lindi harbour, was responsible for the reconnaissance and bombing work, and also made many spotting flights for the *Thistle*.

A minor movement from Lindi was begun early in June, and in this the two naval Voisins and the Short seaplane co-operated. The Voisins proved at first difficult to handle in the bumpy atmosphere in the Lindi area, but the seaplane did good work. The pilot was Flight Sub-Lieutenant C. F. M. Chambers and his observer Petty Officer Mechanic F. Wilmshurst. These two charted the roads for the topographical section, and chiefly on their information the maps were made that were used in the advance. The pilot also took officers of the intelligence staff for reconnaissance flights over the enemy positions, as well as the captain and navigator of the *Thistle*. These two officers were flown over the Lindi estuary to survey the channels, sandbanks, and beaches in connexion with a landing of troops and to select a berth for the ship, inside the entrance, from which she could fire on the enemy positions. On the 2nd of June four bombs, dropped from the seaplane, set fire to the enemy post office at Mingoyo which was gutted.

The Lindi force began to move forward, in two columns, on the 10th of June 1917. The main column advanced to the east of Mandawa from a creek in the coast where a successful landing had been made. The ships in the estuary, which supported the landing, helped with their fire to cover the main column. Next day, when contact with the enemy was made, the seaplane personnel spotted for the *Severn* and *Thistle*, and also reported to headquarters the movements of the British and of the enemy troops. The communication between the base and advanced head-quarters broke down, and the seaplane was then used to provide a connecting link. In the afternoon head-quarters lost touch with the right column. The seaplane pilot reported the position of the column by wireless and message bag, and later landed at head-quarters to receive messages and orders for the column, which the pilot delivered by message bag. When the column was approaching Mayani, later in the afternoon, the occupants of the seaplane realised the troops would quickly be endangered by the fire of the naval guns, and they thereupon signalled the guns to cease fire.

For the next two days the seaplane was used, almost exclusively, as a link between the converging columns. Orders for the columns were communicated to the seaplane by ground-panel from headquarters and were then dropped by message bag. On the 13th of June the initial operations were successfully concluded, the enemy being forced to abandon the area. With the retirement of the enemy inland the seaplane was withdrawn to Zanzibar, and the air work was continued by two naval Voisin aeroplanes.

The advance from Kilwa started at the beginning of July, and during the preliminary moves two B.E.2c's of 'C' Flight of No. 26 Squadron helped to direct the troops by marking the enemy positions with flares and bombs. The enemy forces, after hard fighting, were gradually driven south from the Matandu River towards Lindi.

While the Kilwa force was on the move in July, the Lindi force was preparing to co-operate further. As part of this preparation the survey and mapping of the area ahead of the Lindi troops was done by three naval Voisin aeroplanes, and the more important enemy positions were photographed. One such position, Schaedles Upper Farm, was successfully bombarded on the 4th of July, with the help of aeroplane spotting, by the monitor *Severn*. The commander of the Lindi force, Brigadier-General H. de C. O'Grady, was many times flown over the area before his force moved forward on the 2nd of August. On this day one of the Voisin pilots discovered a strong group of new entrenchments on Tandamuti Hill, ahead of the main advancing column, and this new position, on the 3rd, brought the main column to a standstill.

The commanding officer was kept informed of the movements of his columns and of the tactical position at nightfall by wireless messages from the air and by written reports (some being dropped in message bags), and wireless communication was kept up with the monitors which were spotted for. To overcome the position on Tandamuti Hill, a turning movement south of the hill was made on the 10th of August, and, shortly after the movement was set on foot, a Voisin pilot discovered that the enemy was in retreat. At this time the top of Tandamuti Hill was being bombarded from the sea, and the pilot promptly signalled one of the monitors to switch over to the retreating enemy columns. He spotted for the monitor on the new target, and then asked for rapid fire from both guns. This was immediately forthcoming and the enemy column was broken up. Meanwhile the progress of the turning movement and of the retreat of the enemy was communicated by wireless messages to Brigadier-General O'Grady's headquarters.

By the 18th of August the Lindi forces had pressed the enemy back to a defensive position at Nurunju, but on this day Lettow-Vorbeck arrived at Nurunju with reinforcements from the Kilwa area and brought the retreat to a temporary halt. The Voisins were now used for reconnaissance and bombing of the Nurunju entrenchments, and for co-operation with the 5.9 howitzers and 13-pounder batteries in bombardments of them.

The three Voisins, which had to be kept pegged out in the open without protection, were carefully used to keep them serviceable. They had been shipped from England in January 1916 and had been in service ever since. So far as the operations would permit, one of the three was kept out of action for overhaul, giving place to another when the overhaul was complete.

All was ready for the further advance of both the Kilwa and Lindi forces in the middle of September.

******

> At this time 'C Flight (3 B.E.2c's) was working from a landing ground at Mssindyi. On the 19th of September 1917 the Kilwa front was reinforced by 'B' Flight, which had been re-equipped with three B.E.2C aeroplanes at Dar-es-Salaam.

******

The move forward from Kilwa began on the 19th of September, and its progress was reported by message bags dropped from the air. Pilots and observers helped in the advance by attacking enemy troops with machine-gun fire and bombs, in doing which, on the 20th, every aeroplane received hits from rifles or machine-guns fired from the ground. On the 21st the air observers reported that the enemy was retiring south-west from Mihambia and that British troops had occupied the important Ndessa position. The enemy found his retreat cut off by two battalions of the Nigerian Brigade, and after desperate attempts to break through split up into small parties, which slipped away through the bush. Instructions from the commander-in-chief to the Nigerian Brigade were sent on this and the next day by air, eighteen messages in all being dropped. On the 24th of September and subsequent days, communication with the cavalry column was maintained in a similar manner.

The Kilwa columns continued their southward movement, the enemy offering stubborn resistance the whole way, and the main air work continued to be the reporting of the progress of the British columns. On the 27th/28th of September the enemy, yielding to the combined pressure, evacuated the Nahungu positions and retired southwest, with the obvious intention of concentrating ultimately in the Masasi area.

The whole of the Kilwa force was now concentrated at Nahungu. The time had arrived for the main pressure to be exerted from the Lindi front, and in consequence the bulk of the Kilwa force was ordered thither from Nahungu. The Nigerian Brigade was ordered to make a flanking movement across an eighty-mile stretch of waterless country to strike at the left of the enemy while the Lindi force was pressing from the east. The brigade started off on the 4th of October. The Lindi columns had begun their advance on Nurunju and Mtua on the 24th of September. The enemy positions in these areas and the country in the line of advance towards them had been sketched from the air in a long series of flights by the Naval Air Service Voisins, and before the forward move began the G.O.C. had been given a map of the area made from these sketches. The enemy did not attempt serious opposition. After a brief fight on the 27th, he vacated his positions and withdrew towards Mtama.

By the 11th of October the Lindi columns were making flanking movements against Mtama, but the enemy did not stop to fight, and retired slowly westwards towards Nyangao. The two naval Voisins (the third had been wrecked in a forced landing on the 24th of September) were employed on reconnaissance and bombing during the move on Mtama and were also used to keep touch with the Nigerian Brigade. This brigade, hampered by lack of water and compelled to negotiate the bush track for the most part in single file, was three days late in making contact with the Lindi force. When the brigade failed to appear on the 8th of October a Voisin was ordered to make a search. The pilot found the column and dropped maps and sketches from the air for its use. On the 9th the G.O.C. was anxious to send the Brigade instructions to move with all possible speed against the rear of the enemy forces at Mahiwa on the main Lindi-Masasi road.

These instructions could only go by aeroplane, and although the weather was unfavourable for flying, a Voisin pilot set out and succeeded in delivering the message. On the 11th a relief column, taking food and stores to the Nigerian Brigade, was directed from the air on the position reached by the brigade which had previously been informed by message bag that food was on the way. Acting energetically on the G.O.C.'s instructions, dropped by the aeroplane on the 9th, the column pressed forward with such success that, by the 13th, it had struck across the left flank of the enemy and had gained his food store and rallying centre at Mahiwa. (See *The Empire at War*. Edited by Sir Charles Lucas, K.C.B., K.C.M.G. Volume IV.)

It now became necessary to move the air detachments with both the Kilwa and Lindi forces farther forward. On the 7th of October 'B' and 'C' Flights of No. 26 Squadron moved from Mssindyi to Nahungu, where a small stretch of ground was available in a hill-girt valley. Many trees had to be cut down before the new landing ground could be used with moderate safety, and as the enemy at the time of the transfer was within raiding distance of Nahungu, the aerodrome had to be put in a state of defence. Amongst other measures, Hales bombs, fitted with an electric firing mechanism, were laid out on the exposed sides of the aerodrome, and wires connecting the bombs were carried to a trench from which the bombs could be fired singly or together. The aeroplanes of the naval squadron were transferred from Lindi to a new aerodrome at Mtua on the 13th of October.

From both these aerodromes continuous reconnaissance and occasional bombing flights were made, and the G.O.C. was kept informed of the movements of his columns in the complicated fighting that took place in the middle of October. On the 9th of October a bomb attack was made by five aeroplanes of No. 26 Squadron on the enemy's store *bandas* in the Masasi area, as a result of which a depot was set on fire and gutted, and direct hits were obtained on other objectives in the enemy camps. On the 2 1st and 24th of October, the squadron bombed Tschiwata, causing extensive fires on each occasion.

The severe fighting in the middle of October compelled a halt in the advance until supplies and reinforcements could be brought up, but on the 6th of November the offensive was renewed. In the forward move which followed, the aeroplanes were used to survey the land, more particularly for water, and the reports of the observers were of tactical importance, as the British columns were often directed on water-holes of which the enemy had no knowledge. There was, in addition, considerable spasmodic bombing and occasional photographing of enemy positions, the photographs being dropped on the nearby British columns within a few hours of the plates being exposed. From time to time, also, messages were dropped by bag to give advancing columns bearings on their objectives.

About this time a warning was received from the War Office in London that a Zeppelin flying from Europe might attempt to land, about the 20th of November 1917, with supplies for Lettow-Vorbeck's columns. Arrangements were made to keep a look-out for the airship and to attack her with bombs if she appeared. The Zeppelin did not complete the journey, but her flight constituted a remarkable performance. The chief medical officer of the German East African colonial troops had reported on his arrival in Germany in 1916, as an exchanged prisoner of war, that Lettow-Vorbeck's troops were short of medicines, and his suggestion that an airship should fly out with medical stores was ultimately adopted. In September 1917 the naval

Zeppelin *L.57* had been specially adapted at Friedrichshafen for the long journey to East Africa, but on her trial flight in a strong wind storm she was dashed to the ground and wrecked.

A new Zeppelin, the *L.59*, then under construction at the Zeppelin works at Staaken, near Berlin, was rapidly completed for the second attempt. She set out from Jamboli, in Bulgaria, under the command of Kapitänleutnant Bockholt, on the 16th of November 1917, with a total load, including ballast, fuel, and crew, of about fifty-five tons, of which thirteen and a half tons were medicines, ammunition, rifles, jungle knives, and wireless parts. The Zeppelin had progressed about half-way, and, according to German reports, was over Khartoum when she was recalled by wireless from the German Admiralty in Berlin, in the belief that the German garrison had evacuated East Africa. The *L.59* was turned about and landed safely at Jamboli again after being in the air for ninety-five hours, during which 4,230 miles had been covered. She still had fuel for a further flight of sixty-four hours when she landed, and it was calculated that, carrying a fifteen-ton load, she might have made a non-stop flight from Germany to San Francisco.

The recall of the *L.59* was a wise step. It is unlikely she would ever have found the remnants of Lettow-Vorbeck's forces, and even had she done so she must have been an added source of embarrassment to them. While the Zeppelin was in the air, the main part of the enemy troops had been captured, notably in Tschiwata and Lutshemi, but Lettow-Vorbeck himself, with the remnants of his men, won through the thick bush to the Ruvuma, which he crossed into Portuguese territory at Ngomano on the 25th and 26th of November. Furthermore, Lettow-Vorbeck found an alternative supply of ammunition and medical stores. The Portuguese garrison at Ngomano attempted to delay his movements. The garrison fought bravely, but with little method, and was defeated with heavy loss. Lettow-Vorbeck captured in the Portuguese camp ample supplies of rifles, machineguns, ammunition, equipment, and medicines to enable him to continue his resistance for the remainder of the war.

Of the German commander's further wanderings at the head of his elusive column little more need be said. When the war ended he was still at large in northern Rhodesia, and under the terms of the Armistice he surrendered at Abercorn on the 25th of November 1918 with 155 Europeans and 1,166 natives.

When Lettow-Vorbeck escaped over the Ruvuma, the air detachments which had co-operated with the Kilwa and Lindi forces were

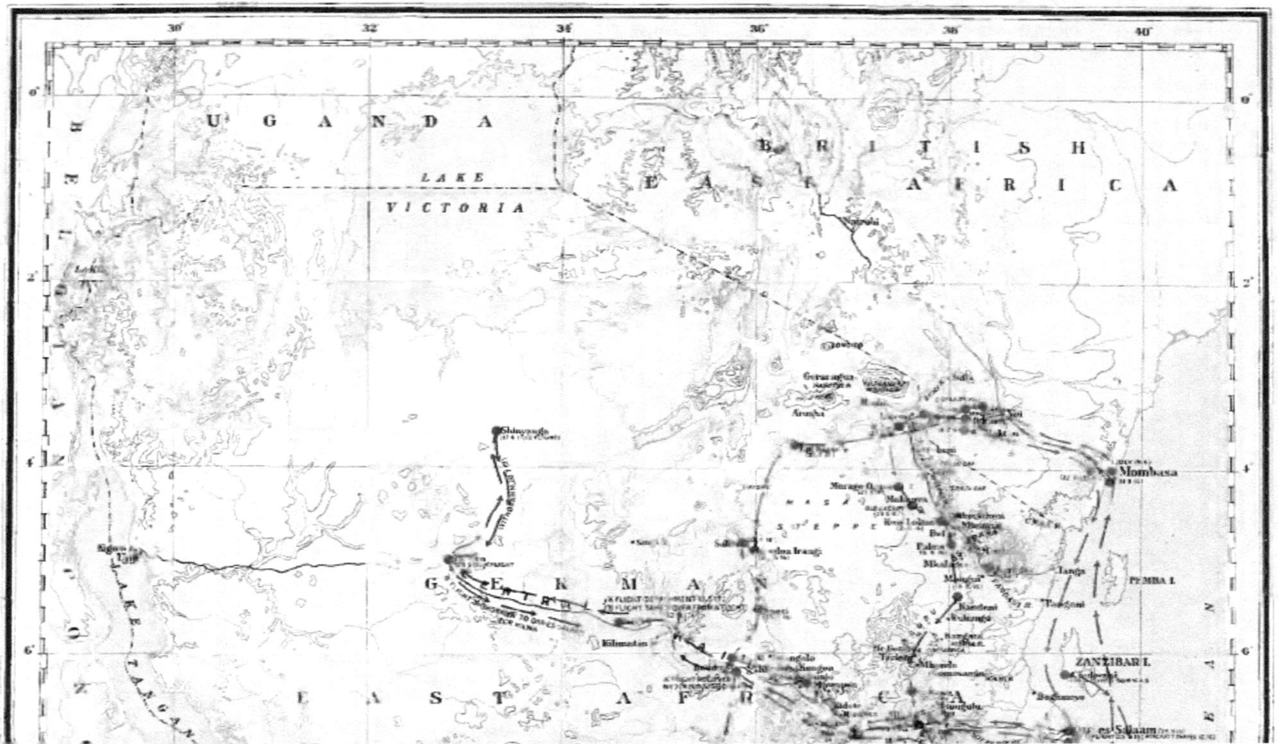
UGANDA
LAKE VICTORIA
BRITISH EAST AFRICA
GERMAN EAST AFRICA
BELGIAN CONGO
LAKE TANGANYIKA
Mombasa
PEMBA I.
ZANZIBAR I.
Tanga
Nairobi
Kilimatinde
Shinyanga
MASAI STEPPE
Arusha
Moshi
Voi
30°
32°
34°
36°
38°
40°
0°
2°
4°
6°

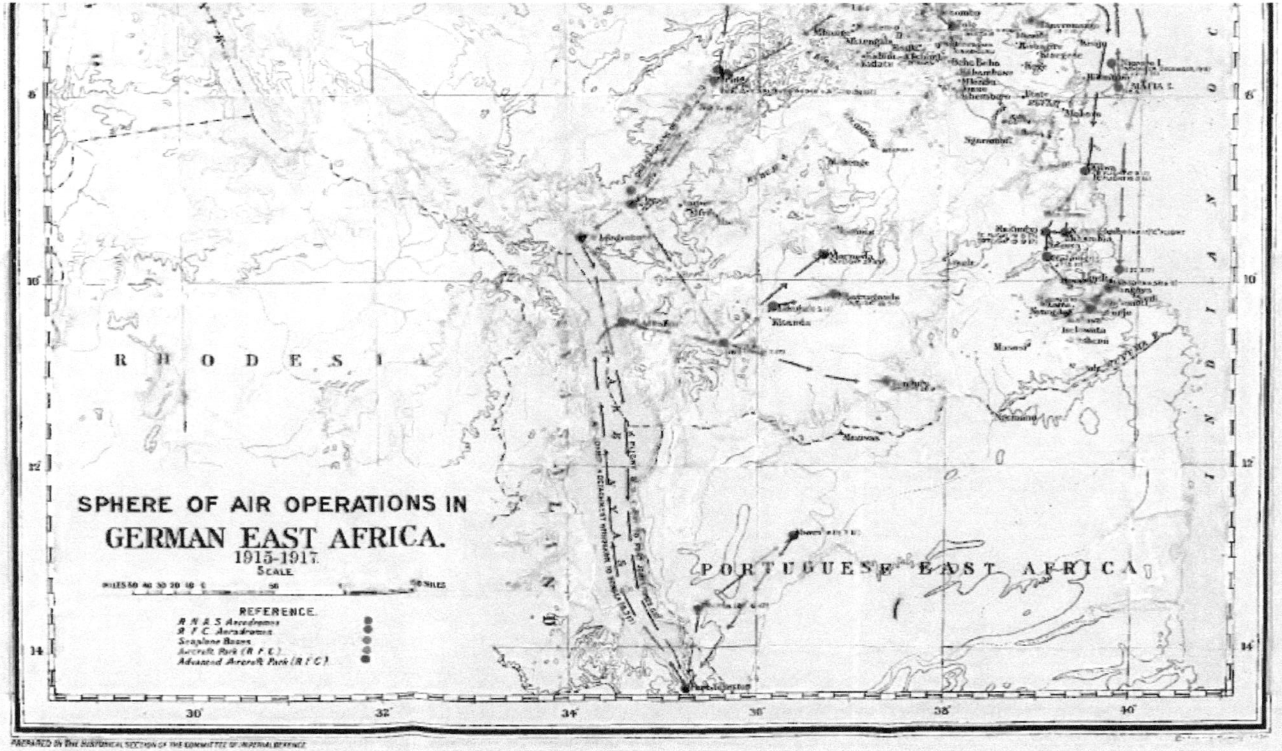
SPHERE OF AIR OPERATIONS IN
GERMAN EAST AFRICA.
1915-1917.
SCALE
REFERENCE.
R. N. A. S. Aerodromes
R. F. C. Aerodromes
Seaplane Bases
Aircraft Park (R. F. C.)
Advanced Aircraft Park (R. F. C.)
RHODESIA
PORTUGUESE EAST AFRICA
30°
32°
34°
36°
38°
40°
8°
10°
12°
14°
PREPARED IN THE HISTORICAL SECTION OF THE COMMITTEE OF IMPERIAL DEFENCE

at Mtua. On the 3rd of December 1917 the naval air personnel left to rejoin their squadron at Zanzibar. The Voisins, which had been kept going for two years, were not considered to be worth tonnage space and were broken up. The squadron, less a small seaplane detachment, left Zanzibar for England in January 1918. In the same month the majority of the officers and men of No. 26 Squadron, left for Egypt. (No. 26 Squadron was formally disbanded at Blandford in July 1918.)

CHAPTER 2

The Air Raids on Great Britain 1914—February 1916

PRE-WAR DEFENCE MEASURES.

In 1899, a year before the first Zeppelin flew and four years before the Wright brothers made their first free flight in a power-driven aeroplane, a Hague Declaration had prohibited combatants from launching projectiles or explosives from balloons or other kinds of aerial vessels. The Declaration was made operative for a period of five years, and when, at the second Hague Conference in 1907, it came up for renewal it was signed by no more than twenty-seven of the forty-four Powers represented. Of the European war belligerents, it was ratified only by Great Britain, the United States, Portugal, and Belgium. As, however, the Declaration contained a provision that the prohibition ceased to be binding when, in a war between the contracting Powers, one of the belligerents was joined by a non-contracting Power, it lapsed automatically in August 1914.

Article 25 of the Land War Convention, an outcome of the 1907 Hague Conference, was the only international rule in existence before the war which touched on air warfare. This stated simply that the bombardment of undefended places 'by any means whatever' was forbidden, the quoted words being expressly inserted to cover attack from the air. The word 'undefended' was not defined, and the latitude of interpretation of which the word admits made the Article nugatory so far as bombardment by aircraft was concerned.

Article 2 of the Naval Convention modified the prohibition of the bombardment of undefended places as follows:

Military works, military or naval establishments, depots of arms

> or war material, workshops or plant which could be utilised for the needs of a hostile fleet or army, and ships of war in the harbour are not included in this prohibition.

This clause embodied traditional practice. But traditional practice had always placed certain restrictions upon the bombardment of this class of objective. The Article took note of these restrictions when it stated that:

> A naval commander may destroy them with artillery, after a summons followed by a reasonable interval of time, if all other means are impossible, and when the local authorities have not themselves destroyed them within the time fixed.

Bombardment from the air, owing to the range and mobility of aircraft, is more analogous to the conditions of the sea than of the land, but the difficulties in the way of applying the above proviso to aircraft are obvious.

The Hague Conference of 1907, then, did not define what were and what were not legal aircraft objectives. There did, however, seem little doubt that these would include places of military importance within the meaning of the Naval Convention. The British Government, therefore, appointed a committee in 1908, under the chairmanship of Lord Esher, to examine the dangers to which this country might be exposed by the development of air navigation. A significant clause in the Committee's report, dated January 1909, stated:

> The evidence before the Committee tends to show that the full potentialities of airships and the dangers to which we might be exposed by their use can only be ascertained definitely by building them ourselves. This was the original reason for constructing submarines, and in their case the policy has since been completely vindicated.

The outcome was the construction of the first naval rigid, the *Mayfly*, the disaster to which, before she had flown, greatly retarded the development of British airships.

At an Admiralty Conference in January 1910 it was put on record that early steps should be taken to provide naval magazines, cordite factories, dockyards, &c, with some form of defence against overhead attack. The minutes of the conference stated:

> There appears to be two forms of protection against airship

attack:

(1) Mobile, (2) Fixed. The mobile defences might be (*a*) Airships or Aeroplanes, (*b*) Balloon guns mounted on motor-cars. The fixed defences might be (*c*) Earth or armour protection above the magazine or cordite factory, (*d*) High angle-fire guns capable of all-round training in the vicinity of vulnerable points.

The Admiralty was alert to the question of protecting naval bases, but the responsibility for making that protection effective lay with the War Office. The determining factor in the shaping of the defensive policy of the British Empire has always been the maintenance of sea supremacy by the navy, and the expulsion of any raiding forces which might elude the Fleet and gain a footing on British territory has always been the concern of the army. In accordance with this long-established tradition, if enemy aircraft crossed the coast the responsibility for resisting them, whether by anti-aircraft gunfire or by aircraft, would automatically rest with the War Office.

The naval views on the subject of air defence, as outlined at the Admiralty Conference in January 1910, were therefore placed before the Army Council, which, in turn, referred the matter to the consideration of the Home Ports Defence Committee.

★★★★★★

The Home Ports Defence Committee, an advisory body, was set up in July 1909. Its President was the Secretary of the Committee of Imperial Defence and its members were prominent Admiralty and War Office representatives.

★★★★★★

This body took the opportunity to survey the airship progress in foreign countries and concluded that airship attacks on Great Britain 'should be regarded as *possible* operations of war'. They quoted the opinion of Colonel J. E. Capper, the *Commandant* of the Balloon School, that aeroplanes were likely to develop in such a manner that they would form an efficient means of defence against airship attack.

In May 1912 came the formation of the Royal Flying Corps. By this time the official German attitude towards the airship had changed considerably. The successes of the privately-operated Zeppelins had turned official indifference into enthusiasm. There was no longer any doubt that German airships could reach vulnerable points in Great Britain. Nor was there much doubt that, in the event of war, they would attempt to do so. In a report to the Committee of Imperial

Defence, dated the 4th of May 1912, the Admiralty stated that, by agreement with the War Office, the navy had undertaken to provide 3-inch semi-automatic guns and mountings capable of being used from the smallest cruisers and even destroyers, and that the army had agreed to provide a 4-inch gun for mounting either in a fixed gun position or on a travelling field carriage. These guns were intended to deal with airships. The Admiralty expected to have their completed gun and mounting ready within six months, but the War Office were less hopeful about the army gun, the production of which was considered by their Lordships 'a matter of extreme urgency'.

Under pressure from the Admiralty, the War Office, as an emergency measure, allotted four 6-inch howitzers for the protection of the Chattenden and Lodge Hill magazines, and the Admiralty were informed, in April 1913, that these howitzers were in position with ammunition available, and that they could 'open fire without delay'. Progress with the anti-aircraft gun defences was, however, slow. When war began only thirty guns were in position, and twenty-five of these were 1-pounder pom-poms of dubious value. The others were one 4-inch at Portsmouth, two 3-inch at Chattenden and Lodge Hill (the 6-inch howitzers having been withdrawn), and one 3 -inch each at Waltham Abbey and Purfleet.

The extent to which aircraft of the Naval Wing should be used in air defence was not definitely settled when the war broke out. In August 1912, soon after the formation of the Royal Flying Corps, the Army Council had considered the question of 'the responsibility for coast defence by aircraft and the line of delimitation between the airships and aeroplanes so employed and those working from the shore for fleet purposes'. They came to the conclusion that such aircraft should be divided into three classes, namely:

Class 1. Aircraft employed for fleet purposes.
Class 2. Aircraft employed in conjunction with Coast Defence Flotillas ('Patrol Flotillas').
Class 3. Aircraft employed in conjunction with the fixed and mobile land defences of defended ports.

The Army Council were of the opinion that the aircraft in Class 1 should be regarded as not in any way available for coast defence, and that those in Class 2 could not be counted upon for this duty as they, like patrol flotillas, would be liable to be withdrawn from the ports at which they had their headquarters whenever the naval situation made such a step necessary. As a corollary to these conclusions the Army Council stated that Classes 1 and 2 would best be provided and maintained by the Naval Wing and that the aircraft for Class 3 should be kept distinct and provided and administered by the Military Wing. The Admiralty agreed with these views but stated also that Class 3 should include all aircraft employed to protect magazines and oil storage tanks.

Such was the agreement, but the War Office did not, in fact, take steps to establish any sort of distinct defence organisation as envisaged under Class 3. The Admiralty, on the other hand, began to set up seaplane stations at several points on the East Coast, which, following the rise of Germany as a maritime power, had become of vital strategical importance.

In November 1913 a number of these naval air stations were already established, and at a conference between the two departments the participation of aircraft of the Naval Wing in the defence was, for the first time, made the subject of an agreement. The position was redefined as follows:

> The War Office to be responsible for our aerial supremacy in the British Isles, or in any land operations in which the army are concerned.
>
> The Admiralty to be responsible for all aerial services of the Fleet.
>
> In order to avoid duplication and overlapping it was agreed that in cases where the naval seaplane stations are close to points of naval importance vulnerable to aerial attack, the Naval Wing should undertake the responsibility for the aerial defence of naval property. Instances of naval seaplane stations so situated are furnished by the Isle of Grain and Eastchurch stations, near Chattenden magazine; the Firth of Forth station, near Crombie magazine; and the Cromarty station, near the Invergordon oil tanks.

This agreement, it will be seen, gave the Admiralty definite responsibility for providing aircraft to protect naval property. Just before the war, however, the General Staff at the War Office challenged the existing position and once more claimed sole responsibility for all air defence, including defended ports and vulnerable points, even where these were of exclusive naval interest. They recommended, however, that at ports where naval aircraft were available the naval pilots should co-operate with the military aircraft allotted to the defence of the ports. In support of their views the General Staff pointed out that coast fortresses have generally fallen from attacks on the land side and that therefore the aircraft of the defence should be manned by personnel trained to co-operate with troops on land. Furthermore, the protection of coast batteries from air attack was, they held, a matter of supreme importance to the fortress commander (a military officer), and this made it essential that the aircraft of the defence should be under his immediate control.

But the War Office was claiming more than it could fulfil. Sir David Henderson had estimated that six squadrons, totalling one hundred and sixty-two aeroplanes, would be essential for the proper protection of the defended ports from Cromarty round the coast to Plymouth alone, yet, when the War Office challenged the Admiralty, the position was that the army had an insufficient complement of aeroplanes for the Expeditionary Force. In fact, in August 1914, almost the whole available fighting strength of the Royal Flying Corps went overseas, and, so far as army aircraft were concerned, England lay wide open to attack. Nor was there any early prospect of military aircraft becoming available for home defence. The navy, on the other hand, had a number of air stations favourably situated for the attack of incoming raiding aircraft and, whatever the paper arrangements might be, the immediate defence by aircraft passed automatically to the Admiralty.

★★★★★★

See *The World Crisis 1911-14*. By the Rt. Hon. Winston S. Churchill. 'The War Office,' says Mr. Winston Churchill, 'claimed on 'behalf of the Royal Flying Corps complete and sole responsibility for the aerial defence of Great Britain. But owing to the difficulties of getting money, they were unable to make any provision for this responsibility, every aeroplane they had being earmarked for the Expeditionary Force. Seeing this and finding myself able to procure funds by various shifts and devices, I began in 1912 and 1913 to form under the Royal Naval Air Service flights of aeroplanes as well as of seaplanes for the aerial protection of our naval harbours, oil tanks, and vulnerable points, and also for a general strengthening of our exiguous and inadequate aviation. In consequence I had in my own hand on the eve of the war fifty efficient naval machines, or about one-third of the number in possession of the Army. The War Office viewed this development with disfavour and claimed that they alone should be charged with the responsibility for home defence. When asked how they proposed to discharge this duty, they admitted sorrowfully that they had not got the machines and could not get the money. They adhered however to the principle.'

******

With the aircraft at their disposal, the Admiralty could aim at nothing more than a limited air patrol of important areas off the East Coast and of the Dover Straits. On the 28th of July 1914 they had given orders for the immediate concentration of naval aircraft at Grain (with advanced bases at Westgate and Clacton), Felixstowe, Yarmouth, Eastchurch, and Kingsnorth (airships). Seaplanes were drawn from the air station at Calshot and allotted to Grain, Yarmouth, and Felixstowe, and aeroplanes from Eastchurch were allotted to Immingham, Felixstowe, and Yarmouth.

On Mr. Winston Churchill's instructions, it was specifically laid down on the 5th of August 1914 that the primary duty of the naval airmen was to repel attacks by hostile aircraft.

******

Mr. Winston Churchill, the First Lord, had minuted on the 29th of July 1914: 'In the present stage of aeronautics, the primary duty of British aircraft is to fight enemy aircraft, and thus afford protection against aerial attack. This should be made clear to air officers, Commander-in-Chief, Nore, and Admiral of Patrols, in order that machines may not be needlessly used up in ordinary scouting duties. After the primary requirement is well provided for, whatever aid is possible for coastal watch and extended defence scouting should be organised. But the naval aircraft are to regard the defence against attack from the air as their first and main responsibility. They must be carefully husbanded.' (See, *The World Crisis 1911-14*.)

******

Lord Kitchener, the Secretary of State for War, was quick to realise that it would be a long time before the army could fulfil its responsibility for the air defence of Great Britain and, with the approval of the Government, he arranged with Mr. Churchill, the First Lord, that this responsibility should formally pass to the Admiralty. The handing over took effect on the 3rd of September 1914. It was part of the agreement that the army would co-operate in the defence with rifle and field-gun fire and with aeroplanes that might be waiting in readiness for dispatch to the Expeditionary Force.

The German airship service, however, was not in a position to begin attacks on this country until the war was some months old. Before the war the German Army fostered the development of the airship more than did the German navy. The army, which had exaggerated views of the value of the early airship as a weapon in land warfare, possessed on the outbreak of war what constituted a strong fleet. There were six Zeppelins, the *Z.4, 5, 6, 7, 8,* and *9*; the Schütte-Lanz ship, the *S.L.2*; a semi-rigid ship, the *M.IV*; and a small Parseval.

★★★★★★

The military Zeppelins were identified, at first by the prefix 'Z' (*Zeppelin*), and later by 'L.Z.' (*Luftschiff Zeppelin*). The naval Zeppelins were given the letter 'L' (*Luftschiff*) throughout. For a complete list of German naval airships, 1912-18, see Appendix 1, and for military airships, 1906-18, Appendix 2.

★★★★★★

The three Zeppelins operating commercially—that is, the *Sachsen, Viktoria Luise*, and *Hansa*—also became part of the army organisation and were fitted with bomb-racks, improved wireless room, &c, and were held ready for special orders from the high command. The *Viktoria Luise,* the *Sachsen*, and the *M.IV*, however, were later handed over to the navy. General staff officers, few of whom had any knowledge of airships, were attached to the early military ships to accompany each flight to point out suitable bombing objectives. At first these staff officers gave the orders, so that the airship commanders were no more than pilots; but these conditions proved unsatisfactory and the arrangement did not last long. The duties assigned to the military ships were long-distance reconnaissance by day and by night and bombing attacks.

Those who looked for great advantages from the Zeppelin in land warfare were soon undeceived. Three of the airships were lost on their first flights. The *Z.*6 while attacking Liege on the 6th of August 1914 was holed by shrapnel and wrecked on landing in a forest near Cologne. The *Z.*7 on a reconnaissance flight over Alsace on the 23rd of August was brought down by gun-fire, and, on the same day, the *Z.*8 was shot down and captured by the French near Badonviller. The loss of these three ships shook the faith of the German High Command in the value of the airship as an army weapon. In fact, too much had been asked of them. They were sent over the battlefront in daylight and, as the target they offered was extensive and their ascending capabilities were small, they stood little chance of surviving gun-fire.

The German Navy, on the outbreak of war, possessed only one airship, the *L.3*. The first of the naval Zeppelins, the *L.1*, had foundered in the North Sea on the 9th of September 1913, and with her was lost Korvetten-Kapitän Metzing, the first chief of the naval airship service. On the day the *L.1* was lost the second naval Zeppelin, the *L.2*, was delivered, but her life was short. On the 17th of October 191 3 she caught fire in the air and was destroyed. In these two disasters the majority of the experienced personnel of the naval airship service perished, and there was some danger that the service might be disbanded. The surviving personnel were without a ship and had no early prospect of obtaining one—a circumstance that made difficult the maintenance of their morale—and, furthermore, those senior naval officers who had no faith in the Zeppelin were quick to raise their voices.

But the Zeppelin had, by now, captured the popular imagination and could not lightly be given up. Kapitänleutnant Beelitz, left in temporary command, gave orders for the dispersal of the personnel to the airship dockyards. Meanwhile the German Admiralty made careful search for a successor to Metzing, and their choice fell on Kapitänleutnant Peter Strasser, a naval officer of energy and courage, with whose personality the work of the naval Zeppelins throughout the war is identified. The third naval Zeppelin, the newly completed *L.3*, was delivered in May 1914. The naval airship base under construction at Nordholz was not ready to receive her and she was berthed in a private shed belonging to the *Hamburger Luftschiffhafen Gesellschaft* at Fuhlsbüttel on the Elbe just north of Hamburg.

When the war began the *L.3* could not cope with the patrol work required by the Fleet, and a Parseval airship was taken into service and housed at Kiel for reconnaissance work over the Baltic, and an agreement was come to with the army whereby every second Zeppelin, as completed, and a few Schütte-Lanz ships, were to be handed over to the navy. No time was lost in completing the naval airship base at Nordholz and in constructing others. Sites were laid out at Tondern, Hage in East Frisia, and Seddin in Pomerania. Hydrogen-producing works were erected near the bases and anti-aircraft guns were provided for local protection. Meteorological stations were opened from the Flemish coast to Königsberg for the transmission of three-hourly reports to the central station at Wilhelmshafen.

The naval airship section also acquired, on the outbreak of war, the services of Dr. H. Eckener of the Zeppelin firm who had, before the war, supervised the training of all Zeppelin crews in Germany—naval, military and civilian. Dr. Eckener, whose knowledge of airship navigation was unrivalled, was stationed at the naval airship headquarters at Nordholz and became the close friend and adviser of Strasser. ('It was Eckener's operating knowledge and Strasser's military spirit that cemented the new organisation into one of efficiency'—Lehmann, *The Zeppelins*.

Early War Activity and Preparations.

While the German airship service was getting ready, the Royal Naval Air Service opened the offensive. Some months before the war the Admiralty view on aircraft defence had been defined as follows:

> Whilst passive measures are useful as safeguards, the real key to the situation will be found to lie in a vigorous and offensive attack on the enemy's air-sheds, &c, and on his aircraft before they reach these shores. (Conclusions of an Admiralty Committee appointed in April 1914 to investigate the question of camouflaging oil tanks and vulnerable points.)

When the navy assumed responsibility for home air defence this policy was restated and amplified by Mr. Winston Churchill, the First Lord, on the 5th of September 1914. His statement envisaged four distinct lines of defence:

> (1) The attack on the enemy's aircraft as close as possible to their point of departure as well as bombing the bases themselves by a special squadron of aeroplanes in Belgium.
> (2) An intercepting force of aeroplanes on the East Coast of Great Britain in close communication with the oversea squadron.
> (3) The concentration of the gun defence at vulnerable points of naval or military importance rather than for the protection of towns.
> (4) The passive defence of London and other large towns by darkening the localities.

Of these methods, the first was considered the most important, and one of the first acts of the Admiralty was the establishment of a naval air base at Dunkirk. On the 1st of September 1914 Commander C. R. Samson's aeroplane unit had been ordered to remain in that port to deny the use of territory within one hundred miles to German airships. On the 3rd of September a detachment from the Dunkirk unit was sent to Ostend to organise attacks from a base at Antwerp on the military airship sheds at Cologne and Düsseldorf. How Flight Lieutenant R. L. G. Marix bombed the Düsseldorf shed on the 8th of October 1914 and destroyed the new Zeppelin, *Z. 9*, has already been told. (Volume 2.) On this day Antwerp was evacuated and the air detachment moved west to reinforce the unit at Dunkirk. Further attacks on the Rhineland sheds were now, for the time being, impossible.

There were, however, other airship bases within reach of aircraft, namely, at Friedrichshafen on Lake Constance, and on the north German coast. The former objective was successfully attacked on the 21st of November 1914, when a Zeppelin nearing completion was damaged in her shed. (See Vol. 1.) Then on Christmas Day 1914 came the seaplane raid on Cuxhaven. (See Vol. 1.) The seaplane pilots failed to find the airship shed (which was, in fact, at Nordholz), but their attempt, following the successful attacks on the Rhineland and Friedrichshafen bases, caused anxiety among the German naval staff, who feared the airships would be destroyed in their sheds before they had struck a blow at England. Consequently, the chief of the German Naval Staff pressed for permission to open attacks on Great Britain.

He urged that London, with its important military centres, must be regarded as a defended area in the sense of The Hague Convention, and that successful raids on London would be of definite military value. All possible care would be taken to avoid doing damage to buildings of historic interest and to private property. He received sanction on the 9th of January 1915 to open the attacks on England, but the *Kaiser* stipulated that the raids were to be expressly restricted to shipyards, arsenals, docks, and military establishments generally, and that London itself was not to be attacked.

In the five months which had elapsed since the outbreak of war something had been done to improve the defences of this country. When the navy took over home air defence, at the beginning of September 1914, only the important magazines (Chattenden, Lodge Hill, Waltham Abbey, and Purfleet) and a few naval ports had antiaircraft guns. In London there were no more than three 1-pounder pom-poms, manned by the Royal Garrison Artillery, which had been mounted on the 8th of August for the direct protection of Government buildings in Whitehall. (The total personnel manning all anti-aircraft guns when the navy took over was 30 officers and 312 other ranks.) On formally assuming the responsibility, Mr. Winston Churchill directed the Third Sea Lord, Rear-Admiral F. C. T. Tudor, whose duty was the provision of material, to report on the whole question of naval anti-aircraft gun resources. Rear-Admiral Tudor reported at once (4th of September) that twelve 3-inch guns would be available almost immediately, that thirty-eight 1½-pounder pom-poms were on order, and that some hundred and fifty 3-pounder and 6-pounder Hotchkiss guns, taken from fleet reserve, would be ready when their mountings had been converted for high-angle fire. He had consulted the Director of the Air Department and he proposed, for the defence of London, twelve gun positions, mounting two guns each, and eighteen searchlight positions, each providing two searchlights. Mr. Winston Churchill was not in agreement with this considerable defence of the capital. He minuted:

> There can be no question of defending London by artillery against aerial attack. It is quite impossible to cover so vast an area, and if London, why not every other city? Defence against aircraft by guns is limited absolutely to points of military value. The Admiralty and War Office with the groups of public buildings in the neighbourhood and the Houses of Parliament constitute a military area and are already sufficiently guarded by the three guns mounted. The effect of these guns will be to compel the airship either to expose itself to dangerous fire or to fly so high that accurate bomb-dropping would be impossible. Searchlights should, however, be provided without delay. Far more important than London are the vulnerable points in the Medway, at Dover, and Portsmouth. Oil-tanks, power-houses, lock-gates, magazines, airship sheds—all require to have their aerial guns increased in number.

Mr. Churchill therefore directed that six of the 3 -inch guns should be sent to the fleet and the remainder to Chatham (2), Dover (1), and Portsmouth (3), and that the Hotchkiss guns should be divided, as they were completed, between the fleet and the defended ports. The small pom-poms were to go mainly to the fleet.

To elaborate the details of his defensive policy, Mr. Churchill set up an expert committee under the chairmanship of Rear-Admiral Tudor. The other members were Rear-Admiral Morgan Singer (Director of Naval Operations), Captain Murray F. Sueter (Director of the Air Department), and Colonel Louis Charles Jackson (Assistant Director of Fortifications at the War Office). The committee first met on the 5th of September 1914 and considered a scheme for the defence of London drawn up by the Director of the Air Department. An independent defence of isolated buildings or localities was thought impracticable. The approved scheme, therefore, treated that part of London extending from Buckingham Palace to Charing Cross as the vital centre of the defensive position and allowed for three pairs of searchlights backed by guns round this area.

At an approximate distance of ten miles from the centre, the establishment of a ring of aeroplane stations was proposed. The system of communication between the guns and the searchlights was modelled on that employed for night defence in a battleship. The gun position in the Admiralty Arch was made the central control for the whole defence under the immediate direction of the officer commanding the gun defences and was linked by telephone with each of the other gun and searchlight positions. No naval personnel could be spared to man the searchlights, and Sir Edward Henry, the Commissioner of Police, provided one hundred and twenty willing special constables for this service. Civilian volunteers also came forward with offers of part-time service.

A Flight of naval aeroplanes was organised at Hendon aerodrome, and emergency landing grounds were prepared in Regent's Park, Kensington Gardens, Battersea Park, and in the grounds of Buckingham Palace. Regular landing grounds for the use of pilots patrolling during daylight were made at Hainault Farm and Joyce Green. The War Office was asked to co-operate in the aeroplane defence by keeping a number of aeroplanes at Brooklands and Farnborough ready to go up if a Zeppelin approached London. On the 9th of October 1914 the ground defence volunteers, who were now beginning to man the guns in addition to the searchlights, were enrolled in the newly-formed Anti-Aircraft Corps of the Royal Naval Volunteer Reserve which was placed under the control of the Director of the Air Department.

Into this force the employees of the Office of Works engaged in erecting gun and searchlight platforms freely enlisted. The personnel of the Corps signed on for day or night duty as they wished, and were called upon, at this time, every other day, going about their ordinary work in the meanwhile. About this time, also, the London defences were expanded following a deputation from the City headed by the Lord Mayor. Arrangements were made to mount additional guns on Tower Bridge and in the Green Park (3-inch); at Waterloo, Nine Elms, and the Temple (6-pounders); and at St. James's Street, Gresham College, Cannon Street Hotel, St. Helen's Court, and Blackfriars (1-pounder pom-poms). Extra searchlights were also provided at Cheapside, Finsbury Circus, King William Street, and near Tower Bridge and Waterloo. Special look-out posts were established and were connected by telephone with the central control. No guns were to fire or searchlights to switch on without orders from this control.

The first regulation giving power to control lights was contained in an Order in Council made on the 12th of August 1914, under the Defence of the Realm Act, Clause 23 of which empowered the competent naval or military authority at any defended harbour to order the extinction, in specified hours, of all visible lights. (On the initiative of Mr. Churchill, the First Lord, schemes had been prepared in 1913 for the immediate extinction of all lights in dockyard areas when in danger from air attack.) On the 17th of September 1914 the first general regulation was made authorising the Home Secretary to issue orders for the extinction or dimming of all or any lights in any specified areas.

The immediate purpose of the regulation was to ensure a reduction of lighting in London. Trips over London had been made at night by naval airships and free balloons to enable observers to study the extent to which lights helped navigation and defined important targets, and these test flights had demonstrated that, in clear weather, nothing short of absolute darkness would prevent a pilot who knew London from finding his way to any locality. But it was not considered worthwhile, until the Zeppelin menace should be more clearly defined, to render London traffic unsafe or to reduce lighting in any district to such an extent that business would be throttled. It was therefore decided that lights should be reduced in such a way that enemy airmen would be unable to pick out salient points.

In long, easily-recognised thoroughfares such as the Mile End Road and the Victoria Embankment, and on bridges, the uniformity of the lighting was to be broken up. The London parks, which would appear to an air observer as tell-tale patches of dark, were to be given a number of lights to bring them into conformity with their surroundings. Elsewhere all abnormal lighting was to be reduced. The Commissioner of Police had issued many public notices requesting that bright lights used for outside advertising should be dispensed with, and that the illumination of shop fronts should be reduced, but the notices had been ineffective.

On the 1st of October 1914, at the commissioner's request, these notices were enforced by an order which required, *inter alia*, that from sunset to sunrise all powerful outside lights be extinguished; that street lamps be extinguished or shaded to break up conspicuous groups or rows of lights; that lighting on railway premises be reduced to the minimum; that lights inside shops and other premises be shaded; and that lights on omnibuses and tramcars be no more than sufficed for the collection of fares. Thus, began the drastic dimming of London, the first outward and visible effect of the airship menace. In December 1914 the order was strengthened by a paragraph prohibiting all outside lights used for advertising.

Meanwhile steps had been taken to reduce lighting in the coast towns, and by the end of 1914 a general reduction, for the most part voluntary, had been effected from Berwick down the East Coast and round the South Coast as far as Weymouth. The only order for lighting restrictions made by the Secretary of State, applicable outside the Metropolis, was for Birmingham, although there was considered to be little likelihood of an air attack on the Midlands.

Arrangements had been made with the Home Office for all police, within a radius of sixty miles from Charing Cross, to report aircraft in flight direct to the Admiralty by telephone.

Meanwhile the mounting of additional anti-aircraft guns, in accordance with the policy laid down by Mr. Churchill, had proceeded rapidly. After consultation with the War Office, twenty-nine of the converted Hotchkiss 6-pounders had been allotted to the Chatham and Medway defences, twelve to Portsmouth, two each to Dover, Harwich, Woolwich, Erith, Waltham Abbey, Tyne, Humber, Rosyth, Ardeer, and Invergordon, and one each to Portland and Windsor Castle. Three 3-pounders had also been sent to Liverpool, seven to Portsmouth, and a number of additional 1½ pounder pom-poms had been variously distributed to strengthen the defences in the above places. Searchlights, provided both from naval and military sources, had been mounted in conjunction with the gun defences of the Medway (24), Portsmouth (16), Dover (6), Woolwich (4), and Portland (2).

All these guns and lights were in position by the middle of December 1914. But the Admiralty had been unable to supply personnel to man either the guns or the lights, and an anomalous position had arisen in a number of defended ports where these guns, operated by the navy, were manned by military personnel. A conference, therefore, was held at the Admiralty on the 16th of October 1914, and, in the result, the naval responsibility for home air defence was appreciably modified.

It was then agreed that the Admiralty should be responsible for the air defence and for manning the guns and searchlights of London and other large cities, classified as undefended, and for attacking all incoming enemy aircraft once they crossed the coast, but that the War Office should man the guns and lights of defended ports and vulnerable points for which the army provided guards. No military aircraft were to be set aside for the protection of any particular locality, but where military aircraft were available they were to cooperate with the naval aircraft in the defence. The effects of this agreement were much wider than might appear on the surface. As the War Office came to provide guards for nearly every place of importance in the United Kingdom, the army virtually became responsible under this arrangement for the anti-aircraft gun defence of the country outside London.

From time to time, after the outbreak of war, reports reached the Admiralty of mysterious aircraft flying over England at night. Little credence was given to them at first, but they became so insistent that a committee was appointed to investigate whether enemy aircraft were flying at night for reconnaissance purposes. Only one report was proved to be founded on fact. This referred to an airship seen near the Humber in the afternoon of the 15th of December evidently reconnoitring in connexion with the naval bombardment of Scarborough, Hartlepool, and Whitby which took place next day. Most of the reports arose from the effects of the illumination of cloud masses by distant searchlights.

By December 1914 anti-aircraft corps, organised similarly to that in London, had been raised for Dover and Sheffield. By this time, too, the arrangements made for direct police reports of enemy aircraft had been extended to the counties of Norfolk, Suffolk, Cambridge, Huntingdon, Northampton, Oxford, Berkshire, and Hampshire. The ordinary telephone lines were to be used, but the call 'Anti-Aircraft, London,' had priority over all other calls. (In the spring of 1915 the arrangements for direct police reports were extended to the whole of England and Wales.)

The bombardment of the Yorkshire and Durham coast by enemy warships on the 16th of December 1914 entailed serious loss of civilian life and property and forced the government to reconsider the question of protection for the civil population of London against air attack. The matter was raised in the Cabinet by Mr. Reginald M'Kenna, the Home Secretary, in a memorandum dated the 24th of December. He stated:

> In earlier discussions on this subject, the protection of the heart of London, with its Royal Naval and Military, and other indispensable buildings, was regarded as sufficient, and it was held that the civil population must run its risk. When, however, the suffering caused by the casualties in the Hartlepools, Scarborough, and Whitby is forced into view, and it is remembered that in a Zeppelin attack upon some of the densely-populated districts of London the loss of life would be infinitely more serious, I am driven to the conclusion that such loss would be regarded as of vital importance by the civil population, whatever its military significance might be.
>
> At the present time the centre of London is fairly protected—that is to say, aircraft which attacked an area covering Westminster and the city would probably be destroyed. Outside this area there is no protection at all against raids from the air except such as may be afforded by aeroplanes, the activities of which are much limited by night. At the time when the Cabinet approved this limitation of the projected area no large supply of anti-aircraft guns was obtainable. By now the shortage may have been made good, and the general question ought to be reconsidered. For my part I should be glad to see provision made for the protection of a circle with a radius of six miles from Charing Cross by an adequate supply of suitable antiaircraft guns and the necessary searchlights. . . .

The effect of this memorandum was strengthened on the following day by the flight of a German seaplane up the Thames as far as Erith and its escape unscathed, and the Government thereupon decided to divert three 3-inch guns which had been allotted to the Fleet to positions approximately six miles from Charing Cross. The sites chosen were at Clapton Orient Football ground (in the line of direction of the north German air bases), at Honor Oak (along the line from Belgium and Northern France), and at Parliament Hill (for the protection of the north-western residential areas). Searchlights were placed near the guns. At the same time an increased number of aircraft were set aside by the Admiralty for defence purposes. Eastchurch was to have as many aeroplanes as possible always ready, Joyce Green four, Hendon four at least, Dover four, and Felixstowe, Yarmouth, and Killingholme three each. In addition, seaplanes were to be kept in readiness at Dover (2), Clacton (2), Yarmouth (4), Westgate (2), Felixstowe (4), Killingholme (4), and Grain (as many as possible). Branch aeroplane stations were to be established as follows: Ramsgate (2 aeroplanes), Chelmsford (2), Chingford (4), and Maidstone (2). The idea behind this disposition was that, in the event of an attempted attack, aeroplanes could be sent up to patrol in such a way as to form a complete screen across the area lying between London and Dungeness (in the path of aircraft from Belgium), and between London and Felixstowe (for Zeppelins coming from the North German sheds). Patrols along definite lines by the naval aircraft based on the coast would, it was hoped, ensure the interception of the raiders on their return journeys.

The German nation, led before the war to expect much from their airships, did not fail to press, from the very beginning, for air attacks to be made on England, but we have seen that, for long, neither the naval nor the military airship service was in a position to respond to the popular clamour. The authorities, however, felt compelled to take some sort of action. One of the earliest projects for the bombing of England, made by the naval air service, was somewhat fantastic. A base was specially equipped in Flanders from which a manned spherical balloon, carrying a ton of bombs, was to be launched against London. Three attempts, all unsuccessful, were made to get the balloon away before the idea was abandoned.

Both services also looked to their heavier-than-air craft as a possible bombing alternative to the airship. In November 1914 a military aeroplane unit was formed at Ghistelles with the special object of raiding Great Britain. For purposes of camouflage, the unit was officially designated the Ostend Carrier Pigeon Squadron (*Brieftauben Abteilung*). Its pilots were chosen from among the best in the military air service. The squadron had been formed on the anticipation that the progress of the German armies would make Calais available as a base within easy reach of England. While waiting, and to gain experience for their major purpose, the bombing pilots made attacks on aerodromes and establishments in the Dunkirk area. But Calais did not fall and, as the aeroplanes with which the squadron was equipped proved unsuitable for long-range attack, the project had to be abandoned and the squadron was moved to Metz in the spring of 1915.

The German naval air service, meanwhile, had established two units in Belgium. Early in December 1914 a seaplane detachment was stationed at Zeebrugge, the railway station hall on the Mole being used as a hangar. The main duties of the unit were sea reconnaissance, spotting for the coast artillery, and bombing. Later in the same month a naval aeroplane squadron arrived in Flanders and took part in the righting on the Yser before it settled at Mariakerke, whence it carried out reconnaissance and occasional bombing flights over the coast of England. It was these heavier-than-air units that opened the bombing campaign.

On the 21st of December 1914, at about 1 p.m., a surprise attack was made on Dover by one aeroplane which dropped two bombs in the sea near the Admiralty Pier and made off before any one quite realised what had happened. Three days later an aeroplane appeared over Dover again at a great height and dropped the first bomb on English soil. This exploded near the castle, but the only damage was broken glass. An aeroplane from Dover went up in pursuit but found no sign of the enemy. On Christmas day a seaplane came in over Sheerness about 12.35 p.m., was engaged by anti-aircraft fire, but flew up the Thames to Erith, on the fringe of London, pursued by three aeroplanes from Eastchurch and Grain. Near Erith one of the aeroplanes overtook and engaged the German seaplane which turned back. On the return journey the enemy pilot, after dropping two bombs harmlessly near Cliffe station, shook off his pursuers and disappeared out to sea.

Meanwhile the German airship service had increased to the point when the long-awaited Zeppelin campaign against England was possible. In the Zeppelin sheds at Friedrichshafen work had gone on day and night. The former Zeppelin station at Potsdam had been turned over to construction and had delivered its first ship on the 11th of November 1914. In all, by the middle of January 1915, nine new Zeppelins, completed after the opening of hostilities, had been taken over by the two airship services. The navy got the *L.4* (28th August), *L.5* (24th September), *L.6* (3rd November), *L.7* (22nd November), and *L.8* (19th December). The army obtained the *Z.10* (13th October), *Z.11* (11th November), *L.Z.34* (6th January), and *L.Z.35* (11th January).

By the middle of January 1915, then, the navy had six Zeppelins of the latest type and the army four. The big naval revolving shed at Nordholz, which would allow the ships to take the air no matter what the direction of the wind, was also ready for use. It was from this shed and from the shed at Fuhlsbüttel, near Hamburg, that the Zeppelins set out on their first bombing expedition to England.

THE OPENING AIRSHIP RAIDS.

(For a statistical summary of airship raids 1915-16, see Appendix 3, Table A.)

For some days after the *Kaiser* had sanctioned attacks on England, at the beginning of January 1915, the weather was unfavourable, but on the morning of the 19th of January the weather conditions improved, and the *L.3* and *L.4* left Fuhlsbüttel and the *L.6* left Nordholz on their first raiding adventure.

★★★★★★

At this time a British force, under Commodore Tyrwhitt, with battle cruisers in support, was on its way to make a destroyer raid, which proved abortive, on the German outer patrol reported to be holding the line between Borkum and Horn Reefs. Although the tracks of the raiding warships and the Zeppelins crossed on the 19th and again on the 20th, when both sets of raiders were returning, they never came within sight of one another.

★★★★★★

The *L.6* (Oberleutnant Freiherr von Buttlar) got halfway across and then turned back with engine trouble. The *L.3* (Kapitänleutnant Fritz) and the *L.4* (Kapitänleutnant Graf von Platen), after a journey through rain and snow squalls, reached the Norfolk coast. Their objective was Yarmouth. The *L.3* crossed the coast at Ingham, soon after 8 p.m., and turned south for Yarmouth, which she began to bomb about 8.25 p.m. The attack on Yarmouth lasted ten minutes, during which nine high-explosive bombs were dropped, killing two persons and wounding three others, besides damaging houses.

The *L.4* meanwhile had turned north-west after making the coast at Bacton, passed over Cromer without taking notice of the town, which was in total darkness, dropped incendiary bombs on Sheringham, Thornham, and Brancaster, a high-explosive near the wireless station at Hunstanton, and then, after attacking Heacham and Snettisham, was attracted by King's Lynn, which was well lighted and offered a clear target. Here her commander dropped the last of his bombs—seven high-explosive and one incendiary. Two people were killed and thirteen injured, and the power station and several houses were damaged.

King's Lynn had no defence, but the airship commander, on his return, reported that he had been attacked near the town by anti-aircraft guns and followed by searchlight. The German official naval historian, evidently in some doubt whether King's Lynn might be included in the specified list of military objectives, says:

> By thus opening hostilities the place in question had itself to thank that the airship defended herself by dropping seven 50 kg. H.E. bombs. (Groos, *Der Krieg zur See*, 1914-18, Vol. 3.)

He would have found it more difficult to explain the attacks on the inland villages of Heacham and Snettisham, which were, in fact, victims of the uncertainties of night bombing. Thus, it became clear, from the opening of the air attacks, that the bombing, if not in intent, certainly in practice, would tend to be indiscriminate.

Less than a month later the *L.3* and *L.4* were destroyed. The two ships set out, on the 16th of February 1915, to look for a British fleet which had been reported off the Norwegian coast, but they found the sea deserted and, on their homeward journey next day, ran into a gale and were forced down in Denmark. The airships, lightened of their crews, soared into the air and were never seen again, the *L.4* carrying with her four of her crew who had failed to jump clear.

As a result of the Yarmouth and King's Lynn raids, during which the airship commanders, who flew low, had avoided the areas of the fixed defences, the Director of the Air Department proposed the immediate formation of a mobile anti-aircraft force. Mr. Churchill approved the scheme, and an eastern mobile section was organised, with headquarters at Newmarket, to cover the whole of East Anglia. (A southern section, formed with head-quarters at Caterham, was disbanded in the middle of June 1915.) The section was equipped with high-angle machine-guns and 1-pounder pom-poms, and with searchlights mounted on motor-chassis. There was no question that the motors of the section should pursue Zeppelins. Their mobility allowed the guns to be moved rapidly, when news of approaching aircraft was received, to positions in the path of the incoming raiders. (The guns and lights were therefore placed at sub-stations at King's Lynn, Chelmsford, Lowestoft, Ipswich, and Shingle Street, in addition to Newmarket.)

The armament of the section, however, was such that it could form no effective menace to the Zeppelin; but there is evidence that the mere presence of the guns and searchlights, variously encountered over a comparatively wide area, considerably disconcerted the airship commanders. In addition, the activities of the section did something towards allaying the uneasiness of the civil population in East Anglia. Orders were also given to each of the East Coast air stations that three aircraft were always to be kept ready for immediate service. Another result of this first raid was the application, by a number of municipal authorities, (Huddersfield, Lincoln, West Bromwich, Wisbech, Coventry, Norwich, Maidstone, Sheffield, Tynemouth, and Wallsend), for compulsory powers, under the Defence of the Realm Regulations, to make a reduction of lighting. It was now becoming clear that lighting restrictions must be considered for the whole country by one central authority. At this time not only the Home Office but also the War Office and Admiralty were issuing separate, and sometimes conflicting, orders. After many conferences between the departments, general orders were finally made on the 8th of April 1915 by the Home Office, and all existing orders made by competent naval or military authorities were revoked. The new orders also took note of the submarine menace, and prohibited all coast lights that might assist U-Boat commanders in their navigation.

Along the whole coast-line of Britain and the Isle of Man all lights usually visible from the sea or any estuary were to be extinguished or completely obscured. The exceptions were authorised navigation lights, indispensable railway and dock lights, and naval and military defence lights. The Isle of Ely and twenty-seven towns on the route from the East Coast to the industrial centres of the Midlands and Lancashire were also brought within the scope of the orders. (During the next few months, inland Orders were made, additionally, for Warwick, Slough, Eton, Datchet, Grantham, Newark, Sleaford, St. Albans, and Stamford. The East Coast Order was also extended to include the whole of Kent and Essex outside the Metropolitan Police District. The object inland was to secure not complete darkness but a uniformity of scattered lighting.)

In the meantime, the War Office was strengthening the gun defences of ports and vulnerable points in accordance with a definite scheme of precedence, under which particular attention was given to centres of munition and other war production. Under this scheme guns and lights were mounted in the first six months of 1915 at Sheffield (six 6-pounders, including two manned by the navy), Birmingham (one 13-pounder and four 6-pounders), Coventry (two 6-pounders), Stowmarket (New Explosive Company, two 6-pounders), Pitsea (British Explosives Syndicate, two 6-pounders), Faversham (Cotton Powder Company, one 3-inch and one 6-pounder), Kynochtown (two 6-pounders), Abbey Wood (one 6-pounder), Chilworth (Chilworth Gunpowder Company, one pom-pom), and, later, at Middlesbrough (one 6-pounder), and Darlington (two 6-pounders). In the same period the existing defences, particularly of the Tyne, Forth, and Humber, and at Harwich and Dover, were strengthened. The main gun and light defences, however, still remained concentrated in the Chatham-Sheerness area.

A respite had followed the first airship attack. Germany was short of ships and the weather was bad. But the first attack on England had led the German people to renew their demands for the bombing of London, and the *Kaiser*, giving way before the pressure, sanctioned, some time in February 1915, attacks on military objectives east of the Tower of London. (Raids on the City of London were sanctioned on the 20th of July 1915.) The naval airship service, anxious to forestall the military service, sent the *L.8* temporarily to the army airship shed at Düsseldorf. Although the weather was unfavourable, the *L.8* set out on the 26th of February to attack London, but she was ultimately foiled by adverse winds and had to land at Gontrode.

There she remained until the weather improved, and in the afternoon of the 4th of March left Gontrode for London again. But she had no better luck. Clouds and high winds made navigation difficult and when the airship, flying low, suddenly appeared near Nieuport, she was attacked and hit by gun-fire and was wrecked after making a forced landing near Tirlemont in Belgium. This was the one and only attempt by the naval airship service to raid from the Belgian bases. (Groos, *Der Krieg zur See*, Vol. IV.) The loss of the *L.8* marked also the end of the naval hopes that the first attack on London would be made by a naval airship.

A new ship, the *L.9*, arrived three days later to replace the *L.8*, and this ship made the next attack on England. In the afternoon of the 14th of April 1915 Kapitänleutnant Heinrich Mathy was over the North Sea in the *L.9*, reconnoitring for British surface craft preliminary to a minelaying sortie by the German Fleet. (The German sortie to lay a minefield off the Swarte Bank was made on the 18th of April.) He flew within 100 nautical miles of Flamborough Head without sighting any British warships, and then, as he had ten 50-kg. high-explosive bombs and forty incendiary bombs on board and the weather conditions were good, he obtained permission by wireless to make a raid at his discretion.

The *L.9* appeared off the mouth of the Tyne about 7 p.m. and moved northwards before turning to bomb the Tyneside towns. Over Cambois she was attacked with rifle fire by the 1st Battalion Northern Cyclists and then passed on to West Sleekburn, where she dropped her first bombs. Mathy, his observation impeded by the scattered lighting below him, was under the impression that his first bombs were dropped into the South Shields timber yards. He then set a winding course over what he thought was Jarrow, Hebburn, Carville, Walker, and Newcastle, dropping bombs all the way.

Actually, he moved from Sleekburn by way of Choppington and Bedlington to Cramlington, dropping fourteen bombs in open fields. He then flew towards Wallsend, dropping a further nine bombs, without doing damage, on the way. Six incendiaries fell on Wallsend, one hitting a cottage and slightly injuring a woman and a girl. The remaining bombs, including two dropped before the *L.9* turned out to sea at Marsden, did no damage. The ineffectiveness of the raid over the crowded Tyne area was due, in large measure, to the drastic lighting restrictions. Following this raid, the First Lord ordered that a 3-inch gun be taken from Whale Island and sent to the Tyne. Later, one 13pounder, two 3-inch (5-cwt.) guns, and two pom-poms were added to the Tyne defences by the army.

When Mathy returned to Hage with his report his apparent success had a stimulating effect on the naval airship personnel, and about midday on the 15th of April 1915 the *L.5, L.6*, and *L.7* set out to raid the Humber under the leadership of KorvettenKapitän Strasser in the *L.7*. None of the ships reached the Humber. The *L.5* (Kapitänleutnant der Reserve Böcker) was known to be off Southwold about 9.40 p.m., but she did not cross the coast until more than two hours later. Henham Hall, Reydon, and Lowestoft received most of her six high-explosive (50-kg.) and forty incendiary (10-kg.) bombs. There were no casualties, but at Lowestoft a timber yard was set on fire and several houses were damaged.

The *L.6* (Oberleutnant Buttlar) crossed the coast at the Naze about 11.30 p.m. and moved across Clacton to the Blackwater, but her commander was under the impression he had been over the sea all the way until he recrossed the coast east of Southminster. He dropped four high-explosive and thirty incendiary bombs on Maldon and Heybridge, which slightly injured one woman and damaged a house. He reported that his ship was found by searchlights and subjected to heavy gun and machine-gun fire. An inspection of his ship, on her return to her shed, revealed two large and six smaller holes and seventeen machine-gun hits. (Groos, *Der Krieg zur See, 1914-18*, Vol. IV.) No searchlights in fact were in action in this raid, and the hits must have resulted from rifle fire from an R.E. Field Company at Brightlingsea and from rifle fire or pom-pom shells fired from Landguard Fort.

The *L.7* (Oberleutnant-zur-See Peterson) dropped no bombs. She came in over Brancaster about 1.40 a.m. and passed south-east along the coast, over Cromer, towards Yarmouth, going out to sea again at Gorleston at 2.35 a.m. Her commander was uncertain of his whereabouts. He never sighted land, and when he abandoned the raid over Yarmouth he thought he was still forty miles distant from the English coast, south-east from the mouth of the Humber. (*Idem.*) Once again a raid had been defeated by the restriction of lighting.

The German military airship service had meanwhile been preparing for a raiding campaign of their own. The army airship sheds in Germany were situated so distant from England as severely to limit the choice of objectives. As soon as the occupation of Belgium was consolidated, therefore, the existing airship hangars at Etterbeek and Maubeuge were enlarged and new ones were built at Berchem-Ste. Agathe, Evere, Gontrode, and Cognelée.

On the 8th of March 1915 the new military Zeppelin, the *Z.12*, was moved from Frankfort to Maubeuge and, on the 16th, set out with about three tons of mixed bombs for London. She met with fog over the English coast and turned back, bombing Calais on the way. An interesting feature of this attack was the lowering, by the *Z.12* over Calais, of an observation car, from which directions were given by telephone to the airship, completely hidden in the clouds. The ship landed in a railway cutting on her return to Maubeuge and was damaged. (The *Z.12* was transferred to the Russian front in July 1915.)

The next raid from the Belgian sheds was made against Paris on the night of the 20th of March. Three ships set out, but one of them was hit while flying over the trenches and she returned to her shed. Paris at this time, unlike London, was still well lighted, and the remaining ships had no difficulty in finding and bombing the capital. One of them, the *Z.10*, was holed by anti-aircraft fire over Noyon, on her return, and crashed near St. Quentin. Nor did her companion in the raid, the *L.Z.35*, much longer survive. On the night of the 12th of April, she set out from Gontrode to bomb the Channel ports and was hit on her return by anti-aircraft fire, probably French, and crashed in a wood.

Both airship services had made a depressing beginning, and their long-distance raids were marked with little military result and considerable airship wreckage. Nevertheless, it was to be expected that the Germans would develop their campaign with characteristic patience in the face of adversity.

The military service was soon in a position to resume. The *L.Z.37* had been delivered on the 28th of February 1915, the *L.Z.38* was delivered on the 3rd of April, and the *L.Z.39* on the 24th of April. These three new ships were the basis for the renewed campaign.

The first raid on England by a military airship was made, at full moon, on the night of April the 29th 1915, by the *L.Z. 38* (Hauptmann Linnarz) from Evere. She crossed the coast at Old Felixstowe and went straight inland by way of Ipswich to Bury St. Edmunds, dropping twenty-six bombs as she went. She circled over Bury St. Edmunds for ten minutes and then dropped three high-explosive and forty incendiary bombs on the town. The ship then followed a winding course to the coast and, after dropping seven more bombs on the way, went out to sea at Orfordness at 1.50 a.m. She was back over Aldeburgh ten minutes later but turned out to sea again almost at once. Six houses were burnt out, two at Ipswich and four at Bury St. Edmunds, but there was no other damage and there were no casualties. No guns, searchlights, or aeroplanes were in action.

The next raids, in May 1915, were made solely by the *L.Z. 38* and included the first attack on London. The first raid was on Southend, on the 10th of May.

★★★★★

> In his report, Hauptmann Linnarz says he could easily have got to London on this night, but that a few hours before the airship set out orders had been received from German General Headquarters forbidding the dropping of bombs on London.

★★★★★

The *L.Z.38* (Hauptmann Linnarz), at 2.45 a.m., appeared over the S.S. *Royal Edward*, moored off Southend as a prisoners-of-war hulk, and dropped an incendiary bomb close to the ship. She passed over Southend from east to west at 2.50 a.m. and dropped four high-explosive and many incendiary bombs as she went. She then turned up the Thames, but ran into anti-aircraft fire at Cliffe, was hit, and turned back to Southend, where the remaining bombs were dropped, together with a piece of cardboard on which was scribbled in blue pencil:

> You English. We have come and will come again soon. Kill or cure. German.'

The number of incendiary bombs dropped on Southend was estimated variously between ninety and one hundred and twenty. A house and a timber yard were burnt out, and several houses damaged, and one woman was killed and two men were injured. Eleven naval pilots went up, but they saw nothing of the raider.

Linnarz appeared again in the early hours of the 17th of May. At 1.40 a.m. he came inland over Margate and flew across Thanet to Ramsgate, where he dropped about twenty bombs, one of which struck the 'Bull and George' Hotel, mortally wounding two people and injuring another. The airship, under rifle fire, went out to sea again and made for Dover, where she appeared about 2.25 a.m. There she was caught and held by searchlights (she was the first airship so illuminated over England), and the anti-aircraft fire which followed induced her commander to release his bombs hurriedly, and about thirty-three of them fell harmlessly at Oxney. He then turned north and hovered over the Goodwins, but engine trouble and the approaching dawn sent him back to his shed in Belgium.

Linnarz had one escape. Flight Sub-Lieutenant R. H. Mulock, who had gone up from Westgate in an Avro, armed with two incendiary bombs and two grenades, came up with the airship as she was dropping her bombs. Linnarz, however, climbed rapidly, and his opponent had no opportunity to get into an attacking position. Although Mulock pursued the *L.Z.38* to the West Hinder light vessel, climbing gradually to 7,000 feet, he could not catch up with her.

Two other airships from Belgium were out that night. One of them, the *L.Z.37*, attacked Calais and got back to her shed without incident. The other, the *L.Z.39*, which apparently dropped no bombs, was attacked by three aeroplanes from Dunkirk, one of which, piloted by Flight Commander A. W. Bigsworth, hit and damaged her with bombs. (See Vol. 2.)

On the 26th of May Linnarz, in the *L.Z.38*, paid his second visit to Southend. He was undoubtedly reconnoitring the route to London and gave special attention to the river Blackwater. He dropped seventy bombs on Southend, where three people were killed and three injured, but no appreciable damage to property was inflicted. Two of five naval aeroplanes that went up in a vain search for the airship were damaged on landing.

Linnarz now seemed confident he could reach London, and this was his next objective. (Linnarz in his report states that as the weather was favourable permission had been given for an attack on the docks and military establishments in London.)

At 9.42 p.m. on the 31st of May the *L.Z.38* appeared over Margate, where she was met with machine-gun fire. She then passed across to the Essex shore, went inland north of Shoeburyness, and made for London. She signalled her arrival over the capital by dropping bombs on Stoke Newington about 11.20 p.m. She then passed over Hoxton, Shoreditch, Whitechapel, Stepney, West Ham, and Leytonstone, dropping a total of thirty grenades and ninety incendiary bombs, or more than a ton of bombs, on her way. She flew over London at a great height apparently unseen and scarcely heard, and none of the London guns came into action against her. She slipped away to sea over the mouth of the Crouch under machine-gun fire from Burnham and anti-aircraft gun fire from Southminster.

Nine pilots went up in search of the *L.Z.38*, but only one saw the airship, and engine failure compelled him to descend before he could do anything. He landed, without damage, in the mud of the river bank at Leigh. One of the other aeroplanes crashed at Hatfield. (The pilot, Flight Lieutenant D. M. Barnes was killed; his observer, Flight Sub-Lieutenant B. Travers, escaped with injuries.)

The casualties caused by this first attack on the capital were seven killed and thirty-five injured. The material damage, to houses and business premises, was valued at £18,596. One other ship, the *L.Z.37*, appears to have set out for England on the same night, but she was attacked by aeroplanes over Dunkirk and, later, by machine-guns south of the Swale, after which she made off without dropping any bombs.

Following this raid, the London gun defences were increased. On the 15th of June the Admiralty agreed to divert three 3-inch guns, earmarked for new ships of the Fleet. The guns were mounted at the beginning of July at Blackheath, Finsbury, and West Ham, and brought the total of 3-inch guns, in and around London, to eight.

By bombing London, the military airship pilots had given their naval colleagues a lead. Orders had already been given that the new naval airships were to be kept primarily for raids on England and that the routine reconnaissances, especially in the Heligoland Bight, were to be made by the older-type airships.

Meanwhile the Admiralty had taken further steps to strike at the naval Zeppelins over the North Sea. Attempts had been made to repeat the seaplane operation of Christmas Day 1914 against the airship bases on the North German coast, but these had ended in failure. (See Vol. 2.) At the end of April 1915 Lord Fisher, the First Sea Lord, in an 'important and immediate' memorandum to Mr. Churchill advocated that a special squadron of light cruisers, armed with anti-aircraft guns, be based on the Humber for the interception of Zeppelins cruising over the North Sea on reconnaissance or on their way to raid England. Mr. Churchill agreed with the proposal, but also put forward an idea of his own which he thought would have better results. This was the placing of half a dozen submarines, armed with anti-aircraft guns, in the Heligoland Bight and its approaches.

Both methods were tried. Six light cruisers were each immediately provided with one 6-pounder and one 2-pounder anti-aircraft guns and assembled at Immingham under the orders of the Admiral of Patrols. The squadron was first designated the Anti-Airship Light Cruiser Squadron, but early in June 1915 it was renamed the 6th Light Cruiser Squadron. The submarine scheme to catch Zeppelins in the Bight was not put into operation until September 1915.

In addition to these arrangements to attack the airships at sea with gun-fire, seaplanes were specially allotted to trawlers and to light cruisers. Aeroplanes which had gone up from coast stations to attack airships had met with no success owing to the impossibility of finding their adversaries in the dark. But although the Zeppelins seldom approached the coast before nightfall they had often been reported by trawlers within fifty miles of the coast an hour or so before darkness fell. The light cruisers of the Harwich Force, and several steam trawlers at Yarmouth, therefore, were fitted, from May 1915 onwards, to carry single seaplanes to sea on days when raids were likely.

On the 4th of June 1915 the *L.10* (Kapitänleutnant Hirsch) left Nordholz with orders to bomb London. She 7 and 8 was accompanied by the *S.L.3* (Kapitänleutnant Boemack), which was to make a long reconnaissance and, if the weather was favourable, go on to the Humber. The *S.L.3* was first reported eighty-five miles east of the Humber at 7.30 p.m., but she cruised about and did not come inland until 11.45 p.m., when she crossed at Ulrome. She went out again almost at once, apparently undecided as to her position, and turned north to Flamborough Head, which was recognised from the breaking of the waves against the headland. She turned inland again at 12.30 a.m. and made for Hull, the distant lights of which could be plainly seen. As the airship approached Hull the city was plunged in darkness, and this fact, together with an increase in the head wind, induced her commander to give up the raid and return. He dropped only three bombs which did no damage.

Nor did the *L.10* reach London. She was engaged by armed trawlers before she made her landfall at Shoeburyness at 11 p.m., and her erratic course afterwards is indicative of the difficulties of navigation.

She made a wide sweep south-east to Whitstable, turned west again to Sittingbourne, where eleven bombs were dropped which injured two civilians and destroyed a house, and then, after a diversion towards Maidstone, made direct for Gravesend. Her commander reported on his return that he gave up thought of attacking London owing to the head wind against him and that he bombed Harwich instead. Actually, his bombs fell on Gravesend, where six people were injured and where the Yacht Club, used as a military hospital, was burnt out, the patients being safely removed to Chatham. The lights of London were seen from the ship when she was over Gravesend, but they were wrongly identified as being in Ipswich. ('Ipswich itself, which was brightly lighted and afforded an excellent ground-mark for navigation purposes, lay to the west.'—Groos, *Der Krieg zur See*, Vol. IV.) Hirsch is reported to have dropped thirty high-explosive and ninety incendiary bombs, but only nine of the former and eleven of the latter were traced.

The 6th Light Cruiser Squadron was at sea during this raid looking for the airships. When the two airship commanders left Germany, they had reported their departure by wireless signals, which were picked up by the Admiralty, but we had, at that time, no clue that the ships were out on anything more than reconnaissance flights. As a precautionary measure, however, the squadron, at 5.30 p.m., had been ordered to a position about midway between the Humber and Borkum. The squadron could not sail until 8.30 p.m., when two cruisers left, but although their track seems to have been along that by which the *S.L.3* approached the English coast, the cruisers did not see the airship and returned with nothing to report.

The next attack was an attempted combined raid by three ships from the military sheds in Belgium (*L.Z.37*, *L.Z.38*, and *L.Z.39*) and by a naval Zeppelin, *L.9*, from Hage in North Germany. Kapitänleutnant Mathy left his shed in the *L.9* on the afternoon of the 6th of June 1915 with the intention, if the weather conditions over England proved suitable, of attacking London. He set a course for the Wash, and was first reported off Mundesley soon after 8 p.m. Here he found a strong head wind from the London direction, so he turned north to his alternative objective, the Humber. He went as far as Bridlington, over patches of fog, before he turned again and made direct for Hull, over which he appeared just before midnight. By means of illuminating flares he located his position over the docks and began his attack. The city had no anti-aircraft protection, and the only opposition Mathy encountered came from the guns of H.M.S. *Adventure*, which was under repair in Earle's Yard. Thirteen high-explosive and thirty-nine incendiary bombs fell on Hull (the German official account says ten high-explosive and fifty incendiary), and did serious damage.

About forty houses and shops were destroyed and many others damaged, a sawmill was burnt out, and twenty-four people were killed and forty injured. Following the attack, rioting broke out in Hull, and many German, or supposed German, shops were sacked before order was restored by troops. From Hull Mathy made for Grimsby, where he dropped seven incendiaries, which did small damage. He was fired at by pompoms from Immingham and Waltham before he disappeared over the sea.

There was fog at the time at the Humber mouth, and the naval air station at Killingholme was unable to send up any aircraft. The 6th Light Cruiser Squadron could not go out, but two of the Harwich light cruisers, with seaplanes on board, were at sea. They were the *Aurora* and *Penelope*, and they had gone out from Harwich about an hour before the *L.9* reached Haisborough, but they took the North Hinder Channel and missed the airship.

Matters did not go so well with the military airships. The *L.Z.38* had developed trouble in the air soon after leaving and was landed again and put back into her shed at Evere. There she was bombed and destroyed by naval pilots from Dunkirk. (See Vol. 2.) Nor could the other two reach England, probably because of the fog over the coast, and they turned for home. It was one of these, the *L.Z.37*, that was overtaken near Ostend on her homeward journey by Flight Sub-Lieutenant R. A. J. Warneford and destroyed in flames. (See Vol. 2.)

The Tyne was singled out for the next attack, which took place, in favourable weather, on the 15th of June 1915. Two airships set out from Nordholz, but one of them, the *L.11*, turned back when ninety miles northwest of Terschelling with a broken crankshaft in one of the engines. The other, *L.10* (Kapitänleutnant Hirsch), was off the coast of England before it was yet dark and cruised at sea for some time before making her landfall north of Blyth at 11.25 p.m. Thence Hirsch moved rapidly for the Tyne and, fifteen minutes later, began to drop his first bombs on Wallsend.

Owing to the rapidity with which the airship approached and to the fact that the telephone warning organisation was not yet fully developed, many of the Tyneside industrial works were taken unawares and were showing a full blaze of light. The lights induced Hirsch to drop his bombs as he had no other clues to his position. All he knew was that there were good targets below him and it mattered little that he thought they might be in Blyth or Sunderland. His bombs on Wallsend did damage to machinery in the Marine Engineering Works to the value of £30,000. He then turned off to Palmer's Works at Jarrow, which were clearly illuminated, and there he made good aiming with seven high-explosive and five incendiary bombs, which did great damage to the Engine Construction Department and killed seventeen and injured seventy-two workmen.

Hirsch recrossed the river to Willington, where he bombed and damaged Cookson's Antimony Works and Pochin's Chemical Works, as well as several houses. He then made for the sea, bombing Haxton Colliery and Bents Ground, South Shields, on the way. He reported that the glare of fires from the raided area was still visible from the airship, thirty miles out to sea. Except a police constable killed at Willington Quay all the casualties occurred at Palmer's Works. The conditions for bombing were as near ideal as any airship commander could wish. The night was moonless, but clear; no searchlights were in action; the anti-aircraft fire was ineffective; there was no opposition in the air; and most of the great industrial targets were well illuminated. The result was, from the point of view of military damage, one of the most effective of the raids carried out by a single airship, and this in spite of the fact that the airship commander had no definite idea what place he was attacking.

No early warning of this raid appears to have been received, and neither the 6th Light Cruiser Squadron nor any of the Harwich cruisers went to sea. The only ship's fire directed at the Zeppelin was from the *Brilliant*, guardship in the Tyne. Two naval aeroplanes went up from Whitley Bay, but Hirsch had left before they got to any height, and they saw nothing of him. It was not to be expected that the defencelessness of the industrial towns of the north and east of England, forcibly demonstrated by the Tyne raid, was to be allowed to continue without considerable public protest, and the attention of the government was directed from many sources to what was described as an impossible state of affairs.

Under the existing agreements, the War Office was responsible for the gun defence and the Admiralty for the aircraft defence of the Tyne area against Zeppelins. The army was already manning at Newcastle one 3-inch, one 13-pounder, two 6-pounders, and two pom-poms, and they took immediate steps to add two 12-pounder Q.F. mobile guns on motor lorries. The Admiralty further decided to take twelve

6-inch guns from various ships and mount them on railway trucks for operation from sidings near likely points of attack on the East Coast.

When the War Office was told of the scheme, the Army Council stated that the East Coast area was regarded as a military defended area throughout and suggested that these 6-inch guns should be handed over to the army. To this the Admiralty agreed on condition that the gun-crews were provided from army artillery personnel. The first gun and mounting was not completed until the end of the year, and, on test in January 1916, was adversely reported upon as an anti-aircraft weapon. Nevertheless, six guns were taken over by the War Office and placed along the East Coast, notably for the defence of the Tyne, Sunderland, the Tees, and the Humber. Two others were sent to Dover, under naval control, and the remainder were mounted by the Admiralty on board the large 'China' class gunboats, *Cockchafer, Glowworm, Cicala*, and *Cricket*, and based at Brightlingsea, Lowestoft, the Humber, and the Wash, respectively, for anti-aircraft purposes.

A more immediate step to strengthen the Tyne defences was the establishment by the Admiralty of a group of additional air stations on the Yorkshire coast. The sites chosen for these new stations were at Redcar, Scarborough, and Hornsea, which, with the existing base at Whitley Bay, formed a defence group with head-quarters at Redcar. Sites for additional night landing grounds were selected at intervals of from fifteen to twenty miles between the Tyne and the Humber. Redcar and Scarborough were equipped at the beginning of July 1915 and Hornsea in the middle of that month, the aeroplanes being Bleriots, Cauldrons', and B.E.2c's.

Although these steps were taken, the Admiralty were not optimistic. Experience had made clear the difficulties which pilots had in finding an airship at night. Searchlights were few, and unless the Zeppelin was caught in a beam, which seemed at this time an unlikely event, or was betrayed by the bursting of her bombs, it was almost impossible for a pilot, once he was in the air, to locate her. Even if an aeroplane got in touch with a raider, the performance of the contemporary aircraft and their armament were such that there was small promise of an attack being successful.

The Admiralty view, therefore, was that as the airship attacks were made after dark, counter-attacks by the existing types of aeroplane were uncertain and precarious and could not be looked upon as offering any security. (Night flying at this time entailed so many casualties that the Admiralty considered the necessity, in view of the small chances of success that night attacks offered, of prohibiting flying by night altogether.)

With the object of striking a blow at the Zeppelins over their own waters, a carefully-planned operation was carried out on the 6th of July 1915. Seaplane reconnaissances of Borkum and the Ems achieved their purpose of bringing the Zeppelins out, but the fighting seaplanes which were to bring the airships to action failed to take off from the rough sea and a great opportunity was missed. (See Vol. 2.)

In August, in order further to intercept Zeppelins making a landfall on the East Anglian coast, a number of night-landing grounds were taken up between the Wash and the Thames Estuary, at Narborough, Bacton, Holt, Sedgeford, Aldeburgh, Covehithe, Goldhanger, and Rochford. To these night-landing grounds aeroplanes and pilots were distributed before dark to be ready to go up on receipt of a warning.

The Campaign against London

(Air Raid statistics for the County of London, 1915-16, are given as Appendix 4.)

The German command, meanwhile, encouraged by the ease and success of the more or less experimental raids of the spring and early summer, was planning concentrated attacks on London. Although London had been an objective, the airship commanders, hitherto, had been ordered to attack only those areas lying east of the Tower and to confine their bombing to arsenals, shipyards, and other military objectives. But the War Office, Admiralty, and other important targets were west of the Tower, and the Chief of the German Naval Staff (Admiral Bachmann) was unwilling that these places should any longer remain immune, and he therefore urged that the existing restrictions be removed. What undoubtedly influenced him was the delivery of new and improved Zeppelins to the navy which made more ambitious bombing possible. So long as London was at the extreme end of the radius of action of the airships the agitation for attacks on the capital was not pressed, but when the new ships made London an easier objective, restrictions became irksome.

Consequently, on the 18th of June 1915, the German Admiralty got into touch with the Chief of the Army General Staff with a view to an agreement for the removal of the existing restrictions. In a memorandum dated the 22nd of June General von Falkenhayn agreed but expressed a warning against 'commencing operations in the present unfavourable period of short nights and with inadequate material'.

(Groos, *Der Krieg zur See*, Vol. 4.) He urged that, as the object of the campaign was to inflict serious damage on the enemy, a big squadron of airships, accompanied by giant and fighter aeroplanes, would be required, and that, therefore, the chief of the military air forces should be entrusted with the whole of the preparations.

Admiral Bachmann was not enthusiastic. Combined action had been tried before and had failed, chiefly owing to the different weather conditions prevailing in the widely separated localities where the military and naval airships were housed. Moreover, the military airship service would require considerable time before it could be ready to co-operate on a big scale, and it was imperative that the dread engendered in England by the airship raids should be kept alive by further attacks. If the campaign were delayed until the autumn, fog and bad weather would then have to be reckoned with.

Admiral Bachmann, therefore, his hands strengthened by Falkenhayn's view that the restrictions should be removed, approached the Imperial Chancellor, who agreed, on the 9th of July, to attacks on the City of London between Saturday afternoon and Monday morning. But the *Kaiser* intervened and, two days later, the approval was withdrawn. Bachmann, however, was not satisfied and, on his further representations, the *Kaiser*, on the 20th of July 1915, finally gave permission for raids on the City, stipulating that buildings of historic interest, such as St. Paul's Cathedral, were to be spared.

The German naval command had got its own way and at once set about opening the campaign. Strasser proposed that the newest airships, the *L.10, L.11, L.12, L.13*, and *L.14*, should be used for the raids against London while the *L.9, S.L.3*, and *S.L.4* simultaneously attacked the Humber and the Tyne and the industrial areas between these two rivers. The remaining naval airships, the *L.6, L.7*, and *P.L.25*, were reserved for reconnaissance work. Strasser obtained permission to conduct the raids personally from one of the Zeppelins.

The first start of the *L.9, L.10, L.11, L.12*, and *L.13* for London on the afternoon of the 9th of August 1915 coincided with the unexpected appearance of British cruisers in the Heligoland Bight. On the 8th of August the German minelayer *Meteor* had appeared off Cromarty Firth and had sunk the armed boarding steamer *Ramsey*. All the available light cruisers had at once been ordered to proceed in the direction of Heligoland to intercept the minelayer. On the following day, the 9th, the hunt was nearing its culmination; the *Meteor* had been cut off from her base and her end was foredoomed. Her commander was aware what was in store for him as the British forces had come under observation from about 7.45 a.m. on the 9th from the patrolling *L.7* and *P.L.25*, and as the *Meteor* was nearing the Bight the former airship informed her by wireless of the approach of British cruisers. The commander of the minelayer thereupon decided to sink his ship, which he did as soon as the *Cleopatra* appeared on the horizon ahead of him about 12.40 p.m.

The British forces were still in the Bight when Strasser sent out a wireless message from over the sea, asking for permission to proceed. The Admiral Commanding the German Fleet was now in a dilemma. Should he recall the new airships for reconnaissance and for attacks on the British Cruisers, or should he let Strasser go ahead? In the event, he decided to carry on with the older airships and gave permission for the raid to proceed. Strasser therefore assembled his fleet of five Zeppelins by wireless orders north of Borkum, and then instructed the *L.9* to proceed to the Humber while he himself with the remaining four ships moved off towards Harwich and London. The airship commanders were given their final instructions, by searchlight signal, some distance off the English coast, as follows:

> Remain together until 8.45 p.m., then each airship will carry out an independent raid, first on the London docks, then the City. For the attack follow a more or less westerly course. Then turn northwards and retire in a north-easterly direction. (Groos, *Der Krieg zur See*, Vol. 4.)

The raid did not come as a surprise. On the 8th of August a message had been intercepted which seemed to suggest an attempted raid, and the air stations had been warned, but no executive orders to sail were given to the 6th Light Cruiser Squadron.

Let us follow first Kapitänleutnant Loewe in the *L.9* to the Humber. He was, indeed, the only one of the airship commanders to get near his allotted objective. He appeared off Flamborough Head about 8.15 p.m. and, a few minutes later, passed over the newly-opened naval air station at Atwick (Hornsea). Two naval aircraft went up in pursuit, and Loewe, made cautious by the twilight, rose rapidly and went out to sea again, where he was quickly lost in the mist. At 9.10 p.m. the *L.9* was off Hornsea again and once more a naval aeroplane went up after her. The airship retreated to sea at once, followed by the aeroplane pilot for thirty-five minutes. She reappeared finally at Aldbrough at 10.5 p.m. and, confused by patches of ground mist, steered an erratic course to Goole, where the lights from the street lamps, although screened from above, were reflected by the wet pavements.

Under the impression that he was over Hull, Loewe dropped eight high-explosive and thirty-four incendiary bombs, which killed sixteen people and wounded eleven, destroyed ten cottages, and damaged two warehouses and several dwelling-houses. The airship then made a wide sweep over Selby (passing across the Olympia Company's oil tanks) and dropped three incendiaries in fields at Hotham on her way out to sea again.

None of the London raiders got within sight of the capital. The *L. 11* (Oberleutnant Buttlar), impeded by rain squalls, ultimately appeared over Lowestoft (which was mistaken for Harwich) at 10.18 p.m., and there seven high-explosive and four incendiary bombs were dropped, killing a woman and wounding seven other people, including three soldiers. Naval 6-pounder aircraft guns came into action against the airship, and twelve rounds were fired without visible effect. The gunners, however, had done better than they knew, as Buttlar reported that it was the bursting of the salvoes close below the forward car that caused him to dispose of his bombs in a hurry. As he reported dropping twenty-eight high-explosive and sixty incendiary bombs, the assumption is that he aimed the majority of his missiles into the sea where we saw what we took to be recognition water-flares. A naval aeroplane pilot from Yarmouth went up in the fog and cruised at 5,000 feet for some time without finding the *L. 11*. The aeroplane was damaged on landing.

The *L. 10* alone kept to the original purpose of bombing London, and when, about midnight, her commander, Oberleutnant zur See Wenke, judged he was on the outskirts of London he proceeded to the attack. Almost at once, he says, searchlights probed the sky and heavy fire opened on him. He therefore dropped all his bombs (twenty-two high-explosive and sixty incendiary), and, although the visibility was bad, he saw some of them fall near ships in the Thames.

What actually happened is somewhat different. The *L. 10* came in at Aldeburgh about 9.40 p.m. and followed a course, roughly parallel to the railway, towards London, but before Chelmsford was reached the ship turned south-east and passed over Shoeburyness just before midnight. This was the moment when Wenke says he thought he was over London. Some of his first bombs, indeed, were heard exploding in the Thames Estuary. He continued his course over Sheppey and actually scored hits on the Eastchurch naval aerodrome, twelve bombs falling in a line about six hundred yards from the sheds; they caused no casualties and did damage only to glass. Two pilots from Eastchurch had gone up some time before and were in the air while the bombs were falling, but in the darkness and fog the pilots saw nothing of the airship. Wenke, aiming his bombs under the impression they were falling on London, came near to wrecking the naval air station at Eastchurch. Of the eighty-two bombs which he reported dropping, only fourteen were traced on land.

The attack by the *L. 10* on Eastchurch was watched from a distance by Mathy in the *L. 13*, the latest naval Zeppelin, on her maiden voyage to England. Mathy never reached the coast. The forward engine in the airship broke down, and ultimately, about 11.25 p.m., Mathy turned for home. He was compelled to drop his 120 incendiary bombs on the Dutch island of Schiermonnikoog before he could finally land at Hage.

There remains the *L. 12* (Oberleutnant Peterson), which was destined not to return. Peterson appeared off, Westgate at 10.48 p.m. He believed he was far north, between Haisborough and Winterton, and as he steered south towards Dover he thought he was moving on Harwich. A naval aeroplane from Westgate went up after him, but the pilot (Flight Sub-Lieutenant R. Lord) lost the airship in the fog and was fatally injured in a crash when he landed again.

About 12.30 a.m. Peterson thought he had reached Harwich, and there he decided to drop his bombs as it was too late to think of getting to London and back. He was, however, over Dover, and he was soon under fire from the anti-aircraft guns. The second or third round from a 3-inch gun hit the airship and she was seen to reel as she dropped her water ballast and swiftly disappeared upwards. Three incendiary bombs from the ship dropped on the Admiralty Pier and a few high-explosive bombs fell in the harbour. Three men were injured, but the material damage was negligible. The *L. 12*, through loss of gas, came down in the sea off Zeebrugge, was towed into Ostend, and there bombed by naval pilots from Dunkirk. During the process of dismantling, a fire broke out in the ship and parts of it only were salved.

This first attempt at a concerted attack on London was a failure. Of the approximate number of four hundred and forty bombs carried in the five airships (some 374 of them for London), only sixty-eight exploded on British soil, and this at the cost of one new Zeppelin lost.

Strasser, however, was not discouraged by the loss of the *L. 12*. On the 12th of August 1915 the *L. 9, L. 10, L. 11*, and *L. 13* set out again, the first for Hartlepool and the others for London. But they were again to meet with failure. A propeller shaft in the *L.9* became loose on the journey across the North Sea and the ship turned back. Mathy's *L.13*, too, was justifying her number. Her port engine broke down and she also returned.

Buttlar, in the *L.11*, reported that he had to fall out with engine trouble off Orfordness just when he was within sight of the coast, but an airship, which we made out to be the *L.11*, appeared off Harwich just before 9 p.m. and moved over the Thames Estuary and Thanet before going home again. She dropped no bombs. On her way back to her shed the *L.11* had to fight through a storm over Terschelling. Lightning encompassed the airship, the points and wire stays emitted electric sparks, and bluish flames ran along the machine-guns while the rain-soaked crew on the top platform were encircled in a ring of light. (See Groos, *Der Krieg zur See*, Vol. 4.) The airship survived the storm and landed safely at Nordholz at 7.37 a.m.

The *L.10* (Oberleutnant Wenke) alone dropped bombs on England. She made her landfall south of Lowestoft at 9.25 p.m., but her commander decided he could not reach London in the teeth of a strong head wind and he therefore turned off for Harwich. Over Woodbridge the airship was attacked with machine-gun and rifle-fire by troops of a London Regiment, and replied with four high-explosive and twenty incendiary bombs which killed seven people, wounded six, and destroyed five houses and damaged sixty-four others as well as a church. Imbedded in one of the incendiary bombs was a machine-gun bullet which had struck the bomb before it left the airship or during its fall.

From Woodbridge the *L.10* went on towards Ipswich, dropping six bombs, without damage, at Kesgrave on the way. Over Rushmere she was attacked by machine-guns of the Eastern Mobile Section, and replied with two bombs, which fell near the lorries, but she then turned away from Ipswich and ultimately appeared over Harwich which, although well darkened, was easily recognised from the outline of the coast. Her remaining bombs (eight high-explosive and four incendiary) were dropped on Parkestone where they injured seventeen people and wrecked two houses. The airship finally went out to sea south of Aldeburgh. Four pilots had gone up from Yarmouth, but they saw nothing of the attack.

The naval Zeppelins were back again within a week. Early in the afternoon of the 17th of August the *L.10, L.11, L.13*, and *L.14* left for England. Before the Zeppelins left, a message had been intercepted which seemed to indicate that operations were to be undertaken by large airships, and four armed trawlers and a seaplane were thereupon sent out from Yarmouth to cruise in readiness off the Jim Howe Bank. The 6th Light Cruiser Squadron was already at sea looking for reported minelayers. Once again Mathy, in the *L.13*, had mechanical trouble and had to turn back. The *L.14*, out on her first raid under the command of Kapitänleutnant der Reserve Böcker, was sighted off the Would lightship at 8.20 p.m. and was thereafter heard and seen off the East Coast until 11.40 p.m., when she disappeared. She never came over the land and her bombs fell in the sea somewhere off Yarmouth. Böcker reported that he gave up the idea of getting to London owing to trouble with two of his engines and he thought he dropped '50 incendiary and 20 high-explosive bombs on the blast furnaces and factory premises in the vicinity of Ipswich and Woodbridge'. (Groos, *Der Krieg zur See*, Vol. 4.)

Buttlar, in the *L.11*, reported, on his return, that he had bombed London. The German naval historian tells how Buttlar followed the course of the Thames, was fired on by batteries in the eastern quarter of London and dropped his bombs on Woolwich. (*Idem*). The actual course of the *L.11* was different. She came in over the pier at Herne Bay at 9.30 p.m. according to our observation, passed over Canterbury to Ashford, where she dropped twenty-one bombs, turned north to Faversham, dropping forty-one bombs on Badlesmere and Sheldwich on the way, and eventually passed out to sea again near her original landfall. She met with nothing more than spasmodic rifle-fire during her two-hour flight over Kent, and her bombs fell in open country.

Wenke, in the *L.10*, alone reached and bombed London, and was the first naval airship commander to do so. The ship came overland at Shingle Street at 8.56 p.m. and thence her commander steered an unhesitating course for the capital. He was over Walthamstow about 10.34 p.m. and dropped three bombs. The crowded district of Leyton, where sixteen high-explosive and ten incendiary bombs fell, suffered most. From here the *L.10* passed over Leytonstone (four bombs) and Wanstead Flats (ten bombs) before going back in the same direction as she had come. Two other bombs fell, without doing damage, at Chelmsford.

In Leyton nine people were killed and forty-eight injured, Leyton railway station was partly wrecked, the tramway depot damaged, and a great number of houses demolished or damaged. The only other casualty of the raid was a man killed in Leytonstone. Wenke met with no opposition over London. Two rounds were fired at him from the Waltham Abbey pom-pom as he came in, but thereafter he was unseen and untroubled by any gun-crew. Four aircraft which went up from Yarmouth and two from Chelmsford failed to get in touch with the enemy. One of the Chelmsford aeroplanes was blown up by its own bombs on landing. (The pilot of this aeroplane, Flight Sub-Lieutenant C. D. Morrison, who had seen and then lost the airship, was injured, but his observer, Flight Sub-Lieutenant H. H. Square, was not hurt.)

One of the Zeppelins, on her incoming journey, had been sighted by the Yarmouth armed trawlers, which thereupon proceeded eastward in the hope they would intercept the airship on her return. But she went homeward by a different route and the trawlers waited in vain.

The military airship service was now ready once more to take a part in the campaign. On the night of the 7th of September 1915 three military ships from the Belgian sheds appeared over the coast, bound for London. They were not sighted from the sea before coming overland and no other intimation had been received that a raid was impending. They were the Zeppelins *L.Z.77* (Hauptmann Horn), the *L.Z.74* (Hauptmann George), and the Schütte-Lanz *S.L.2* (Hauptmann von Wobeser). The first raided the county of Suffolk while the two last-named reached and attacked London. The first ship to approach the coast, the *L.Z.77*, came in at Clacton-on-Sea at 10.40 p.m. and steered an erratic course to Hatfield Broad Oak, the most westerly point to which she penetrated. From this place the searchlights sweeping the London skies must have been visible to the airship personnel. The ship then turned back and dropped seven bombs before she went out again at Lowestoft, off which town further bombs were heard exploding in the sea. The only damage done by this raider was to a reaping machine. An aeroplane pilot who went up from Yarmouth failed to get in touch with the airship.

The second ship to come overland, the *S.L.2*, was over the Crouch at 10.50 p.m., flying low, whence she moved, with some directness, on London, reaching Leytonstone just before midnight. Here she turned south and followed the left bank of the River Lea, making straight for Millwall. There her first bombs fell and others followed on Deptford, Southwark, New Cross, Greenwich, Charlton, and Woolwich. Eighteen high-explosive and twenty-six incendiary bombs fell, and eighteen people were killed and thirty-eight injured. The damage, mostly to private houses, was small. The ship went out again at Harwich and, after wandering over Holland, appeared over her shed at 7.45 a.m. with only one engine working. She got out of control when descending, struck a house, and was severely damaged. She went back, after local repair, to Germany, where she was partly rebuilt, but she made no further flights over England. (Her commander, who later commanded the *S.L.10*, was posted as missing in the Germany casualty lists on the 28th of July 1916. He was probably lost at sea.)

The third raider, the *L.Z.74*, was the first airship to penetrate to the City of London. She approached the capital along the Lea Valley from Broxbourne, but for some reason, difficult to determine, Cheshunt received the full force of the attack. Eighteen high-explosive and twenty-seven incendiary bombs fell there. They caused no casualties and did most of their damage to glasshouses and cottages. The airship now came under fire from the Waltham Abbey guns, but her commander persisted on his course and appeared over Fenchurch Street at twenty minutes past midnight. There he dropped one incendiary bomb on a store which started a fire that was quickly put out. This was the only bomb dropped on London. (Hauptmann George thought he dropped bombs on Leyton and on the East London docks, &c.) Cheshunt certainly saved the City that night. The *L.Z.74* was fired on without effect by the Purfleet guns on her way out to Harwich in company with the *S.L.2*. This was the last occasion on which a military airship penetrated the London area.

The weather remained ideal for raiding, and the successful military attack brought out the naval airships on the next night. The City of London was not this time to get off so lightly; indeed, the damage which the City then suffered was the greatest caused in any raid.

The renewed activity by the German naval airship service did not take the Admiralty by surprise. It had been expected that the enemy would take advantage of the September period of moonless nights (the moon was new on September the 9th), and with the object of attacking the Zeppelins near their bases a new plan had been tried. Seaplane attacks had been disappointing, and the Admiralty therefore turned to Mr. Churchill's idea of using submarines.

The submarines *E.4* and the *E.6,* each fitted with four 6-pounder high-angle anti-aircraft guns, had been sent out on the 1st of September with orders to cruise together for five days on the western side of the German Bight. They were to attack, in close co-operation, any airships met with, but early on the 2nd of September they had to dive to avoid discovery, and when they came to the surface again they were out of touch with one another. For the rest of the cruise they acted independently. The *E.4* during her patrol sighted only one airship, and this was too far off to attack. She did, however, arrest and bring back to Harwich a German trawler. The *E.6,* on the 4th of September, opened fire on a Zeppelin and thought she scored a hit.

The airship—*L.9*—was, however, not hit; she merely moved off rapidly to open the range, and she reported the presence of the submarine by wireless. Aeroplanes and destroyers were sent out to hunt for the *E.6*, which was compelled to dive. The submarines had failed to damage any Zeppelins, but while they were in the Bight one airship, the *L.10*, was destroyed by the elements. On her return from a reconnaissance flight over the Bight on the 3rd of September she was struck by lightning and destroyed in flames with her crew.

The anti-airship patrols by the Yarmouth trawlers with seaplanes were kept up continuously throughout the early part of the month in the neighbourhood of the Swarte and Jim Howe Banks, but the patrols passed without incident.

At about 1 p.m. on the 8th of September 1915 we intercepted signals from four German airships that they had only 'H.V.B.' on board. We now knew exactly what this message meant. A copy of the German code-book known as H.V.B. (*Handelsschiffsverkekrsbuch*), which served as the official instrument of correspondence with the German Mercantile Marine, had been captured in Australia early in the war, and another copy had been fished up later from the depths of the sea by a Lowestoft trawler. The Germans knew that this code-book was compromised, but they continued, with frequent changes of ciphering key, to employ it in official correspondence, and the Zeppelins, when they raided England, also used the book, as its capture, if the airship fell into British hands, would be of no importance.

When the airship commanders set off on a raid, however, they always left behind the more confidential naval signal book, a fact which they reported by wireless, using the words 'Only H.V.B. on board'. This signal we invariably picked up, and to us it came to mean in effect 'We are now leaving for a raid on the British Isles'.

Except the *L.9,* destined for the north of England, the airship commanders had London as their objective. One of the latter Zeppelins, the *L.11*, had to turn back, shortly after starting, with engine breakdown, but the other two, the *L.13* (Kapitänleutnant Mathy) and the *L.14* (Kapitänleutnant der Reserve Böcker), continued their westerly flight side by side.

The *L.9* (Kapitänleutnant Loewe) had as her special target a benzol factory, unspecified, but presumably the one which had been erected before the war by German contractors at the Skinningrove Iron Works. Loewe came in at Port Mulgrave, between Whitby and Kettleness, about 9.15 p.m., and dropped six bombs, without doing damage, before he appeared over Skinningrove at 9.35 p.m. There he dropped his main load, nine high-explosive and twelve incendiary bombs, on the iron works. He stated that he could not find the benzol factory, but he did, indeed, aim better than he knew. One incendiary bomb made a direct hit on the benzol house, but it failed to penetrate the concrete. Another, a high-explosive, fell within ten feet of it, and, although the bomb broke the water-main and the electric-light cables and did other minor damage, it failed to damage the benzol house. Had the bomb hit this or the tanks, which held 45,000 gallons of benzol, not much of the works could have survived.

The works had one other extraordinary escape, as a bomb which made a direct hit on a T.N.T. store failed to explode. Many other attacks were to be made on the Skinningrove Iron Works, but none was to come so near destroying them as this one, although the damage actually done was slight and there were no casualties. The *L.9* went out again at Sandsend at 9.45 p.m., having encountered no opposition during her brief flight overland. Three naval pilots went up from Redcar, but they saw nothing of the airship.

The trawlers *Conway* and *Manx Queen* of the Humber patrol were cruising in wait off the Haisbro' Light Vessel when the *L.14*, flying low, came within range of the *Conway*, which fired eight rounds from her 1-pounder gun, and caused the airship to rise at a sharp angle. The airship commander, in fact, mistook the trawler patrol for a light cruiser squadron and he promptly made off northward. A quarter of an hour later, the *L.13* came within range of the *Manx Queen*, which fired nine rounds at her without result. The *L.14* crossed the land west of Cromer, but soon developed engine trouble, and her commander thereupon gave up the raid on London and bombed instead 'Norwich and the extensive industrial district and the railway there'. (Groos, *Der Krieg zur See*, Vol. 4.) So he thought, but his bombs fell on Bylaugh (15), East Dereham (31), and Seaming (9). Four men were killed and seven people injured in East Dereham, but there was no material damage, although the airship report states that explosions occurred at factory buildings in the south-west part of Norwich. (*Idem.*)

It was Mathy, in the *L. 13*, who did the damage. He came in at the Wash and flew straight to London. The night was clear and, from over Cambridge, the airship personnel could see the distant glare of their objective. At 10.40 p.m. the first bombs were dropped on the residential suburb of Golder's Green; they fell in fields and gardens and did no damage. The airship then proceeded slowly to Euston, where bombing was resumed with serious effect. From the neighbourhood of Euston Station across to Theobald's Road, down Gray's Inn Road, Hatton Garden, Farringdon Road, Smithfield Market, the Wood Street area, Moorgate Street, Liverpool Street, and Norton Folgate, the passage of the airship was marked by fires and destruction.

In all, fifteen high-explosive and fifty-five incendiary bombs fell and twenty-two persons were killed and eighty-seven injured. The greatest material damage was done within the City of London, especially in Silver Street, Wood Street, Addle Street, and Aldermanbury, where several blocks of business premises were entirely burnt out or seriously damaged by fire. The money value of the damage done in the City was estimated at £510,672 out of a total for the whole raid of £534,287. One of the bombs, the first of its size to be dropped on England, weighed 660-lb. (300 kg.), 'in the crater of which a whole row of lights disappeared all of a sudden'. (*Idem.*) This fell in Bartholomew Close.

As seen from the ground the airship gave an impression of unhurried calm. Every one of the twenty-six guns in the vicinity of London, including those at Woolwich, fired on the airship at one time or another. When Mathy first came under fire he was at 9,000 feet, and he reports that some of the shells almost reached him, but he at once climbed on a zig-zag course to 11,000 feet, and there he was out of harm's way. He was, however, taken by surprise at the volume of fire opened on him. He reported on his return that:

> The anti-aircraft defence was so extensive that in future with clear sky airships would only be able to remain quite a short while over the City, and that it would be hardly possible to seek out special objectives. (Groos, Vol. 4.)

Three naval pilots who went up from Yarmouth had already landed when Mathy passed over the town out to sea again.

******

> One of the pilots, Flight Sub-Lieutenant G. W. Hilliard, was killed by the explosion of his bombs when he landed in a field

at Bacton. Another Yarmouth pilot, Flight Lieutenant J. M. R. Cripps, forced down with engine failure, jumped from his bomb-loaded aeroplane just before it reached the ground and was unhurt. The aeroplane landed almost intact.

******

A relic of this raid, dropped from the *L.13* near Barnet in a bag attached to a parachute, is a scraped ham-bone. Round the shank is painted a band of the German tricolour, and below this, on one side, is a crude drawing of a Zeppelin dropping a bomb on the head of an elderly civilian labelled 'Edwart Grey', against whom is the inscription: '*Was fang ich, armer Teufel, an?*' ('What shall I, poor devil, do?'). On the other side of the bone are the words: '*Zum Andenken an das ausgehungerte Deutschland*' ('A memento from starved-out Germany').

On the same night, a military airship, the *L.Z.77*, was reported between 8.40 p.m. and 10.40 p.m. off the coast between Dunwich and the Dover Straits, and bombs which exploded near the Galloper Lightship were attributed to her.

The London Press was quick to seize on the attacks on the City as demonstrating the weakness of our defences, and it was urged in many quarters that the defence of London should be the definite and sole responsibility of one officer. On the 10th of September 1915 the Board of Admiralty decided that henceforth the defence of the Metropolis should be treated as outside the ordinary duties of the Director of Air Services and that a Flag Officer with special qualifications should be appointed with direct responsibility to the Board for the gunnery defence of London. The appointment was given on the 12th of September to Admiral Sir Percy Scott, who was, however, informed that the question of the transfer of the general responsibility for all air defence to the army was under consideration.

Although the appointment of Sir Percy Scott, a gunnery expert of wide experience, reflected the faith of the Board in the gun as the effective anti-aircraft weapon, Sir Percy Scott himself had, or quickly developed, faith in the aeroplane. He urged that night flying by the naval aeroplanes on the East Coast should be taken in hand seriously. Aeroplanes, he said, when their pilots had been trained for night flying, were going to be 'the Zeppelins' worst enemy'. They would, in the future, play a much more important part in the defence of London than people thought. He held the view that the defence of London by aircraft started at the Zeppelin sheds and that the defence by gunfire began on the English coast. The mobile defences in the country should be increased so that they could turn back any attempted air raid and, while no Zeppelin should ever be allowed to reach London, there should be sufficient heavy guns strategically distributed near the capital to make hitting a certainty if an airship got through.

Sir Percy Scott, indeed, soon began to make his presence felt. It was not long before he wrote to the First Lord threatening to resign unless he was given a free hand in getting, how and best he could, what he wanted. He promptly discarded all the pom-pom guns, which, he held, were useless and dangerous, and put forward detailed proposals for new gun stations, which would require an extra 104 anti-aircraft guns and at least fifty searchlights.

******

> The shells fired from the pom-poms were too small for the fitting of time fuses, and they therefore burst only on impact, a fact which made them dangerous to life in a thickly-populated area. When the London pom-poms were withdrawn, they were handed over to the Eastern Mobile Section.

******

He pressed the First Lord to divert guns and searchlights from the Fleet, which, he suggested, had fifty more sub-calibre guns than it required. He at once began the preparation of a number of additional gun and searchlight stations and sent Lieutenant-Commander A. Rawlinson to Paris to bring back a sample of the best existing French anti-aircraft gun. (Before the next raid on London, on the 13th/14th October, three additional 3-inch guns had been mounted at Barnes Common, King's Cross, and Dollis Hill.) By the 19th of September this officer was back in London with a 75mm. gun on a special motor-mounting, complete with equipment. This gun, manned by ratings from the disbanded armoured car squadrons, was the nucleus of the London Mobile Section which was formed under Lieutenant-Commander Rawlinson at the Talbot Works, Shepherd's Bush, in the middle of October 1915.

At the beginning of December, the Section moved to Kenwood House, Hampstead. By this time its strength had been increased by six 3-pounder high-angle Vickers guns, mounted on Lancia light lorries, (two further 3-pounder Vickers guns were added almost at once), and by two mobile searchlights. Two of the guns were temporarily detached for the defence of the Hampton Waterworks and one each to the waterworks at Kempton and Surbiton. The remainder moved to pre-allotted positions on the receipt of a raid warning.

The aeroplane defence of London was considered by a sub-committee, under the presidency of the Director of the Air Services (Rear-Admiral C. L. Vaughan-Lee), on the 16th of September 1915, and it was concluded that the defence should be started with a minimum of forty aeroplanes and twenty-four pilots, and that four stations additional to Hendon and Chingford would be necessary. Before anything further was decided the committee wished to have statements on the Paris defence methods. A member of the committee, Squadron Commander J. T. Babington, was sent to France to study the defences of Paris. His report, made on the 27th of September, brought about a reversal of opinion on the value of night flying. The defence of Paris consisted of guns, searchlights, listening posts, and darkness, and, although some sixty pilots and thirty aeroplanes were employed, aircraft played a very minor part. French opinion seemed unanimous that aeroplane pilots had the greatest difficulty in finding an airship in the dark.

As a result of this report, the Director of the Air Services was reluctant to embark on an ambitious scheme of aeroplane stations. He now proposed that the expansion of this side of the defence should be confined to an improvement of the existing landing grounds between the Wash and London and that night-flying instruction, under fairly safe conditions, should proceed. His proposals were discussed by the Board of Admiralty on the 28th of September and generally approved. The Board affirmed that the overseas naval air units had first claims on all trained pilots and that East Coast requirements must, for the time being, be met by less trained airmen. This decision meant, in effect, the cessation of effective night flying. The Naval Air Service contribution to the aeroplane defence of London was now centred in four specially-trained pilots stationed at Hendon and Chingford.

Meanwhile there had been two attacks by single military airships from Belgium. One ship, the *Z.Z.77* (Hauptmann Horn), came in south of the Blackwater about 11.15 p.m. on the 11th of September 1915 and made direct for London. There was fog in the Epping Forest district and the airship commander was confused as to his exact position. Under the impression that he was attacking London from east to north, he dropped all his bombs (eight high-explosive and fifty-two incendiary) on the Royal Field Artillery Camp near North Weald Bassett. The safety appliances had not been withdrawn from the high-explosive bombs and they did not detonate.

No damage was done by the bombs nor were any casualties caused.

Another military ship, the *L.Z.74* (Hauptmann George), came again next night, but there was a thick ground fog over much of East Anglia and the raid was a failure. The airship commander was misled by fire from the machineguns of the Eastern Mobile Section into the belief that he was over a town, probably Southend, and he therefore dropped his twenty-seven bombs, which fell in open country or on small villages between Colchester and Woodbridge. There were no casualties, and the only material damage was to glass and fences. On each of these two nights a naval aeroplane went up, but the pilots saw nothing.

★★★★★★

The *L.Z.74* was shortly afterwards destroyed. On the 8th of October 1915 she ran against a hillside in the Eifel and her gondolas were torn off and the occupants thrown into a wood. What remained of the airship came down, with one or two men taking refuge in the gangway, near the German headquarters at Mézières.

★★★★★★

The last raid of this moonless period came on the following night and was made by naval airships. Towards midday on the 13th of September 1915 the *L.11, L.13*, and *L.14* left North Germany for London, announcing, as usual, that they had only 'H.V.B.' on board. They ran into squally weather, and Buttlar in the *L.11* and Böcker in the *L.14* turned back when near the English coast. Mathy alone persisted. He was approaching Felixstowe at 11.37 p.m. when he came under fire from a 6-pounder anti-aircraft gun, and it appeared to the gunners that one shell made a direct hit. He at once turned north, went overland over Bawdsey Marshes, and made his way to Harwich. There the low clouds prevented the searchlights from reaching the airship and no fire was opened. Without dropping any bombs, Mathy moved off again, and, a little later, came under fire from a detachment of the Eastern Mobile Section at Levington Heath.

He reports that his airship hereabouts received a direct hit from a shell which came up vertically from below, penetrated two gas-bags, and fractured the petrol lead and the wireless leads. He therefore gave up all idea of raiding London, or even Harwich, and, to escape further anti-aircraft fire, dropped his bombs in the open. They were forty-six in number and caused no casualties and only slight damage to cottages. As we did not know at the time that the *L.13* had been hit we found it difficult to understand why Mathy so promptly turned back. Petrol, oil, water, and records were jettisoned on the homeward trip, but the airship forcibly struck the ground on landing and was further damaged. All the damage, it is claimed, was repaired within four days.

According to the German official naval history, Buttlar, in the *L.11*, set out for London again on the 15th of September, but was met by head winds and low clouds when he reached the English coast, was 'suddenly fired on from all sides by ships with screened lights', and therefore dropped all his bombs on the ships and on four guns on the coast which also opened fire on him. 'A huge column of fire and two specially loud explosions' showed that the bombs had taken effect, and Buttlar, still under fire, climbed rapidly and made for Nordholz. (See Groos, *Der Krieg zur See*, Vol. 4.) No airship came near our coasts that night, and there is no record that any British ships or shore guns were in action against aircraft.

From September the 13th the cruisers of the Harwich Force carried out a nightly Zeppelin patrol. Three cruisers were detailed one to each of a defined beat.

******

> The *Arethusa* left Harwich at 6 p.m. to patrol between Cromer Knoll and Newarp, and the *Undaunted*, and *Penelope* at 8 p.m., the former for a beat between Cross Sand Light Vessel and a line drawn E. by S. through Southwold Light, and the latter between this line and a position, four miles east of the Sunk Light Vessel.

******

There was only one encounter with an airship. At 10.50 p.m. on the 13th of September the *Undaunted*, near Aldeburgh Napes, sighted and opened fire on an airship, which, however, quickly disappeared apparently untouched. These cruiser patrols continued, without incident, up to the 18th when, in view of the bright moonlight, air raids were considered unlikely, and the Admiralty approved that the patrol should not go to sea unless reports of the approach of aircraft were received.

Meanwhile a further attempt was made by submarines to attack the airships patrolling in the Bight. On the 14th of September four submarines proceeded to the Outer Bight, the *E.17* and *D.3*, for the usual form of patrol, and the *E.4* and *E.6* for attacks, as before, against airships. Bad weather separated the submarines on the 15th. An airship (*S.L.3*) was seen by the *E.4* on the 21st near Horn Reefs and was at once engaged by the submarine with her four 6-pounder anti-aircraft guns. The airship accepted the challenge and made straight for the submarine, which was compelled to submerge when the airship was nearly overhead. The submarine had barely got under when she felt the shocks of three bombs, but she suffered no damage and eventually returned to her base with nothing further to report.

Now that the Zeppelin campaign was getting well under way, and the naval airships were bombing or claiming to have bombed London, the German army staff were seized with uneasiness. They foresaw there might be some hitting back, and that if this came the towns within the German army area on the western front would be the ones to suffer. Accordingly, the Chief of the General Staff approached the Chief of the Naval Staff:

> With the request that for the time being only the docks and wharves of London should be raided and that the City itself should not be bombed so long as the enemy refrained from raiding the open towns of Germany. (Groos, *Der Krieg zur See*, Vol. 4.)

The Chief of the Naval Staff in the interests of the conduct of naval warfare and in view of the military importance of air raids on the City was unable to agree specifically, but:

> Gave orders that in future air raids should be restricted once more as far as possible to those parts of London on the banks of the Thames, as to which no restriction had been made by the German authorities, and that the northern quarter of the City inhabited chiefly by the poorer classes should as far as possible be avoided. (*Idem.*)

The next raid, the last of the year, was to try our defences severely. It was the most ambitious and, from the German point of view, the most successful as yet undertaken, but it was to teach us much. Atmospheric conditions, it was anticipated by us, would be favourable for Zeppelin attacks during the second week in October and, at the beginning of the month, the War Office, in conference with the Admiralty, had prepared an experimental scheme of defence to deal with airships attempting to approach London from the north. The plan provided for:

> (1) Cordons of ground observers, supplied by local commands, in telephonic communication with Home Defence headquarters.
> (2) Two aeroplanes and pilots at Joyce Green and at temporary landing grounds at Hainault Farm and Suttons Farm.

(3) A ring of mobile 13-pounder guns (provided by military anti-aircraft sections mobilizing at Woolwich for overseas), and searchlights, round the north-eastern outskirts of London.

The observer posts were to be placed on the coast, and at selected points on an eighty-mile, sixty-mile, and thirteen-mile radius from London. The observers were provided with rockets of various colours which, on sighting a Zeppelin, they were to fire as an indication to the searchlight and gun crews, and also to the waiting pilots, of the direction in which the airship was going. The observer posts were so disposed that the rate of the advance of the incoming airships could, it was hoped, be calculated and pilots ordered into the air in good time to climb to 8,000 feet before the Zeppelins arrived. The aeroplanes, guns, and searchlights were ready for action on the 5th of October 1915 and the ground observers on the following day.

It was originally intended that the experiment should end on the evening of the 12th, but as no raid had taken place it was suspected that the plan had become known to the enemy. A warning message was thereupon sent to the mobile 13-pounder commanders to hold themselves in readiness to return to Woolwich. This message was for the information of enemy agents and was followed by secret orders for three of the four guns to move to new positions at Romford, Loughton, and Broxbourne. Two additional 13-pounder guns were sent, on the 13th of October, to Suttons Farm and Hainault Farm to work in co-operation with the Royal Flying Corps detachments.

The first warning of the impending attack came from France at 5.0 p.m. on the 13th of October, when messages from the British wireless direction-finding stations indicated Zeppelins moving towards the East Coast. Half an hour later the Admiralty had news of a Zeppelin sighted from a patrol vessel, forty-five miles east of the Haisbro' Light Ship.

Five airships, the *L.11, L.13, L.14, L.15*, and *L.16*, had, in fact, set out from north Germany at midday. At this time a detachment of the Harwich Force was escorting a mine-laying expedition in the German Bight.

******

At midnight and at intervals afterwards messages were sent by the Admiralty to Commodore R. Y. Tyrwhitt ordering him to watch for the airships near Terschelling, at daylight, on their return from England. A watch was kept, but the British ships saw nothing of the Zeppelins.

★★★★★★

No firing by the British armed trawlers along the coast is recorded by us, but most of the airship commanders, on their return, said they had been fired on by darkened vessels when approaching the English coast. It had been originally agreed by the German naval command that the airship attacks, in the dark October nights, should be primarily directed against Liverpool, but the weather conditions on the 13th were deemed not good enough for such an extensive raid and all five ships were ordered to attack London instead. Three of them reached London or its outskirts, one got as near as Hertford, and the other made a brief incursion into Norfolk.

The last, the *L. 11* (Buttlar), may be shortly dismissed. Her commander claimed that he came in at Southend, followed the Thames, which was full of shipping, and, held by fifteen or twenty searchlight beams while the anti-aircraft shells burst about him, bombed West Ham and Woolwich. The *L. 11*, according to our own observation, came in at Bacton at 8.25 p.m., long after the other ships had passed on their way. She was fired on by machine-guns of the Eastern Mobile Section and lost little time in getting rid of her bombs (twenty-three) which were dropped at Horstead, Coltishall, and Great Hautbois. They all fell in open fields and did no more than shatter windows in cottages. The *L. 11* then went out to sea again north of Yarmouth, having been fired on by a Territorial Royal Horse Artillery gun at Mousehold Heath on her way.

The four remaining ships had come in over Bacton, more or less together, about 6.30 p.m. The first to reach London was the *L.*15 (Kapitänleutnant Breithaupt) on her maiden visit to England. She had come under fire from the mobile 13-pounder at Broxbourne at 8.40 p.m. and had replied with four high -explosive bombs, three of which fell near enough to blow down the gun detachment by the force of their explosions. Breithaupt kept his remaining bombs until he was well over the City. Showing coolness and judgement he turned off west to Edgware so as to move across London with the wind behind him, and, judging his position from Hyde Park and the Thames, he began to bomb when he was in the neighbourhood of Charing Cross. By this time the *L. 15* was encircled by searchlight beams and shells were bursting below the ship. Along the Strand to Lincoln's Inn, Chancery Lane, Gray's Inn, Hatton Garden, Farringdon Road, and then on to Finsbury Pavement, Houndsditch, Aldgate, the Minories, and Limehouse, bombs fell in succession. Breithaupt had four bombs left which had failed to release over London and these he dropped harmlessly on his return journey in reply to an attack by a pom-pom detachment of the Eastern Mobile Section at Rushmere, east of Ipswich.

We counted thirty of Breithaupt's bombs on London, and the damage which they did was serious. One, which fell in front of the Lyceum Theatre, killed seventeen people and injured twenty-one. In Aldwych, near the Strand Theatre, four were killed and fifteen injured. The sixteenth-century stained-glass windows in Lincoln's Inn Chapel were seriously damaged, as also were Gray's Inn Hall and many private business premises. In the East Central and City districts, a number of buildings were destroyed. The total casualties caused by this one airship were twenty-eight killed and seventy injured.

Breithaupt's attack on the City was seen by Oberleutnant zur See Peterson, in the *L.16*, who was near Chipping Ongar at 9.30 p.m. Peterson, as he says, thought he would take the opportunity to slip into London from the north while the defences were concentrating on the *L.15*. He therefore made a wide sweep and came in, he reported, over Tottenham and, as his attack was unexpected, he met with comparatively slight opposition, but the town was well darkened and he found it difficult to pick up the details of the ground below him. However, guided by what he thought was the Thames (actually the River Lea), he made his attack on such buildings as he could see. What he did was to attack Hertford with fourteen high-explosive and thirty incendiary bombs, which destroyed ten buildings, slightly damaged 141 others, and killed nine and injured fifteen people.

Kapitänleutnant Böcker, in the *L.14*, in some confusion as to his position, went far south out of his course. He was near Shorncliffe at 9.15 p.m. and, apparently attracted by lights and fires, he dropped four high-explosive bombs in Otterpool Camp where fifteen soldiers were killed and eleven injured. Two more bombs near Westenhanger Camp did no damage. The ship then skirted the sea near Hythe and proceeded to make a wide sweep west and north-west towards London. Seven bombs were dropped at Frant and three at Tunbridge Wells on the way, but they caused no casualties or damage. Near Oxted, the *L.14* crossed the path of the *L.13* (Kapitänleutnant Mathy) which had made a westerly sweep to Guildford. Böcker went on direct to Croydon which he bombed at 11.20 p.m. Seventeen of his eighteen bombs fell on villa residences, and the other exploded by the railway, slightly damaging the permanent way. In Croydon nine persons were killed and fifteen injured. Over Bickley, on the return journey, the *L.14* narrowly averted a collision with the *L.13* which was on her way to Woolwich.

Mathy, in the *L.13*, had dropped his first bombs on his way in to London near an anti-aircraft gun which opened fire on him at Birchwood Farm near Hatfield, and he then went on by way of Watford and Staines to Guildford. He apparently mistook the River Wey for the Thames, and under the impression that he was attacking Hampton, dropped twelve high-explosive bombs which fell in Shalford and did minor damage to private houses. Mathy then turned off towards London, coming up, as has been told, with the *L.14*.

As Mathy went on his way to Woolwich he looked back and watched the bombs from the *L.14* exploding in Croydon. Mathy flew direct over the whole length of the barracks and Arsenal at Woolwich, and on these two targets he dropped four high-explosive and twenty-eight incendiary bombs. Four men were injured in the barracks and nine (one of whom died later) in the Arsenal, but nothing vital was hit and the material damage was slight. A final high-explosive bomb was dropped in the magazine area on Plumstead Marshes, but again no damage was done. Mathy did not know that his attack had been made on the Arsenal; he thought he had bombed the Victoria Docks, and so reported.

All five Zeppelins, hampered by fog, got back to Germany, but one of them, the *L.15*, made a rough landing in the mist near the Nordholz base and received damage which put her out of commission for eight days. A thousand men man-handled her back into her shed.

The total number of bombs accounted for during this attack, was 102 high-explosive and eighty-seven incendiary. (The German official account says 6,100 kg. of high-explosive and 157 incendiary. See Groos, Vol. 4.) The full casualties of the attack were seventy-one killed and 128 injured, a greater number, in proportion to the ships engaged and bombs dropped, than were inflicted by any other airship raid of the war.

The value of the observer cordons throughout this raid was well demonstrated. Reports poured in to Home Defence headquarters from which the courses of the incoming ships were plotted, and warnings were issued to everyone required to take action. The dispositions of the six mobile 13-pounder guns proved sound, every one of them coming into action. Had these guns been manned by more experienced personnel, held their fire longer, and been provided with a high-explosive shell with time fuse, it is doubtful whether the Zeppelins could have escaped undamaged.

★★★★★★

> Following this raid, anti-aircraft sections, during the period of their final training for overseas, were regularly sent to positions on a twelve-mile radius covering the approach to London. By the end of December 1915 there were twelve 13-pounders and eight 6-pounders, with twenty-one searchlights, so disposed.

★★★★★★

In addition to these 13-pounders, all guns of the London defences as well as those of Woolwich, at Waltham Abbey, and of the mobile section in East Anglia, were engaged. The airship commanders reported a great increase in the London defences, but no ship suffered damage from gun-fire.

No naval aeroplanes went up in the raided area, but the information sent in by the observer cordons gave the waiting Royal Flying Corps pilots at Joyce Green, Hainault Farm, and Suttons Farm, ample time to get their height before the airships approached London. Five pilots ascended in spite of ground fog, but only one saw a Zeppelin. This was Second Lieutenant J. C. Slessor who found an airship caught in the beam of a searchlight. He set off in pursuit, but had to fly through thick cloud and, when he got clear again, the airship had disappeared. After a fruitless two-hour patrol, the pilot landed in the mist, breaking his undercarriage. Two other of the patrolling pilots crashed in the fog on landing but escaped injury.

They had had no luck, but their flights were not made in vain. Breithaupt, referring to his passage across London says:

> The *L. 15* was caught in the beams of a large number of searchlights, the illumination, especially above the City, being as bright as day. Unusually violent anti-aircraft defence fire opened and the airship was soon surrounded by bursting shrapnel. Even more sinister was the appearance of another danger in addition to the anti-aircraft guns. Four aeroplanes, at first observed by the flames from the exhaust and then clearly shown up in the beam of the searchlights, endeavoured to reach the airship and shoot her down with incendiary ammunition . . . not until the *L. 15* had dropped all her ballast was she out of reach of the enemy. (Groos, *Der Krieg zur See*, Vol. 4.)

The experiences of the Royal Flying Corps pilots made clear the need for more continuous searchlight illumination of the Zeppelins. It had already been suggested that enough searchlights should be ringed round London to ensure that no airship could enter without being lighted up. But an airship passed from the range of any one light with rapidity and so gave a pilot little opportunity to get into an attacking position. It was decided, therefore, to establish an inner ring of lights to pick up the airships as they neared the limit illuminated by the outer ring. This was the principle on which the War Office set to work at once.

As part of the scheme nine electric tramcars were fitted to carry searchlights (six belonging to the Metropolitan Electric Tramways, two to the Ilford Urban District Council, and one to the Croydon Corporation) and were distributed to the tramcar depots on the outskirts of London whence, as occasion demanded, they could be run out to allotted positions. Seven of the cars were ready for action in December 1915, and the remaining two by the first week in January 1916. These searchlight tramcars, of limited mobility, remained in use until the end of 1916 when they began to be withdrawn, the last one being dismantled in March 1917.

Although the War Office was now co-operating more closely in the air defence, the responsibility was still a naval one. No naval aeroplanes rose to the attack in this October raid on London, and the question of increasing the defence aircraft was raised at the Admiralty. A letter was sent to the naval commands on the East Coast pointing out that every effort must be made to intercept and destroy Zeppelins. The letter stated:

> It was with this object in view, that the executive control was taken from the Air Department and transferred to Senior Naval Officers on the coast when the Air Service was recently reorganised.

The senior naval officers were enjoined to maintain an air patrol along their coast-lines, especially at twilight, whenever weather conditions were favourable. The Admiral of Patrols promptly replied that he had less than half the required number of aircraft to ensure patrols of his area, and he proposed that light draught paddle steamers should be equipped to carry four seaplanes each and sent out, before sunset on favourable nights, along a line, fifty to sixty miles, east of the coast from the Tyne to the Wash. A similar suggestion had been made by the senior naval officer at Lowestoft, and as it was obvious that Zeppelins could be more effectively attacked in daylight than in the dark, the Admiralty adopted the proposal. In the result, at the end of March 1916, two paddle steamers, the *Killingholme* and *Brocklesby*, capable of crossing the minefields, were fitted to carry two or three Sopwith Schneider Cup seaplanes and were based at Killingholme and Yarmouth respectively.

The Attack on the Midlands, 31st January 1916

For three and a half months, following the October attack on London, there was no attempt by the airship commanders to reach England. But when the next raid came, at the end of January 1916, it proved to be ambitiously conceived, and a serious beginning of the campaign of the new year. The attack was directed against the Midlands, and the Zeppelin commanders had the special task of getting to the west coast, where they were to bombard Liverpool. The area of attack was still almost defenceless, and, from the German point of view, the conditions for carrying out the project were as favourable as they could be.

The whole force of the new standardized-type naval airships left their sheds at Nordholz, Tondern, and Hage towards midday on the 31st of January 1916. They were the L.11 (Buttlar, and carrying Korvettenkapitän Strasser, the commander of the Naval Airship Detachment), *L.13* (Mathy), *L.14* (Böcker), *L.15* (Breithaupt), *L.16* (Peterson), *L.17* (Ehrlich), *L.19* (Loewe), *L.20* (Stabbert), and *L.21* (Max Dietrich). We intercepted the usual 'H.V.B.' signals about noon from which we knew that six or more airships were setting out. The anti-aircraft trawlers at Lowestoft were ordered out, and Commodore Tyrwhitt was instructed to make a Zeppelin patrol with his light cruisers if the weather were clear. Two of the Lowestoft trawlers, the *Kingfisher* and the *Cantatrice*, had been fitted to carry seaplanes specially for attacks on Zeppelins.

The *Kingfisher* was ready and left at once, with another armed trawler as guard, but fog enshrouded the coast before the *Cantatrice* was ready and she, as well as the Harwich light cruisers, could not go out. The fog also descended on the *Kingfisher* about the time the Zeppelins were approaching and she saw nothing of them. When the airships got near the English coast, they found the whole area obscured by a deep cloud layer and the commanders were compelled, in the main, to depend for navigation on bearings relayed to them by their wireless telegraphy stations, which are stated to have been unreliable.

(See Groos, *Der Krieg zur See*, Vol. 5.)

Before the coast was crossed the ships flew into rain and snow clouds and their weight was increased by the formation of ice on the envelopes. The airships, consequently, could not be forced higher than 6,500 feet and even to get this height petrol and a few bombs had to go overboard as ballast. At this period, also, three of the airships (*L.16, L.17*, and *L.20*) developed engine trouble and their commanders had to abandon the idea of reaching Liverpool and decided, instead, to attack suitable objectives nearer the East Coast.

The detailed account in the German official history, (*ibid*) of the movements and doings of the airships is of small value as a check on our own observations that night. The German historian admits the difficulties and uncertainties of navigation during this raid. What is clear, is that the airship commanders, for the most part, came in much farther south than they thought they did and that this initial mistake continued to confuse their subsequent navigation. Broadly stated, the Germans were under the impression that they bombed Sheffield three times in succession, Immingham and Yarmouth once each, Manchester by two airships simultaneously, Liverpool twice at short intervals, and Goole and Nottingham once each. Of the nine airship commanders, four, it is claimed, reached the west coast although only two bombed there, but both of these were emphatic that their bombs had fallen on Liverpool.

In fact, no bomb fell on any one of these towns. Nor did any airship get near the west coast, the most westerly point reached being near Shrewsbury. One of the Zeppelins, the *L.19*, remained in the air over England for about eleven hours (she was to pay for her temerity); another was over England for eight hours, and the rest for lesser periods, and they all steered complicated courses so that the paths of their flights cross and recross. It is possible that our own observations as to the movements of any particular ship are sometimes at fault, but what is beyond dispute is the locality in which bombs were dropped.

Let us consider first the three ships which developed engine trouble. The *L.16* crossed at Hunstanton about 6.10 p.m. and wandered about Norfolk until 9.5 p.m. when she went out again at Lowestoft. Her only bombs (two high-explosive, of which one did not explode) were dropped on Swaffham and they did no damage. (The German account says *L.16* dropped 'all her bombs on various factories and industrial works at Yarmouth'. See Groos, Vol. 5.)

The *L.17* drifted in over Sheringham at 6.40 p.m. and was caught by the searchlight from the Naval Air Service landing ground at Holt. She promptly dropped her load of bombs, of which we counted forty on Bayfield and one on Letheringsett; they fell mostly in open fields, and the only damage was a barn destroyed and a house partly demolished. There were no casualties. No other bombs came from this airship which went out south of Yarmouth at 8.30 p.m. (The *L.17* commander thought he made his landfall near Immingham. He reported dropping his first salvo of bombs on a searchlight and the remainder on 'the industrial works assumed to be in the vicinity'. See Groos, Vol. 5.)

The *L.20* penetrated farther inland than her two partly-crippled consorts. She came overland at the Wash about 7.0 p.m. and dropped her first bomb at Uffington near Stamford; it did no damage beyond breaking windows. She continued in a westerly direction and her commander seems to have been attracted by the lights of Loughborough, which had not been reduced, and he made straight for the town, leaving Leicester, which lay in darkness, untouched. Four bombs fell on Loughborough at 8.5 p.m. and killed ten and injured twelve people and did slight damage to buildings. Bennerley and Trowell were next attacked with seven bombs which damaged a cattle-shed and a signal-box. At 8.30 p.m. the airship appeared over Ilkeston and signalled her arrival with fifteen bombs which fell in, or near, the Stanton Iron Works, Hallam Field.

The moulding and blacksmiths' shops, and a stable and a schoolroom were damaged, and two men were killed and two others injured. The airship then turned on her tracks and made off south-westward towards Burton-on-Trent, which was fairly well lighted, and here, about 8.45 p.m., a dozen or more incendiary bombs were thrown. This was the first attack on Burton, which was visited by three airships between 8.45 p.m. and 9.45 p.m. It is impossible to distinguish between the bombs dropped at Burton by the three different ships and to assign particular damage to a particular ship. The total damage in the town is stated below. From Burton, the *L.20*, all her bombs gone, turned for home, passing Cromer, on her way out to sea, just before midnight. (Her commander reported he had dropped most of his bombs on a town that appeared to be Sheffield. See Groos, Vol. 5.)

Mathy, in the *L.13*, was one of those who penetrated well inland, as he was one of the first to come overland. He came in north of Mundesley with the *L.21* about 4.50 p.m. and steered a direct westerly course south of Nottingham and over Derby to Stoke-on-Trent where he was at 8.15 p.m. Six bombs dropped at Fenton Colliery, south of Stoke, broke a few windows by concussion, but did no other damage and caused no casualties. From Stoke, Mathy turned north-west, possibly in the hope of finding Manchester, but a low-lying cloud-sheet confused him. He was seen to drop flares to locate his whereabouts and, so far as our observers could make out, he turned again south-east, and, it seemed, was one of the commanders who bombed Burton-on-Trent. It is clear, however, from the German account that Mathy did not attack Burton.

Groos (vol. 5) says:

> The airship, with the aid of flares and wireless telegraphy bearings from Bruges, felt her way presumably towards the Humber and at 23.45 hours dropped the rest of her high-explosive and 60 incendiary bombs through the clouds on a blast furnace and other extensive factory premises near Goole.'

Mathy, in fact, did not quite get to Goole, but his account is approximately accurate. His bombs fell at Scunthorpe, south of the Humber, where the Frodingham Iron and Steel Works, which had received no warning, were in full blast, and, with their untapped furnaces, must have offered an easy mark. We counted sixteen high-explosive and forty-eight incendiary bombs. All of them missed the Frodingham Works, but several fell on the Redbourne Iron Works, which were closed down and in darkness. Two men were killed, but the material effects were inconsiderable, involving only slight damage to the engine- and boiler-house. In Scunthorpe itself, four workmen's houses were demolished, and one man was killed and seven people injured. The *L.13* then went out to sea direct just before midnight.

At the time, we thought the Scunthorpe attack had been made by the *L.11* and it is easy now to see how we made our mistake. The *L.11* carrying Korvettenkapitän Strasser, dropped, according to Groos, no bombs at all. After crossing the East Coast, the airship commander was much hampered by fog and mist and, although one or two towns appeared below the airship on her westward journey, they were not definitely recognised and no bombs were therefore dropped on them. About 10.0 p.m. it appeared from calculation that the *L.11* was over the west coast, but in view of the fog it seemed unlikely that Liverpool could be located, and the airship was therefore turned about and, as no further definite objectives presented themselves, carried her whole load of bombs home again.

An airship was credibly reported in the sparsely-inhabited Peak district, and there is little doubt now that this was the *L.11*. She never got near the west coast, but turned back somewhere east of Macclesfield and, on her return journey, crossed the path of the *L.13*. From this point our own records transpose the two ships. We show the *L.11* going north to the Humber and the *L.13* going straight out to sea, whereas it is now clear that it was Mathy who went to Scunthorpe while the *L.11* went home direct.

It is pleasant to pay tribute to Korvettenkapitän Strasser for his high conception of his duty. He had been over British soil for four hours or more and had sighted a number of possible targets, but as he recognised no objective of definite military importance he was content to take his bombs back as he had brought them.

The course flown by the *L.21* on her first flight over England was direct. She came in north of Mundesley, close behind the *L.13*, but soon out-distanced her consort. She passed south of Nottingham and north of Derby (which Kapitänleutnant Max Dietrich, her commander, identified as Manchester), and then turned south-west towards Wolverhampton. Hereabouts, Dietrich, who calculated he was over the west coast, saw fog below him, but he soon came upon the bright lights of two towns, separated by a river, which he took to be Liverpool and Birkenhead. He therefore made a wide sweep, as he thought out to sea, before coming in to deliver his attack.

Actually, he was over the congested area midway between Wolverhampton and Birmingham, and his bombs, of which we counted twenty-seven high-explosives and twenty-one incendiaries, fell in succession on Tipton, Lower Bradley (near Bilston), Wednesbury, and Walsall. They killed thirty-three people, including the Mayoress of Walsall, and injured twenty, but the material damage was not great, although a number of private houses were wrecked. Dietrich then steered an unswerving course for home. On his return journey he thought he again passed over Manchester and reports that the city was shrouded in fog, but that he saw the betraying blaze of a blast furnace on which he dropped the remainder of his incendiary bombs. The blaze which attracted him was from the Islip furnaces at Thrapston at which six incendiary bombs were thrown at 9.15 p.m.; they fell in fields and did no damage. The *L.21* went out, south of Lowestoft, at 11.35 p.m. Dietrich, having mistaken Thrapston for Manchester, concluded he had crossed to sea again near the Humber.

The Tipton-Wednesbury area suffered a second raid that night. The commander of the *L.19*, who had steered a hesitating course, was probably attracted to the area by fires and lights which were showing after Dietrich's attack. He reported by wireless, on his homeward journey, that after reaching the fog-enshrouded west coast and vainly seeking Liverpool, he dropped all his bombs on industrial works near Sheffield. His most westerly point, however, was Bewdley, from which he turned east and then north, missing Birmingham, which was in total darkness, and beginning his attack at Wednesbury about midnight. (He seems previously, on his incoming flight, to have dropped a few incendiary bombs on Burton-on-Trent.)

Twenty high-explosive and seventeen incendiary bombs fell on Wednesbury, Dudley, Tipton, and Walsall. They inflicted no further casualties and did only minor damage. Of the seventeen bombs which were aimed at Dudley all, except one, fell in fields or in the castle grounds. The *L. 19* went out again along a winding course and crossed the coast at 5.25 a.m. some hours behind the last of her companion ships. She seems to have developed engine trouble, possibly owing to shortage of petrol, on her return journey. She was seen cruising, at a low height, over the Dutch Islands, and was there fired upon and is reported to have been hit, after which she disappeared in a northerly direction. The Germans feared she was in trouble, but, owing to the high south wind, airship reconnaissance to search for her could not be made. Aeroplanes, however, were sent out from Borkum, but their pilots saw nothing and two of them failed to return.

Meanwhile, at dusk on February the 1st, it was reported that a Zeppelin, in difficulties, had been seen off Cromer, and Commodore Tyrwhitt was ordered to send out vessels to search for her. At daybreak on the 2nd of February the Harwich Force of light cruisers and destroyers sailed and made an unrewarded search until 4.50 p.m. when the Force was recalled.

Nothing was known of the fate of the airship until a fishing trawler, the *King Stephen*, arrived at Grimsby. Her skipper, who had been fishing in a prohibited area, reported that at 7.0 a.m. on the 2nd of February, he saw a white object on the water about 120 miles east of Spurn Light Vessel which he found, on investigation, to be the *L. 19* in a sinking condition. A group of men were in a roughly constructed shelter on the top of the envelope and, from inside the airship, came the sound of knocking, which seemed to the fishermen to be caused by attempts by the remainder of the crew to caulk the leaks in the hull. The commander of the airship hailed the skipper of the *King Stephen* with a request that the airship crew be taken on board, but the skipper replied: 'No. If I take you on board you will take charge,' for it was his conviction that his few hands could, and would, be easily overpowered by the Germans, even if they were unarmed. He therefore steamed off to find and report to a patrol boat, but it was not until he put in to the Humber on the morning of the 3rd of February, that he found a vessel to receive his report. Then it was too late. The *L. 19* had gone down with all hands.

★★★★★★

The last report of her commander was washed up in a bottle at Marstrand, on the Norwegian Coast, some months later. It read: 'With 15 men on the platform of *L. 19*. Longitude 3° East. The envelope is floating without any car. I am trying to send the last report. We had three engine breakdowns. A very high head-wind on the homeward flight hampered progress and drove us in the fog over Holland when we came under rifle-fire. Three engines failed simultaneously. Our position became increasingly difficult. Now, about one o'clock in the afternoon, our last hour is approaching. Loewe.' See Groos, Vol. 5.

★★★★★★

There remain the *L. 14* and *L. 15*, the former penetrating farthest west of all the airships. She came in north of Holkham at 6.15 p.m. and dropped her first bomb, an incendiary, at Wisbech. Her next, a high-explosive, fell near Knipton. The airship then flew south of Nottingham and Derby, and north of Stafford, to Shrewsbury, where she appeared at 10.5 p.m. Her commander thought he was now over the west coast and tried in vain to pierce the fog below him for a target. As he could see nothing, he eventually turned and flew east again until he was attracted by the light of some pipe-furnaces at Ashby Woulds, where he dropped two bombs which exploded on a cinder-heap. Four more followed on Over seal and three on Swadlincote, without damage, before the *L. 14* appeared over Derby where the main attack was made. (The *L. 14* reported dropping her bombs on blast furnaces and factory premises in the vicinity of Nottingham.)

Twenty-one high-explosive and four incendiary bombs struck the town. Nine of the explosive bombs fell on the Midland Railway Works and damaged the engine-sheds and killed three men and injured two. Three hit the 'Metalite' Lamp Works, doing considerable damage, yet causing no casualties. The remaining bombs had small effect, the only additional casualties being a man killed and a woman who died of shock. From Derby the *L. 14* went out direct, crossing the coast of Lincolnshire, north of the Wash, soon after 2.10 a.m.

The *L.15*, whose flight we followed with some difficulty, seemed to have been responsible for the dropping of a load of forty bombs in the open fen district near Isleham, but it is possible that these came from the *L.16* which was wandering in this vicinity for a considerable time. As far as we could make out, the *L.15* then cruised tortuously into Lincolnshire, and other bombs which fell ineffectively at Welbourn Hill Top (nine incendiaries) and Holland Fen (one incendiary) were credited to her. But Breithaupt, a reliable commander, reported that he flew due west and came upon an extensive inhabited area, bisected by a river, which he took to be Liverpool and Birkenhead. He then says that while the lights below him were gradually extinguished, he flew along the river bank four times and dropped the main load of his bombs. It is possible that his attack was actually made on Burton-on-Trent where a number of bombs, estimated at twenty-five, fell about 9.15 p.m.

The casualties inflicted at Burton, as a result of the three attacks made on the town, were serious, fifteen people being killed and seventy injured. Nine houses and a malthouse were wrecked, a church, a mission room, and two breweries badly damaged, and many other houses and buildings slightly damaged. The figures for the whole raid are 205 high-explosive and 174 incendiary bombs which killed 70 people and injured 113.

The defence during the attack was negligible. Thirty-four rounds were fired at one airship near the Humber by the Waltham one-pounder pom-pom and one round was fired by a 4.7 gun at Mundesley. Fourteen pilots went up in two relays, from the mist-enshrouded aerodromes near London, but they naturally saw nothing, and seven of the aeroplanes were damaged, three of their pilots being injured. (Two of them died of their injuries. They were Majors L. da C. Penn-Gaskell and E. F. Unwin of the Royal Flying Corps, both of whom crashed in the mist as they were getting away from their aerodromes.) Two aeroplanes which went up from Castle Bromwich under similar difficult conditions patrolled fruitlessly: one was wrecked on landing, the pilot escaping injury. Four aircraft from Yarmouth also searched in vain.

This first raid on the Midlands brought about an extension of the lighting restrictions. Some of the towns which had been attacked, for example Burton-on-Trent and Walsall, were, at the time of the raid, not covered by the Lights Orders, and, owing to a breakdown in the local warning arrangements, the airships were over the towns before precautions could be taken. Although general instructions had been issued to chief constables in May 1915, the arrangements for the collection and communication of raid information had not, in some areas, been worked out, and a further difficulty, during the attacks, arose from a congestion of the telephone lines which were overloaded with unnecessary calls by members of the public. To prevent a recurrence of this latter difficulty the telephone exchanges were instructed to keep police circuits free for official messages, and an appeal was issued to the public to restrict telephone calls, during an attack, to what were necessary and urgent.

Now it was clear that the Midlands, and even the western parts of the country, were no longer immune from attack, it was agreed that the lighting restrictions should be extended to the whole of England except Cumberland, Westmorland, Hereford, Monmouth, Somerset, and Cornwall, and orders were made on the 8th of February 1916 to come into force on the 16th. But the public were by now thoroughly roused, and many authorities in the exempted districts asked to be included in the restricted areas. Pending the working out of a detailed scheme, applicable to the whole of England, four interim orders were made: for Monmouthshire, Cardiff, and the urban districts of Penarth and Barry; for Cumberland and Westmorland; for Somerset; and for Exeter and Plymouth. The orders came into force on the 14th of April 1916.

The problem of lighting was more easy of solution than that of warning. The Lord Mayor of Birmingham, who strenuously voiced the feeling of the Midlands, proposed that the whole of the Midland munitions area should be divided into districts, each with an appointed centre to which warnings could be sent and from which they could be distributed locally. Between this area and the coast, he proposed the setting up of a cordon of observers whose sole duty it would be to watch for and report the approach of hostile aircraft, so that warnings could be sent to the munition district centres in time for street lights, &c, to be extinguished and other precautions to be taken.

These proposals embodied some of the ideas of the scheme on which General Headquarters of the Home Forces had been working for some time. But until the control of air defence passed formally and definitely to the army, G.H.Q. Home Forces were not in a position to put their scheme into operation, and a promise was given to the Lord Mayor of Birmingham by the Admiralty, on the 4th of February 1916, that a special warning of the approach of hostile aircraft would be sent to Birmingham for distribution to neighbouring areas. At the same time, an interim arrangement with G.H.Q. Home Forces and the Post Office was made, whereby the trunk telephone systems were to be used for sending from London to Chief Constables in coast counties and the Midlands a confidential notification of the arrival of hostile aircraft over the country, and of their subsequent movements.

How chaotic the existing warning arrangements were, and how nervous the general public had now become, is evidenced by happenings on the nights following the great Midland raid. Not until the beginning of March 1916 did airships again approach our coasts, but Zeppelins were being continuously reported in the interim. On the 2nd of February 1916 Zeppelins were independently reported in the Birmingham, Derby, and Manchester districts and lights in railway stations and munition works were extinguished for a time. On the two following nights there were alarms, accompanied by the extinction of lights, in south Lancashire and Staffordshire.

On the 10th of February a report that a Zeppelin had been seen off Scarborough during the afternoon was widely disseminated, with the result that railway lights were put out at places so variously distant as Nottingham, Bath, Gloucester, and Worcester, while traffic was held up on the Hull and Barnsley railway and on the North Eastern Coast lines, and work came to a standstill in two Government factories at Gloucester. These Zeppelins existed only in the public imagination, which was stimulated by a complete lack of faith in the official warning arrangements. There was a grave risk too, that the output of munitions would be seriously curtailed by the refusal of workers to keep going at night unless they were assured that warnings would be timely and reliable. On the 12th of February a representative of the Ministry of Munitions stated:

> Our position is that workmen are refusing to work at night at all unless guaranteed that warning will be given in sufficient time to enable them to disperse. It is not merely a question of putting out lights.

In the result, it became necessary to issue a circular to chief constables asking them to arrange to notify all munition factories in their areas when hostile aircraft were approaching. This was to be done either by telephone or by some system of public warning such as hooters or sirens.

The attack on the Midlands of the 31st of January 1916 closed the period of the most formidable airship raids regarded from the point of view of frequency, casualties inflicted, and material damage caused. This is shown clearly in the following table where statistics for the raids culminating in the Midland attack are compared with similar figures, for airship attacks, applicable to the whole war period.

	Number of Raids.	*Number of Bombs.*	*Casualties.*		*Estimated monetary damage.*
			Killed.	*Injured.*	
January 1915/January 1916 (Inclusive).	21	1,900	277	645	£869,698
Whole war period, i.e. January 1915/April 1918.	51	5,751	556	1,357	£1,527,585

What makes the comparison more striking is that the number of ships and the weight of bombs increased, so that the potential destructive force of the later raids is far greater than is implied in a comparison of the figures given above. Yet for the period ending with the Midland attack of January 1916, very nearly as many casualties were inflicted and rather more material damage was caused by the airships than during the remainder of the war.

The explanation is that from the beginning of 1916 technical developments, and reorganisation, put the defence on an effective basis. At first gradually, and later, rapidly, it caught up with and then finally overtook the offensive powers of the Zeppelins. During our time of defencelessness, as was to be expected, we suffered most, but we might have suffered far more. Luck was with us time and again. One may instance the attack on the Skinningrove Iron Works by the *L.9* on the night of the 8th of September 1915, when, by the merest chance, we escaped a disaster that must have had an enormous effect on the morale of the workers in the northern and midland industrial centres.

Nor did the enemy take full advantage of his position. He had developed his special weapon over a number of years and for long we failed to produce any effective counter-weapons. Our anti-aircraft guns were few and not many of them could send shells high enough to harass the airship commanders. Our aeroplane and seaplane pilots had the will, but they had none of the other essentials of successful attack. Patrolling to be effective must be so ordered that attacking pilots are in the probable line of the enemy's approach. Thanks to our system of wireless interception, we usually had warning, hours in advance, of impending raids, but we profited little from our knowledge.

Our system of observation and deduction, once the airships reached this country, was inadequate and laborious, with the result that the heavier-than-air craft patrols were haphazard and not co-ordinated. Furthermore, the importance of the searchlight as an aid to the night-flying pilot was, for long, not properly appreciated. A pilot in the air may be attracted to the proximity of a raiding airship by the bursting of anti-aircraft shells or by the explosion of bombs on the ground, but he requires the illumination of the airship by searchlight to direct him on his target.

An airship moves with comparative rapidity, and if it is to be kept illuminated searchlight stations must be precisely spaced and planned, and their operations closely co-ordinated. What searchlights there were, in this early period, were attached to the scattered anti-aircraft guns with the sole idea of lighting up their targets to the gunners. Even, however, had these aspects of the ground defence been perfectly realised and provided for, our pilots, with few exceptions, had not the aircraft that would take them near or above the Zeppelins, nor did they have ammunition which would give them a reasonable chance of bringing an airship down if they did get within striking distance. Indeed, the ramming of the Zeppelins was envisaged as a form of attack and was the subject of instructions to pilots.

★★★★★★

> The instructions issued by Squadron Commander J. C. Porte, commanding the R.N.A.S. station at Hendon, included: 'If the aeroplane fails to stop the airship by the time all the ammunition is expended and the airship is still heading for London and shows no sign of being turned from her objective, then the pilot must decide to sacrifice himself and his machine and ram the airship at the utmost speed.' A similar order had been issued by an overseas Squadron Commander of the Royal Flying Corps. 'I certainly think in those days', says Air Marshal Sir Robert Brooke-Popham, 'a great many officers would have deliberately charged a Zeppelin if they had met it.'

★★★★★★

Training in night flying, too, was meagre and casual, and the lighting arrangements on the aerodromes, and on alternative landing grounds, an all-important safety factor, were primitive.

There was, indeed, little or nothing effectively to impede the enemy coming and going as he wished on every favourable occasion, and that he came comparatively seldom is a cause for thanksgiving.

Nor did his choice of objectives reveal sound strategy. He was unduly attracted by the lure of London and neglected the industrial centres of the Midlands at a time when they lay wide open to attack. One great advantage of the airship as an attacking weapon was its power to strike anywhere over a wide area, and had the airship commanders turned their eyes away from the capital, and systematically bombed the industrial centres of the north, who can say what the material and moral effect might have been? Because he concentrated his attacks towards London, the enemy played into our hands as he enabled us also to concentrate our slender defensive forces.

Yet even here the enemy did not persist when he still had the opportunity that was later, and for ever, to pass from him. A lack of sympathy between the German naval and military airship services had reactions which told in our favour. We had ample warning, by wireless interception, when the naval Zeppelins came out to raid England. The military airship commanders, however, kept silent, and the first we knew of their intentions was usually that they were crossing the British coast. Combined raids by military ships from Belgium and by naval ships from the North German sheds may have been a failure from the German point of view.

But on nights when naval Zeppelins were over England, the presence also of military airships added elements of general doubt and confusion which made more difficult the task of those directing the defensive measures. We much preferred to deal with the two airship services on different nights and, thanks to German policy, we were usually enabled to do so. The conclusion cannot be avoided that the German authorities, having once committed themselves to Zeppelin warfare, failed to exploit it to the full.

Aeroplane and Seaplane Attacks

(For a statistical summary of aeroplane and seaplane raids 1914-16 see Appendix 3, Table B)

The raids by heavier-than-air craft for the first two years of the war were of the 'tip and run' kind, usually by single aircraft, and they offer few features of interest, although the aeroplane raids were, in the end, to prove more formidable than those made by airships. Fortunately, however, the airship menace had already been disposed of before we were called upon to meet the determined aeroplane attacks. The two raids by heavier-than-air craft in 1914 have already been referred to. In 1915, there were three daylight attacks on this country and one by night. The first took place on the 21st of February, when a single aircraft came in over Clacton at 7.45 p.m. and flew as far as Braintree, near which two incendiary bombs were dropped. They did no damage; it was reported that one of them was picked up by a soldier and thrown into the River Blackwater. The aircraft then returned over Coggeshall (one high-explosive bomb: no damage) and over Colchester where a high-explosive bomb, dropped near the Artillery Barracks, damaged a house and a shed.

There were about this time occasional attacks on shipping in the Downs and off the Essex coast. On the 26th of February 1915 two seaplanes abortively attacked the *Cordoba* near the Sunk Lightship. It was known that a third seaplane had set out at the same time to raid Essex, but nothing further was heard of it until the next day when a tug put into Lowestoft with two German aviators on board. They had fallen in the sea on their way over on the 26th and had spent the night, in snowstorms, clinging to the wreckage of their seaplane.

On the 20th of March four aeroplanes were seen making for the Downs. One dropped six bombs near a coasting steamer, but none made a hit.

There was quiet for nearly a month. Then, just before noon on the 16th of April, a single aeroplane came in over Kingsdown and flew to Sittingbourne where four bombs were dropped, one of them falling near a military camp. The aeroplane then went off over Faversham where five bombs fell in reply to anti-aircraft fire. They were possibly aimed at the Faversham Explosive Works, but, like those dropped at Sittingbourne, they exploded in open fields.

There was little activity after this until September. On the 23rd of May 1915 unsuccessful attacks were made by single aircraft on shipping near the Goodwins and off Dover, and on the 3rd of July two aircraft appeared off Harwich where one of them dropped bombs in the sea, but it was not until September that the first casualties of the year were caused. On the 13th of this month a seaplane appeared suddenly over Cliftonville and dropped ten bombs, four of which fell on the foreshore and six in streets and gardens. Two women were killed and two men and four women injured, but the material damage was slight and none of it of military importance.

In January 1916 there were four attempted attacks, all aimed at Dover. In the afternoon of the 9th, one aircraft approached the town, but was turned back by anti-aircraft fire. In the early hours of the 23rd nine bombs from a single aeroplane fell near the Garrison Headquarters and wrecked the Red Lion Hotel and a malthouse. One man was killed and two men, one woman, and three children injured. Twelve hours later, towards 1.0 p.m., the alarm was raised again. The anti-aircraft fire seems to have diverted the attack, made by two aircraft, from Dover to Folkestone where five bombs were aimed at the airship sheds at Capel. They scored no hits and there was no damage. A seaplane appeared over Capel and Dover again next afternoon but dropped no bombs.

During these spasmodic attacks by the heavier-than-air craft, naval and military aeroplanes and seaplanes went up to engage the raiders, but only once did a British pilot get near enough to attack. That was on the 24th of January 1916, when one of four pilots who pursued the Capel-Dover raider opened fire with his Lewis gun at a range of 300 yards. He was gaining on his adversary when his gun jammed and the German aircraft disappeared in a cloud. The attacks, indeed, were difficult to meet. The raiders came in, high up and without warning, and had usually passed on their way before any British aeroplane could approach their height.

CHAPTER 3

The Air Raids on Great Britain February to December 1916

AIR DEFENCE AS AN ARMY RESPONSIBILITY

It is true that in the first attack on the Midland towns the German airship commanders claimed to have bombed many industrial centres which they did not, in fact, get near. It is true, also, that in proportion to the number of bombs dropped the material damage was not great. But it would be misleading to dwell on these features of the raid. What was important was that the Zeppelin commanders found many vulnerable targets and that the manufacturing areas over which they flew were, for the most part, undefended. The airship menace, indeed, was at its height, but a reorganisation of the defences, destined to defeat the Zeppelin as a raiding weapon, was about to take place.

The existing arrangement whereby the responsibility for air defence was arbitrarily divided between the Admiralty and the War Office was pleasing to neither of the two departments. The system was dogged by all the evils of divided control—indecision, lack of co-ordination, conflict of purpose and of policy, and a sapping effect on the driving power from above. The Admiralty, mindful of the temporary nature of their responsibility, never took full charge of the situation. There was no properly worked-out scheme for the air defence of the country as a whole which could be progressively put into force.

Nor did the naval staff have much faith in the aeroplane as an attacking weapon against night-flying airships. The War Office viewed the situation with intermittent disquiet. They never departed from the principle that home defence, by land or by air, was an army responsibility, and they watched the Admiralty with the critical eye of one whose child was being mishandled by someone *in loco parentis*.

Soon after the appointment of Mr. Arthur Balfour as First Lord in May 1915, the Admiralty had decided to ask the War Office to relieve them of the responsibility for home air defence and the request had been formally put forward on the 18th of June 1915. The ultimate decision was a matter for the government, but meanwhile representatives of the two departments met to explore the problems of a possible transfer. It cannot be said that the War Office representatives came to the conferences with enthusiasm. It was one thing to be keen on the principle, but another and different thing to accept the responsibility with no early prospect of having the material and personnel to discharge it efficiently. At the second of two conferences, in July 1915, it was stated, on behalf of the War Office, that if no fresh calls were made on the Royal Flying Corps the army might be in a position to meet home defence air requirements about January 1916, but the War Office representatives could express no opinion on the question of taking over anti-aircraft armament.

Had the matter been carried to a decision at this stage, much confusion would have been avoided. If the Army Council had been pressed to fix a time, some months ahead, when they could reasonably expect to be ready, both departments would have known what to prepare for. But there followed months of drift and procrastination.

The question was in abeyance until the War Office was informed, on the 12th of September 1915, of the appointment of Admiral Sir Percy Scott to the command of the London gun defences, whereupon the Army Council replied by again raising the subject of a transference of responsibility. But when the Board of Admiralty came to consider the matter they had before them the report of the naval officer who had been sent to study the air defences of Paris. This report showed that the French relied chiefly on guns, searchlights, listening posts, and darkness, and that aeroplanes played a minor part in the defence scheme. The Admiralty, therefore, in reply to the War Office, observed, on the 3rd of November 1915, that:

> At the time of the July conferences, it was assumed that aeroplanes were indispensable for the defence of London, but it has been necessary to modify this opinion and it is not possible for the Admiralty to propose any definite arrangements for the transfer pending further experience.

The Admiralty went on to suggest a conference between the two departments about the middle of December, presumably when the lessons of this further experience might be available, but the Army Council were no longer acquiescent and, on their firm representations, the conference was fixed for the 10th of November 1915.

At this conference it was stated on behalf of the Admiralty that:

> So far experience had shown that aeroplanes were not at the present time of much use for the defence of a city like London, and therefore no elaborate scheme had been drawn up on the subject.

The Admiralty representatives freely admitted that the existing defence position was unsatisfactory but, in answer to Sir David Henderson, the Director-General of Military Aeronautics, they thought that the provision of a few aeroplanes by the Royal Flying Corps was of little use. They would prefer, if the question of responsibility as between the two departments was again to be considered, that the army should take over the whole defence from some twenty miles inland of the coasts. Sir David Henderson, who was agreeable to this arrangement, had no authority to pledge the Army Council, and he suggested that the proposal should be put forward formally to the War Office. This was done, by letter, two days later.

The Army Council, in a reply dated the 26th of November 1915, resisted the delimitation of responsibility by an arbitrary line drawn at a distance of twenty miles from the coasts and proposed instead that the navy should undertake to deal with all enemy aircraft approaching the coasts while the army undertook to deal with all those which succeeded in reaching our shores. Under such an arrangement the whole defence on land would be the task of the army. This modification was accepted by the Admiralty and, on the 29th of November 1915, Mr. Balfour placed the matter before the War Committee of the Cabinet. But the indecision which dogged this question was not to end. Lord Kitchener, the Secretary of State for War, was temporarily absent at the Dardanelles and the War Committee were possibly reluctant to give a formal decision before they were made aware of his views. Consequently, they merely 'took note' that the Admiralty and the Army Council had agreed in principle on the transfer of responsibility.

The two departments, however, went ahead on the assumption that the transfer was approved, and the army began gradually to take over guns and searchlights in the London area. The detailed arrangements were proceeding steadily when, in the middle of January 1916, the matter first came before Lord Kitchener, now back from the Dardanelles. The Secretary of State for War at once took the view that, in face of the calls from the western front, the army had no aircraft and no anti-aircraft guns to spare for home defence, and, on the 18th of January 1916, the Army Council addressed a letter to the Admiralty in which they said they were now averse from making an important change during the progress of hostilities:

> More especially as the arrangements for the defence of the United Kingdom against aerial attack are still in a very incomplete state.

There was, however, the difficulty that the army had already begun to man lights and guns in the London area, and the War Office proposed to surmount this by placing the military personnel at the disposal of the Admiral Commanding the London air defences.

This letter threatened to throw the whole matter into the melting pot again. At a meeting of the Board of Admiralty on the 21st of January 1916 their Lordships expressed their 'great surprise and regret' that the Army Council should propose to suspend further action in the matter. They must, they said, adhere to their agreed policy and:

> Press the Army Council to carry out an arrangement decided some six months ago for which a great many preparations have already been made and agreed to by both departments.

The Admiralty felt so strongly on the matter that Mr. Balfour, the First Lord, had a series of talks with Lord Kitchener and, as a result, the question was again referred to the War Committee of the Cabinet and was discussed at meetings held on the 26th of January and the 10th of February 1916. The decisions arrived at are recorded as follows:

> (*a*) The Navy to undertake to deal with all hostile aircraft attempting to reach this country, whilst the Army undertake to deal with all such aircraft which reach these shores.
> (*b*) All defence arrangements on land to be undertaken by the Army, which will also provide the aeroplanes required to work with the Home Defence troops and to protect garrisons and vulnerable areas and the Flying Stations required to enable their aircraft to undertake these duties.
> (*c*) The Navy to provide aircraft required to co-operate with and assist their Fleets and Coast Patrol Flotillas and to patrol the

coast and to organise and maintain such Flying Stations as are required to undertake these duties.

In the result, the responsibility for London passed to Field-Marshal Lord French, the Commander-in-Chief of the Home Forces, on the 16th of February 1916, and for the rest of the country a few days later. (Sir John French had been appointed Field-Marshal Commanding-in-Chief, Home Forces, on the 19th of December 1915.)

Under the November 1914 agreement, by which the War Office had become responsible for the gun defences of garrison ports and vulnerable points, the majority of the defences outside the London area were, at the time of the changeover, already manned by military personnel under army administration. So far as the gun and searchlight defences were concerned, therefore, the change in responsibility was chiefly confined to London.

In anticipation of the transfer a general scheme of antiaircraft defence had been drawn up by the staff of the Home Defence Directorate at the War Office. This scheme, based on the assumption that the whole of Great Britain was open to air attack, provided for the protection of magazines and munition or explosive factories grouped in the following areas:

(1) Scotland.
(2) Newcastle.
(3) Leeds.
(4) Sheffield.
(5) Liverpool.
(6) Birmingham.
(7) London and the Thames.
(8) Portsmouth.

Other objectives for protection were garrison ports, a number of munition or explosive factories not situated within the above areas, and certain populous districts specially exposed to attack. The anti-aircraft guns were to be so placed that raiding aircraft met an increasing volume of fire as they approached the defended vulnerable points or the centre of each defended area. In addition, mobile guns and lights, mounted on motor lorries, were to operate from 'surprise' positions in advance of the fixed defences in each protected area.

For the defence of London, the comprehensive plans in process of development by Admiral Sir Percy Scott were adopted. These provided for a central defended area with a five-mile and a nine-mile circle of twin gun positions. The War Office extended this system to include Woolwich and Waltham Abbey. For London, there was also to be an outer ring of searchlights, known as 'Aeroplane Lights', in advance of the extreme defence line, for the help of aeroplane pilots. (By the 6th of March 1916, 18 of these special searchlights were ready for action and positions for 29 others were under construction.)

It was estimated that the full scheme would require 475 guns (including 72 mobile) and 500 searchlights (including 72 mobile and 60 'Aeroplane Lights'). The position when the War Office took over was that, excluding the London area, there were 197 guns manned by military personnel, and 33 manned by naval personnel. In the London area, there were 65 guns. But of this total of 295 guns of all calibres, 53 were pom-poms of no fighting value, and, of the others, no more than 80 met the War Office definition of efficient anti-aircraft guns. (The remainder, improvised 140 6-pounders, 20 3-pounders, and 2 2-pounders, were to be replaced as supplies of 3-inch guns became available.)

In addition to the guns actually mounted, Admiral Sir Percy Scott had made provision for a further 60 guns for the defence of London and of the coast, all of which the Admiralty handed over, as they were converted, to the army.

******

These guns included four 6-inch on railway mountings, ten 47-inch, one 3-inch (20 cwt.), twenty-eight 75 mm., five 6-pounders, and twelve 2'95-inch Russian guns. The last were never mounted owing to lack of ammunition.

******

The Admiralty had further agreed to allot to the War Office 86 anti-aircraft guns for which naval contracts had been placed. By the middle of February 1916, seven of these had been transferred (two 3-inch, three 3-pounder, and two 2-pounder), but further deliveries were curtailed to meet the urgent need of arming merchant vessels against submarine attack, and only an additional twelve 3-inch and two 3-pounder were received by the army.

Meanwhile a great number of guns were on order for the army. By December 1915 contracts for anti-aircraft guns, placed by the Ministry of Munitions on behalf of the War Office for home and overseas, totalled 326 3-inch and 62 13-pounder (9 cwt.) guns. With Admiralty approval the War Office also withdrew 12-pounder (12 cwt.) guns from defended ports and converted them for high-angle fire. Thirty-four of these guns were in action by the middle of 1916 and three more had been added by the end of the year.

To tide over the time required for the manufacture of the 3-inch guns on order, ninety 18-pounder Q.F. guns were adapted, as a make-shift, for anti-aircraft fire. It was hoped they would all be quickly replaced, but more and more guns had to be diverted to arm merchant ships to meet the U-boat threat, and these 18-pounders, although initially recognised as inefficient anti-aircraft weapons, were retained until the end of the war.

In strengthening the ground defences, the War Office gave their first attention to Woolwich and Waltham Abbey. By the end of March, when the first raid of 1916 on the Woolwich area was made, the local gun defences had been increased from one 3-inch to nine, and the consequent volume of fire not only made the attack abortive, but, as will be seen, led to the destruction of the raiding Zeppelin. Woolwich was given preference and Waltham Abbey did not receive its first additional gun (a 3-inch 5 cwt.) until the beginning of April, but it was in position to resist a raid on the night of April 2nd/3rd 1916.

As the light-calibre guns were replaced in the more important areas, they were used, temporarily, to strengthen the defences in places less liable to attack.

In September 1916 the country was divided in accordance with the degree of preparedness required from the anti-aircraft defences. This was done to effect economies in the personnel required to man guns and lights. There were places which might be attacked by airships at night and a much wider area by aeroplanes, at night or by day, without preliminary warning. These were incorporated in an *Ever Ready* zone which included the coastal area from the north of Scotland to the Wash, and the whole of south-eastern England east of a line which was drawn from the point where the Norfolk boundary meets the Wash, passed east of Luton and Windsor, west of the London anti-aircraft defence area, and thence east of Chilworth to a point on the South Coast, west of Newhaven. Inside this zone, full detachments for guns, observation posts, &c, by day and by night, and for searchlights by night, were to be ready for immediate action.

The remainder of Great Britain constituted the *Inner Zone*, in which it was improbable an attack by day or by night could develop without warning being given to the anti-aircraft defences. In this zone the crews of guns, lights, &c, were not required to be continuously ready, but they were to be present or near enough to their posts to be ready for action within fifteen minutes of a warning being received at the gun station. (In April 1917, the *Ever Ready* zone was divided into Zones 'X' and 'Y' and the *Inner Zone* then became Zone 'Z'.)

Home Defence Squadrons

Although the organisation of the aeroplane defence dates from the time of the retransfer of responsibility to the War Office, a number of minor defensive measures had been taken by the Royal Flying Corps from the beginning. In January 1915, all military air stations, except those west of Farnborough, had been instructed to keep two aeroplanes ready for action on receipt of warning of an impending night attack. In the following month, landing-grounds for the use of night-flying pilots had been prepared at Wimbledon, Romford, Blackheath, Enfield, and Eynsford. They were located near a military unit which was made responsible for the aerodrome lighting arrangements. The system of lighting on each ground was made distinctive so that a pilot in the air could tell at a glance which landing-ground he was over. It was further arranged that when night flying was in progress the military aerodromes at Hounslow and Northolt would be illuminated.

In May 1915, it had been laid down that the stations at Brooklands, Northolt, Hounslow, Joyce Green, Dover, Shoreham, and Farnborough would be primarily responsible for the Royal Flying Corps contribution to the defence when a raid was in progress, and that one aeroplane at each station was to be kept continuously ready. The most suitable aeroplane, at this time, was, it was stated, the Martin-Handasyde Scout, and the most suitable weapon, the bomb. During the airship attacks which took place in the summer of 1915, pilots from these stations went up, but with no success. When the attacks on London, in the autumn of 1915, revealed the complete ineffectiveness of the defences, Lord Kitchener had sent for Sir David Henderson. 'What are you going to do about these airship raids?' he had asked, to which the Director-General of Military Aeronautics replied that the responsibility rested with the Royal Naval Air Service. Lord Kitchener retorted:

> I do not care who has the responsibility. If there are any more Zeppelin raids and the Royal Flying Corps do not interfere with them, I shall hold you responsible.

Sir David Henderson was in a difficult position as he was finding it increasingly hard to fulfil the approved programmes for the expansion of the Royal Flying Corps in France. But he told the Admiralty he would do what he could to help them, although he could make no permanent arrangements. He gave instructions that trained military pilots, waiting to go overseas, were to be sent to newly chosen landing-grounds at Hainault Farm, Suttons Farm, and Farningham, as well as to Joyce Green, where they were to hold themselves in readiness to repel raiding airships. In addition, steps were taken to establish a ring of searchlights which would ensure that an attacking airship would be continuously illuminated over the London Area. When it seemed certain that the responsibility for the air defence would pass back to the War Office, the aeroplane arrangements were considerably extended.

At the end of December 1915, it was ordered that two military B.E.2c's, manned by pilots specially trained in night flying, were to be maintained on a ring of ten aerodromes encircling London. (Hounslow, Wimbledon Common, Croydon, Farningham, Joyce Green, Hainault Farm, Suttons Farm, Chingford, Hendon, and Northolt.) In addition to the pilots, the detachments included about six mechanics and a Royal Engineer party with a searchlight. The pilots took it in turn to sleep in the hangar within hearing of a telephone on a direct line from the War Office from which warnings and instructions were issued.

These detachments were provided by several different training squadrons, but it was soon clear that, for efficient co-ordination, they must be grouped in a single command and, on the 1st of February 1916, they were placed under Major T. C. R. Higgins, the officer commanding the newly formed No. 19 Reserve Squadron at Hounslow. There were, in addition to these defensive detachments, at the time of the transfer, two military aeroplanes each in readiness at Brooklands and Farnborough for the local defence of the Royal Aircraft Factory and the powder factory at Chilworth, and three at Cramlington for the defence of Newcastle.

★★★★★★

> The Royal Flying Corps had been made responsible for the local defence of Newcastle on the 1st of December 1915, by which date three military B.E.2c's were in readiness at Cramlington. They formed the nucleus of No. 36 Squadron which was formed on the 1st of February 1916.

★★★★★★

When the responsibility of the War Office for air defence was made definite, the position of the G.O.C. Royal Flying Corps was changed. Sir David Henderson, under the direction of the Chief of the Imperial General Staff, had now to meet the aircraft requirements of Field-Marshal Lord French in exactly the same way as he did those of Commanders-in-Chief overseas. (The allotment of all aircraft to the various theatres of War was the ultimate responsibility of the C.I.G.S. who was advised on technical matters by the Director-General of Military Aeronautics.) Subsequent air operations were directed by Lord French, as Commander-in-Chief, Home Forces, and the aeroplane defence schemes were drawn up by his staff in consultation with the General Staff at the War Office.

The initial aeroplane scheme of the new command had been worked out in some detail while the change in responsibility was still under discussion. At the beginning of December 1915, steps had been taken to secure night-landing grounds in the Eastern Counties, the Midlands, and in Northern England.

★★★★★★

> By the 1st of March 1916, grounds were ready or being prepared as follows: in the Newcastle and Tees Valley area, 7; in the area of the Humber defences, 5; Leeds area, 3; Nottingham area, 3; Birmingham area, 2; Eastern Counties, 20; and in Kent and Sussex, 4.

★★★★★★

Under the scheme, a varying number of aeroplanes were to be permanently allotted for the close protection of each defended area or garrison port, with additional aeroplanes in advance of those areas for mobile defence. The task of the latter was the interception of enemy airships making for defended areas, and it was hoped that this interception would be ensured by a series of patrols along the probable lines of approach.

The scheme envisaged the organisation of special home defence squadrons, but these could not be formed at once owing to a shortage of equipment and of personnel. As an immediate measure, therefore, three additional B.E.2c's were allotted to those training squadrons favourably situated to meet an attack (Norwich, Thetford, Doncaster, and Dover), and six B.E.2c's were sent to reinforce No. 5 Reserve Squadron in the defence of Birmingham and Coventry. All these additional aeroplanes were ready for action at the beginning of March 1916. For the defence of Leeds and Hull, it was arranged that No. 33 Squadron should be moved from Bristol to Bramham Moor and No. 34 Squadron from Castle Bromwich to Beverley near York. The latter move, however, did not take place and the defence of Hull was provided, first by No. 47 Squadron, formed at Beverley on the 1st of March 1916, and, later, by a detachment of No. 33 Squadron which duly moved to Bramham Moor in April. The senior Flying Corps officer at each station was solely responsible for ordering his pilots to patrol on receipt of a warning that a raid was imminent. The idea was that the aeroplanes from each station should make their patrols, in succession, at a height of 8,000 to 10,000 feet over their own landing grounds. The normal patrol for each aeroplane lasted two hours and a second aeroplane was sent up after an hour and a half to ensure continuity. The aeroplanes were armed with high-explosive bombs and with Ranken darts, which had to be dropped from above an attacking airship, and it was essential to success that pilots should be given sufficient preliminary warning to get their height before the airships arrived.

In March 1916 the home defence aircraft establishment was laid down as ten squadrons, which were to be drawn from the total of seventy service squadrons sanctioned for the Royal Flying Corps in December 1915. As a result, certain squadrons already formed or about to be formed in England were designated Home Defence Squadrons. At the same time the aeroplane defence of London was reorganised. A new Wing—the Eighteenth—was formed on the 25th of March 1916 under Lieutenant-Colonel F. V. Holt to include all the air defence detachments in the London area. These detachments, hitherto administered by No. 19 Reserve Squadron, became No. 39 Home Defence Squadron, with head-quarters at Hounslow, on the 15th of April. The commanding officer was Major T. C. R. Higgins and his squadron was to do more than any other to counter the Zeppelin. The policy now was to concentrate the detachments on aerodromes east of London. Accordingly, in May and June 1916, two Flights of six aeroplanes each were concentrated at Suttons Farm and Hainault Farm. The third Flight of No. 39 Squadron was at Hounslow until August when it moved to North Weald Bassett, the headquarters of the squadron taking up new quarters at Woodford, Essex.

The War Office hoped that the home defence squadrons would be able to combine their specific duties with advanced instruction to pilots under training. It had indeed been laid down at the end of May that 50 *per cent*, of home defence aeroplanes could be used also for training purposes, but Lieutenant-Colonel F. V. Holt pointed out that the experiment of mixing home defence duties with training had been tried in the Eighteenth Wing, had met with failure, and had been abandoned. Officers under instruction were apt to handle the aeroplanes in such a way that the craft were often unfitted for night-flying. Nor was it to be expected that a pilot could properly and efficiently combine the responsibilities of instruction by day and anti-airship patrol by night.

In the result, the War Office decided that training could not form part of the duties of the home defence squadrons and that these should be grouped in a special Home Defence Wing which would be independent of the Training Brigade (VI Brigade). The Home Defence Wing (at first called the Sixteenth Wing) was formed by Lieutenant-Colonel F. V. Holt, with headquarters at Adastral House, on the 25th of June, and comprised Squadrons No. 33 at Bramham Moor, (this squadron absorbed two half-Flights of No. 47 Squadron, the latter squadron was re-formed as a service squadron.) No. 36 at Cramlington, No. 38 forming at Castle Bromwich, No. 39 in the London area. No. 50 at Dover, and No. 51 at Norwich. Searchlight units were attached to the Home Defence Squadrons (six lights each) and were placed under the direct orders of the squadron commander.

In the middle of July, a new scheme which involved an entire change of policy with regard to the location of air defence units was put forward by Brigadier-General W. S. Brancker, the Director of Air Organisation.

******

The Military Aeronautics Directorate had been reorganised in April 1916 to embody two subordinate directorates, for Organisation, under Brigadier-General W. S. Brancker (D. Air O.) and for Equipment under Brigadier-General D. S. MacInnes (D.A.E.).

******

The scheme had been worked out by Lieutenant-Colonel F. V. Holt in close co-operation with the staff of Lord French. The basis of the original scheme had been the defence of specified vulnerable areas. It had been accepted, when the scheme was drawn up, that pilots could only patrol and fight over their own landing-grounds owing to difficulties of navigation and to the danger of forced landings at night. It had been considered certain, also, that a pilot could not pursue a Zeppelin at night. Night-flying stations, therefore, had been situated, for local action only, close to the vulnerable areas, and wide gaps had been left through which enemy aircraft could penetrate. Experience had falsified some of the accepted beliefs. Pilots had often been forced down on grounds which were strange to them and had landed successfully. Over country which was well lighted they had had no difficulty in patrolling wide areas. Further, it had been proved that once a pilot got within sight of an airship he could give chase.

Now that it was clear the aeroplane patrols could be extended, it was suggested that the Flights situated near Birmingham, Sheffield, and Leeds should be moved farther east as a step towards the ultimate establishment of a barrage-line of aeroplanes and searchlights parallel with the east coast of England. A line of stations was proposed about twenty miles apart with enough searchlights to allow double lights every three and a half miles along the line. There was a good stretch of country, suitable for night-flying operations, running north and south near the East Coast, and the number of aeroplanes sanctioned for the original scheme would suffice for a barrage patrol that should prevent the enemy getting through in normal weather.

At a conference held at the Horse Guards on the 15th of July 1916 this change in policy was generally approved. The detachments of the Home Defence Squadrons were now to be placed along a line between Dover and Edinburgh in conjunction with a barrage-line of searchlights stretching from the London anti-aircraft defence zone to Blyth, with interlying barrage-lines in Kent, Essex, and Norfolk. It was realised that much time must elapse before the scheme could be fully operative; it was begun at once and gradually developed. It was, however, never completed, although the principles on which it was based were not departed from throughout the remainder of the war.

The original decision that the number of Home Defence Squadrons should be ten had twice been modified. In May 1916 the number had been reduced to eight and in June, as a result of urgent demands from overseas, to six. With the adoption of the new barrage-line scheme it was decided to form, when possible, the remaining four squadrons originally sanctioned. These were Nos. 37 and 76, formed on the 15th of September, and Nos. 75 and 77, formed on the 1st of October 1916. It had been laid down at the end of August 1916 that the establishment of the Home Defence Squadrons was to be eighteen aeroplanes, except Nos. 37, 39, and 50 Squadrons which were to have twenty-four aeroplanes.

******

No. 37 Squadron was originally formed as an Experimental Squadron at Orfordness on the 15th of April but ceased to exist a month later when the nucleus Flight of the Squadron was absorbed by the Experimental Station at Orfordness.

******

At the end of September, the home defence units were augmented as a result of a flight by a Zeppelin over Portsmouth. Before this flight, which was made on the 25th of September, it had been assumed that the air stations at Dover and Dunkirk would constitute an effective barrier against Zeppelins attempting the journey through the Dover Straits. Lieutenant-Colonel Holt, on the 28th of September, proposed that an additional squadron should be formed on the barrage-line of lights, south of London, to carry the aeroplane defences to the South Coast, as far west as Littlehampton. The proposal was sanctioned and No. 78 Squadron (establishment, twenty-four aeroplanes), was formed with headquarters at Hove on the 1st of November 1916.

At the end of December 1916, the Home Defence Squadrons were located as shown in the table and map later on. No figures are available for the aeroplanes the squadrons possessed at the end of 1916, but it is certain the number was less than one-half the establishment total. With the exception of a few F.E.2b's (120 and 160 horse-power Beardmore engines), all these home defence aeroplanes were of the B.E. type. They were the B.E.2C, B.E.2e, and B.E.2d (all with 90 horse-power Royal Aircraft Factory engines), and the B.E. 12 (140 horse-power R.A.F. engine).

The aeroplane patrol and the searchlight barrage systems were briefly as follows. The searchlights, under the direction of the squadron commander, were situated along the patrol line of the aeroplanes, and the searchlight crews were connected with the squadron headquarters by telephone. When news was received that enemy aircraft were approaching, the normal practice was to send up two or three aeroplanes from each Flight for the patrol of specified areas, the pilots receiving instructions to go as high as they could before they began their patrol. The squadrons south of Melton Mowbray received general orders to patrol from the officer commanding the Home Defence Wing who acted on information received from G.H.Q., Home Forces. The squadrons situated from Lincoln northwards to the Forth were in direct communication with the Warning Controllers of their areas, and the squadron commanders ordered their patrols in accordance with the information given them by the Controllers.

The early armament of the aeroplanes was either the bomb or Ranken darts. The bombs were the 20 lb. Hales high-explosive and the 16 lb. incendiary, of which two each were carried. Experience, however, had proved that the chances of a pilot seeing an airship from above at night were small and that his chances of scoring a direct hit, even if he found a Zeppelin, were smaller, while there was the risk of his bombs finding targets on the ground. The Lewis gun was therefore taken into use. There was, at first, no thought of destroying the airship by machine-gun fire. All that was expected was that three or four drums of Lewis-gun ammunition fired into an airship would so puncture the gas-bags that the ship would be forced down on the sea by loss of gas before she could make her base. But when, in June and July 1916, efficient incendiary and explosive bullets were produced, the end of the Zeppelin as a raiding weapon was in sight, although, until the value of these bullets was proved by actual results, their effectiveness as anti-airship missiles was questioned.

★★★★★★

Those used in 1916 were the Buckingham, the Brock, and the Pomeroy. The Buckingham, designed by Mr. J. F. Buckingham of Coventry, lighted at the muzzle of the gun and combined a smoke trace with incendiary qualities. The Brock was the design of Squadron Commander F. A. Brock, of the Naval Air Service, an inventive genius who lost his life in the attack on Zeebrugge on the 23rd of April 1918. This bullet, which was both explosive and incendiary, functioned on impact. The Pomeroy bullet, the prototype of which had been submitted to the War Office in August 1914 by Mr. J. Pomeroy, an engineer of Canadian extraction, had qualities similar to the Brock. The Lewis-gun drums were loaded with a mixture of the various types of bullets. For a summary of the war-time development of explosive and incendiary ammunition see Appendix 5.

★★★★★★

This was due to a belief—erroneous, but firmly held by some of those in authority—that the Zeppelins were protected by a layer of inert gas which would prevent the airships from catching fire. It was this belief that engendered faith in the use of the bomb and militated against the earlier development of incendiary and explosive ammunition.

The Home Defence Squadrons worked under active service conditions, and accommodation on the aerodromes was of the simplest. As the landing-grounds were chosen for strategic reasons, they were sometimes cramped and of poor surface. The headquarters of the squadron, usually hired buildings with sufficient out-buildings for technical stores and simple workshops, were, at first, situated at some

Squadron No.	*Date of Formation.*	*Head-quarters and Commanding Officers.*	*Flight Stations.*
33	12.1.16	Gainsborough. (Major A. A. B. Thomson, M.C.)	Brattleby (Scampton), Kirton Lindsey, Elsham.
36	1.2.16	Newcastle. (Major A. C. E. Marsh.)	Seaton Carew, Hylton, Ashington.
37	15.9.16	Woodham Mortimer. (Major W. B. Hargrave.)	Rochford, Stow Maries, Goldhanger.
38	14.7.16	Melton Mowbray. (Major the Hon. L. J. E. Twisleton-Wykeham-Fiennes.)	Stamford, Buckminster, Leadenham.
39	15.4.16	Woodford. (Major A. H. Morton.)	North Weald Bassett, Suttons Farm (Hornchurch), Hainault Farm (Ilford).
50	15.5.16	Harrietsham. (Major M. G. Christie, M.C.)	Dover, Bekesbourne, (Canterbury), Throwley (Faversham).
51	15.5.16	Hingham. (Major H. Wyllie.)	Harling Road (Roudham), Mattishall, Marham.
75	1.10.16	Goldington (Bedford). (Major H. Petre, M.C.)	Yelling (St. Neots), Old Weston (Thrapston), Therfield (Baldock).
76	15.9.16	Ripon. (Major E. M. Murray, M.C.)	Copmanthorpe, Helperby, Catterick.
77	1.10.16	Edinburgh. (Major W. Milne, M.C.)	Turnhouse (Edinburgh), Whiteburn (Grant's House), New Haggerston (Berwick-on-Tweed).
78	1.11.16	Hove. (Major H. A. Van-Ryneveld, M.C.)	Telscombe Cliffs (Newhaven), Gosport, Chiddingstone Causeway (Tonbridge).
11 Reserve (Home Defence Training Squadron).	1.11.15	Northolt. (Major B. F. Moore.)	

central point about equidistant from each detached Flight. In 1917, however, accommodation was provided on the aerodromes of each central Flight for the squadron headquarters staff.

The aids to navigation by night up to the end of 1916 must be mentioned. Early in 1916 lighting sets were provided for the instrument boards in the aeroplanes, and, as an extra precaution, the instruments were made luminous. Each aeroplane was fitted to carry two parachute flares to facilitate a forced landing. Up to April 1916 the flares used on night-landing grounds were cans filled with petrol and waste, but for home defence stations there was no standard distance between flares nor was the number of flares to be used defined. In April, however, standard methods of placing flares on first, second, and third-class landing-grounds were introduced, and, at the same time, a new type of flare came into use. This was the Money flare, formed of asbestos packed into a wire cage, which was soaked in a bucket of paraffin. It was economical, consuming only 1.2 gallons of paraffin for an hour's burning, simple, and required little attention, and its light penetrated mist and fog with some success; in addition to the flares, small Lyons searchlight sets, or oxy-acetylene sets, were used on aerodromes further to illuminate the flare path while the aeroplanes were landing.

The lighting arrangements on the detached night-landing grounds were, up to the end of 1916, normally in charge of volunteers, but, for various reasons, this arrangement was not successful, and at the end of 1916 the duty was taken over by detachments of the Royal Defence Corps.

The Reorganisation of the Warning System

One of the most important effects of the change in responsibility was the revision of the intelligence and warning organisation. It has been told how, after the great Zeppelin attack on the Midlands at the end of January 1916, the general public had become nervous. This nervousness had led, during some nights in early February, to many scare reports of Zeppelins. The alarms had spread from one end of the country to the other with great rapidity. One of the worst was on the 10th of February when a report of a Zeppelin, supposed to have been seen at Scarborough, had plunged great tracts of the country in darkness and had brought about a widespread cessation of work. Two government factories, as far remote from the source of the scare as Gloucester, had temporarily closed down. Following this last disturbance, the Government took action. Field-Marshal Lord French was

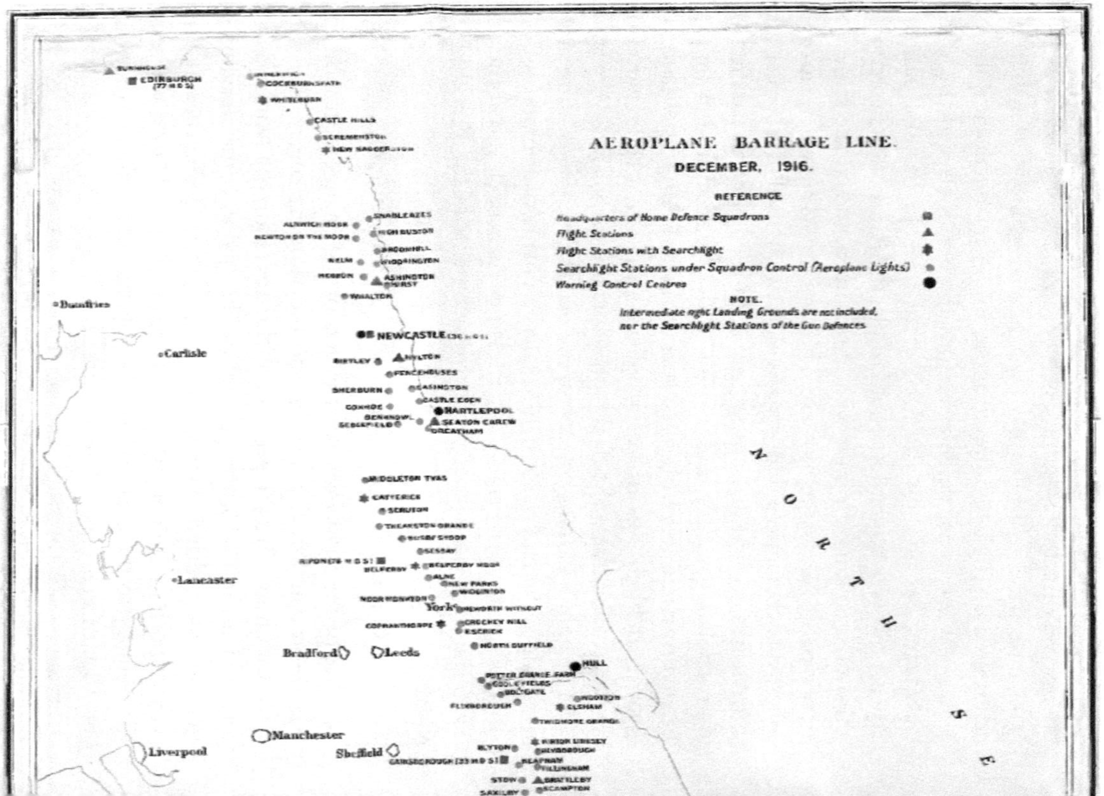

AEROPLANE BARRAGE LINE.
DECEMBER, 1916.
REFERENCE
Headquarters of Home Defence Squadrons
Flight Stations
Flight Stations with Searchlight
Searchlight Stations under Squadron Control (Aeroplane Lights)
Warning Control Centres
NOTE.
Intermediate night Landing Grounds are not included, nor the Searchlight Stations of the Gun Defences.
EDINBURGH
CASTLE HILLS
NEWCASTLE
HARTLEPOOL
SEATON CAREW
MIDDLETON TYAS
CATTERICK
HULL
Dumfries
Carlisle
Lancaster
York
Bradford
Leeds
Manchester
Liverpool
Sheffield
N O R T H S E

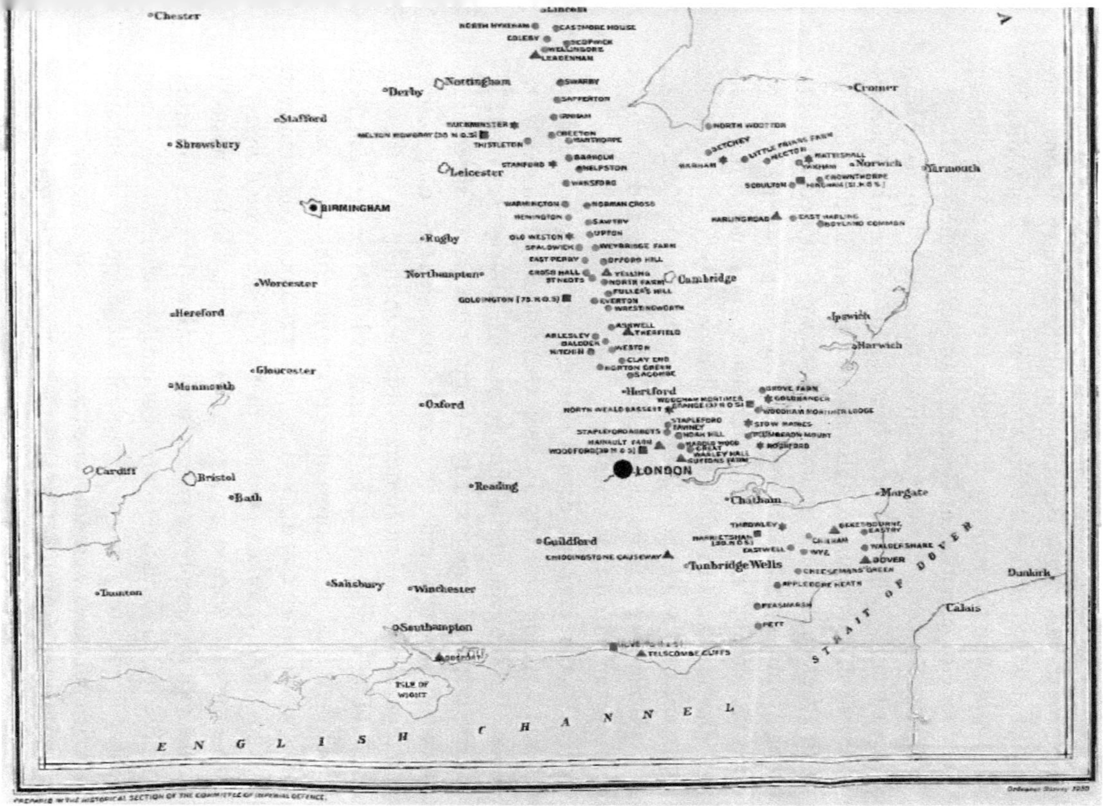
Chester
Lincoln
Derby
Nottingham
Cromer
Stafford
Shrewsbury
Leicester
Norwich
Yarmouth
BIRMINGHAM
Rugby
Northampton
Cambridge
Worcester
Hereford
Ipswich
Harwich
Gloucester
Monmouth
Oxford
Hertford
Cardiff
Bristol
Bath
Reading
LONDON
Chatham
Margate
Guildford
Tunbridge Wells
Dover
Taunton
Salisbury
Winchester
Southampton
Dunkirk
Calais
ISLE OF WIGHT
STRAIT OF DOVER
ENGLISH CHANNEL
PREPARED IN THE HISTORICAL SECTION OF THE COMMITTEE OF IMPERIAL DEFENCE.

summoned to a meeting of the Cabinet and was asked to prepare, urgently, a scheme of warnings which would stop the spreading of rumour and of false reports. Lord French gave a promise that he would have a scheme ready within three days. The Staff Officer responsible for making this promise effective was Lieutenant-Colonel Philip Maud who decided at once that any efficient warning system must be based on the telephone organisation of the country. A conference was called at which attended representatives from the Post Office, the Home Office, and the Railway Executive Committee. Maps showing the telephone organisation in Great Britain were studied.

In the result it was decided to divide the country in accordance with what may be called the main 'watersheds' of the telephone system. First of all, England and Wales and that part of Scotland deemed liable to attack (all except the north-west), were divided into eight. Warning Controls, each to be under a Warning Controller who was to act as the representative of the Commander-in-Chief of the Home Forces. The headquarters of the Controllers were to be located at one of the main centres of the telephone system in each Control area. The Controllers were to be responsible for collecting and passing on information and for issuing warnings.

For the latter purpose, each Control area was subdivided into numbered Warning Districts. To keep the dislocation caused by the presence of a Zeppelin at the minimum, each District was made approximately 30 to 35 miles square. Assuming the average speed of the enemy airships to be 60 miles an hour, the passage across each District would thus take about half an hour. Districts in the path of the Zeppelin could be warned in succession and, with a few exceptions, need only put their final precautions into effect when the danger was near. In other words, work could go on to the last moment consistent with safety. This sub-division ensured also that a Zeppelin would always be in the centre of a 'warned' area. As the Districts had to be adjusted to conform with the telephone system, their boundaries were sometimes decidedly irregular. This led to minor anomalies when warnings came to be issued, but alterations were made in the telephone organisation, and the irregularities were smoothed away.

The Warning Controller had many sources of information as to the movements of enemy aircraft. His most important source, once the enemy was over this country, was the system of observer posts which were set up throughout the land. So far as the telephone organisation allowed, the Warning Districts in which the important industrial centres were situated were provided with cordons of observers about thirty miles distant from the District boundary on the sides most exposed to attack. (There was, later, a special cordon for London about forty-five miles out to give warning of attack by aeroplanes.) In addition, there were outer observer cordons at a distance of fifty to sixty miles, coastal cordons, and cross cordons to prevent enemy aircraft moving unobserved between, or parallel with, the main cordons.

The observations from the cordons were passed to each Warning Controller direct. In addition, he was in telephonic touch with General Headquarters, Home Forces, with the various Anti-Aircraft Defence Stations, and with each adjoining Warning Controller. He also received reports from the police, railway officials, troops, or naval stations in his control area.

To avoid confusion in plotting the paths of flight of the Zeppelins, once a raid was in progress, it was necessary to adopt some device whereby each airship could be separately identified. The specific number of each Zeppelin was, at the outset, not always known and, furthermore, even when this information was available, the numbers *L.14*, *L.15*, &c, lacked the distinction essential to accuracy when messages were being passed frequently and rapidly over the telephone. Each airship, therefore, when it was first picked up, was given a temporary name by which it was identified at the various headquarters throughout its subsequent flight over this country. Girls' Christian names such as *Annie*, *Mary*, and *Jane* were reserved for German naval airships and boys' names, *Tom*, *Dick*, or *Harry* for military airships. The names chosen, by chance or design, had nothing ogreish about them. On the contrary, they tended, by association, to endow each Zeppelin with a personality of a kind to inspire confidence rather than fear.

In the various headquarters, when a raid was being made, the strain was considerable. Information from many sources had to be continuously sifted. The value of each message had to be judged at a glance. Decisions involving important consequences had to be taken swiftly. Into this atmosphere of tension, the recurrence of the familiar English Christian names brought a touch of the commonplace, even of humour.

The new warning organisation assured in theory, and almost invariably in practice, that each Warning Controller received reports of hostile aircraft movements within a few minutes of the observations being made. If he judged that the aircraft were approaching his control area, he issued his warning message to the telephone exchange manager in the town where his headquarters was situated, and he specified by numbers the districts to which the warning was to be transmitted.

******

> On receipt of the first intimation that airships were leaving Germany for a possible raid on England, the Post Office authorities were informed. They thus usually had ample time in which to assemble their telephone staffs.

******

The dissemination of the warning now passed to the telephone operators. It was at once distributed to the various exchanges in each specified district and passed thence to individual subscribers in accordance with a 'Warning List' in the hands of each telephone operator. These lists were divided and subdivided so that priority was given to those firms and authorities who were required to take urgent preliminary precautions. Separate lists were kept for warnings by day when the question of the extinction or reduction of lighting did not arise.

The warning lists were made up by the chief police officer of each district, who was also responsible for making the necessary arrangements with the district telephone manager. Naval authorities and stations were placed on the warning lists by senior naval officers, and military stations, including those of the Royal Flying Corps, by the competent military authorities.

Everyone on the warning lists had, under penalties imposed by the Defence of the Realm Regulations, to answer a warning call, at any time of the night, within fifteen seconds. If no answer came in this time, the telephone operator passed to the next name on the list, but when he had gone through the list, he again called those who had not answered. The persons or firms who failed to answer were prosecuted, but those required to take air-raid action were fully alive to the importance of the efficient working of the system and such prosecutions were rare.

It was an underlying principle of the warning scheme that no person should communicate any warning he received to any person other than those who had definite action to take. There were a few special exceptions to this rule. Certain police officers, military telephone exchanges, and industrial establishments were made responsible for passing on the warning. Some of these (in London certain police stations and fire stations after July 1917) made the warning public by means of sound signals.

The railways were exempted from the official warning scheme. The Railway Executive Committee, made up of the managing directors of the important railway systems, requested authority to issue their own warnings direct. Their organisation was such that they could do this efficiently, and the dislocation of traffic on the railways would be less if the warnings were centrally controlled than if they were issued for different areas by diverse warning authorities. Lord French's staff readily agreed and the Committee were made responsible for warning all railway authorities. Close touch with the Committee was maintained by G.H.Q. Home Forces. When raids were in progress, the Committee made their warnings conform, as far as possible, with those issued for successive Districts by the military authorities.

The warnings issued by the Warning Controllers were stereotyped. They were four in number:

(*1*) 'Field-Marshal's Warning Only.'
(After Field-Marshal Lord French gave up his command, on the 8th of May 1918, the formula was still retained for convenience.)
This was passed to persons or authorities on the 'Special Warning Lists' and, so far as possible, was issued to reach them when the enemy aircraft were still about fifty or sixty miles distant from the nearest boundary of the district. On receipt of this message, preliminary precautions were taken.
(*2*) Field-Marshal's Order: Take Air Raid Action.
This was communicated to all persons on the warning lists and was timed to reach them when the enemy aircraft were fifteen to twenty miles from the district boundary. At once, on receipt of this message, all final prearranged precautions were taken.
(*3*) Field-Marshal's Order: Resume Normal Conditions.
This was issued generally when immediate danger of attack on a district had passed. It was a signal to revert to the, conditions which obtained before the issue of message (*2*).
(*4*) Field-Marshal's Notice: All Clear.
This indicated that all emergency precautions might be withdrawn.

******

Later, after a system of public warnings was introduced for London, the order of the third and fourth messages was reversed. In London the All Clear notice was issued before the enemy was known to have left the country. The final Order (Field-Marshal's, Military, or Police), thereupon became: Resume Normal Conditions.

******

At a later stage code words were used by Controllers in passing these messages to the Trunk Exchange Managers. They were green, red, white, yellow, followed in each instance by the numbers of the Districts for which the messages were intended. This code was derived from the coloured lights which were shown behind the appropriate Warning Districts on a transparent map in the Operations Room at the Horse Guards, thus enabling the Controller to see, at any moment, the Districts in which warnings or orders were in force. It will be seen that the warning messages gave the recipient no information as to the number or direction of enemy craft. All he had to do was to initiate or relax the precautionary arrangements for which he was responsible.

There were two exceptions to the rule that the sole authority for the issue of general warnings was the Controller. On the east and south-east coasts, it was possible an attack might develop with comparative suddenness and without giving time for the information to reach the Controller and be communicated by him to the District affected. Certain areas, therefore, were constituted 'Warning Sub-Districts', and the local Anti-Aircraft Defence Commander, or other military authority, was authorised to issue, in emergency, the following messages:

(*1*) Military Order: Take Air Raid Action.
(*2*) Military Order: Resume Normal Conditions.
(*3*) Military Notice: All Clear.

The second exception was that a Chief Constable, or any police officer authorised by him, could issue local air raid warnings if communication was interrupted by a breakdown of the General Post Office telephone system, or if a bombardment occurred or hostile aircraft were seen in the immediate vicinity of a town where no previous warning had been issued. (Police Order: Take Air Raid Action; Police Order: Resume Normal Conditions; Police Notice: All Clear.)

The principle of the new warning scheme, that each person required to take action should receive the appropriate message direct from the military authorities through the telephone, was in complete contrast with the arrangements existing hitherto whereby each chief constable had been the authority responsible for the distribution of warnings to his subordinates and to any factories or other industrial establishments within his jurisdiction. The fact that the boundaries of the new Warning Districts did not coincide with police boundaries made a continuance of the old system impossible. On the 'intelligence' side, however, the work of the police was continued, and indeed extended.

The permanent Warning Controls came into operation on the 25th of May 1916, as shown following. (As an interim arrangement, three centres for receiving and transmitting information of hostile aircraft movements had been set up on the 14th of February 1916. They were Scottish Command Headquarters, Edinburgh (for Scotland); Northern Command Headquarters, York (for the north of England); and G.H.Q., Home Forces (for the south of England).)

Warning Controls.

Headquarters.	Controllers.
Edinburgh Garrison	Commander, Forth Garrison.
Newcastle Garrison	Commander, Tyne Garrison.
Leeds	Anti-Aircraft Defence Commander.
Sheffield	Anti-Aircraft Defence Commander.
Liverpool Garrison	Commander, *Mersey* Garrison.
Birmingham	Anti-Aircraft Defence Commander.
London	General Headq., Home Forces.
Portsmouth	Garrison Comm., Portsmouth Garr.

★★★★★★

In December 1916 the Leeds and Sheffield Warning Controls were amalgamated and the control headquarters for the combined area was transferred to Hull. In June 1918, however, the headquarters was transferred back again to Leeds, and Hull was constituted a Sub-District Control headquarters with emergency jurisdiction over the whole of the Warning District in which it was situated.

On the 15th of February 1917 the headquarters of the Liverpool Control was transferred to Manchester, a new sub-district being established at Liverpool. There were also minor alterations and extensions in the Harwich, Newhaven, and Middlesbrough sub-districts.

Sub-District Controls: Cromarty, Aberdeen, Dundee, West Hartlepool, Hull, Gorleston, Lowestoft, Harwich, Chatham, Dover, Newhaven, Weymouth, Devonport, Falmouth, Cardiff,

Swansea, Pembroke, Barrow, and Greenock.

******

Air-raid warnings by day were first introduced in June 1917. They extended only to the five Warning Districts, covering roughly Suffolk, Hertfordshire, London, Essex, Kent, and Surrey. After a few weeks it was deemed advisable to establish a Special Day Warning District, to include the area east of a line drawn through Norwich, St. Albans, Windsor, and Worthing, and that any warning should be given to the whole of this district. This was done because hostile aeroplanes flew high and at great speed and made the issue of timely successive warnings to small districts almost impossible. The disadvantages of issuing a wide warning to involve many places that could not be visited, led to the abolition of this Special Day Warning District on the 1st of January 1918. From this time onwards, Day Warnings were issued by successive districts in the same way as at night.

******

The Sub-District Controllers were the local Garrison Commanders or the Officers Commanding Troops.

Reference has been made to the issue of public warnings—a question which aroused widespread controversy. The *raison d'être* of the warning system was to enable precautions to be taken which could not be maintained permanently without great inconvenience or loss, and it follows that the efficiency of the system was dependent on the issue of the warning at the latest moment consistent with putting the precautions into force, and on its cancellation immediately the danger ended. The effect of making a warning public was a maximum disturbance of all normal activities in the affected area and an increase of the risk that the alarm would spread to adjoining areas.

What were the objects of a general public warning? They may be briefly stated. The public would be able to extinguish lights under their own control which might not be properly obscured, and they would have the opportunity to seek the best available shelter. Another advantage was merely psychological. If the public knew they would receive definite warning of an imminent attack, it was argued, they would the more readily and freely pursue their ordinary avocations. It may be noted that underlying these arguments were three assumptions—that people would seek cover on receipt of a warning; that the choice of action should be at the discretion of each individual; and that the authorities were in a position to give prompt and reliable warning of an impending attack.

But many raids had come and gone before it became at all certain that a warning would clear the streets. During the first attack on London, and during some subsequent raids, people flocked into the streets to get the best view of what was going on. Those who set their faces against a general public warning argued that it would have the effect of attracting into the streets people who might otherwise remain indoors. The question arose, should theatres and other places of amusement be warned in time to allow their patrons to disperse? At first consideration, it would seem that such a warning would have the effect of diminishing the chance of heavy casualties.

But, although a direct hit on a crowded auditorium must have entailed a heavy loss of life, the chances of such a hit were small, and this risk was counted less than the risk incurred if the public were given the opportunity to disperse. Unless the warnings were given in ample time there was the danger that the public would be caught in the streets, or, as traffic would be interrupted, they might congregate at the railway and tram termini, where the shelters were of the poorest description, and where they might, especially in the railway centres, be much more liable to attack. The argument that the choice of action should be left to the individual was a good one but was only valid if the choice was made with knowledge of the comparative risks, and the public were in no position, in the early days, to assess the risks.

But what governed the position was that for the first two years of the war it was impossible to give a prompt and reliable warning. Until the army took over home defence no adequate system for the collection and transmission of air-raid information existed, and it was not until the early summer of 1916 that the military warning system was fully operative. Until that time there was no guarantee that enemy aircraft would not approach unobserved or unreported, a possibility that was fatal to any sense of security based on public warnings. Furthermore, the lack of adequate information often led to precautionary action being taken on uncorroborated reports and the issue of warnings on many occasions when no attacks eventuated.

For example, up to February 1916, the police at Ipswich had received warning of the approach of hostile aircraft on forty-four occasions, but on only six of these did aircraft pass over the town, and on none of these occasions were bombs dropped. Again, had a system of public warnings been in operation in London in 1915 it would probably have been necessary to issue the warning on sixty-four occasions during the year, whereas the number of attacks on London was five.

In some provincial towns where public warnings had been tried, the effect was to bring excited crowds into the streets and, after a time, the system had been abandoned. In others, for example Hull, the system was continued because the public had become accustomed to it. Writing in October 1915, the Chief Constable of Hull stated that he would have hesitated to introduce sound signals had he known at the beginning what the effect would be.

> The buzzer was intended, and in theory is still used, for the purpose of extinguishing lights rapidly, for calling out the Special Constables, and for assembling the ambulance workers . . . but in practice it is regarded as a warning to the population. It has been opposed by a good many of the upper classes, but there is an almost unanimous desire for it among the other classes, and I have insisted on its being kept, having once started it, because (1) it gets all lights out in from 10 to 20 minutes; (2) the result of it is that on ordinary nights the people are perfectly "careless and secure"... But the result of it also is that when it sounds great numbers of people leave their houses and troop out with their children into the country, and in some cases stay there for hours in the fields . . . They are perfectly orderly and show no signs of panic, but it must be a very harassing thing for the women and children, and as a matter of fact the schools do not open the morning after. Sick people, old people, others who cannot leave their houses, and many of the better classes, who prefer to stay at home, are always greatly upset on "buzzer" nights.

With the introduction of the military warning system in 1916 the difficulty of giving reliable warning of an attack began to disappear. When, too, the warning arrangements over the whole country were surveyed by the War Office, it was deemed impossible, in a few areas, to convey the warning with sufficient rapidity to the numerous munition factories unless a system of public warning was utilized. The matter was referred to the Cabinet, who decided:

'To approve of the principle of public warning of air raids, not as a universal measure, but as one to be adopted in places where the local conditions require it. The Field-Marshal Commanding-in-Chief, Home Forces, should have authority for giving warnings by this method to munition factories and elsewhere, as required, when other effectual means are not available'.

On this decision power was taken, in March 1916, under the Defence of the Realm Regulations, to require hooters to be used under preconcerted schemes and, conversely, to prevent their unauthorised use for warning purposes.

In the same month, the proposal was renewed by G.H.Q., Home Forces, that all places of public worship and public amusement in the London area should be warned of approaching raids. The suggestion was approved and, in June 1916, churches, theatres, &c., were placed on the Warning Lists. Theatre managers who took advantage of this arrangement (which was not made compulsory) were required, on receipt of the message 'Take Air Raid Action', to interrupt the performance and communicate the warning in a prescribed form to the audience. About half the places of entertainment in the Metropolitan district at once accepted the arrangement.

During the remainder of 1916 and the early months of 1917 there was no further important development in the public warning arrangements, but, for London particularly, the whole question was placed on a new footing when the enemy inaugurated his daylight aeroplane attacks in June 1917. It was this change in the form of attack which led to the institution in July 1917 of public warning arrangements for London. (The warning devices for London and their effects will be considered in a later volume.)

One other question considered from time to time by the Home Office may be mentioned. This was the control of sounds which might serve as a guide to hostile aircraft. In November 1915 the War Office and the Admiralty had expressed the view that, under certain conditions, the chiming of church bells and the striking of public clocks might afford navigational data or reveal the whereabouts of a town which might otherwise escape observation. Chief Constables had, therefore, been advised, in December 1915, that the use of church bells and clock chimes should be discontinued between sunset and sunrise, particularly in places within ten miles of the sea from Northumberland round the coast to Hampshire.

This was followed, in March 1916, by a new Defence of the Realm Regulation, which prohibited the ringing of bells or the striking of clocks within any area in which a Lights Order was in force and during the hours when the Order was operative. (In May 1916 it was made clear that the regulation referred to bells and clocks 'audible at such a distance as to be capable of serving as a guide for hostile aircraft'.) Many other suggestions for securing silence were put forward by responsible authorities, but they were not seriously considered by the Home Office. These included proposals to prohibit singing, whistling, or shouting in the streets, or even the barking of dogs.

It took some months before the full fruits of the reorganisation were apparent, but the improvement in the defences, especially of London, was steady.

Airship Attacks with Fleet Support

But the second airship attack in 1916 was not made on London. The airship operations, indeed, formed part of a wide plan in which the whole of the German High Sea Fleet was involved. Admiral Scheer had been appointed to the command of the High Sea Fleet by an Order in Council dated the 24th of January 1916. The loss of the *L. 19* in the North Sea after the raid on the Midlands a week later led to a decision that future air raids must be made in conjunction with destroyer sweeps. The airship commanders were to keep the destroyers informed of the presence and composition of any British forces which they saw at sea, and the destroyers, in their turn, were to help the airships in case of accidents.

Such was the general scheme, but the first airship raid planned under the direction of Admiral Scheer went beyond this. A further sweep was to be made well to the southward of the route of the returning Zeppelins by the German 1st and 2nd Scouting Groups, in the hope that they might meet and overwhelm any British light forces sent out in pursuit of the airships. The channels of exit from Harwich, Dover, and the Thames were to be mined by U.C. boats during the night in which the air raid took place, and seven U.B. boats were to be stationed in hopeful positions between Yarmouth and the Dover Straits. The whole operation was to be backed up by the High Sea Fleet in force. We knew nothing of these intentions at the time.

Arrangements were completed for the Zeppelin raid to take place on the 3rd of March 1916, but there was delay, and not until the 5th of March did the movement from the Bight begin, although the U.C. boats had carried out their part of the programme on the 3rd, mining Dover, the Edinburgh Channel, the Black Deep, and the southern and northern exits from Harwich. Three airships, the *L. 11, L. 13*, and *L. 14*, left at noon on the 5th. They were to make a reconnaissance of the British Fleet in its northern bases, in preparation for the proposed action of the German High Sea Fleet, and then, if possible, to bomb the naval establishments in the Firth of Forth and on the Tyne and Tees. Soon after midday we intercepted messages from the airships that they were bound on a north-westerly course 'with only H.V.B. on board' and knew they were on their way with bombs. The three airships had not gone far before they ran into strong north-westerly winds, accompanied by snow and hail squalls, and their progress was slow.

All three commanders eventually gave up the intended raid on Rosyth. The *L.11* (Korvettenkapitän Victor Schütze) changed her objective to Middlesbrough, and the *L.14* (Kapitänleutnant Böcker) and *L.13* (Kapitänleutnant Mathy) steered for the Tyne. All three ships made their landfall considerably farther south than they had intended. The *L.14* came in at Flamborough Head about 10.30 p.m. and wandered, apparently in doubt as to her position, until midnight, when she dropped six bombs near Beverley, which fell in open fields. The Humber now showed up against the snowy landscape like a dark ribbon, with Hull clearly visible, and the airship thereupon bore down on the city and began to attack it at 12.5 a.m. Hull was defenceless, not a single anti-aircraft gun being mounted in the vicinity. For ten minutes Böcker remained over the city dropping his bombs with deliberate aim. We counted seven high-explosive and thirteen incendiary bombs, four of the latter falling in the river. The main damage was to houses near the docks. The German naval historian says:

> The most striking result, was the collapse of whole blocks of houses in a street running north and south, and these afterwards showed up against the snow as big black patches. (Groos, *Nordsee*, Vol. 5.)

From Hull, Böcker turned towards Grimsby and came under fire from the 1-pounder and 6-pounder Hotchkiss anti-aircraft guns at Killingholme, one of which was probably responsible for a hit stated to have been received over Hull. Grimsby was now obscured by cloud, and Böcker turned north again, dropping seven more bombs, without doing damage, on his way out to sea near Tunstall.

The attack on Hull by the *L.14* was followed by a second attack, an hour later, by the *L.11*. This ship had come in near Tunstall at 9.45 p.m. and had made a fairly direct course to Lincoln through squalls which covered the Zeppelin with snow. The airship missed the town of Lincoln and shortly afterwards turned north again. When the snow clouds cleared, her commander found he was within sight of Hull, which was under attack from the *L.14*, and he decided to drop his bombs on the same objective. But almost at once the clouds closed over the town again and the airship had to wait until they had cleared. At about 1 a.m. the clouds drifted away and Hull now offered a perfect target. Schütze reported:

> The town, though very well darkened, showed up clearly under the starlit sky like a drawing, with streets, blocks of houses, quays and dock basins, beneath the airship. A few lights were moving about in the streets . . . During a period of twenty minutes incendiary and high-explosive bombs were dropped on the harbours and docks . . . and the effect of each was carefully noted. The first H.E. bomb struck the quay, big portions of which went up, and another hit the lock-gate of one of the harbour basins. The burst was so directly on the gate that it might have been taken for a gun fired off there. Buildings collapsed like houses of cards. One hit had a specially far-reaching effect; radiating round the burst more and more houses collapsed and finally showed up, in the snow-covered harbour area, as a black and gigantic hole. A similar, bigger dark patch in the neighbourhood seemed to be due to the raid of *L. 14*. . . . With binoculars it was possible to see people running hither and thither in the glare of the fires. In the harbour, where the lock-gates were hit, ships began to move. (Groos, *Nordsee*, Vol. 5.)

The damage, in fact, was less than appeared. From the town the airship seemed to hover at a low height (estimated at 3,000 to 4,000 feet), and the light shown by the opening of the bomb-dropping trap was seen clearly. The first bomb fell in the river opposite Earle's Shipyard and caused the partial collapse next day of a 3,000-ton steamer that was on the stocks in the yard. Twenty more bombs came from the *L. 11* and destroyed a number of houses, broke water-mains, set fire to the Mariners' Alms-houses and to a dock shed, and damaged the roof of the Paragon Station, the windows of Holy Trinity Church, and the offices of the Chief of the Royal Artillery. In the two attacks on the city the casualties were seventeen killed and fifty-two injured. From Hull the *L. 11* passed south over Killingholme, where she came under antiaircraft fire, to which she replied with four bombs, which killed a man, but did no material damage. The ship finally passed the Spurn on her way out to sea at 1.40 a.m.

There remains Mathy in the *L. 13*. He made a remarkable flight. From the Dogger Bank onwards towards England the *L. 13* flew through blinding snowstorms, and Mathy never knew when he crossed the land. When the storm abated he calculated he was over Carlisle, and thereupon turned back to make for the Humber, but he again flew into a storm area with winds of hurricane force. Owing to the weight of the snow and the failure of one engine the ship lost height, and Mathy dropped bombs as ballast he knew not where. These, which did no damage, fell between the village and church at Sproxton (thirty-two incendiaries) and in fields in the parish of Thistleton (fourteen high-explosives), the explosion of the latter being heard at Norwich, eighty-five miles distant.

Mathy, in fact, had not been near Carlisle. He had crossed the Lincolnshire coast, south of Spurn Head, at 9.14 p.m., and had made a south-west course to Lincoln and Newark. He circled east of the latter town and then flew off south-east, at great speed, across many counties, dropping his bombs, as stated above, on the way. At about 1.30 a.m. he appeared over the Thames Estuary, where he came under fire from Shoeburyness and Sheerness. The weather was now clearer, and Mathy discovered to his surprise that he was not over the Humber but the Thames. Over Sheerness the *L. 13*, bows to the wind, hovered almost motionless, and was held in the searchlights for five minutes, but the only anti-aircraft guns in the fortress were six-pounders, and their fire, although heavy, was without effect. The airship then passed across Kent and out to sea south of Deal, and eventually made a safe landing, after further trouble with storms over the Channel, at Cognelee, a station of the German military airship service.

The Harwich light cruisers had been kept at one hour's notice throughout the night ready for an attempt to intercept the returning airships, but the courses of the Zeppelins were too erratic to warrant a search in any particular direction, and further, by 7 a.m. on the 6th of March, it seemed that the Harwich Force might be required for more definite work elsewhere. The German High Sea Fleet had, according to plan, gathered in the outer roadstead on the evening of the 5th, and had set a course, westwards. In the morning of the 6th of March, we had learnt by directional wireless that the High Sea Fleet was at a point about twenty miles north of Terschelling. This became known to the British Chief of Staff at 7 a.m.

The unusual position of the German Fleet seemed to portend an invasion or a bombarding raid, and counter movements were at once set on foot. Efforts were made to get all merchant shipping on the East Coast into harbour, and all vessels of the auxiliary patrol along the coast, including the drifters of the Dover barrage, were recalled. The Harwich Force was sent to reconnoitre north-eastward from the North Hinder with orders to retire on the Dover Straits in front of the enemy, if necessary, and the Grand Fleet was ordered to concentrate in the Long Forties. For some hours, while these movements were afoot, the situation was obscure and tense.

At 11 a.m. the surprising information came in that the flagship of the German High Sea fleet had turned north from Terschelling, and when we learnt later that the High Sea Fleet was about to return to harbour it became clear that there was now no chance of contact. The German movement was over, and conditions on the East Coast returned to normal. The Admiralty concluded at the time that the German sortie was merely an exercise. From the enemy point of view the operation was a failure. The Fleet had gone to sea to catch British light naval forces which, it was hoped, would be induced to come out to follow up the returning Zeppelins, but the High Sea Fleet returned to harbour without having seen a British vessel. Nor did the mines laid by the U.C. boats do any damage. Indeed, the only result of the operation, apart from the bombing of Hull, was the sinking of two fishing smacks off Lowestoft by the U.B. boats.

Great feeling was aroused in Hull by the attack. That Zeppelins should be allowed to hover near the town for an hour without any attempt to attack them from land or from the air led to many forceful protests. (The feeling was such that Royal Flying Corps transport was attacked and damaged by a crowd in Hull, and a Royal Flying Corps officer was mobbed in Beverley.) The General Officer Commanding-in-Chief the Northern Command (Major-General H. M. Lawson) was deputed to meet the Lord Mayor of Hull and the local members of Parliament and prominent citizens. These voiced their complaints with vigour. They were assured that the scheme for the anti-aircraft defence of Hull and of the Humber had been settled and that guns would be mounted as soon as they were available.

Meanwhile two 13-pounder guns of the Mobile Section were sent temporarily to Hull until the guns permanently allotted should arrive. By the end of May two 3-in., one 12-pounder, and one 6-pounder guns were in position at Hull, and the Humber defences had been strengthened by the placing of extra guns at Immingham, Killingholme, Waltham, Spurn, and Hornsea.

★★★★★★

The anti-aircraft guns of the Humber Garrison at the end of

May were: Killingholme, two 12-pounders, two 6-pounders, two 1-pounders; Immingham, one 12-pounder, two 1-pounders; Waltham, one 12-pounder, one 1-pounder; Spurn, one 3-pounder; Hornsea, one 3-pounder; and Hull, two 3-in., one 12-pounder, and one 6-pounder.

******

For the moonless period, at the beginning of April 1916, the German command organised a series of raids which were planned to cover the British Isles from the Firth of Forth to London. By this time the dimming of lights at night was general throughout the country, and many improvements had been made in the anti-aircraft defences. The moon would be new on the 2nd/3rd of April, and the first attack of the series was planned for the 31st of March. Seven Zeppelins left their sheds in North Germany about midday on the 31st.

On this occasion we did not intercept the usual messages from the airship commanders that they had only 'H.V.B.' on board, but from other indications we were able to predict that seven airships would attempt to attack the south of England that night. Two of the airships were first sighted by a Lowestoft minesweeper at 6.50 p.m. At 8 p.m. the Admiralty ordered two destroyer divisions out from Harwich, one to be off Cromer and the other off Lowestoft, to deal in daylight with any Zeppelins which might be brought down. (The Harwich destroyers returned next day with nothing to report.)

Meanwhile two of the seven airships had turned back when they were north-west of Terschelling. They were the *L.9* and *L.11*, which had developed defects. The remaining five continued their westward flight, their main objective being London. But engine trouble developed in the *L.22* (Kapitänleutnant Martin Dietrich), which took four hours to put right, and her commander abandoned the raid on London and went to the Humber instead. This airship reached the Lincolnshire coast near Mablethorpe about 1 a.m. on the 1st of April, and then turned north.

Under the impression that he was attacking dockyards at Grimsby, Dietrich dropped fourteen high-explosive and twelve incendiary bombs on Humberston at 1.35 a.m. Five of the bombs did not explode and the only damage was to a farmhouse. There were no casualties. The next bombs (six high-explosive) fell on Cleethorpes where a chapel used as a billet by men of the 3rd Manchesters was destroyed and twenty-nine soldiers were killed and fifty-three injured. A wing of the Town Hall was also damaged, but otherwise only window-glass suffered. The *L.22* went out to sea, south of Spurn Head, under fire from anti-aircraft guns in a paddle minesweeper in the Humber.

Two of the remaining ships made the Suffolk coast shortly before 8 p.m., the *L.13* (Kapitänleutnant Mathy) north of Aldeburgh and the *L.15* (Kapitänleutnant Breithaupt) south of Southwold. Mathy decided that the barometric conditions would prevent him from getting the height which he judged necessary for a direct descent on London and he looked round for more immediate objectives on which to drop some of his great weight of bombs. (The airships, according to Groos, vol. 5, carried an average of 2,040 kg. of high-explosives and 2,388 kg. of incendiaries.) He made first for the New Explosive Works at Stowmarket, north-west of Ipswich. He found Stowmarket, but he could not locate the works, and while he was looking for them he was picked up by a searchlight and came under anti-aircraft fire, to which he replied with twelve high-explosive bombs aimed at the battery.

Mathy, in fact, was over the Explosive Works, and the guns which engaged him were two 6-pounders allotted to their defence. The bombs, in consequence, fell close to the works, but they broke only window-glass. Mathy then went off west to Haughley, but he was apparently still anxious to find the Explosive Works, and he turned back again to Stowmarket. He was attacked once more by the anti-aircraft guns, and one shell appeared to the gunners to have made a direct hit. This was confirmed in a curious way. A signal form, apparently blown overboard before it reached the wireless operator in the airship, was picked up next morning near Stowmarket. On it was scribbled:

> Chief of Naval Staff, High Sea Fleet, 10 p.m. Am hit; have turned back. Will land at Hage about 4 a.m. *L.13*.

As soon as Mathy discovered he was hit (half the gas had escaped from one gas-bag) he made off. He reported that he dropped his remaining bombs at Lowestoft on his way out. Actually, he went out north of Southwold and his bombs fell without inflicting damage at Wangford (eleven high-explosive and five incendiary) and on the aerodrome at Covehithe (seven high-explosive and twenty incendiary). The height of the airship, during this attack, was estimated at 2,000 feet, but after the bombs had been released the *L.13* rose sharply and made for home at full speed, reaching her shed safely at 2 a.m.

Breithaupt, in the *L.15*, steered a direct course for London, but he dropped a few bombs and flares on the way. His first two bombs fell in the sea before he made his landfall at Dunwich, and his third, without damage, at Yoxford. He was over Ipswich at 8.20 p.m. and dropped three more, two of which damaged houses, killing three persons and injuring two. At 8.45 p.m. one bomb was dropped harmlessly on Colchester, but no others fell until the airship was within sight of London.

The *L. 15* approached the Thames near Grays and then turned west, with the river on her port beam. She was picked up by the Perry Street searchlight and almost at once came under fire from the Dartford anti-aircraft guns. About this time, too, Second Lieutenant C. A. Ridley, who was in the air from the Joyce Green aerodrome, saw the airship and gave her twenty rounds from his machinegun before he lost her in the darkness. It was not long before the *L. 15* was illuminated again, and heavy fire was opened on her by the guns at Purfleet, Abbey Wood, Erith, Erith Marsh, Southern Outfall, Plumstead Common, and Plumstead Marsh.

To avoid the fire Breithaupt turned north, and when, at 9.43 p.m., he judged he was over the northern suburbs of London, he dropped twenty high-explosive and twenty-four incendiary bombs. In fact, these fell in fields at Rainham and did no damage. Two minutes later the Zeppelin was hit by a shrapnel shell from the Purfleet gun, which made a large rent in her side. Breithaupt at once decided to make for home. His troubles, however, were only beginning. He was overtaken, east of Brentwood, by Second Lieutenant A. de B. Brandon in a B.E.2c. aeroplane from Hainault Farm. From above the airship, this officer dropped explosive darts without apparent result, and then flew alongside to attack from the rear, and he was met with machinegun fire from the airship as he went, several of the shots hitting his aeroplane. He made a further unsuccessful attempt to bring the Zeppelin down with an incendiary bomb and explosive darts before he suddenly lost sight of his quarry. Breithaupt, indeed, had changed his course with the idea of getting his crippled ship to Belgium. He jettisoned every movable object to lighten the ship before he crossed the coast near the Crouch.

His determined effort to save the *L. 15* was of no avail. At 11 p.m. the back of the airship broke and she fell into the sea near the Knock Deep. Before she fell she sent a call for help, and a reply was made that destroyers would come out from Zeebrugge. The Admiralty ordered Commodore Tyrwhitt and the Admirals at the Nore and Dover to send out destroyers to attack the damaged Zeppelin and any forces attempting to help her. But the *L. 15* was beyond attack. She had, in fact, come down in the middle of a flotilla of net-drifters guarded by the armed trawler *Olivine*. The *Olivine* opened fire but ceased after a few rounds as there was no resistance, and as she went alongside the airship a voice from inside was heard to say, 'We surrender; have no arms; come alongside'. The crew were taken off; only one man was lost, drowned while the airship was under fire. Shortly afterwards some of the Nore destroyers arrived and with great difficulty took the airship in tow, but off Westgate she suddenly collapsed and sank.

Both the remaining ships, the *L.14* and the *L.16*, were credited with attacks on London. The guns and searchlights which had proved fatal to the *L.15* showed the *L.16* (Oberleutnant zur See Peterson) the way. So, says the German naval historian, (Groos, *Nordsee*, Vol. 5), who goes on to recount how the *L.16* dropped her bombs in the Hornsey district. Peterson's bombs, however, fell on Bury St. Edmunds, where they damaged thirty-seven houses and killed seven people and injured five. After this attack the *L.16* went out again direct, dropping one more bomb on Lowestoft as she went. This damaged a tramcar shed but inflicted no casualties.

The *L.14* (Kapitänleutnant Böcker), which carried Korvettenkapitän Strasser, the commander of the naval airship division, came farther south. Under the impression that he was attacking 'several big factories in the otherwise admirably darkened town' of Cambridge, her commander dropped his first bombs (eight high-explosive and nineteen incendiary) on Sudbury, where five persons were killed, one was injured, and dwelling-houses were damaged. Next came three bombs on Braintree (seven casualties, four fatal). The German account then tells of the *L.14's* attack on London 'in the vicinity of Tower Bridge and the docks', where houses were seen to collapse and fires break out, while the airship was caught in the beams of searchlights and continuously fired at.

But the further course of the *L.14* was less direct than this implies and her bombs more scattered. From Braintree Böcker continued towards London, but west of Brentwood he turned right about and went back nearly to Sudbury again, from which he came south once more to the Thames Estuary, whence he turned north-east and made his way home, crossing the coast south of Dunwich. His further bombs fell at Blackmore (9), Doddinghurst (2), Springfield (1), Stanford-le-Hope (1), and Thames Haven (14). None of these bombs inflicted casualties and the material damage was negligible, but the oil tanks at Thames Haven narrowly escaped destruction. Incendiary bombs made direct hits on two tanks at the works of the Asiatic Oil

Company, but it happened that both the tanks were empty.

Two military airships were also reported to have been out during this attack. One of them approached the Suffolk coast, but did not cross, and the other appears to have come overland as far as Ipswich without dropping any bombs.

******

> Three military ships, the *LZ.88, LZ.90*, and the *LZ.93*, set out to attack England. The *LZ.90* claimed to have attacked Norwich, but we traced no bombs from her. The other ships turned back as the weather conditions were unfavourable.

******

The raid had been a failure. What little had been achieved was at the cost of one Zeppelin destroyed and another hit and damaged. Furthermore, the fact that a pilot had, for the first time, succeeded in dropping bombs on a raiding Zeppelin at night, although it had not led to the destruction of the airship, gave encouragement to every pilot of the defence. In all, eight naval and thirteen military pilots had, in spite of local ground mist, gone up during the raid, (one pilot, Second Lieutenant J. W. Bailey, was killed getting off the ground, no other pilot was injured, but three aeroplanes were completely, and two partly wrecked), but Second Lieutenant Brandon alone came within striking distance of a Zeppelin, although two other military pilots saw the *L. 15* from below, but could not catch up with her.

Two interesting points were brought out during this attack. One was that the lighting arrangements on some of the landing-grounds were so complicated as to confuse pilots and make landing hazardous, and the other was the great difficulty of finding an airship from above. One pilot was for a time directly over the *L. 15*, but he saw nothing of her.

It seemed to us at the time that after the wireless message was sent out from the *L. 15* calling for help, the other airships, which presumably took this message in, developed hesitancy, and that the sting went out of the raid from that moment. When, therefore, the German Admiralty published *communiqués* after the raid claiming successful attacks on London, it was thought that these were prompted by disappointment. But it is clear that the German authorities believed what they claimed and that their belief persisted. In the third volume of the British official naval history, published in 1923, Sir Julian Corbett refers briefly to this raid. His reference calls forth the following comment from the German naval historian:

The official British report (*Corbett, Naval Operations*,Volume 3) at any rate satisfied itself with the laconic remark that bombs had been dropped at Cleethorpes (just east of Grimsby) and Bury St. Edmunds, a few miles north-west of Stowmarket, and that these had 'killed and injured a number of soldiers.The report, however, omitted to state the fact that three airships had reached and bombed London. At the time the British Press was very strictly censored and only allowed to publish general information, but this showed that the effect of this raid put that of all previous raids in the shade.

Although the docks and arsenals were immediately closed to the public so that no one might see the results of the raids and no foreigners were permitted to leave the British Isles for eight days, important details were soon received from agents. At Grimsby, in addition to the post office and several other houses, a battleship in the roadstead was heavily damaged by a bomb and had to be beached. At Kensington an aeroplane hangar was wrecked, near Tower Bridge a transport ship damaged, in Great Tower Street a factory wrecked, and north of the Tower a bomb fell in George Street only 100 metres away from two anti-aircraft guns.

It was reported that a big fire had broken out at West India Docks, and that at Tilbury Docks a munition boat exploded (400 killed). Specially serious explosions occurred at the Surrey Commercial Docks and at a factory, close to the Lower Road, at which shells were filled with explosives. A railway train already loaded with these shells was stated to be completely wrecked. Further, all reports from the airship commanders showed that the anti-aircraft artillery defence of England was being gradually strengthened, which meant that in time the position on the Western front in France would be easier for the Germans, owing to the withdrawal of artillery. In London the number of guns was said to be so high that it was impossible to count them from the air. Camouflage, however, made accurate sighting of objectives impossible, but the probability of good hits with a shower of shells was great, hence it was only advisable to carry out raids on London from a very high altitude. (Groos, *Nordsee*,Vol. 5.)

No time was lost in carrying on the attacks. At midday on the 1st of April the *L.11* and the *L.17*, duly assisted by the High Sea Fleet, set out to raid London. On the way the wind became unfavourable for this enterprise, and the airship commanders received instructions, by wireless, to bomb the Midlands or the north of England instead. About dusk the *L.17* (Kapitänleutnant Ehrlich) was off Flamborough Head, where she cruised for an hour, but just as her commander decided it was dark enough to go overland, the propeller shaft of the after-engine broke. The airship was brought to a standstill and the propeller was secured, but before this could be done all the bombs had to be dropped as ballast: their distant explosions in the sea were heard at Tunstall. The *L.17* returned home safely.

The *L.11* (Korvettenkapitän Victor Schütze) was fired on, but not hit, by patrolling trawlers off the Dogger Bank on her way in. She crossed the coast at Seaham about 11 p.m. and dropped her bombs at Eppleton Colliery (2), Hetton Downs (2), Philadelphia (2), Sunderland (21), Port Clarence (1), Middlesbrough (2), Brotton (2), and in the River Tees (2). Except in Sunderland, the damage was negligible, and the casualties were confined to two men injured at Middlesbrough. In Sunderland much damage was done to shops and houses and twenty-two people were killed while twenty-five were seriously and one hundred and three others slightly injured.

Only one shell was fired at the *L.11*, from a 6-inch gun in Fulwell Quarry, Sunderland, and four aeroplane pilots who went up from Whitley Bay, Redcar, and Cramlington failed to find her.

The *L.11* landed at Nordholz at 9 a.m. on April the 2nd, and, three hours later, four of her consorts set out again for a new objective. This time they were to raid the Firth of Forth, especially the naval base at Rosyth and the Forth Bridge. Mathy in the *L.13* had engine' trouble soon after leaving and had to turn back. The remaining ships, the *L.14* (Kapitänleutnant Böcker), *L.16* (Oberleutnant zur See Peterson), and *L.22* (Kapitänleutnant Martin Dietrich) continued on their course. From their reports of position sent out as they proceeded, and intercepted by us, the Admiralty came to the conclusion that the airships were making for a northern objective and, at 5.25 p.m., warned Admirals Jellicoe and Beatty and the Admiral, Rosyth.

Meanwhile a northerly wind in the western half of the North Sea drove the airships southward of their objective. The first to arrive was the *L.22*, which came in north of Berwick-on-Tweed about 9 p.m. and dropped most of her bombs on what was thought to be a single big factory in Newcastle, but in reality, in fields north and inland of Berwick. They did no damage. The *L.22* then went out to sea and skirted the coast to Edinburgh, where she arrived just as the city was being attacked by the *L. 14*. She added three bombs of her own, which did no more than break glass in Colinton and Liberton, before she finally went off.

The *L. 14* was the only one of the airships to approach the Firth of Forth direct. On her way in, off St. Abbs Head, she had been pursued and fired on by destroyers which she eventually outdistanced, but for some time thereafter she made slow progress, and her commander could see little below him. About 11 p.m. he caught sight of a few lights in Leith and Edinburgh, and these enabled him to fix his position, but as he steered towards them they were gradually extinguished and the airship was picked up by a searchlight. Nothing could now be distinguished of Rosyth or the Forth Bridge, and Böcker gave up all idea of trying to find them and dropped his bombs instead on 'the docks and harbour works at Leith and Edinburgh'. (Groos, *Nordsee*, Vol. 5.) Böcker was not unacquainted with the geography of the docks. In the years before the war he had visited Edinburgh and Leith as an officer in a Hamburg-Amerika ship.

Nine high-explosive and eleven incendiary bombs fell in Leith. A man and a child were killed, three houses were wrecked or burnt, the whisky bond warehouse of Messrs. Innes and Grieve was destroyed with its contents (damage, £44,000), and a grain and a tannery store were damaged. How little the town anticipated airship raids is shown by the fact that the bonded warehouse which was demolished was, like several other buildings in Edinburgh and Leith at that time, not insured against damage by aircraft. One of the early bombs thrown from the *L. 14*, a small incendiary, fell into a room in Commercial Street in which an old lady was in bed. The bomb crashed through the floor into the room beneath where it burst into flames. The woman got out of bed and poured water through the hole in the floor until she had put out the fire below.

From Leith the *L. 14* passed to Edinburgh, on which were dropped eighteen high-explosive and six incendiary bombs. Although many of these burst harmlessly, eleven people were killed and twenty-four injured, four houses, a spirit store, and three hotels were seriously damaged, and Princes Street Station and a large number of houses less seriously hit. The last bombs were thrown about 12.15 a.m., and the *L. 14* then made off at full speed. The only fire she met with over land came from two machine-guns which fired a few rounds from the southern slopes of Arthur Seat.

While the *L.14* was attacking Edinburgh the *L.16* was making an abortive journey into Northumberland. Her commander thought he was attacking blast furnaces and factories south of the Tyne, but he was well north of the river, and none of his forty-one bombs on Ponteland, Cramlington, and Broomhill inflicted damage or casualties. The Ponteland bombs (23) were attracted by flares burning on the landing-ground at High West Houses, and those which fell at Cramlington (11) by similar flares on the local aerodrome. The remaining seven exploded in fields near Broomhill Colliery.

While the naval Zeppelins were raiding Scotland and Northumberland, without opposition, two military airships from Belgium crossed the East Coast. Although the two ships, between them, dropped thirty-six high-explosive and one hundred and twenty-eight incendiary bombs, they inflicted no casualties, and the damage was confined to four houses at Waltham Abbey. The latter damage was the result of the complete load of bombs (90) dropped by one of the airships which was apparently trying to reach London. (This was the *L.Z.90;* Oberleutnant Lehmann. Her commanding officer was under the impression that his attack was made on London. The visibility was very poor.)

They were dropped when the Zeppelin came under heavy fire from the guns of the Waltham Abbey defences, and they fell along a line between Woodridden Farm and Windmill Hill, near Waltham Abbey. When the last had been thrown, the airship escaped from the searchlight beams by rising sharply and made her way out to sea again at Clacton. The second military ship came inland south of Orfordness, passed twice across Ipswich, and ultimately dropped all her bombs (74) at Alderton, Ramsholt, and Hollesley. The only effect was broken windows at Ramsholt. She met only machine-gun fire from the naval mobile anti-aircraft section.

******

> This airship, the *L.Z.88* (Hauptmann Falck), had London for objective. She was, however, blown out of her course by the wind, and, as time was short, her commander made for Harwich. He apparently mistook the River Deben for the Orwell and his bombs fell on villages north of the former river.

******

A number of aeroplanes had gone up to attack the raiders, but they had no luck. In Scotland seaplane pilots stationed at Dundee tried, but failed, to get away, and one aeroplane pilot who went up from

East Fortune saw nothing; his aeroplane was wrecked on landing. Two military aeroplane pilots who went up from Cramlington in search of the *L.16* (which later bombed their landing ground) also failed to locate the airship. One of the aeroplanes caught fire on landing and was blown up by its own bombs, the pilot escaping unhurt. In search of the military Zeppelins, pilots took the air from Hounslow, Croydon, Suttons Farm, and Hainault Farm, and although an airship was sighted she could not be overhauled. Three of these aeroplanes were damaged on landing.

To catch the Zeppelins returning from Edinburgh and Northumberland, Admiral Jellicoe had ordered out a light cruiser squadron and four destroyers from Rosyth. They sailed at 10 p.m., nearly two hours before the Edinburgh attack took place, and patrolled during the early hours of April the 3rd along the probable tracks of the returning airships, but saw nothing, and were recalled at 7 a.m. Had they gone farther east they might have run into three German flotillas which were sweeping the area between Horn Reefs and the Northern end of the Dogger Bank to engage any forces we might send so far to intercept the airships.

Four Harwich destroyers which had been ordered out to the North Hinder along the track of the military Zeppelins did not leave until 4.30 a.m., by which time the airships were nearly home again. One of the military Zeppelins, however, had been met on her return, and fired at, by some of the Lowestoft trawlers specially armed with anti-aircraft guns. She was very high, but a trawler's crew imagined they saw a hit, although the airship continued on her course and disappeared.

In the afternoon of the 3rd of April 1916 there was again activity in the North German sheds. The *L.11* and *L.17* left at 2 p.m. with London as their objective, but they ran into strong winds on the way over, and, although the *L.17* got near the coast, at Haisborough, she made such little headway that her commander abandoned the raid and returned home. The commander of the *L.11* (Korvettenkapitän Victor Schütze) made his landfall at Sheringham soon after 1.30 a.m. on the 4th of April, but the visibility was poor, and, as the hour was late, he decided to attack Norwich, Yarmouth, and Lowestoft. He failed, however, to find any of these places, and had gone out to sea again at Caister when he saw what he thought to be flashes from guns firing near Yarmouth. He turned back and dropped three groups of bombs, which were heard exploding in the sea off Caister.

It is possible these so-called distant gun-flashes were the lights from the funnels of destroyers which had been ordered out from Harwich by the Admiralty at 8.5 p.m. on the 3rd and passed the Corton Light Vessel in the early hours of the 4th, just about the time the *L. 11* passed overhead. The deck logs of the destroyers, however, do not mention Zeppelins or bombs. Only four bombs, all incendiaries, fell on land, and these did no damage. They were dropped while the airship commander was searching for objectives in the hope, which proved vain, that they would bring guns and searchlights into action.

On the 4th of April five Zeppelins set out to bomb the Midlands in conjunction with three torpedo-boat flotillas which were to sweep in a north-westerly direction. Strong winds caused this operation to be abandoned not long after the airships started.

Next day, the 5th of April, three airships set off once again. They were the *L. 11, L. 13*, and *L. 16*. The *L. 13* (Mathy) had engine trouble on the way and turned back. The *L. 11* (Korvettenkapitän Victor Schütze) shaped a course for the Firth of Forth but was driven south by rain squalls and made her landfall at Hornsea Mere on the Yorkshire coast at 9.10 p.m. and thence proceeded inland with the idea of attacking Sheffield. When, however, the *L. 11* approached Hull she was picked up by searchlights and came under immediate attack from anti-aircraft guns. Schütze had bombed Hull in leisurely fashion only a month before when the town was defenceless, and the fire from the newly-placed guns came as a shock to him.

The airship was much shaken by shrapnel bursting near her, and her commander was unwilling to risk a passage across the town. He therefore dropped four bombs and retreated to sea again. It was his intention, he says, to steer southward along the coast and go inland again when the moon had set, but the after-engine failed, and Schütze turned north, to keep to windward, towards Hartlepool. On the way the outline of the coast and the rivers showed up in the clear air as on a map. Before Hartlepool was reached the forward-engine in the *L. 11* failed, and this objective also was given up.

As Schütze turned for home he was attracted by the brightly-lit smelting furnaces of an ironworks, towards which he steered. These were the Skinningrove Works, at which nine high-explosive and twenty incendiary bombs (six of the latter failing to explode) were aimed. These appeared to Schütze, watching from above, to cause explosions which wrecked the works. But only the laboratory at the works was destroyed. There were no casualties, and the damage otherwise was confined to the Council School, a Co-operative Society's building, and two dwelling-houses. The crew of the 6-inch gun at Skinningrove, who had not yet received their allotted searchlight, did not see the airship and could not fire.

Oberleutnant zur See Peterson in the *L.16* thought he made his landfall north of Scarborough and that he proceeded direct to Leeds. His bombs, he thought, fell on Leeds and on junctions between that city and York. Actually, he came in north of Hartlepool and passed over Bishop Auckland to Evenwood where, apparently attracted by fiery waste-heaps, he dropped twenty-three bombs at Evenwood and Randolf Colliery. Fifteen miners' cottages were wrecked and seventy damaged, and a man and a child were injured.

The airship then proceeded on her homeward journey and dropped twenty-seven other bombs on collieries south-east of Bishop Auckland, where miners' cottages again suffered and a child was killed and a woman and two children were injured. No damage was done to the colliery works. The *L.16*, before she got home, was caught in a whirlwind, and was tossed about for a long time without making any progress. She escaped at dawn by going down low, where the weather conditions were better.

Military pilots went up from Beverley and Cramlington and a naval pilot from Scarborough, but they failed to find any airship. One of them, Captain J. Nichol, crashed into a house and was killed. The sloop *Poppy*, from the west end of the Dogger Bank, sighted one of the returning airships for a short time, but could take no action, and destroyers which were sent out from the Tyne and the Humber were too late to see anything of the raiders.

Throughout the whole of this week of air activity the Lowestoft trawlers, the *Kingfisher* and *Cantatrice*, specially fitted to carry seaplanes, were out, with two others as guards, in the neighbourhood of Smith's Knoll, patrolling for an opportunity to intercept Zeppelins, but they sighted nothing.

Thus, ended an ambitiously-planned series of raids. They taught the airship commanders that the day of 'the usual little gun-fire which the Zeppelin had come to look upon as both innocuous and normal when raiding in England' was over. (A statement by Kapitänleutnant Breithaupt who was taken prisoner from the wrecked *L.15*.)

The next raids again coincided with a period of moonless nights and anticyclonic weather. They were made by both the naval and military airship services, but the operations of the former service were of more than ordinary significance. The first naval Zeppelin raid of this series was connected with the bombardment of Lowestoft, which, in turn, had its origin in political events in Ireland. The German General Staff had agreed with Roger Casement, the Irish rebel, to send rifles, machineguns, and ammunition to Ireland to help the rising planned for Easter Sunday. The Irish insurgents also urged that the rising should be accompanied by a strong demonstration by the High Sea Fleet against the East Coast, and this proposal found favour with the German naval staff.

The Irish rebellion duly broke out on the 24th of April, but the German co-operation did not pass off exactly as planned. The German ship *Libau*, disguised as a Norwegian, got through with her arms to Tralee Bay, and was there captured by the British sloop *Bluebell*, which was waiting for her. The Lowestoft raid was a day late. A sweep by the Grand Fleet into the North Sea on the 22nd/23rd of April had caused alarms and excursions in the High Sea Fleet which led to a postponement of the sortie against the East Coast, and the Lowestoft bombardment did not take place until the early hours of the 25th of April. This bombardment was preceded by an airship attack which had a threefold object: the infliction of damage on London, which would add to the moral effect expected to result from the German Fleet's activities; the influencing of British Fleet movements by causing detachments of light forces to be sent out to follow up the returning airships with the chance that they would run into, and be annihilated by, the oncoming High Sea Fleet; and, finally, reconnaissance by the airships to screen the German Fleet movements.

The raiding Zeppelins, the *L. 11, L. 13, L. 16, L. 17, L. 21*, and *L. 23*, made their landfall one after the other from 10.15 p.m. to 1.35 a.m. on the night of the 24th/ 25th of April. Except the *L. 17*, which came in late north of the Wash, all the airships crossed the coast between Cromer and Southwold. The German official history mentions also the *L. 20* as having taken part in the raid, but we have no record of this ship coming overland. The airship commanders discovered that the whole of the coastal area south of the Wash was now well provided with anti-aircraft equipment, and the Zeppelins were occasionally picked up through the clouds by searchlights and came under fire from various batteries with shrapnel and incendiary shells.

Only one of them, however, was hit, some shell splinters striking the fore gondola of the *L. 13* (Kapitänleutnant der Reserve Prölsz). The airship commanders found a strong south-west wind blowing over England, and they soon gave up the idea of getting to London and began to search for alternative objectives. In this they had little better luck. Fog, rain, banks of clouds, and the unlighted country made observation difficult, and the airship commanders, after hours of fruitless searching, dropped their bombs more or less haphazardly, although two of them (in the *L. 13* and *L. 16*) were under the impression that they attacked Cambridge and Norwich. Neither of these places was flown over.

The *L. 16*, the first airship to come in, dropped a parachute, to which was attached a bundle of German illustrated papers, at Kimberley, and then went on to Newmarket, where she was fired on by machine-guns, to which she replied with eighteen high-explosive bombs and one incendiary bomb. They injured one man, wrecked five houses, and damaged a hundred others. Two more bombs in the open outside Newmarket did no damage, and five at Honingham, on the way out, were also ineffective. The *L. 16* crossed the coast again near Mundesley at 1.35 a.m. Her commander, Oberleutnant Peterson, mistook Newmarket for Cambridge and Honingham for Norwich.

The German official naval history states that the majority of the remaining airships went to sea again without dropping even a part of their load of bombs. According to our own observation, bombs which fell on Honing Hall (4), and Dilham (45) came from the *L. 11*; off Kessingland (2 in the sea), Old Newton (9), and Witton (1), from the *L. 21*; on Caister (3), Ridlington (9), and Bacton (6), from the *L. 23*; and, in Lincolnshire, on Alford (3) and Anderby (1), from the *L. 17*. A woman died of shock at Dilham, but there were no other casualties, and the material damage was confined to sheds and window glass.

The last Zeppelin to go out crossed the coast at 2.5 a.m. on the 25th of April. At this time, the German battle cruisers, which were to effect the bombardment, had reached a position about sixty-five miles east of Lowestoft. Screening them ahead and on the flank were six light cruisers in three divisions with four destroyers to each division. The main German fleet was in support in the rear. Three airships had been ordered for reconnaissance duties by Admiral Scheer. The *L. 6* was to be over the Dogger Bank for patrol at dawn on the 25th, and the *L. 9* and *L. 7* were to accompany the battle fleet. The *L. 7*, however, escorted the battle cruiser *Seydlitz* back to harbour after she had struck a mine on her way out on the 24th. The *L. 7* subsequently landed at Hage and was not ready to take the air again until 2.30 a.m. on the 25th, so that she had got no farther than the Ems by daylight.

The *L.6* was driven north, out of her reckoning, and she had steered from the Dogger Bank towards Terschelling at 3.20 a.m.

The *L.9*, scouting between the main fleet and the battle cruisers, was flying at 2,600 feet about forty miles east of Lowestoft at 4.38 a.m. when she was attacked by two aeroplanes (B.E.2c's) from Yarmouth, piloted by Flight Lieutenant V. Nicholl and Flight Lieutenant F. G. D. Hards. The airship, which narrowly escaped disaster, beat a hasty retreat and was, in consequence, prevented from seeing anything of the Harwich Force when Commodore Tyrwhitt turned to follow the enemy at 5.40 a.m. (The *L.9*, shortly afterwards, was recalled by wireless from Germany.)

Only one of the Zeppelins, on the way home from raiding England, seems to have come within sight of the German fleet. This was the *L.21*, which, for a time, obeyed orders to remain by the battle cruisers and screen them from the north. This airship had previously been pursued by three Bristol Scout pilots from Yarmouth, but they could not gain on her and had to give up the chase.

When the German battle cruisers opened fire on Yarmouth, three seaplanes, fitted with wireless, went up on patrol. One pilot, Flight Sub-Lieutenant H. G. Hall, sighted the German squadron at 4.15 a.m. and at once came under fire: he was wounded, but remained in the air for forty-five minutes and then landed his damaged seaplane safely. Two aircraft also went up from Felixstowe and one of these made an unsuccessful attack on a German submarine (probably the U.B.12). Although other attempts at bombing the enemy ships were made by the Yarmouth seaplanes, none was hit.

The effect of the bombardment of Lowestoft and Yarmouth was, in view of the strength of the bombarding fleet, not great. Two hundred houses were wrecked in Lowestoft, but the loss of life was small, and Yarmouth was scarcely touched. The returning enemy ships were pursued across the North Sea by the British fleet, but touch could not be gained and there was no engagement. There is, however, one feature of this pursuit that calls for mention. The *L.9* had been recalled to her base by wireless soon after Admiral Scheer turned for home. This left only the *L.6* to screen the retirement, which she did until 7.30 a.m., when she too was recalled by wireless from Germany. Scheer speaks of the open waters north-west of Terschelling as favourable for offering battle, and he had intended, he says, to pause in these waters, on his homeward journey, in the hope that he would have the opportunity of giving battle to an inferior force of the British pursuing fleet.

He judged, however, that to wait was useless and he continued his homeward journey in some haste. Had he waited, he might, in due course, have had the opportunity he was seeking, for Admiral Beatty would have come up with him before noon. The German naval historian is inclined to blame the departure of the L.6 for the fact that there was no fleet action. He says:

> If the weather and the order sent by the airship division to return had not prevented *L.6* from cruising on the look-out line ordered by the Commander-in-Chief, south-west of the Dogger Bank, it would probably not have escaped her, and through her the fleet command, that the whole British battle cruiser fleet passed this line soon after 10.0 a.m., making at high speed for the very area where the German fleet, according to the original plan, had expected, with sound foresight, to meet the enemy's counter thrust, and was willing to meet him in battle. Perhaps *L.6* would also have reported that for a long distance behind the British battle cruiser fleet no other forces were supporting it, and thus Admiral Scheer was offered the very opportunity, which the bombardment aimed at, of cutting off a portion of the enemy forces before the main body could come to its support. Unfortunately, the German Commander-in-Chief did not possess the means of gaining an idea of the enemy's movements comparable with that which the latter, by the aid of a superior deciphering system, had so royally at his disposal. (Groos, Vol. V.)

This statement is not entirely convincing. Had Scheer wished to give battle he could have detached his light cruisers to scout for the approach of the British ships in the ordinary way. This he made no attempt to do. Moreover, if the German operation aimed at anything more than a belated and hurried demonstration against the East Coast to enhance the effect of the Irish insurrection, the diversion of the best Zeppelins to a raid on England was a tactical error. Those airships, specifically disposed in advance of the fleet as a scouting screen, might have kept Scheer informed of the general movements of the British pursuing ships. If Admiral Scheer envisaged contact, the place for his Zeppelins was with the fleet.

The next raid by naval airships did not take place until the night of the 2nd/3rd of May and once again was closely connected with wider operations by the German fleet. Meanwhile, the weather was too favourable for any respite, and the attacks were taken up by military Zeppelins. Five of these approached our coasts, without previous warning, on the 25th of April. One never came overland and another (*L. Z. 87*), after dropping eight bombs, without effect, near the steamer *Argus* in Deal Harbour, was turned back by the Walmer guns and, although she cruised off the coast as far as Ramsgate, she made no further attempt to come in, and eventually returned to Belgium.

A third ship (*L. Z. 93*) bombed the area of Harwich, but, although her high-explosive bombs were of a heavy type, weighing some 240 lb., they inflicted neither casualties nor damage. Two of these heavy bombs which fell close to Government House failed to explode. Another bomb, an incendiary, fell between two dormitories in the Royal Naval Training Barracks. The fourth airship (*L. Z. 88*) came in near Whitstable, and, after passing over Canterbury, dropped her first bombs (nine incendiaries) in fields near Preston. Thirteen other bombs fell on Sarre and on Chislet Marshes, and fifteen more were dropped before the airship left the coast at Minnis Bay. They did no damage.

The journey of the fifth airship was more purposeful. This was the *L. Z. 97*, commanded by Hauptmann Linnarz, who had made the first of the Zeppelin attacks on London in May of the previous year. Linnarz came in over the Blackwater River about 10 p.m. and approached London from the north-east. He mistook the River Roding for the Thames and dropped forty-seven incendiary bombs in a line between Fyfield and Ongar, the only damage being a shed partly destroyed at Ongar. An officer of the *L. Z. 97* tells how these Ongar bombs fell on London. He says:

> Far, far away we discern a light, and soon afterwards a second. They lie on our course. A short calculation follows. We must be right over London. Impenetrable shadows envelop the gigantic city, only pierced here and there by minute pinpricks of light. . . . Did they really hope we should not find their London? At high speed we steer for the city, the Commander standing ready on the bombing platform . . . "Let go!" he cries. The first bomb has fallen on London! (Neumann, *The German Air Force in the Great War.*)

From Ongar the *L. Z. 97* continued to follow the Roding and then turned south-west over the gun at Dog Kennel Hill, which opened fire at 11.8 p.m. The airship eventually reached Barkingside, where twelve high-explosive bombs were dropped, damaging a few cottages, but causing no casualties, and then she passed by way of Newbury Park (one bomb) towards Ilford, but was turned back abruptly over Seven Kings by anti-aircraft fire and aeroplane attacks. She made off rapidly, dropping only two more bombs between Goodmayes and Chadwell Heath. One fell in a field, the other destroyed a house from which the occupants were absent.

The gun-fire which met the *L.Z.97* over Seven Kings was heavy, but the aeroplane pilots who were in the air reported that the shells burst well short of the airship, which had risen to 12,000 feet when fire was opened. The effectiveness of the threat of the aeroplane attacks was a gratifying feature of the raid. Eight night-flying pilots had gone up, three from Hounslow, three from Suttons Farm, and two from Hainault Farm. Two got near the Zeppelin and one attacked her with machine-gun fire at long range. This officer was Lieutenant W. Leefe Robinson, whose experience was to stand him in good stead later in the year.

A single military ship came in again next night, the 26th of April, over the Kent coast near Kingsdown. She had previously dropped three bombs in the sea off Deal, where she was fired on. The ship passed northwards across Kent and out to sea again east of Margate without dropping any bombs on land. (The *L.Z.93*, Hauptmann Schramm. Engine trouble compelled her commander to turn back.)

Then came the second naval airship raid of this moonless period. The main objective was Rosyth and the Forth Bridge. Eight airships, the *L.11, L.13, L.14, L.16, L.17, L.20, L.21*, and *L.23*, left their sheds and flew across the North Sea, in formation, on the 2nd of May. It so happened that we, too, were on the eve of carrying out a bombing operation, with seaplanes, on the German sheds at Tondern, in conjunction with mining operations in the Bight. (For the account of the seaplane operations see Vol. 2.) The British enterprise, supported by the Grand Fleet, was planned with the two-fold object of enticing out the High Sea Fleet and inducing the enemy command to recall or retain High Sea Fleet vessels intended to operate in the Baltic against the Russians, who, at this time, were re-laying mine-fields destroyed by the ice of winter.

The first part of the British forces to leave for this operation was the submarine division from Harwich for the Horn Reefs, at 3.30 p.m. on the 2nd of May, followed by the submarines from Blyth at 8 p.m. By this time directional wireless had made it clear that seven or eight Zeppelins were approaching the north of England or the south of Scotland. The naval commands concerned had been informed, and Admirals Jellicoe and Beatty had been warned to have their ships at two hours' notice until required to sail for the Tondern operation in case any Zeppelin should be damaged and the enemy should send out ships to the rescue.

When the Zeppelins were a hundred miles or so off the Firth of Forth adverse winds were encountered and, except the *L.14* and *L.20*, the airships turned off to attack alternative objectives in the Midlands. The *L.11* (Korvettenkapitän Victor Schütze), after being fired at by patrol ships east of St. Abbs Head, crossed the coast of Northumberland at Holy Island and passed out to sea again at Amble. Only two bombs came from her and they did no harm. She seems to have been blinded by snow, and her commander, after vainly searching for objectives, went home again, carrying away the main load of his bombs as he had brought them. The five remaining Zeppelins which had turned away from Scotland cruised over Yorkshire. Their commanders claimed on their return that they had bombed blast furnaces, factories, and other important objectives at Blyth, Shields, Stockton, Middlesbrough, and Hartlepool, but none of these places was attacked, and it is clear from the airship reports that, in the snow-squalls and clouds, the Zeppelin commanders experienced great difficulties of navigation.

The L.23 (Kapitänleutnant von Schubert) dropped her first incendiary bomb on Danby High Moor and set the heather on fire. She afterwards saw 'a blast furnace near Shields' (actually the Skinningrove Iron Works) and dropped eleven bombs which partly wrecked a storehouse and dwelling-houses but inflicted no casualties. She was illuminated by searchlight, and fire was opened on her by the 6-inch railway gun at Brotton, and she was erroneously believed to have been hit, but she passed on her way to Easington (six bombs, which wrecked a dwelling-house and injured a child) and then went out to sea without dropping any further bombs.

The heather on Danby High Moor was blazing extensively when the *L.16* (Oberleutnant Peterson) appeared in the neighbourhood. Peterson at once bore down on the conflagration and dropped a large number of bombs on the wastes of the moors. He thought he caused 'great damage to buildings and railway tracks'. Further bombs from this Zeppelin fell at Lealholm (5) and Moorsholm (5). The only effect was damage to a farm building.

The Danby fire was now burning stronger than ever and diverted yet another attack. The *L.17* (Kapitänleutnant Ehrlich) had come in at Saltburn and had made straight for Skinningrove. She dropped thirteen high-explosive and four incendiary bombs on Carlin How, which wrecked six dwelling-houses and damaged others, but caused no casualties, and then turned inland over the moors, where she was soon attracted by the Danby fire, to which she also contributed an unknown number of high-explosive bombs. She then went off, passing out to sea north of Whitby.

The *L.13* (Kapitänleutnant der Reserve Prölsz) hoped to make Leeds, but her commander, caught in blinding snowstorms, could not fix his position and he soon abandoned the Leeds attack. He dropped a large number of bombs on a town which he thought was Hartlepool, but as he was over the Danby Moor area when the heather was blazing, it is possible that he added yet another load of bombs to the fire. Only two bombs from this ship were definitely traced elsewhere, and these fell at Fridaythorpe and Seamer.

The *L.21* (Kapitänleutnant der Reserve Max Dietrich) penetrated farthest inland of this group of airships. She came in north of Scarborough and steered a direct course for York, over which she appeared about 10.40 p.m. Eighteen of her bombs had already exploded on Dringhouses, where they shattered glass and slightly wounded an officer and a soldier on duty. In a ten-minute attack on York, sixteen bombs fell along a line across the southern and eastern part of the city. They destroyed eighteen dwelling-houses and considerably damaged many others, killed nine people and injured twenty-seven. Dietrich reported, on his return, that he had bombed 'the industrial area of Middlesbrough and Stockton'.

Of the two airship commanders who had held to their main objective, Böcker, in the *L.14,* thought he had got through to the Forth area. He saw what appeared to be two warships, and he aimed five bombs at them at 11.30 p.m., but although he searched the Edinburgh area in the snow, he did not find the Forth Bridge or any other target, and he eventually turned for home without dropping any more bombs. He did not find the Forth Bridge because he was searching the wrong estuary. He was, in fact, over the Tay and the 'warships' he had seen were either fishing-vessels or lights ashore. Some of his bombs fell in a field near Arbroath.

The commander of the *L.20*, Kapitänleutnant Stabbert, found navigation even more difficult. He crossed the land at Redcastle, Lunan Bay, and steered straight across Forfarshire. He ran into snow and fog and sent out repeated wireless calls asking to be informed of his bearings, but none of his calls reached the German wireless stations. Soon after midnight, Stabbert got a glimpse of land below him (he was at this time near Loch Ness), and he then turned south and, later, east. He was now far beyond the area to which lighting restrictions applied, and, on his way to the coast, he passed across Craig Castle, which was lit up. Six bombs were promptly dropped here, falling within forty feet of the house, the windows and roof of which were damaged. There were no casualties. Eight more bombs were dropped in fields as the Zeppelin passed on her way to the sea, which she reached near Peterhead at 2.40 a.m.

At 5.0 a.m. the *L.20* was sighted by a trawler about ninety-five miles due east of Aberdeen. Her journey to the Caledonian Canal had taken her beyond the limit of her radius of action, and by this time her commander realised he had insufficient petrol to make Germany and he therefore headed for the nearest land, the Norwegian coast. He eventually made a rough landing south of Stavanger, at 10.0 a.m., where the destruction of the *L.20*, already considerably damaged, was completed by her crew.

The other Zeppelins which had taken part in the raid returned, thickly coated with ice, to their sheds, but they had had a hazardous journey. In particular the *L.11, L.14, L.17*, and *L.21* were handicapped by a novel form of damage. Ice which formed on the stays and bracings was shaken loose by the air-screws and shot through the gas-bags immediately behind the engines. These gas-bags, which became riddled with holes, gradually emptied, and the airship commanders reported by wireless that it was doubtful whether they could reach Germany. Naval forces were thereupon sent out to be ready to help them, but at 9.0 a.m., more reassuring reports from the commanders made it clear that the airships would reach port, and the surface ships were then recalled.

One other airship, a military one, was reported off the Lincolnshire coast during this attack, but she never came over land. (This was the *L.Z.98* (Oberleutnant Lehmann). Her objective was Manchester, but her commander gave up the attack as the weather proved unfavourable.)

Three months passed without any further attempted raids by the airships. This was because the nights were neither dark enough nor long enough to allow the Zeppelins to approach, attack, and get away without running considerable risks from pursuing aircraft. Furthermore, German naval activity, which was to culminate in the battle of

Jutland, made the risk of using Zeppelins for raiding unacceptable.

Airship activity was resumed on the 28th of July, and between that date and the end of August six raids took place, five of them by naval Zeppelins.

Ten Zeppelins left North Germany on the 28th of July 1916, but only six (*L.11, L.13, L.16, L.17, L.24*, and *L.31*) crossed our coasts. The *L.31* was the newest ship, a so-called super-Zeppelin. The six airships pushed only a little way inland into Yorkshire, Lincolnshire, Norfolk, and Suffolk. Fog at sea and a thick ground mist inland effectively defeated the raid. We counted sixty-nine bombs from the attackers, but they did no damage beyond breaking glass, burning a straw-stack, and killing or wounding cattle. Only one ship, the *L.13* (Kapitänleutnant Prölsz), penetrated much beyond the coastal area. She came in at North Somercotes at 12.37 a. m. on the 29th of July and steered a direct course for Lincoln. Two bombs were dropped at Fiskerton, east of Lincoln, and the *L.13* then continued towards Nottingham, but, east of Newark, turned south and circled while her bombs dropped on villages south-east of that place. She then went out direct over the Wash and was heard to drop a final bomb somewhere out to sea off Cromer Lighthouse. (The majority of bombs from the *L.13* fell near the railway. Her commander, in his report, says he was attracted by lighted trains.)

The aircraft-carrier *Vindex* had been ordered to go out, but she was kept in harbour by the thick fog. Next day general orders were issued to the *Vindex*. She was to be at one hour's notice from 8.0 p.m. to daylight to proceed with four destroyers to a position about fifteen miles off Southwold, to be ready to attack, with her Bristol Scouts, Zeppelins on their way home.

On the night of the 30th/31st of July reports were received from a number of observers that two Zeppelins had been seen near Wells-next-the-Sea. There had, however, been no indication of an impending raid, nor did any attack take place. Aeroplanes went up from Bacton, Holt, Killingholme, Yarmouth, Felixstowe, and Covehithe to search for the enemy, and at 5.15 a.m. on the 31st of July, Flight Sub-Lieutenant J. E. Northrop, in a B.E.2c, found an airship, thirty miles east of Covehithe. He attacked her with his Lewis-gun and was firing off his third drum of bullets when the drum came off the gun and hit him in the face. When the pilot recovered control, the airship had disappeared.

On the same day, the 31st of July, ten naval Zeppelins set out across the North Sea for England. They were the *L.11, L.13, L.14, L.16, L.17, L.21, L.22, L.23, L.30, and L.31.* Two of the raiders (*L.21* and *L.30*) turned back before they reached the coast. Four of the remaining ships were sighted on their inward journey by the trawler *Adelaide*, at 8.30 p.m., about fifty miles off the Humber, and one of them, the *L.11*, went close to the trawler, but did not attack her. Of the eight airships which came over land, the *L.16* raided Lincolnshire and the eastern part of Nottinghamshire, the *L.11, L.13, L.14, L.17, L.22*, and *L.23* attacked Norfolk, Suffolk, and the Isle of Ely, and the *L.31* raided East Kent. (The *L.11*, later, had engine trouble. One member of the crew, overcome by gas fumes, fell overboard near Texel on the way home and was drowned.)

The weather conditions were unfavourable and the attack was ineffective. An uncertain number of bombs fell in the sea. Of those which fell on land fifty-seven high-explosive and forty-six incendiaries were traced, and they inflicted no casualties and did no damage beyond the breaking of windows and telegraph wires. The commander of the *L.31* (Mathy), who flew along the coast of Kent and dropped his bombs off Ramsgate and Sandwich, was under the impression that his attack was made on London. (Mathy flew high—13,000 feet—and encountered strong and variable winds. He was surprised to find himself, on his return, over Holland.)

The airship commanders avoided the areas where anti-aircraft guns were located. Many pilots went up, but they were impeded by the mist and returned with nothing to report. The *Vindex* had gone out with her destroyer escort on Zeppelin patrol, but she too saw nothing and returned next day.

Another raid followed quickly. Three Zeppelins were reported over the Bight of Heligoland in the afternoon of the 1st of August, and two of them, in the evening, headed west, but although they approached the East Coast, they did not come over land. The *Vindex* had sailed from Harwich on the look-out for them but saw nothing. She returned next day, the 2nd of August, and was sent off again at 3 p.m., this time with the *Conquest* as well as her four escorting destroyers, with orders to go farther out, about fifty miles east of Lowestoft. Her departure was timely, for six Zeppelins rose that afternoon and made for England. The Admiralty warning went out at 6.40 p.m. to the Rear-Admiral, East Coast, and to the Commodores at Harwich and Lowestoft. Ten minutes before this warning was sent, the *Conquest*, which had reached a point, forty miles east of Lowestoft, sighted a

Zeppelin ahead. She increased to full speed and, at long range, got off twenty rounds of 6-inch and 4-inch shrapnel, in face of which the airship turned and disappeared to the southward, apparently not hit.

Meanwhile the *Vindex*, some distance off to the eastward, was also making full speed in pursuit of another Zeppelin, but the airship soon out-distanced the carrier. At 6.52 p.m. Flight Lieutenant C. T. Freeman left the *Vindex* in a Bristol Scout to make a search, and it was not long before he sighted two more incoming airships. He made three attacks, determined but unsuccessful, on one of them (the *L.17*) before he was forced to alight on the water, whence he was rescued by a Belgian ship and taken to Holland. (See Vol. 2.) While Flight Lieutenant Freeman was delivering his attacks, two other Zeppelins were being engaged by the *Conquest*. They were both heavily fired on and went back the way they had come and disappeared from sight.

Ultimately all six Zeppelins crossed the East Coast in the following order from north to south: *L.21, L.13, L.16*, and *L.17* (attacked Norfolk and Suffolk); *L.11* (attacked Suffolk); and *L.31* (attacked south-east Kent). Of these, the *L.21* (Hauptmann Stelling) penetrated farthest inland. She came in at Wells-next-the-Sea at 11.55 p.m. and flew straight to Thetford, where, attracted by aerodrome flares, five high-explosive bombs were dropped which did no damage. She then changed her course east and made for the sea. Four more of her bombs fell at Covehithe and eight in the water close by, but again they had no effect. The three other airships of this group operated in a more restricted area. Eighty-seven bombs came from them, mostly aimed at Norfolk villages, but the only results were cottages damaged and cattle killed. Two of these airships passed close to Norwich, but the town escaped attack. (One of these airships, the *L.17,* was hit by shell fire and made a slow return. Four gas cells showed 127 holes.)

The commander of the *L.11* (Korvettenkapitän Victor Schütze) made a bolder, but equally unsuccessful, attempt on Harwich, over the defences of which he circled, under fire, for twenty minutes. His bombs, of which no more than thirteen were traced, fell over the county border, in Suffolk, the nearest to Harwich being on the parade ground at Landguard Fort. One bomb injured a boy at Kirton—the only human casualty of the night's raid—and others on the same place damaged six cottages.

The *L.31* (Kapitänleutnant Mathy), the newest Zeppelin, crossed Deal at 1 a.m. and thereafter circled along and off the Kentish coast, slipping out to sea each time she came under gunfire. None of her bombs fell on land, but a number were heard exploding in the sea off Dover.

******

> Mathy, who again flew high (13,000 feet), was once more the victim of variable meteorological conditions. He could see little, but believed he was attacking London from west to east.

******

Many pilots went up in search of the Zeppelins; one of them, from Yarmouth, came up with a Zeppelin over Burgh Castle and emptied three drums of ammunition into her without result, and another, also from Yarmouth, found and pursued a Zeppelin, but lost her in the clouds. The latter officer eventually came down on the sea off Cromer and was picked up by a steamer.

A few days passed without any further alarms. Then, on the 8th of August, about 6.30 p.m., we began to intercept the usual informative wireless messages. The Commodore, Harwich, was warned to send out Zeppelin patrols at his discretion, and the Commodore, Lowestoft, was ordered to send out the paddle seaplane-carrier *Brocklesby*. Later in the evening, when further intelligence was received, there were indications of an enemy plan to attack ships attempting to intercept the Zeppelins, and the *Brocklesby* was recalled.

Eleven Zeppelins started, but only nine reached the coasts. The weather conditions favoured a northerly raid, and, except the *L.16*, which flew over the north-west coast of Norfolk, all the ships came in between Berwick and the Humber. The most northerly, the *L.14* (Hauptmann Manger), which entered south of Berwick, made a sweep inland and went out again at Alnmouth. Her bombs, of which eight were traced, fell in fields. Along the coast from Tynemouth to Whitby six Zeppelins (*L.11, L.13, L.21, L.22, L.30*, and *L.31*) operated, but they penetrated only a slight distance inland. Seventy-six bombs came from them on land, and an unknown number in the sea, and for these the total of the material damage was a house and an office wrecked. The casualties were five people injured at Whitley Bay. Only two antiaircraft guns were in action against this northerly group, one at Hunley Hall, Saltburn (6-inch, four rounds) and one at Whitley Bay (3-inch, four rounds). The Whitley Bay gunners claimed a hit with their second round, but, in fact, no Zeppelin was damaged by gun-fire.

The attack by the *L.24* (Kapitänleutnant Robert Koch) on Hull was more serious in its effects. Forty-four bombs fell on the town and killed ten people and injured eleven; a number of houses and shops were destroyed. Patches of ground mist effectively blinded the Hull anti-aircraft gunners, and only eight rounds were fired. Hull, indeed, was the chief sufferer of the raid, for the bombs (thirty-five) of the ninth Zeppelin, *L. 16*, on villages south of the Wash, were ineffective.

The ground mist which hampered the anti-aircraft defenders, also prevented aeroplanes from going up except at Redcar, whence Flight Lieutenant B. P. H. de Roeper took off, in a B.E.2c, soon after midnight. He found a Zeppelin over Saltburn caught in the beams of a searchlight, but he could not get to her height. He pursued her out to sea, dropping his bombs in the water to get more height, but he failed to get near enough to attack, and finally lost the Zeppelin in the mist twenty miles from the coast.

The two airships which approached England but never came over land, the *L. 17* and *L. 23*, were engaged by the armed trawler *Itonian* (one six-pounder). The *L. 17* was first attacked by the trawler off Whitby and replied with all her bombs aimed at her assailant and at the fishing fleet off the Tyne. They made no hits and the *L. 17* turned and went home. The *L. 23* was also attacked by the *Itonian* later off Scarborough, and she went off without dropping any bombs. The yacht *Miranda II* engaged the *L. 21* off Skinningrove with her three-pounder, but without success. Three bombs were aimed at the *Miranda*, one exploding four hundred yards from the vessel.

The damage done at Hull and the comparative impunity with which the Zeppelins flew, once again led to many protests. At an Air Board meeting a week after the raid it was hinted that the seaplane-carriers were not doing all they might to intercept Zeppelins, and that the plea of risk from submarines would not satisfy public opinion. The report of the meeting called forth some incisive comments in the Admiralty. These emphasized that the army was responsible for defence against aircraft attack and that the seaplane-carriers were intended to act as eyes of the fleet. Fleet requirements, they said, could not give way to helping the military to do their work. An Admiralty report showed that on the 8th of August 1916 no fewer than 114 vessels, armed with high-angle guns, were along the East Coast from the Forth to Dover, ready and able to fire at Zeppelins.

The next attack was made by a military Zeppelin, the *L. Z. 97* from Belgium, on the night of the 23rd/24th of August. She dropped thirty-four bombs in open fields near Trimley, Walton, and Old Felixstowe, and as she was never seen during her overland journey, no action could be taken against her. When the Zeppelin had been first reported off the coast, the *Undaunted* and four destroyers had put to sea, but although the engines of the airship were heard from the ships she was not seen and no seaplanes were sent up.

We had early warning of the next attack, made on the night of the 24th/25th of August. By wireless interception on the 24th, twelve airships were located in the North Sea, and at 3 p.m. the East Coast naval commands were warned. The *Brocklesby* with her seaplanes was ordered out from Lowestoft, and from Harwich went the *Conquest* with four destroyers at 5 p.m., followed by the *Carysfort* and the *Canterbury* and a division of the 10th Flotilla at 7 p.m. The *Vindex* remained in harbour. At 6.43 p.m. the *Conquest* was informed of the positions of two incoming Zeppelins, as indicated by directional wireless, and she steered at once towards them. She came upon one of them, at 7.24 p.m., thirty miles east of Orfordness and, in unfavourable light, got off two rounds from her 6-inch gun before the airship disappeared.

At 9.45 p.m. the *Conquest* sighted another Zeppelin and opened fire with her 3-inch gun, following which the airship dropped half a dozen bombs in the water and made off hastily. She was the *L.13*, and she had received a hit, for she reported by wireless that she had been fired at and damaged and asked for destroyers to help her. (The *L.13* had a narrow escape. A shell went through her and exploded above her back. With gas escaping from two compartments, she made a slow and cautious journey to her base.)

Before 10 p.m. six of the raiders had turned back, four on account of the weather and the other two possibly as a result of the attack by the *Conquest*. Of the remaining six, no more than four came over land, but one of these, the *L.31* (Kapitänleutnant Mathy), raided the London area, and was the first airship to do so since October of the previous year. The *L.31* had crossed Belgium in company with the *L.32* (Oberleutnant Peterson with Korvettenkapitän Strasser on board), another super-Zeppelin. While, however, the *L.31* made a direct dash for London, the *L.32*, apparently delayed by strong winds, got no farther than the Kentish coast.

Eventually she was driven out to sea by the combined fire of the Dover defences and by an aeroplane attack, and she dropped her bombs in the sea off Dover and Deal. The aeroplane attack was made by Captain J. W. Woodhouse, who went up from No. 50 Squadron at Dover and came up with the airship at the moment when she was caught in the Dover searchlights. The *L.32* turned away over the Channel with Captain Woodhouse in pursuit. After a while he lost her in the clouds, but he found her again and fired into her from below, without effect. He was changing his drum when the airship vanished from his view and could not again be found.

Mathy, in the *L.31,* met with favourable conditions for his attack on London. He flew up the Thames Estuary to Canvey Island and then overland to Barking whence he turned south to Millwall. There his first bombs were dropped. Others followed on Deptford, Greenwich, Blackheath, Eltham, and Plumstead. A great number of houses were destroyed or damaged and nine persons were killed and forty injured. In all eight incendiary and thirty-six high-explosive bombs fell in these crowded residential areas; a house, on which a heavy bomb weighing 660 lb. made a direct hit, disappeared with its occupants.

For a long time, the searchlights failed to pick up the *L.31* through the clouds and mist, and she was unmolested by the guns of the London defences until after she had bombed Eltham at 1.35 a.m. Then she was found by the Erith lights and 120 rounds were fired at her. She turned quickly north across the river, disappeared into a cloud-bank in the direction of Rainham, and eventually went out to sea east of Shoeburyness, where she was again protected from the defences by the clouds. (On the homeward journey, strong rain made the *L.31* heavy and she made a hard landing at her base. One of her gondolas had to be replaced.)

The two remaining ships did nothing of note. One, the *L.16*, flying high above the clouds, got nearly to Ipswich, but dropped her twenty bombs between Woodbridge and Bealings, without effect. The other, the *L.21*, seems to have dropped some of her bombs in the sea off Felixstowe, before she came overland at Frinton. Her bombs on land fell in the area of Great Oakley and Pewit Island and narrowly missed the works of the Explosive and Chemical Products Company. Their only effect was to do slight damage to farm buildings.

Fifteen pilots went up during this raid, but they were hampered by the poor visibility in the air, and although some of them caught momentary glimpses of the Zeppelins, Captain Woodhouse alone got near enough to attack.

Meanwhile, there was activity at sea. The *L.13*, it will be recalled, had turned back from the raid, damaged by gunfire. To assist her and any other Zeppelins which might need help, all available German submarines were ordered to proceed on a westerly course, and, in addition, destroyers were specially ordered out in the direction of the *L.13*. There came indications, also, that the German 1st Scouting Group was moving, and counter-orders thereupon went out to the commodore, Harwich. Nothing, however, came of these various movements, and the Harwich Squadrons eventually returned without incident.

Eight Zeppelins set out again on the 29th of August, but they encountered heavy thunder-storms and were recalled.

The Defeat of the Zeppelin

The next effort was the most ambitious we had yet been called upon to face. The comparative ease with which Mathy had attacked London on the night of the 24th/25th of August possibly induced the German command to make their biggest demonstration against the capital. In the afternoon of the 2nd of September, sixteen airships, twelve naval and four military, set out for a combined raid with the city of London as the sole objective. Their departure was known at the Admiralty about 5 p.m., and the usual warning went out to the East Coast.

Of the great load of bombs carried by the airships, 261 high-explosives and 202 incendiaries were destined to fall on English soil, but not one of them on the city of London. And the casualties for this load of about sixteen tons, were four killed and twelve injured, while the material damage was negligible.

The ineffectiveness of the raid was due in part to unfavourable weather conditions, but chiefly to the moral effect produced by the first night-flying victory for the defence aeroplanes, achieved against the only one of the four military airships which we definitely identified. (*L.Z.90, L.Z.97, L.Z.98*, and *S.L.11.*) This was the Schütte-Lanz, *S.L.11* (Hauptmann Schramm), which came in unheralded from Belgium, at Foulness Point, about 10.40 p.m. and made a wide sweep over Essex and Hertford to approach London from the north-west. She was over St. Albans at 1.10 a.m. and ten minutes later dropped her first bombs—three high-explosive and three incendiaries—on London Colney, where they exploded without doing damage.

Other bombs followed on North Mimms (four), Littleheath (three), Northaw (one), Gordon Hill (three), Clayhill (nine), Cockfosters (three), and Hadley Wood (two). From Hadley Wood the airship passed on to Southgate (three bombs) and thence to Wood Green, where she was picked up by the Finsbury Park and Victoria Park searchlights. From now onwards she was well illuminated by the lights and suffered heavy anti-aircraft fire, which turned her off towards Edmonton (six bombs, two of which fell in Messrs. Eley's Explosive

Works), and thence on to Ponders End (two bombs). The next bombs, six high-explosive, fell along Enfield Highway, and the last, twelve high-explosive, on Forty Hill and Turkey Street. Not one of the sixty bombs which came from the *S.L.11* caused casualties, and the damage was confined to houses and to water-mains.

During the time the bombs were being dropped the gun-fire directed against the airship did not cease, but although many of the shells exploded near, none actually hit the ship. On the approach of the raider, aeroplanes had gone up from the three detached Flights of No. 39 Home Defence Squadron at Hainault Farm, Suttons Farm, and North Weald Bassett. Each Flight sent up single aeroplanes at two hours' interval, the first pilots leaving their aerodromes about 11 p.m. Lieutenant Leefe Robinson from Suttons Farm was to patrol the line Suttons Farm-Joyce Green; Second Lieutenant C. S. Ross, from North Weald Bassett, had the line North Weald-Hainault; and Second Lieutenant A. de B. Brandon, from Hainault, the line Hainault-Suttons Farm. The second set of patrols, for which the pilots ascended about 1 a.m., was slightly different. Second Lieutenants F. Sowrey and B. H. Hunt were given the line Joyce Green-Farningham, and Second Lieutenant J. I. Mackay, the line North Weald-Joyce Green.

Three of these officers, Lieutenants Leefe Robinson, Mackay, and Hunt, sighted and pursued the *S.L.11.* It is difficult to see how the airship could have escaped. Lieutenant Leefe Robinson came up with her first, when she was between Enfield Highway and Turkey Street. Shells at this time were bursting round her, but Leefe Robinson went straight in to attack. This is his report of his adventures, which included an earlier attempt to engage an unidentified military airship (the *L.Z.98*), that made an abortive attack in the neighbourhood of Gravesend:

> I have the honour to make the following report on Night Patrol made by me on the night of the 2nd/3rd instant. I went up at about 11.8 p.m. on the night of the 2nd with instructions to patrol between Suttons Farm and Joyce Green. I climbed to 10,000 feet in 53 minutes. I counted what I thought were ten sets of flares—there were a few clouds below me but on the whole, it was a beautifully clear night. I saw nothing till 1.10 a.m. when two searchlights picked up a Zeppelin about SE. of Woolwich. The clouds had collected in this quarter, and the searchlights had some difficulty in keeping on the aircraft. By

> this time, I had managed to climb to 12,900 feet, and I made in the direction of the Zeppelin which was being fired on by a few anti-aircraft guns—hoping to cut it off on its way eastward. I very slowly gained on it for about ten minutes—I judged it to be about 800 feet below me, and I sacrificed my speed in order to keep the height. It went behind some clouds, avoided the searchlights, and I lost sight of it.
>
> After 15 minutes' fruitless search I returned to my patrol. I managed to pick up and distinguish my flares again. At about 1.50 a.m. I noticed a red glow in NE. London. Taking it to be an outbreak of fire I went in that direction. At 2.5 a.m. a Zeppelin was picked up by the searchlights over NNE. London (as far as I could judge). Remembering my last failure, I sacrificed height (I was still 12,900 feet) for speed and made nose down in the direction of the Zeppelin. I saw shells bursting and night tracer shells flying around it.
>
> When I drew closer I noticed that the anti-aircraft aim was too high or too low; also, a good many, some 800 feet behind—a few tracers went right over. I could hear the bursts when about 3,000 feet from the Zeppelin. I flew about 800 feet below it from bow to stern and distributed one drum along it (alternate New Brock and Pomeroy). It seemed to have no effect; I therefore moved to one side and gave it another drum distributed along its side—without apparent effect. I then got behind it (by this time I was very close—500 feet or less below) and concentrated one drum on one part (underneath rear). I was then at a height of 11,500 feet when attacking Zeppelin.
>
> I hardly finished the drum before I saw the part fired at glow. In a few seconds the whole rear part was blazing. When the third drum was fired there were no searchlights on the Zeppelin and no anti-aircraft was firing. I quickly got out of the way of the falling blazing Zeppelin and being very excited fired off a few red Very's lights and dropped a parachute flare. Having very little oil and petrol left, I returned to Suttons Farm, landing at 2.45 a.m. On landing I found I had shot away the machine-gun wire guard, the rear part of the centre section, and had pierced the rear main spar several times.

The *S.L. 11* fell at Cuffley: she was a wooden ship and burned for nearly two hours on the ground. (Lieutenant William Leefe Robinson was awarded the Victoria Cross. He continued to serve at home until March 1917, when he returned to France as a Flight Commander with No. 48 Squadron.) The destruction of this military Schütte-Lanz, the first airship brought down on British soil, was the beginning of the end of the airship menace. Its immediate effect was to kill the attempted great raid on the city of London. The *S.L.11* had tested the defences, and the crews of many of the other airships were witnesses of her fate. The heart went out of them, as well it might, and their bombs seemed to us to be dropped indiscriminately, not to destroy, but to lighten the ships and so give them greater height and performance.

★★★★★★

> A military airship, the *L.Z.90*, lowered an observation car which broke away and fell near Mistley in Essex. The car, fourteen feet in length and of stream-line form, is made of light sheet aluminium. It contained a mattress on which an observer could lie full length to carry out observations through celluloid windows. He communicated with the ship above him by telephone. There is no reason to suppose that, on this occasion, an observer was in the car when it fell. The car is housed in the Science Museum, Kensington, London.

★★★★★★

Whatever the views of the German High Command might be about the failure of the Zeppelin as a raiding weapon, it was not to be expected that the attacks would be lightly given up.

The next raid, however, was to demonstrate that Lieutenant Leefe Robinson's victory was not fortuitous. On the afternoon of the 23rd of September, eleven Zeppelins set out for England, but on this occasion only the super-Zeppelins, the *L.31, L.32*, and *L.33*, the last-named on her maiden voyage, approached the London area. Of the eleven ships, nine came over land, two of them, the *L.31* and *L.32*, making their approach to London from across Belgium. The other London raider, the *L.33*, came in over the Crouch. The commander of the last-named ship, Kapitänleutnant Böcker, steered a direct course, dropping a few bombs on the way, and appeared over the outskirts of London about midnight. He came in across Wanstead and West Ham and began to drop his bombs on Bromley-by-Bow, on Bow itself, and on Stratford, under a fierce bombardment by the anti-aircraft defences. The airship seemed, to the gunners, to receive a direct hit, but there was no immediate effect. Twenty-seven bombs on East London were accounted for, and they did considerable damage to houses and factory premises and killed eleven people and injured twenty-six.

The anti-aircraft gunners were not deceived. During the bombardment to which the *L.33* was subjected over East London, one shell passed through her body, another damaged a propeller, and shell splinters punctured her gas-bags. Losing gas, she tried to make for home. Near Chelmsford she was met by Second Lieutenant A. de B. Brandon, who, for twenty minutes, kept up a running attack, firing at every favourable opportunity, but, although he saw his shots streaming into her body she failed to catch fire. Eventually the Zeppelin crossed the coast at West Mersea, but her commander soon realised he had no hope of getting his ship home, and he turned back and landed in a field between Little Wigborough and Peldon. There the *L.33* caught fire, but she had lost so much gas that the fire burnt itself out without doing any appreciable damage to the structure. The latest type of Zeppelin thus fell into our hands to form the basis for the design of the British *R.33* class. (See Vol. 2.)

The two remaining London raiders had come in together at Dungeness. Mathy, in the *L.31*, made a bold flight to London direct, but his companion, Peterson, in the *L.32*, seems to have had trouble soon after making his landfall. He hovered about for some time before he finally turned off towards Tunbridge Wells, over which he appeared at 12.10 a.m. Thence he turned north and at 12.50 a.m. aimed seven bombs, without damage, at the Crockenhill searchlight which had opened on him. He now made for the Thames, which he crossed east of Purfleet. South of the Thames, mist had shrouded the *L.32* from the defences, but north of the river the airship flew into clear air and was at once illuminated by many lights. Fire was opened and at least two hits were claimed.

The majority of the remaining bombs from the *L.32* (twenty-three high-explosive and twenty-one incendiary) were dropped in a line between Aveley and South Ockendon where they shattered windows. Peterson was escaping, as quickly as he could, from the ring of anti-aircraft fire, but he was, unaware, running into another danger. Second Lieutenant F. Sowrey, who was on his patrol line from Joyce Green to Suttons Farm, caught sight of the *L.32* just as her last bombs were bursting, and he made for her direct, opening his attack about 1.10 a.m. To another patrolling pilot in the distance, it appeared that the Zeppelin was 'being hosed with a stream of fire', and it was not long before she met her fate. Here is Second-Lieutenant Sowrey's report of his patrol, which included an earlier, but unsuccessful, attempt to catch up with the *L.33*:

> I have the honour to report the following on my action during the night of 23rd/24th September, 1916. At 11.25 p.m. I received orders to patrol between Suttons Farm and Joyce Green and at 11.30 p.m. I left the aerodrome. The weather was clear with a few thin clouds at 3,000 feet. At 4,000 feet I passed another machine proceeding in a northerly direction. I was then flying due south. I continued climbing as hard as possible and at 12.10 a.m. I noticed an enemy airship in a southerly direction. It appeared to be over Woolwich. I made for the airship at once, but before I could reach it, the searchlights lost it. I was at this time at 8,000 feet. There was a certain amount of gunfire but it was not intense.
>
> I continued climbing and reached a height of 13,000 feet. I was still patrolling between Suttons Farm and Joyce Green. At 12.45 a.m. I noticed an enemy airship in an easterly direction. I at once made in this direction and manoeuvred into a position underneath. The airship was well lighted by searchlights but there was not a sign of any gunfire. I could distinctly see the propellers revolving and the airship was manoeuvring to avoid the searchlight beams. I fired at it. The first two drums of ammunition had apparently no effect, but the third one caused the envelope to catch on fire in several places; in the centre and front. All firing was traversing fire along the envelope.
>
> The drums were loaded with a mixture of Brock, Pomeroy and Tracer ammunition. I watched the burning airship strike the ground and then proceeded to find my flares. I landed at Suttons Farm at 1.40 a.m. 24th instant. My machine was B.E.2c 4112. After seeing the Zeppelin had caught on fire, I fired a red Very's light.

The *L.32* fell at Snail's Hall Farm, Great Burstead, south of Billericay, where the wreckage burnt for forty-five minutes, many of the crew being charred beyond recognition. The descent of the flaming mass was seen from a British submarine in the Dover Straits.

Mathy, in the *L.31*, was rewarded for his bold handling of his ship. He dropped ten bombs near Dungeness, to lighten the ship, but he wasted no more bombs on his inland journey across Tunbridge Wells, Oxted, and Carshalton, and illuminating flares which he dropped on his approach to the Metropolis had the effect of blinding the searchlights so that he was little troubled by the south-eastern defences. He crossed London, swiftly and at a good height (estimated at 12,000 feet; Mathy, in his report, gives his height as 3,800 metres), and got clear away without injury. His bombs fell in Kenley (four), Mitcham (four), Streatham (thirty-two), Brixton (twenty-three), Kennington (one), and Lea Bridge Road and Leyton (ten).

Twenty-two people were killed and seventy-four injured, and the material damage, mostly to dwelling-houses, was large. Three of the high-explosive bombs which fell weighed 300 kg. (660 lb.) each. Mathy was helped on his flight across the northern defences of London by a mist which completely shrouded the airship from the gunners, and not a shot was fired at him. He went out to sea south of Yarmouth under heavy, but ineffective, fire from shore and fleet guns.

Of the five Zeppelins which came in between the Humber and the Wash (*L. 13, L. 14, L. 17, L. 22*, and *L. 23*), one only, the *L. 17* (Kapitänleutnant Kraushaar), penetrated an appreciable distance inland. She got to Nottingham (bombing North Muskham, Colwick, and Sneinton on the way) and began to attack the city, from a height estimated at 14,000 feet, at about 12.40 a.m. Eight high-explosive and eleven incendiary bombs fell in crowded areas and did much damage to property and killed three people and injured sixteen. There was mist in the Trent valley and the airship was not seen during her passage across the town. Another bomb followed on Mapperley, after which the airship went out again over the Humber, and further bombs from her were heard exploding at sea.

The remaining four of the northern Zeppelins were engaged by anti-aircraft guns, particularly over the Humber area, and dropped their bombs with little direction, many of them falling in the sea. Of those which exploded on land, one hundred and eighteen were accounted for and these were scattered over Lincolnshire. The only result other than broken glass was damage to a church, a farm building, and telegraph wires. A notable feature of this raid was the respect paid by the airship commanders to the anti-aircraft guns, a fact which saved important targets from attack. The *L. 13* bore down upon Sleaford, but when she was attacked by the guns, which had been placed well clear of the town, she dropped her bombs, mostly in open fields, and made off. A similar thing happened at Lincoln and at Stowmarket. As the *L. 14* approached Lincoln she was picked up by searchlights and then by the Canwick gun, and she dropped her cargo of forty-four bombs harmlessly in their neighbourhood and turned about. The *L.21* was held off Stowmarket by the anti-aircraft guns and she ultimately dropped her thirty-six bombs near Suffolk villages with no result.

Of the nine airships which came over land during this attack, two did not leave again, but the number might have been greater. Patrolling pilots from No. 39 Squadron were in the air ready to pounce upon the *L.31* as she made her way out of London, but the mist in the Lea valley, which kept the searchlights out of action, probably saved Mathy. The *L. 13*, which attempted the attack on Sleaford, was unsuccessfully engaged by a naval pilot from Cranwell aerodrome. Other naval pilots went up from Westgate, Eastchurch, Covehithe, Yarmouth, and Bacton. Two Yarmouth pilots had made attacks on Zeppelins as they approached the coasts.

Flight Lieutenant B. D. Kilner, in a Short seaplane, delivered one of these attacks, without result, forty-five miles east of Yarmouth, and he was, later, forced down on the water, where he was adrift all night. The second attack was made by Flight Lieutenant C. J. Galpin, who fired a drum of explosive ammunition into a Zeppelin near Lowestoft, but she did not catch fire and disappeared in the darkness. Flight Lieutenant E. Cadbury, from the Yarmouth air station, had not long returned from a flight, for lack of petrol, when a Zeppelin passed across the area which he had been patrolling. He went up again, but towards the end of his patrol, during which he saw no trace of the raiders, he was temporarily blinded by his goggles becoming displaced, and he dived into the sea. He was injured but was flying again within a week.

The bombardment of Nottingham once more stirred up the Midlands. The blame for the attack on the city was laid on the railways, which, it was stated, failed to extinguish lights and also ran lighted trains. The city authorities demanded that measures should be taken to ensure the extinction of railway lights and the stopping of all railway trains when air-raid action was ordered. The Mayor of Nottingham was joined in his demands by the mayors or representatives of a great number of cities and towns in the Midlands and Eastern Counties. The outcome was the reception, by Lord French, of a deputation consisting of representatives from twenty-five towns. The deputation was informed of the reply made by the Secretary of State for War to a similar deputation from Sheffield. This was to the effect that the War Office was resolutely opposed to anything in the nature of stopping railway traffic. It was essential not only to transport munitions, but to carry goods for the commerce of the country and food for the people, and the shutting down of the railways for hours would mean tremendous dislocation.

Although this might look a small thing in one place it might mean, in fact, the cessation of traffic all over the East Coast of England. This temporary paralysis of the business of the country would be exactly what the enemy was aiming at. The Mayor of Nottingham said, in reply, that the deputation could only accept the decision, but he feared the people would not look at the matter in the same light and that there might be trouble.

The Zeppelins came out again on the 25th of September and there were indications, also, of considerable High Sea Fleet activity. Eight Zeppelins set out, but the *L.13* turned back with engine trouble before she was half-way across and the *L.23* followed suit later. Bombs believed to come from the latter ship were heard a long way out to sea off Cromer. The *L.30* also was not seen to cross the coast. She was reported wandering up and down between Cromer and Yarmouth and a large number of heavy bombs from her were heard exploding at sea.

The actual raid comprised two distinct attacks. Four Zeppelins attacked Lincolnshire, Yorkshire, and Lancashire, while the remaining naval Zeppelin made a remarkable flight along the south coast of England. The most ambitious flight of the northern Zeppelins was made by the *L.21* (Oberleutnant Frankenberg). This airship came in at Sutton-on-Sea at 9.45 p.m. and passed over Lincoln and across the northern outskirts of Sheffield into the Peak district. She disappeared from observation for a time over the uninhabited moorland and was then picked up again, just before midnight, at Todmorden.

Her first bombs (two) fell near Newchurch, and others followed at irregular intervals on Rawtenstall (two), Ewood Bridge (seven), Holcombe (seven), Ramsbottom (two), Holcombe Brook (two), and on Bolton (nine high-explosive and eleven incendiary). Thirteen people were killed and ten injured at Bolton and a woman was killed at Holcombe, but the material damage, mostly to private houses, was slight. The ship dropped a final bomb, which did not explode, at Bolton Abbey on her way out. (Frankenberg thought his main attack was made not on Bolton, but on Derby. He says he found the town well lighted.)

An hour after the *L.21* had quietly skirted Sheffield on her way to the Bolton area, the *L.22* (Kapitänleutnant Martin Dietrich) appeared over the city. She had, just before, heralded her approach by dropping seven incendiary bombs, without doing damage, near Tinsley Park Colliery. The *L.22* passed direct across the great armament works at

Sheffield and marked her passage with fifteen high-explosive and fifteen incendiary bombs. By some good fortune no damage was done to any of the works with the minor exception that one incendiary bomb struck the machine shop at the Atlas Works of Messrs. John Brown & Co., causing a slight fire. Otherwise the damage was confined to small cottage property, with the result that twenty-eight people were killed and nineteen injured. There were considerable patches of mist in the Sheffield area, and the *L.22*, which flew at a great height, was not seen over the city. Two rounds were fired in the apparent direction of the airship by the three-inch gun at Shire Green, following which the Zeppelin dropped no more bombs in the Sheffield area. What she had left fell in the Humber off Immingham as she went out again under fire from the Humber defences.

The *L.14* made York, but after she had dropped nine bombs she was turned away from the city by the light and the gun at Acomb, and she then made a wide sweep, bombing intermittently on the way, with the apparent intention of approaching Leeds from the north. She turned east before she reached Leeds, and when she was picked up by the gun and light at Collingham, she promptly dropped her remaining bombs. None of her forty-three bombs caused casualties, and the sum total of the damage was a house wrecked in York and a cottage damaged in Collingham. The *L.16* was even less effective. She came inland, unseen, at a great height, but no more than three bombs from her were traced, and none of these, inflicted damage.

The flight along the south coast of England was made by Mathy in the *L.31* and is notable as being the only occasion on which a Zeppelin flew across the dockyard at Portsmouth. Mathy flew down the Channel and made Portsmouth from the direction of the Isle of Wight. He flew straight over the harbour and was illuminated by the searchlights. Fire was opened by the guns of the defences, but the shells burst well below the airship which was flying at an estimated height of 11,000 feet. From Portsmouth, Mathy turned east and passed out to sea near Hastings. No bomb came from his ship over land. About 2.30 a.m. he seems to have dropped three bombs in the sea off Dover before turning for home through Belgium.

It appeared at the time that the flight of the *L.31* was made for reconnaissance purposes, but the author of this history has been privileged to examine Mathy's official reports and these, throw new light on the episode. Mathy's original objective was London, but he had received orders, if the night proved clear, not to take undue risks

(*Zurückbaltung geboten sei*). When he came to Dungeness he judged the night to be too bright for an attack on London, so he diverted to Portsmouth. He was carrying four 300 kg., fifteen 100 kg., and fifteen 58 kg. high-explosive bombs, and thirty incendiary bombs. As he came over Portsmouth he was, he says, blinded by the searchlights and he could see no details of the town. He decided to drop his complete load of bombs and proceeded to do so in an intense two-minute attack, which was made, as he thought, on the centre of the town. What happened to these bombs is a mystery. They fell, presumably, in the sea.

A military airship was reported as far west as Pevensey half an hour later than the L.31, but no bombs came from her. There was other airship activity in and near the Dover Straits, but no other ships came over land, and it is possible that their activity was by way of demonstration in connexion with the German naval movements.

Seven naval and eight military pilots went up during this raid. One of them, from Calshot, sighted a Zeppelin but could not overtake her, and the others came down with nothing to report. Two aeroplanes were damaged, in the mist, on landing.

The fleet movements which had been set in motion, consequent on the raid, passed off without incident. The German torpedo flotillas had run down the Flanders Bight as far as the latitude of Lowestoft, but they saw nothing of the Zeppelins or of British craft, and they turned back to Terschelling, where they joined the 3rd Scouting Group about 4 a.m. and continued their journey home. At 8.5 a.m. the order went out on the British side for the resumption of normal conditions.

It was calm over the southern portion of the North Sea on the 1st of October, and Zeppelins once again set out to attack England. Of the eleven which started, no more than seven crossed the coasts; they were the *L.14, L.16, L.17, L.21, L.24, L.31*, and *L.34*, the last-named ship being the most recent addition to the naval airship fleet. Three other ships were heard in the vicinity of the coast, and one of them, the *L.22*, dropped bombs in the sea off Bacton when she came under fire from the gun at that place. (The *L.22, L.23*, and *L.30* had engine trouble and turned back. The *L.13* also turned back on account of unfavourable weather.) The *L.14, L.16,* and *L.21* raided Lincolnshire, and from these ships we counted fifty-eight bombs on land, which killed cattle, but caused no other damage or casualties. The *L.17* made a brief journey into Norfolk, where she dropped two bombs west of Norwich. She seems to have dropped a number of others in the sea, both on her inward and outward journeys.

The *L.34* (Kapitänleutnant Max Dietrich), the newest ship, achieved little. She pushed into Northamptonshire and, on being picked up by the Corby light and fired on by the gun, she dropped thirty bombs between Corby and Gretton, which fell in woods and open fields.

The handling of the two remaining ships was bolder. The *L.24* (Kapitänleutnant Robert Koch) came in west of Sheringham and steered a fairly direct course towards Cambridge with the evident intention of making London. Just before midnight a glare in the southern sky told her commander of the disaster which had overtaken one of his colleagues, but although his course afterwards showed hesitancy, he moved on west of Cambridge and was ultimately attracted by flares on a night-landing ground east of Hitchin, where he let fall all his bombs (twenty-eight high-explosive and twenty-six incendiary). They did no material damage, but a soldier of the Royal Defence Corps on duty on the landing-ground was killed. (The commander of *L.24* thought he attacked north-east London and specially mentions Stoke Newington and Hackney.)

The victim that night was Mathy, in the *L.31.* He came in north of Lowestoft about 8 p.m. and, with characteristic decision, steered an unswerving course towards London. At 9.45 p.m. he was at Kelvedon Hatch, where he was picked up by the searchlight. He was now approaching the eastern defences and he seems to have changed his mind about the direction of his attack, for he promptly turned off north-west. He had got almost to Buntingford at 10.30 p.m. before he decided to turn back again. He then made a wide sweep south of Hertford and Ware, and from the latter place steered south at high speed, with the evident intention of attacking London from the north. But he had not gone far before he came under heavy fire from the guns at Newmans and Temple House, and at this stage he abandoned hope of attacking London and got rid of his bombs on Cheshunt. Thirty high-explosive and twenty-six incendiary bombs fell in quick succession.

At least five of the explosive bombs each weighed 660 lb., all of which fell on the Recreation Ground, where they did no serious damage. But other bombs caused damage to three hundred and four dwelling-houses, and glass-houses covering an area of six and a half acres were demolished. The only casualty, however, was one woman injured. To escape from the gunfire, Mathy turned sharply to the west, and he must now have become aware of aeroplanes in his vicinity.

He did his utmost to shake off the searchlights and so win through to darkness and comparative safety, but he was relentlessly held. He dropped a final bomb at Potters Bar and then his end came.

Four pilots who were in the air from the aerodromes north and east of London had seen the *L.31* illuminated by the searchlights and had set off in pursuit. The first to come up with her was Second Lieutenant W. J. Tempest, who had left the North Weald aerodrome at 10 o'clock to patrol the line Hainault Farm-Joyce Green, he says:

> About 11.45 p.m., I found myself over SW. London at an altitude of 14,500 feet. There was a heavy ground fog on and it was bitterly cold, otherwise the night was beautiful and starlit at the altitude at which I was flying. I was gazing over towards the NE. of London, where the fog was not quite so heavy, when I noticed all the searchlights in that quarter concentrated in an enormous "pyramid". Following them up to the apex, I saw a small cigar-shaped object, which I at once recognised as a Zeppelin, about 15 miles away, and heading straight for London. Previous to this I had chased many imaginary Zepps only to find they were clouds on nearing them. At first, I drew near to my objective very rapidly (as I was on one side of London and it was the other and both heading for the centre of the town): all the time I was having an extremely unpleasant time, as to get to the Zepp I had to pass through a very inferno of bursting shells from the A.A. guns below. All at once, it appeared to me that the Zeppelin must have sighted me, for she dropped all her bombs in one volley, swung round, tilted up her nose and proceeded to race away northwards climbing rapidly as she went. At the time of dropping her bombs I judged her to be at an altitude of about 11,500 feet. I made after her at all speed at about 15,000 feet altitude, gradually overhauling her. At this period the A.A. fire was intense, and I, being about five miles behind the Zeppelin had an extremely uncomfortable time. At this point misfortune overtook me, for my mechanical pressure pump went wrong and I had to use my hand-pump to keep up the pressure in my petrol tank. This exercise at so high an altitude was very exhausting, besides occupying an arm, thus giving me "one hand less" to operate with when I commenced to fire.
>
> As I drew up with the Zeppelin, to my relief I found that I was

free from A.A. fire, for the nearest shells were bursting quite three miles away. The Zeppelin was now nearly 15,000 feet high and mounting rapidly. I therefore decided to dive at her, for though I held a slight advantage in speed, she was climbing like a rocket and leaving me standing. I accordingly gave a tremendous pump at my petrol tank, and dived straight at her, firing a burst straight into her as I came. I let her have another burst as I passed under her and then banking my machine over, sat under her tail, and flying along underneath her, pumped lead into her for all I was worth. I could see tracer bullets flying from her in all directions, but I was too close under her for her to concentrate on me.

As I was firing, I noticed her begin to go red inside like an enormous Chinese lantern and then a flame shot out of the front part of her and I realised she was on fire. She then shot up about 200 feet, paused, and came roaring down straight on to me before I had time to get out of the way. I nose-dived for all I was worth, with the Zepp tearing after me, and expected every minute to be engulfed in the flames. I put my machine into a spin and just managed to corkscrew out of the way as she shot past me, roaring like a furnace. I righted my machine and watched her hit the ground with a shower of sparks. I then proceeded to fire off dozens of green Very's lights in the exuberance of my feelings.

I glanced at my watch and saw it was about ten minutes past twelve. I then commenced to feel very sick and giddy and exhausted, and had considerable difficulty in finding my way to ground through the fog and landing, in doing which I crashed and cut my head on my machine-gun.

The wreckage of the *L.31* fell at Potters Bar. Such was the end of Heinrich Mathy, the greatest airship commander of the war. It is possible that, had he not turned off at Kelvedon Hatch, he would have survived. The first of the Flying Corps pilots to get away from the London aerodromes did not leave the ground until five minutes after the *L.31* altered her course. Had she kept on across London and out again to the south, there is small chance that the aeroplanes would have caught up with her. Mathy entered the German Navy in 1900. He was, before the war, twice attached for short periods to the airship service, but when war came he was in command of a torpedo boat.

He was transferred to airships in January 1915, and his subsequent record as a raiding pilot has been told in this history. Those who are minded to condemn the Zeppelin commanders for their attacks on this country may be referred to the words inscribed over the grave, in a Suffolk churchyard, of the crew of a later Zeppelin:

> Who art thou that judgest another man's servant. To his own master he standeth or falleth.

The loss of Mathy in the *L.31*, following close on the disasters to the *L.32* and *L.33*, was a severe blow to the German Airship Service. Germany, however, was loath to admit defeat and, eight weeks later, she made her final attack of the year. This time the well-defended south was left alone, but the precaution was of no avail. The event was to show that the defences elsewhere had now got the measure of the Zeppelin.

On the afternoon of the 27th of November ten airships left their sheds for the north of England. They were the L. *13, L. 14, L. 16, L. 21, L. 22, L. 24, L. 30, L. 34, L. 35,* and *L.36*, the two last-named, super-Zeppelins, out on their maiden voyage to England. The *L.30* turned back, with engine-trouble, half-way across the North Sea. The remainder made their approach in two groups. The first group, of five ships, came in between Scarborough and the Humber, and the second group, of four, diverged towards the Tyne area. The first of the latter group to cross was the *L.34* (Kapitänleutnant Max Dietrich) which came in over Black Halls Rocks at 11.30 p.m. and went inland over Castle Eden, where she was picked up by the Hutton Henry light. She dropped thirteen high-explosive bombs near the light without doing damage. At this point she was seen by Second Lieutenant I.V. Pyott, who was in the air on his second patrol from the aerodrome of No. 36 Squadron at Seaton Carew. This officer says in his report:

> I had been in the air for approximately an hour, when I sighted a Zeppelin between Sunderland and Hartlepool in the beam of a searchlight (Castle Eden) coming south and towards me. At this moment I was at 9,800 and the Zepp seemed a few hundred feet below me. I flew towards the Zepp and flew at right angles to and underneath him amidships, firing as I went under. I then turned sharp east, the Zepp turning east also. We then flew on a parallel course for about 5 miles, firing 71 rounds at the Zepp. I estimate his ground speed to be approximately 70 m.p.h. I was aiming at his port quarter and noticed first a small

> patch become incandescent where I had seen tracers entering his envelope. I first took it for a machine-gun firing at me from the Zepp, but this patch rapidly spread and the next thing was that the whole Zepp was in flames. I landed at 12 midnight, engine and machine O.K. The Zeppelin, which fell into the sea at the mouth of the Tees, was still burning when I landed.

Just before the Zeppelin caught fire she began dropping bombs on West Hartlepool. Sixteen high-explosives fell and did considerable damage to houses. Four people were killed and eleven injured.

The destruction of the *L.34* was seen from great distances. A pilot in the air above Melton Mowbray, one hundred and thirty-six miles away, saw the flaming airship falling. The disaster was witnessed also by the crews of the airships which had come in with the *L.34*. Only one of them, the *L.35*, had crossed the coast at the time and she turned without dropping any bombs. It was well for her she did, for had she persisted any farther, it is unlikely she could have evaded encounters with other aeroplane pilots who were patrolling in the vicinity. (Her commander reported that thick ice had formed on his ship, and that the valves were caked with it. He also reported seeing two aeroplanes.) The *L.36* was preparing to cross when the *L.34* went down in flames, and her commander thereupon dropped an unknown number of bombs in the sea and went home. (The commander of *L.36* stated that he gave up because the night was too light. He had engine trouble and dropped his bombs to trim the ship.) The *L.24* also turned back before she reached the coast and no bombs came from her. The destruction of the *L.34* had effectively killed the northern attack.

The southern group of airships penetrated farther inland, but their movements betrayed nervousness. The *L.14* (Hauptmann Manger) wandered about the East Riding of Yorkshire for an hour avoiding aeroplanes, searchlights, and guns, and when she was finally fired on, near Hull, she turned back and made for home. Her bombs (forty-four) were dropped at Mappleton in answer to fire from mobile guns at Cowden and did no damage. It was thought at the time that aeroplanes which had gone up from Elsham were seen by the crew of this ship and induced her commander to turn back, but his official report shows he had engine trouble.

The *L.22* was steering for the northern industrial Midlands when she was fired upon unexpectedly by the guns of the Howden area and, according to our observation, she turned back and went out again without dropping any bombs. She had, in fact, been hit, and only just managed to get home. When she was berthed in her shed it was found she had about 150 holes in her envelope caused by shrapnel. During part of her journey over land we followed the course of the *L.22* with some difficulty. She claimed attacks on New Malton and York. No incoming ship passed near the former town, but it is not impossible that the *L.22* followed close behind *L.13* (as her navigating officer has stated) and that some of the bombs which fell on Barmby Moor and York, attributed by us to the *L.13*, came from the *L.22*.

The *L.13*, after dropping twenty-four bombs in open fields on Barmby Moor, got as far as York, but there she was met by accurate anti-aircraft fire, and she quickly scattered her remaining bombs (two high-explosive and twenty-one incendiary) on the eastern outskirts of the city and retreated. Her bombs on York damaged houses and wounded two people.

The *L.16* ventured as far as Barnsley and Wakefield, but neither of these places was attacked. Her bombs, of which thirty-nine were traced, were mostly distributed over the West Riding of Yorkshire, where they did no damage and caused no casualties. On her return journey, the *L.16* was turned away from York by the Acomb gun, and she dropped her remaining bombs, ineffectively, in the East Riding. She was again heavily fired at as she went out south of Scarborough.

There remains the *L.21* (Kapitänleutnant Frankenberg) which made a remarkable flight and was destined not to return. She came over land at Atwick, north of Hornsea, about 9.20 p.m., and on being engaged by the Barmston guns went out to sea. She shortly returned farther north but seemed to become aware of aeroplanes in her vicinity and deviated considerably from her course to avoid them. Steering at first with hesitancy, but later with decision, she bore down on Leeds, which she approached, under fire from the Brierlands gun, at 11.34 p.m. Although her height was estimated at 12,000 feet, the *L.21* was easily visible to the gunners over their open sights, and their fire seems to have turned her away from Leeds, for she changed course to the south, dropping her first bombs (one high-explosive and two incendiary) on Sharlston, east of Wakefield, which had been attacked an hour previously by the *L.16*. It is possible that lights, consequent on the earlier attack, attracted her.

The *L.21* next appeared over Barnsley, but the town was well darkened and escaped attack although three bombs fell at Dodworth, two miles to the south-west. The Zeppelin then moved on over the

Peak district to Macclesfield, but the whole Midland area was so darkened that her commander was baffled. He hovered over Macclesfield for a few minutes, without dropping any bombs, and then made off south-west towards the congested towns of the Potteries. Bombs fell at Kidsgrove (1), Goldenhill (3), and Tunstall (3). From over Tunstall a glare of lights was visible to the west, and the airship commander, apparently grateful for the sight at last of a definite target, promptly turned off and attacked.

The glare came from ironstone-burning hearths at Chesterton, on which sixteen high-explosive and seven incendiary bombs were dropped. They caused no casualties and no damage beyond the breaking of glass. Burning waste-heaps in collieries between Fenton and Trentham attracted the next bombs—four incendiaries, but these also had no effect. Hanley, Stoke-on-Trent, Newcastle-under-Lyme, and the other towns of this district which had been in the path of the airship, undoubtedly owed their escape to the efficacy of their darkening. The *L.21* turned away from Trentham about 1.30 a.m. and steered a deviating course towards Yarmouth. North of Peterborough she had her first encounter with aeroplanes. Two pilots found her, but the airship was skilfully handled and neither pilot got near enough to attack with any likelihood of success, although a few rounds were exchanged at long range.

She shook off her pursuers and eventually took up her eastward journey again, but she was attacked near East Dereham in Norfolk by Lieutenant W. R. Gayner, who was attracted by a light she was temporarily showing. Just as the pilot was getting within striking distance, however, the engine of his aeroplane failed, and he watched the *L.21* open out her engines and escape at full speed. She next appeared over Yarmouth, drifting slowly, at 6.5 a.m. She was fired on and passed out along the coast towards Lowestoft, where she again came under fire. Dawn was now breaking and military and naval aeroplanes were on her track. Three naval pilots came up with her. They were Flight Lieutenant E. Cadbury and Flight Sub-Lieutenants E. L. Pulling and G. W. R. Fane. Flight-Lieutenant Cadbury got under her at a distance of about 700 feet and fired into her after-part. He put all his Lewis gun ammunition—four drums—directly into her, but without immediate effect.

Flight Sub-Lieutenant Fane now took up the attack. He approached within a hundred feet of her and tried to open fire, but his gun jammed, the oil having frozen in the cold air. Flight Sub-

Lieutenant Pulling, who had witnessed the two previous attacks, now came up within fifty feet of the airship and fired two rounds. He was himself under fire from her machine-guns. At the second round his gun jammed and he turned away to clear the obstruction. Almost at once the *L.21* caught fire and within a few seconds was, in the pilot's words, 'a fiery furnace'. Until they were consumed by the flames, the crew of the airship's machine-guns kept up an unceasing fire on Flight Sub-Lieutenant Pulling. The *L.21* fell into the sea about eight miles east of Lowestoft and disappeared, leaving only an oil patch to mark her passing.

The naval airship service had to face another disaster before 1916 came to its end. On the 28th of December the *L.17* and the *L.24*, lying alongside one another in their sheds at Tondern, caught fire and were destroyed. On the same day eight Zeppelins had set out with orders to bomb the south of England, but after they had been at sea three hours reports of bad weather led to their recall.

The operations of the German airships over this country have been set down in some detail as a matter of historical record. The reader cannot fail to have been struck by the comparative ineffectiveness of the attacks, but it would be misleading to lay stress on the direct results. It should be remembered that the primary duty of the Zeppelins, and one which they splendidly fulfilled, was reconnaissance work over the North Sea, and that the raids on Great Britain used up only a minor part of their time and energies. Yet had the Zeppelins been built and maintained solely for the raids, it must be admitted that, from a purely military standpoint, they would more than have justified the money and ingenuity that went to their building. The threat of their raiding potentialities compelled us to set up at home a formidable organisation which diverted men, guns, and aeroplanes from more important theatres of war.

By the end of 1916 there were specifically retained in Great Britain for home anti-aircraft defence 17,341 officers and men. There were twelve Royal Flying Corps squadrons, comprising approximately 200 officers, 2,000 men, and no aeroplanes. The anti-aircraft guns and searchlights were served by 12,000 officers and men who would have found a ready place, with continuous work, in France or other war theatres. There was an observer corps of officers and men, and, in addition, some part of the energies of the police force and of the personnel of the telephone, fire brigade, and ambulance services was diverted to home defence activities.

And it must be remembered that this considerable force had to be kept in a high state of readiness all over the country, that it was, as it were, on constant active service against an enemy who, enjoying the advantages of the initiative, came from his sheds to raid when he chose.

There were many other effects of the raids, real and powerful, but difficult to assess. When raids were in progress, or even threatened, vital war work was held up all over the country. Until the dissemination of raid warnings became efficient and their reliability unquestioned, the general life of the community, during a raid, tended towards temporary paralysis. The dislocation on the railways in particular was widespread. On the 19th of March, 1916, for instance, when there was a brief raid by heavier-than-air craft on the Kentish coast, a warning order led to a complete stoppage of traffic throughout the South-Eastern Railway system, on all other lines in and out of London, and on many lines on the East Coast. After every such stoppage it took a long time to return to normal working conditions.

A further disquieting feature of this traffic dislocation was a threat of chaos in the event of the railways being called upon to make an urgent emergency movement such as the conveyance of troops to some point on the coast where a landing was being attempted—and it seemed certain that any attempt at a landing would be preceded by widely dispersed demonstrations by hostile aircraft. Up to the spring of 1916, such air activity would have meant the maximum disorganisation of all inland communications.

In April 1916 the arrangements governing the conduct of the railways during a raid were drastically revised. Up to this time, the orders were that when danger threatened trains must stop running, all lights be extinguished, and work in goods yards and stations cease, and it was the effect of these orders on the deliveries of war material that led to their rescission. So serious were the resultant delays and congestion that it was decided that traffic must be kept running at all costs. When Air Raid Action for specified areas was ordered, passenger trains were to reduce speed to fifteen and goods trains to ten miles an hour and enough light was to be kept going in the yards and stations to ensure a continuance of work.

These instructions led to many protests from railwayman and from munition workers. In some areas the latter threatened to prevent railwaymen working after raid warning had been received, and some of the railwaymen themselves made a threat to 'down tools' in the danger period. When, however, the reasons which prompted the orders were fully explained to the men the trouble was, for the most part, overcome.

More important than the disturbance on the railways, which was, to some extent, remedied when the new orders were put into force in April 1916, was the effect of the raids on industry. A good idea of the effects of a raid, or even of an alarm, on an industrial works is conveyed in the following statement, made in April 1916, by Messrs. Palmer's Shipbuilding and Iron Company.

> There have been three such alarms recently, namely, on the first, second, and fifth instant, the result in each instance being such as to seriously restrict our output at the time and to delay the progress of work on the following days. The position at our blast furnaces on each of the nights was one of extreme gravity, the whole of the plant being in positive danger of destruction by explosion at times. The definite pronouncement from the Military Authorities that we must on no account show a light prevented regular slagging or releasing of the iron from the furnaces, with the result that on two occasions the slag broke out at the region of the blast-pipe.
>
> The state of things is accentuated and reaches a grave position when, as has happened, the men from the boilers cease, the steam pressure thereby falling away and the blast engines coming to a standstill. With the exception of the actual back and front men on the furnaces, everybody clears out when the alarm signal goes, the engines, boilers, and blasts being practically left to themselves. The furnaces are thrown into an abnormal condition and a good portion of the next day is spent in trying to get them worked round, the loss of output of course being considerable and the quality of the products materially decreased.
>
> The position in the steel works, whilst the plant is not so open to disaster and wreckage by the condition of its working being interfered with, is that it is seriously open to large and costly repairs and wasting of material. In this department, on the alarm signal being received, practically everybody leaves the place. Metal is left in the large furnaces and also in ladles, or in whatever manner the circumstances find it. The whole aspect of these air raids on a steel works is one of extreme gravity

> and very little realised except by those who are in actual touch with the details, *and it is our opinion that in the event of a sustained number of such raids sooner or later much material harm will be done to the plant.*

It came to be generally accepted by works managers that on the morrow of a raid not more than 10 *per cent*, of outside workers would be in their places at their usual time and that 20 *per cent*, would stay away all day. Also, for some time after a raid or an alarm it was difficult or even impossible to induce workers to agree to overtime.

The suppression of the fires of blast furnaces on the approach of aircraft was always costly and sometimes serious in its effects. In many instances the metal was wasted. The loss for each furnace stopped was calculated, in Derbyshire, to be about £20 an hour, with the added risk that the furnace might be put out of action. Nor was it possible to confine the stoppage to the danger period. After the order to resume normal conditions was given it sometimes took eight or nine hours before work was in full blast again, with a consequent widespread drop in output figures.

In Cleveland there were thirteen weeks in 1916 in which there were Zeppelin alarms. In each of these weeks the fall in the production of pig-iron averaged 30,000 tons or a total drop for the year of 390,000 tons, a figure which represented approximately one-sixth of the whole annual output of pig-iron for the Cleveland industrial area. (Figures supplied by the Iron and Steel Institute.) This fall was not due to bomb-dropping but was the direct result of the orders which compelled the dowsing of blast furnaces whenever air raid warning was given. The effect reached its peak in 1916. From 1917 onwards to the end of the war, the industrial north and midlands enjoyed comparative immunity from attack.

It must be emphasised that the figures quoted above are indicative only, and that factories and works, large or small, producing every kind of war material, were affected.

In London one of the strangest sights resulting from the raids was provided by the rush of people to the cover of the Underground railways. For many nights following the attack on the capital on the 23rd/24th of September 1916, many thousands of people flocked to the tube railways without waiting for any warning. Many of them began to take up their places about 5.30 p.m. prepared to camp out until the danger, real or imaginary, was over. They went in family parties and carried with them pillows, bedding, provisions, and household treasures.

The air-raid menace, more, perhaps, than any other aspect of the war, was responsible for a temporary revolution in English social and general life. Night brought the unrelieved gloom of darkened streets and a brooding sense of danger. The reader, with the full facts before him, may reflect on the paucity of the means which brought this about. The air war was fought out on the Continent of Europe, and the bombing of Great Britain was episodic. It is not difficult to imagine circumstances in which we might have been called upon to meet the full force of Germany's air strength over this country. Unless the reader ponders what that implies, the air raids will not be viewed in their proper perspective, nor will the potentialities of air attack be made clear.

Bombing Attacks by Aeroplanes and Seaplanes

November 1916 was notable for the first attack on London by an aeroplane. Two of the earliest raids by heavier-than-air craft, namely, on Christmas Day 1914, when an enemy seaplane flew along the Thames to Erith, and on the 21st of February 1915, when Braintree and Colchester were bombed, might justifiably have been looked upon as preliminary to a widely directed campaign. In fact, those two efforts proved to be more ambitious than any which followed until the November 1916 attack on London. The reason is not far to seek. The enemy had no men or material to spare from the dominant theatres of war, and the attacks on England by heavier-than-air craft were no more than demonstrations. In some instances, too, reconnaissance of naval bases, such as Dover and Sheerness, and of aerodromes, was the primary object of the enemy flights, and bombs were only dropped incidentally.

Down to the end of 1916, the Kentish coast towns, particularly Dover, were the chief objectives of the enemy pilots. On the 9th of February two seaplanes passed over the North Goodwin lightship together, but on approaching the coast one turned off to Broadstairs and the other to Ramsgate. Four bombs from the former fell on a girls' school and three in the grounds. Part of the roof crashed into a class of girls, but only one was hurt, while a maid in the building was slightly injured. Two other bombs fell in an outlying part of the town and injured a woman. The pilot who flew to Ramsgate dropped his four bombs near a crowded tramcar, but they exploded without doing damage. There was only one other attack in February, made on the 20th simultaneously on Walmer and Lowestoft by two pairs of seaplanes. Nineteen bombs fell at Lowestoft, but their chief effect was to sever telephone lines in the grounds of the 5th Provisional Brigade head-quarters, where an officer and a clerk were cut by glass.

One of the Walmer raiders aimed his bombs, without success, at shipping near the Kentish Knock, while the other pilot dropped a bomb on the Marine Barracks, another in the Dover Road, one in Beach Road, and three in the sea. A boy was killed and another severely injured, and windows were broken, but there was no other damage. Twenty-six British pilots who went up to meet the attacks were too late to engage the raiders.

The Kent coast was visited again twice in March. On the 1st, three bombs from one seaplane fell in Cliftonville and four in Kingsgate. In the former town a child was killed and houses were damaged, and in Kingsgate only windows broken. The next attack, on the 19th of March, was more serious. At Dover and Ramsgate fourteen people were killed and twenty-six injured, but two of the attacking aircraft were shot down. (See Vol. 2.)

Reconnaissance flights were made over Dover by single aeroplanes on the 23rd and 24th of April, and on the 3rd of May a single aircraft attacked Deal with nine bombs which injured four people. On the 20th of May came a moonlight attack by five aircraft on Dover, St. Peters, Sholden, and Ringwold. Little damage was done and, once again, one of the raiders was shot down. (See Vol. 2.)

Many weeks of quiet followed. On the 9th of July an enemy pilot made what appeared to be a reconnaissance flight to Manston aerodrome. No bombs were dropped. One of the pilots who went up overtook the raider forty miles out to sea and fired two drums of ammunition from his Lewis gun without apparent effect. That same night an aircraft appeared over Dover and dropped seven bombs which did no damage. The next two attacks were also on Dover, in the afternoon of the 12th of August (four bombs, seven injured), and the 22nd of September (seven bombs, one injured). The raiders, who came in without warning, were pursued across the Channel, but were not brought to action.

In October there were two minor attacks. In the early hours of the 22nd an aircraft was heard off Sheerness and heralded its arrival with four bombs, three of which fell in the harbour and one in the dockyard railway station, breaking windows but doing no other damage.

Another enemy pilot came up the Thames Estuary an hour later but dropped no bombs. Next morning a single aeroplane dropped three bombs on Margate, and one in the sea. The bombs wounded two people but inflicted little material damage.

Then came the first aeroplane raid on London, and the last attack of the year. It was made by one aeroplane piloted by Deck-Offizier Paul Brandt with Leutnant Walther Ilges as his observer. The aeroplane left Mariakerke in the morning of the 28th of November 1916, with the object of attacking the Admiralty offices in Whitehall. (It was an L.V.G. with a 225 horse-power Mercedes engine: speed 80 miles per hour and radius of action about 200 miles.) The weather was fine, but hazy, and the enemy aeroplane, flying high, was seen by no more than two people on its way to London and these did not identify it as German.

The first that was known of its presence over London was when bombs began to fall just before midday. Six 10-kg. bombs exploded between Brompton Road and Victoria Station. They did little damage but injured ten people. The German observer took twenty photographs of aerodromes, military camps, and ammunition works on his way in to London. These photographs were destined not to be developed. On the homeward journey the engine gave trouble, the camera and plates were thrown overboard, and the aeroplane was eventually landed near Boulogne, where it was captured.

CHAPTER 4

Administration, Supply, Recruitment, and Training 1914-16

It was clear before the Somme struggle ended, in the autumn of 1916, that the future growth of the Royal Flying Corps would be dominated by air fighting. The formation of the German pursuit squadrons, the *Jagdstaffeln*, equipped with Halberstadt and Albatros single-seater fighters, superior in performance to any contemporary Allied aeroplane, marked the beginning of a new 'Fokker' period, which was to have effects on the supply and administrative organisation in England.

Major-General Trenchard when framing his proposals, or programmes as they were called, for the expansion of the Royal Flying Corps on the western front, had to reckon with many difficulties. The character of the air war changed rapidly. The auxiliary services rendered by the Flying Corps to the army grew in scope and intensity, and the satisfaction of the army's demands came to depend more and more on success in combat. The G.O.C. Royal Flying Corps in France had to look far ahead and judge what the needs of the army would be; but before he could outline his own future requirements he had to forecast the development—administrative, tactical, and technical—of the German air service.

Nor was this all. He had also to see that his demands were in accordance with what he could reasonably expect to get. It is one of the greater achievements of Major-General Trenchard's command that his approved programmes, few and progressive, stood the test of time. They would, had they been strictly fulfilled, have ensured superiority to the Royal Flying Corps in France. But they were not strictly fulfilled. They were subject to continuous postponements and disappointments.

In June 1916, before the Somme battle opened, MajorGeneral

Trenchard, looking ahead to the spring of 1917, had asked that the number of squadrons in France should be increased to fifty-six. His demands contemplated equal numbers of fighting and artillery (or corps) squadrons. But in September 1916 he was quick to read the lessons of the Somme battle and he intimated to the War Office that ultimately the number of fighting squadrons with each army must be increased from four (as asked for in the June programme) to eight. This would mean twice as many fighting as artillery squadrons. On the 16th of November 1916 this became a definite proposal on the application of Sir Douglas Haig for twenty fighting squadrons, extra to those asked for in the June programme. The application was intended to be a form of guidance for the future, so that the War Office could initiate the necessary production without delay.

This application for additional squadrons, however, came at a time when the Royal Flying Corps sources of supply were drying up, and it was obvious that there must be a general stocktaking of the national resources. Before the position in the autumn of 1916 can be appreciated it will be necessary to review the broad development, from the beginning, of the supply organisation for the two air services, with its co-related problems of administration, recruitment, and training.

The reader must first have some idea of the material required to maintain a squadron once it was in the field. The mobilization store table for the original 1914 establishment for a squadron of twelve aeroplanes, included six heavy and seven light aeroplane tenders, four motor repair lorries, three shed lorries, six trailers, four reserve equipment lorries, six motor-cycles, three portable sheds, and a variety of miscellaneous stores such as brass, copper, gun-metal, solder, mild-steel, tool-steel, tin, copper-tubing, wire, carpenters' and metal-workers' tools, signalling lamps, heliographs, acetone, beeswax, paint, soda, soap, tallow, varnish, carbide, oil, fire-extinguishers, and timber. In addition, there were spare engines and other aeroplane and motor-transport spare parts. As the activities of the squadrons expanded there were added wireless sets, Lewis guns, magazines and mountings, Vickers guns, bombs, carriers, sights and release gears, and cameras and photographic equipment.

In March 1916 the establishment of a squadron was raised to eighteen aeroplanes and the general equipment and spares proportionately increased. The squadron was further raised, in March 1917, to twenty-four aeroplanes, although it was not until 1918 that the material was forthcoming to enable squadrons to be equipped according to this higher establishment.

Apart from the expansion in demands consequent on the growth of the squadrons, in numbers and in size, there was the problem of allowing for wastage, including battle casualties, accidents, and the replacement of obsolete types. New aeroplanes, additional to those originally supplied to equip squadrons or to raise them to the higher establishments, were delivered to the Royal Flying Corps in France, as follows: 1914, 84; 1915, 399; 1916, 1,782; 1917, 4,641; and 1918 (to the end of October), 7,230. These figures give interesting results when they are apportioned between the average numbers of squadrons for each year. In 1914, new aeroplanes had to be supplied to replace 33 *per cent*, of the aircraft in all squadrons *each month*. In 1915, the figure was 26 *per cent.*, in 1916, 37 *per cent.*, in 1917, 47 *per cent.*, and in 1918, 52 *per cent.*

That is to say, in 1914 allowance had to be made to re-equip all squadrons in France, in aeroplanes, every three months, while by 1918 the figure had dropped to just under two months. (Naval Squadrons working with the Royal Flying Corps up to the formation of the Royal Air Force, on the 1st of April 1918, were maintained by the Admiralty and are not included in the above figures.) Some of the early difficulties which attended the production of aircraft, such as the lack of factories, plant, machinery, and experienced personnel, were common to all other munitions of war. But there was the additional and powerful disadvantage that the aircraft industry, when war began, was in its infancy. The Royal Flying Corps, always short of money, had done little to foster the growth of the industry.

★★★★★★

> Speaking before the Bailhache Committee on the Administration and Command of the Royal Flying Corps, in 1916, the Chief Engineer to the Daimler Company said: 'The aviation vote in the Army Estimates for the year preceding the war was not more than sufficient to keep a decent-size firm for a year, yet it had to provide for the whole establishment of the Flying Corps, buildings and personnel, as well as engines and aeroplanes.'

★★★★★★

In August 1914 there were no more than twelve aircraft manufacturing firms in England, of which three specialised in seaplanes. There were also, two leading ordnance firms which had contracts for aeroplanes of Government design. The outstanding orders in course of fulfilment by these various firms included one hundred and fifteen aeroplanes for the Flying Corps and fifteen aeroplanes and thirty-four seaplanes for the Naval Air Service. The approximate output for the whole country was at the rate of one hundred aircraft a year. The crucial weakness of the industry was the lack of suitable British aero engines. The government, alive to this weakness, had offered a £5,000 prize for a British-designed engine, which had been won in the spring of 1914 by the six-cylinder water-cooled Green of one hundred horsepower.

Twenty of these were ordered, but the engine proved too heavy for its power and its use was abandoned. The only other possible British aero engines, of proprietary design, existing in August 1914, were the eight-cylinder (100 horse-power) and twelve-cylinder (200 horse-power) Sunbeams. These showed promise, but they were at that time unsuitable on account of their great weight and petrol consumption. The Sunbeam firm, however, developed these engines, with Admiralty encouragement, and they were subsequently used by the Naval Air Service. The manufacture of the 120 horse-power Austro-Daimler (re-named Beardmore) had been started on a small scale in the Arrol-Johnson Works.

******

> When it was decided, in the autumn of 1913, that the navy should develop all lighter-than-air craft, the small military non-rigid airships were handed over to the Admiralty. Colonel J. E. B. Seely, the Secretary of State for War, used the credit transferred to the War Office as a result of this transaction, for the building of 24 Factory R.E.5 aeroplanes. Austro-Daimler engines for these were at once ordered from Messrs. Beardmore. The Austro-Daimler became the Beardmore, and the Beardmore resulted in the B.H.P. (Beardmore-Halford-Pullinger, 200-230 horse-power) and the Siddeley-Puma (230 horse-power).

******

There was, however, an engine of official design of which one model had just been produced, and for which detailed drawings were available, so that firms new to aircraft work might be expected to take up its manufacture. This was the ninety horse-power stationary air-cooled engine of the Royal Aircraft Factory (R.A.F.1) which had been based on, but promised to be superior to, the French seventy horse-power Renault. A second Factory engine, a twelve-cylinder water-cooled model of two hundred and fifty horse-power (R.A.F.3) was in the design stage and one complete engine was on order from the trade. Drawings for a third model (R.A.F.4) similar to the R.A.F.1, but of twelve cylinders and to develop one hundred and forty horse-power, were in hand.

None of the above engines was in production until 1915, so that for the first six months of the war the air services had to rely on engines of French design. Of these, drawings of the 70 horse-power Renault and of the 80 horse-power Gnome were in the possession of British firms. A serious difficulty which was, for the first two years, to place a grave handicap on engine production at home, was British pre-war dependence on Germany for magnetos. The whole British magneto output, hopelessly inadequate, was centred in one firm whose product was of a simple type, and the Admiralty and War Office endeavoured to meet their early war requirements by direct importation, chiefly of existing German-built instruments.

By the middle of 1915, however, this source was nearing exhaustion and the Admiralty Air Department undertook to foster the supply of home-produced magnetos for all the fighting services, a work which they continued until early in 1917, when it was handed over to the Ministry of Munitions. The magneto shortage reached its most acute stage in the summer of 1916, when the supplies of German-built instruments came to an end. American magnetos were forthcoming, but they had been built primarily for road transport and they proved unreliable in aircraft. British manufacturers suffered twelve months of repeated failures before they produced magnetos of fair reliability, and not until the autumn of 1916 were British magnetos being delivered, and then only in small quantities (twenty to thirty per week). The manufacturers had to contend with great difficulties.

None of the essential material was procurable at home. There were no suitable British magnets, nor hard rubber insulating material, nor fine copper enamelled wire, nor oiled silk or paper for insulation. The best quality enamelled wire came from America and the fabric for the oiled silk from Japan, but it became increasingly difficult to import supplies, and the production of these essentials at home had to be organised. Meanwhile, the shortage of these basic materials was such that none could be set aside for the repair of damaged magnetos, and the demand for spare magnetos could only be met by withholding parts from new production.

Such was the engine problem. The aeroplane problem was less acute, but here again we were greatly dependent on the French. When war began there were only two proprietary aeroplanes of British design of which sufficient experience was available to justify large orders, namely, the Vickers (100 horse-power Monosoupape Gnome) two-seater pusher and the Avro (80 horse-power Gnome) two-seater tractor. In addition, the Sopwith, Bristol, and Martinsyde firms all had new designs in a more or less experimental stage. Of French-designed aeroplanes, the manufacture of which had been begun in England, there were three considered good enough for quantitative production, namely, the Maurice Farman, and the Henri Farman, both of which were two-seater pushers, and the Bleriot monoplane.

There were, however, a number of aeroplanes, designed at the Royal Aircraft Factory, notably the B.E.2a, B.E.2b, and B.E.2c, for which drawings and specifications were sufficiently ready to allow of orders being placed with firms which had never before had anything to do with the construction of aeroplanes. The employment of agricultural implement makers, furniture and piano manufacturers, &c., was only made possible by supplying them with detailed drawings and by subjecting their work, at every stage, to rigid inspection. In addition, their managers and foremen were put through an intensive course of instruction at the Royal Aircraft Factory. It thus happened that a large number of officially designed aeroplanes was ordered at the beginning of the war. They were delivered at the Factory, less engines and instruments, and were there completed and tested before being handed over to the air services.

The development of aircraft supplies is bound up with the organisation for administering the air services in each of the two great war departments. At the War Office, the Military Aeronautics Directorate was a self-contained and independent department.

★★★★★★

In July 1914, the Directorate was organised as follows:

D.G.M.A.	Brigadier-General Sir David Henderson.
M.A.1. (General Staff) — Policy, administration, personnel.	Major W. S. Brancker, R.A., G.S.O.2. Major W. G. H. Salmond, R.A., G.S.O.3. Major B. D. Fisher, 17th Lancers, G.S.O.3.
M.A.2. (Equipment) — Supply and inspection of material; Inventions and experiment; Administration of the Royal Aircraft Factory and the Aeronautical Inspection Department.	Colonel W. MacAdam, R.E., A.D.M.A.) Captain J. T. Dreyer, R.A.

M.A.3. (Contracts) — Purchase and sale of aeronautical material.	Mr. A. E. Turner. Mr. F. R. Stapley.

******

Its duties were to advise the General Staff on all air matters, to administer and to prepare schemes of development for the Royal Flying Corps, to recruit, appoint, and train personnel, and to provide all technical equipment. This Directorate, in short, had in it the germs of the eventual Air Ministry, for it had vested in it, to a great extent, the duties of the principal departments of the War Office so far as the air is concerned. Notably, it had its own Contracts Branch, rendered necessary by the technical complications involved in arranging contracts for engines and aircraft equipment. The duties of the Contracts Branch were wider than the title implies. Among other things, the Branch dealt with labour for aircraft supply, advised on the subject of export licences relating to aircraft material, urged deliveries by correspondence, and regulated traffic facilities for aeronautical supplies. The Director-General of Military Aeronautics (Sir David Henderson) dealt directly with the Secretary of State for War, and, as a pilot and head of the Flying Corps, he could speak with authority on all matters affecting his service.

At the Admiralty, on the other hand, the Naval Air Service was treated like any other branch of the navy, the administration being divided between the different Sea Lords. The Director of the Air Department (Commodore M. F. Sueter) was responsible for advising the First Sea Lord as to exercise and the general use of aircraft, the Second Sea Lord as to personnel and training, the Third Sea Lord on matters affecting airship design and construction, and the Fourth Sea Lord on aviation stores. The Royal Naval Air Service, therefore, was not directly represented on the Board of Admiralty, none of whose members had any personal knowledge of aeronautics.

Commodore Sueter was empowered to deal direct with the air staff at the War Office on matters of detail, but decisions on general air questions were communicated officially by correspondence between the secretaries of the two Departments. The Royal Aircraft Factory was, nominally, a technical department for both air services, but the Admiralty made small use of the Factory, preferring to develop a technical department of its own.

In the two years before the war the two branches of the Air Service had, to some extent, been controlled and led to co-operate by a Joint

Air Committee, presided over by the Secretary of State for War (Colonel J. E. B. Seely). Admiral Sir J. R. Jellicoe, as Second Sea Lord, was for some time Vice-Chairman of this Committee, and its members included the officers commanding the two Wings and the Central Flying School, the Director of the Air Department, and the Superintendent of the Royal Aircraft Factory. It might be said to have formed a sort of Air Council, but it had no executive powers, and when war came it ceased to meet. Some of its members took the field and the others were too busy to spend time on a committee which could only talk and not act. In a word, when the crisis came, all central control between the naval and military wings disappeared.

Sir David Henderson took the field in command of the Royal Flying Corps and Lieutenant-Colonel W. S. Brancker was appointed Deputy Director of Military Aeronautics at the War Office. Liaison with the Naval Air Service now became a personal matter between Lieutenant-Colonel Brancker and Commodore Murray Sueter. As a step towards establishing some sort of co-operative policy, Lieutenant-Colonel Brancker conferred with Commodore Sueter and it was agreed that the majority of the aeroplanes in the British Isles should be allotted to the War Office and all seaplanes to the Admiralty.

Certain aircraft and engine manufacturers were verbally allotted to each service and a few others who were supplying both services were made common to both. The necessity for water-cooled engines of high power for seaplane work had been realised by the Admiralty from the earliest days, and, as has been told, the Sunbeam firm, with the encouragement of the Admiralty Air Department, had produced before the war an engine of 200 horse-power. On the outbreak of war Messrs. Rolls-Royce were also approached by the Air Department and undertook the design of an engine of 250 horse-power. Shortly afterwards Messrs. Napier were requested by the War Office to develop a high-powered engine for aeroplanes. The experts of the Royal Aircraft Factory gave the two firms all possible data, and the existing drawings of the R.A.F.3 (250 horse-power) water-cooled engine were handed to them.

Although the Joint Air Committee had ceased to meet, there were hopes that co-operation between the two services would be close and amicable. Indeed, so long as the supply problem was confined to the rapid organisation of the existing means of production, there was little or no cause for friction.

The two departments worked on different lines. The Admiralty policy was to buy aircraft, engines, and spares in any available market. The War Office, on the other hand, while it bought from the trade whatever appeared suitable, particularly after war began, had, in the Royal Aircraft Factory, a manufacturing concern of its own. The factory attracted considerable criticism. It was looked upon by some sections of the trade as a competitive organisation, and there was an uneasy feeling—unjustified, be it said—that the designs of private manufacturers were not protected from the too-prying eyes of rival designers at the factory. Furthermore, official designs made competitive tenders possible and so reduced profits.

Not that the factory was a fully-fledged aircraft-producing firm. Chiefly it concerned itself with experimental construction of all kinds—aeroplanes, engines, balloons, armament, bombs, instruments, and sundries—from which drawings were produced for the use of private firms, but it did manufacture spare parts, and it did, also, in emergency, produce a number of complete aeroplanes. (For statements of the duties of the Royal Aircraft Factory and of aeroplanes built at the factory 1911-18 see Appendix 6.)

The impartial critic must admit that, whatever may be thought about the policy of the Government being in business on its own account as aircraft designers and manufacturers, the exacting standard set by the Royal Aircraft Factory greatly helped towards the ultimate superiority of British-designed aircraft in safety, workmanship, and performance. Air Vice-Marshal Sir Sefton Brancker said:

> Practically all private designers, although some of them may have been bitterly opposed to the policy followed in connexion with the Royal Aircraft Factory, admit that they owe much to the high standard set and to the information distributed by this Government institution.

When the initial war orders for military aeroplanes and engines were placed, there was no experience from which the future requirements of the Expeditionary Force might be gauged. It was obviously necessary to limit the number of types employed so far as possible, but it was also obvious that existing resources must be developed to produce aeroplanes and engines quickly, and that standardization could only be achieved, if at all, at some later date. The War Office therefore placed orders for Avros, Farmans, and Bleriots to the full extent of the factories concerned.

The Vickers Fighter was also ordered in considerable numbers, although the latest model of the aeroplane was untried and it was still doubtful whether its engine, the hundred horse-power Monosoupape-Gnome, would be forthcoming in numbers, or, if forthcoming, would run reliably.

On the urgent recommendation of the Superintendent of the Royal Aircraft Factory, it was decided to standardize the B.E.2c, instead of the B.E.2a or B.E.2b, although experience of the two, last named, was greater and the drawings more complete. The B.E.2c had a better performance and was stronger than its prototypes, and it was, in addition, stable. Large numbers of B.E.2c's were therefore ordered from the trade. The Daimler Company and G. and J. Weir, Limited, of Glasgow, were the first firms, outside those already concerned with aircraft production, to accept large orders for the B.E.2c aeroplane. The Daimler firm also undertook orders for the R.A.F.1 engine, in other words, for complete aeroplanes, and an aerodrome, for delivery, was constructed adjacent to the Daimler works. Another factory aeroplane, the R.E.7, an improved type of the R.E.5, designed to carry a greater useful load, was also ordered in quantities, contracts being placed with Messrs. Austin, the Coventry Ordnance Works, Messrs. Napier, and Messrs. Siddeley-Deasy.

The necessity for developing the aeroplane for fighting purposes was recognised. The value of the two-seater pusher type seemed likely to be greater than that of the single-seater tractor, as it would give a clear field of fire forward. Therefore, work at the factory on the drawings of the F.E.2 was proceeded with at full speed. In addition, small orders for the Bristol Scout and Martinsyde Scout were placed to fill the untried role of single-seater fighters.

Large orders were placed with motor manufacturing firms for the Gnome and Renault engines, and other orders, in anticipation of the completion of the drawings, were placed for the Factory R.A.F.1 engines. (This engine had a set-back when the first of its type, under test in the air by Second Lieutenant E. T. Busk, on the 5th of November 1914, caught fire and destroyed the aeroplane with its pilot.)

Until the orders placed began to bear fruit it was necessary to keep the Farman aeroplanes in the fighting-line. It was realised that as soon as the B.E.2c orders were in full swing, the Bleriots and possibly the Avros, both of which could only be obtained in small numbers, could be relegated to training. Meanwhile all possible experiments were encouraged. In the Royal Aircraft Factory an improved S.E.2, the S.E.4, which in the summer of 1914 actually flew at a little more than 130 miles an hour with a one hundred and sixty horse-power Gnome engine, the F.E.2 and the F.E.4 (a two-engined aeroplane designed to carry a 1½-pounder gun, which was under experiment) were given precedence. The Vickers firm took up the problem of developing a single-seater fighter of high performance, and a large two-engined bomber. The Aircraft Manufacturing Company undertook to produce single-seater and two-seater pusher fighters, and the Martinsyde firm began to develop a single-seater fighter to take the Austro-Daimler (or Beardmore) engine. Finally, Messrs. Armstrong-Whitworth, on receiving orders for B.E.2c's, undertook to produce an equally efficient, but more easily manufactured aeroplane, and were given permission to do so.

Thus, before any definite policy had been laid down, and before any real experience had been gained in France, a great amount of aircraft and engine production had been initiated in England. As illustrative of the difficulties which attended the initiation of types of aeroplanes at home, before experience in the Field had crystallized, one or two instances of early demands from France may be mentioned. When the first British aeroplane was shot down, by rifle fire from the ground, there came a demand for armour-protected aeroplanes. Although armour-plating was fitted to a few B.E.2c's, this demand was not seriously considered until 1918, and then only for special type aeroplanes designed for low-flying.

Again, during the retreat from Mons, there was an occasion when bad weather and approaching darkness brought a threat that many of the Flying Corps aeroplanes must be left behind to fall into the hands of the enemy. This incident led to a request for aeroplanes that would fold up for towing along a road, a request that was never met. Similarly, experience during the retreat, in which rapid movement was essential, induced the command in France to report later on that Bessonneau hangars would be useless; but when the lines became stabilised, the Bessonneau hangar came to be the standard accommodation for the Flying Corps in the Field.

The British firms worked at top pressure on the government orders, but much time must always elapse between initiation and output, and, in the meanwhile, recourse had to be had to French sources of supply. In October 1914 a Flying Corps officer was sent to Paris to organise a department to deal with the purchase of French aircraft supplies. The Paris office, which dealt through the French Ministry of War, became known as the British Aviation Supplies Department, and, in December 1914, an Admiralty representative joined the department to watch over the interests of the Naval Air Service and to place orders on behalf of the Admiralty Air Department. The Paris office did not work smoothly. From the outset the War Office and Admiralty representatives were, by nature of their different allegiance, in competition with one another.

Each was there to get all he could for his own service, and the consequent friction led to disappointments which, in view of the fact that many of the high-performance aeroplanes in use by the Royal Flying Corps were French, had its repercussions in the field. The result was that Major-General Trenchard found it essential to make many personal visits, with the Flying Corps representative in Paris, to the French firms. Furthermore, French manufacturers were in no real position to meet the British demands. The French were, however, as much in need of certain essential materials, such as steel in the raw and treated, aeroplane cable, ball-bearings, and Lewis guns, which we could supply, as we were in need of French aircraft engines and aeroplanes.

The matter therefore became one of bargaining, or, to use a more polite word, of reciprocity. It became a common occurrence for orders to be held up on both sides on the plea that reciprocal orders were not being fulfilled. In June 1915, for example, there was a threat that deliveries of aeroplanes and engines from France would cease as a consequence of the failure of Great Britain to maintain a promised delivery of Lewis guns amounting to fifteen per cent, of her total output. At this time outstanding orders with French manufacturers included one hundred and eight complete aeroplanes and one hundred and seventy-six engines. Sir Edward Grey, the Secretary of State for Foreign Affairs, was informed by the British Ambassador in Paris that:

> General Joffre intends to stop entire supply of aviation material to His Majesty's Government....

Had this threat become effective the aircraft supply problem must have become critical, and the government therefore reviewed the whole question of reciprocity in the provision of different classes of war material. In the result, the French were reassured and the supplies from France continued. In October 1915, on the suggestion of the French Under-Secretary of State for Aeronautics, it was agreed that representatives of the two Allied air services should meet to discuss the supply problem each month. At an early meeting lists were submitted by the French representatives showing the requirements of their government in a variety of materials. Something of the diversity of these items of bargaining may be gathered from the fact that they included steel, copper, white metal, bronze, machine tools, enamelled wire, Palmer wheels, Italian hemp, acetate of soda and of lime, acetone, trichlorethylene, chloride of sulphur, and benzine.

An attempt to lessen the competition and friction between the Flying Corps and Naval Air Service representatives in Paris was made in January 1916, when a joint Commission was set up under the direction of the British naval *attaché* (Captain Fitzmaurice Acton, R.N.). (The British Aviation Commission was formed on the 1st of January 1916. The naval air representative on the Commission was Squadron Commander I.T. Courtney, and the military, Captain Lord Robert E. Innes-Ker.) The work of the Commission was facilitated by an undertaking, made by those Allied Governments who disposed of raw material needed by the French, to give the French demands more sympathetic consideration than they had received in the past.)

How this enforced reliance on the French aeronautical industry confounded estimates of Flying Corps expansion and affected the equipment of squadrons may be seen from one or two definite examples. Towards the end of 1915 the 110 horse-power Le Rhone engine came into service in the Royal Flying Corps with the Morane Biplane. Early in 1916 other French aeroplanes, namely, the Morane Bullet and Parasol, and the Nieuport Scout (the last-named in use by the Royal Naval Air Service) were delivered with the 110 in place of the 80 horse-power Le Rhone. The performance of these new aeroplanes was so improved that it was at once decided to discard the lower-powered engine, and every effort was made to ensure delivery to the Royal Flying Corps of sufficient 110 horsepower Le Rhone engines to maintain the improved types. In the fourth quarter of 1915 one hundred and fifty of the higher powered Le Rhones had been asked for from the French Government, but only twenty-four were allotted, and, of these, ten only were actually delivered. In the first quarter of 1916, twenty-four were delivered in satisfaction of demands totalling one hundred and thirty.

******

Captain J. D. B. Fulton had reported, after a visit to France before the war, on the technical efficiency of the Le Rhone engine, not then taken up by the French authorities, and he had urged that an agreement be made with the Le Rhone company for its manufacture for the Royal Flying Corps. His proposals were not adopted.

******

The delivery of French aeroplanes, as apart from engines, although much below demands, reacted higher proportions. The French, indeed, were in an invidious position. They certainly possessed a small aircraft industry when war came, but in the rapid development of that industry they had to face many of the same difficulties which made progress slow in England. For long it was more than they could do to meet the demands of their own air services, but they had, in addition, to build aeroplanes and engines for the British, Russian, and Italian Governments. The wonder is, not that they could not satisfy the demands of those governments in full, but that they could meet them at all. Let it be stated clearly that it was the help given by the French which tided over the time while the British aircraft industry was developing and so enabled the British air services to carry on in the early part of the war.

The difficulties and delays attendant on the purchase of aero engines manufactured in France were clear in the spring of 1915, and the War Office thereupon took energetic measures to foster the construction of all French-designed engines in England. By the middle of 1916 every type of French engine in use by the Royal Flying Corps was being built in this country, although the output was small and large orders were still being placed in France. There were many incidental difficulties which delayed production at home. Much experimental work and modification of tools was necessary before manufacturers of motor-car engines could cope successfully with aero engines. Protracted negotiations relative to patents and royalties delayed the production of all engines of foreign proprietary design. In 1915, for example, the 150 horsepower Hispano-Suiza, of Spanish origin, came into prominence. The factory single-seater fighter, the S.E.5, was designed to take this engine, and large orders for the Hispano-Suiza were placed with French firms which had taken up its manufacture.

******

The first order for Hispano engines (50) was placed in August 1915. This was on the recommendation of Lieutenant-Colonel H. R. M. Brooke-Popham, who had inspected a specimen engine in Paris. The engines of this order were delivered between August and November 1916.

******

At the same time arrangements were begun for the building of the engine in England, but negotiations with the patentees in Barcelona and with the French manufacturing firms consumed valuable time and the construction of the Hispano-Suiza was not begun in England until the spring of 1916.

It has been told how the Rolls-Royce and Napier firms were encouraged, at the beginning of the war, to take up the development of a high-powered water-cooled engine. The Napier firm used the drawings of the Factory 250 horse-power engine and produced the 200 horse-power Napier Raf.3a. Messrs. Rolls-Royce, however, proceeded with their own independent designs, and by March 1915 had produced the first of the *Eagle* type. The earliest deliveries of the approved engine, which gave 250 horsepower at 1,800 revolutions, did not begin until October 1915. Thereafter there were various modifications of the *Eagle* which culminated in the *Eagle VIII* of 375 horsepower, of which delivery began in February 1918. Two other Rolls-Royce engines were designed in 1915, namely, the 190 horse-power *Falcon* and the 90 horse-power *Hawk*. As with the *Eagle*, various modifications of the *Falcon* appeared, culminating in 275 horse-power. It was not until June 1916 that the Royal Flying Corps in France began to receive aeroplanes with Rolls-Royce engines, the first so fitted being the F.E.2d's with which No. 20 Squadron was re-equipped.

Meanwhile, the aeroplanes decided on in the early part of the war were coming forward in quantities, more especially the Factory-designed B.E.2c. Of sixteen squadrons in France at the end of 1915, twelve were equipped with this aeroplane. Of the others, two had Vickers and two had Moranes. The first F.E.2b squadron did not arrive until January 1916, and, as this aeroplane did much to combat the Fokker predominance, it will be of interest to investigate whether it should and could have appeared earlier. The F.E.2a, which had its prototype in an aeroplane designed by Mr. Geoffrey de Havilland and bought by the War Office in 1910, was designed at the factory as a fighter in August 1913, and in August 1914 the factory had received orders to build twelve of the improved type.

The first was ready in January 1915, but the 100 horsepower Green engine, to take which the F.E.2a was designed, proved unsatisfactory, and it was decided to try again with the 120 horse-power Beardmore. This change of engine necessitated many minor alterations to the design of the aeroplane, and the first completed aeroplane with the Beardmore, was not delivered until May 1915. By November of that year the twelve aeroplanes ordered on the outbreak of war had been delivered. Had the Green engine proved satisfactory, or, alternatively, had the original design been made for the Beardmore, the F.E. must have appeared in France much earlier than it did and the day of the Fokker shortened. The other single-seater which outfought the Fokker, Mr. Geoffrey de Havilland's D.H.2, was first tested in July 1915, and was ordered in quantity the following month, the first aeroplane of this contract arriving in France in December 1915. The first squadron of D.H.2's did not reach France until February 1916.

A pusher similar to the D.H.2 and designed to take the same engine—the 100 horse-power Monosoupape Gnome—was the factory F.E. 8 which was designed in May 1915, during which month the main working drawings were completed. The first F.E. 8 was not finished at the factory until October 1915, and then in the following month, after it had been tested and approved, it was broken on landing by an inspector of aeroplanes. Spare parts were made into a second aeroplane, which was sent to France in December and was at once reported on favourably. Many difficulties, however, ensued with contractors in England when the aeroplane was put into production, and the first F.E. 8 squadron (No. 40) did not appear in France until August 1916. In October 1916 a second squadron (No. 41) was equipped with this aeroplane, which continued in service in France until July 1917. It was the last single-seater pusher to be flown in the field.

The period of the Fokker predominance brought to the surface in England much latent misgiving that all was not well with the administration of the Royal Flying Corps. By the end of 1915 public opinion in favour of some coordination between the two air services was strong. It was advanced, and was the subject of discussion in Parliament, that there should be an Air Minister with entire control of the air services and with status equal to that of the First Lord of the Admiralty and of the Secretary of State for War.

But public opinion was in advance of the feeling in Whitehall, and on February the 15th 1916 Mr. Asquith, the Prime Minister, appointed a new committee, known as the Joint War Air Committee, under the chairmanship of Lord Derby, 'to collaborate in and to co-ordinate the question of supplies and design for material for the Naval and Military Air Services'. The committee was a strong one, its members being, in addition to the chairman, Lord Montagu of Beaulieu as an independent advisor, three Admiralty representatives (Rear-Admiral C. L. Vaughan-Lee, Commodore Murray F. Sueter, and Squadron

Commander W. Briggs), and two from the War Office (MajorGeneral Sir David Henderson and Lieutenant-Colonel E. L. Ellington), with Sir Maurice Hankey and Major C. L. Storr of the Committee of Imperial Defence as Secretaries.

******

> Sir David Henderson had returned from France to the War Office on the 19th of August 1915 and resumed his duties as Director-General of Military Aeronautics. He became a member of the Army Council on the 22nd of February 1916.

******

But the committee, which was set up as a permanent one, lasted a bare two months. While Sir David Henderson, as a member of the Army Council, could speak as a plenipotentiary for the War Office, the leading Admiralty representative was not a member of the Board of Admiralty and he could settle nothing without reference to the Board. This tended to sterilise the Admiralty contribution to the committee from the start. But chiefly the committee had no executive powers and therefore no authority to resolve conflicting ideas of policy between the two services. Lord Derby sent his letter of resignation to the Prime Minister on the 3rd of April 1916, stating as his main reasons that:

> (1) The Committee had no executive power and no authority.
> (2) A fundamental disagreement was found to exist between the two branches of the service, each having its own organisation, *esprit de corps,* and aspirations.
> (3) The terms of reference were so narrowly limited as to preclude the committee from deciding any question of policy.

Lord Derby went on to say that he found no existing division of duties between the Naval and Military Air Services and no general principles on which co-ordination was possible. He says:

> To sum up the matter, it appears to me to be quite impossible to bring the two Wings closer together than they are at the present moment, unless and until the whole system of the Air Service is changed and they are amalgamated into one service as personally I consider they ultimately must be. To make this great change would be a difficult and lengthy operation in peace time. I am inclined to think it would be practically impossible in war time. . . .

Lord Montagu of Beaulieu, in his letter of resignation, stated that he became a member because he thought the committee would soon become the nucleus of a Board of Aviation and he could see no chance of this happening.

The papers put before the committee, during its brief existence, by the naval and military representatives, reveal conflicting views between the two departments and contain charges of overlapping and interference in design, supply, and contract work. Sir David Henderson, in a memorandum before the deadlock, pointed out that what was required was 'something more positive than the mere 'prevention of overlapping and competition, namely very 'close co-operation', and he went on to suggest that this could only be brought about by a closer fusion of the two Supply Departments.

Lord Curzon, the Lord President of the Council, took up the question of the air administration. In a memorandum in which he analysed the reasons for the failure of the Joint War Air Committee, he examined also the type of body which should take its place. He explored all possibilities, especially the formation of an Air Ministry and a separate Air Service. He realised this might be difficult, and eventually suggested an Air Board with greatly increased functions which should be regarded as preliminary to an Air Ministry on the possible formation of which the Air Board itself would report. Lord Curzon's memorandum called forth many comments, notably from the War Office and the Admiralty. Lord Kitchener thought the proposed Air Board might give valuable assistance although it should, he said, he made clear that:

> The heads of the naval and military aeronautical services on the Board could not bind the Board of Admiralty or the Army Council to any decision except in regard to such matters as fall distinctly within their responsibility as heads of their respective branches. It would be necessary, therefore, for proposals of policy either to receive the assent of the Admiralty and War Office, or to be referred to, and decided by, the War Committee....

Mr. Balfour, speaking for the Admiralty, took a firmer line:

> A fighting department should, as far as possible, have the whole responsibility (subject to Treasury and Cabinet control) of the instruments it uses, the personnel it commands, and the operations which it undertakes. From this it follows that in so far as air operations are directly ancillary to sea operations, the navy should not have to consult any outside department under any

of the three heads above mentioned. It should be autonomous. I fully admit that the present situation is, from a Parliamentary and political point of view, a serious one. I think it is quite possible that if the government refuse to do anything of their own free will, some dramatic change may be forced on them by the House of Commons. If this be the view of my colleagues, I shall of course raise no difficulties in the way of any change they deem necessary; and when it is effected I shall do all I can to make the new system work. Others, of course, must explain and defend it in Parliament and the Country. . . .

The whole matter was debated at a meeting of the War Committee, held on the 11th of May 1916 when the decision to set up an Air Board was recorded as follows:

1. The Board to be composed of:
The President who shall be a Cabinet Minister. One Naval representative who shall be either a member of the Board of Admiralty or shall be present at its meetings when matters connected with the work of the Air Board are under discussion. An additional Naval representative who need not always be the same individual.
One Military representative who shall be a member of the Army Council.
An additional Military representative, who need not always be the same individual. A member of independent administrative experience.
A parliamentary representative in the other House to the President.
2. The Board will be an Advisory Board in relation to its President, *i.e.* the decisions will not be arrived at by voting.
3. (*a*) The Board shall be free to discuss matters of general policy in relation to the air and in particular combined operations of the Naval and Military Air Services, and to make recommendations to the Admiralty and War Office thereon.
(*b*) The Board shall be free to discuss and make recommendations upon the types of machines required for the Naval and Military Air Services.
(*c*) If either the Admiralty or War Office decline to act upon the recommendations of the Board the President shall be free to refer the question to the War Committee.

(*d*) The Board shall be charged with the task of organising and co-ordinating the supply of material and preventing competition between the two Departments.

(*e*) The Board shall organise a complete system for the interchange of ideas upon air problems between the two services and such related bodies as the (Naval) Board of Invention and Research, the Inventions Branch of the Ministry of Munitions, the Advisory Committee on Aeronautics, the National Physical Laboratory, &c.

4. The Board shall have a Secretariat to assist in the conduct of the business that comes before it.

It will be seen that the Board had no executive powers and, although it was charged with the duty of organising the supply of material and preventing competition, it had no authority to lay down policy on which the nature of the aircraft orders placed must depend. This inherent weakness was to bring about a deadlock, but before that happened the Board did much useful work. Lord Curzon of Kedleston was appointed President and, at the first meeting of the Board, held on the 22nd of May 1916, he made it clear, in an opening speech, that he took a very wide view of the Board's duties.

******

The members were: Naval, Rear-Admiral F. C. T. Tudor (Third Sea Lord) and Rear-Admiral C. L. Vaughan-Lee (Director of Air Services); Military, Lieutenant-General Sir David Henderson (Director-General of Military Aeronautics) and Brigadier-General W. S. Brancker (Director of Air Organisation); Lord Sydenham; and Major J. L. Baird, M.P. (Parliamentary representative in the House of Commons). The Secretary was Sir H. Paul Harvey and the Assistant-Secretary Commander R. M. Groves, R.N. The offices of the Board were at 19 Carlton House Terrace.

******

Whereas the Joint War Air Committee was restricted by the terms of its reference, he explained, there was no question connected with the air which might not come within the province of the Board. The duties of the Board, as defined by the War Committee, would comprise, not only the settlement of points of detail, but formulation of policy, and the President would ultimately be expected to advise the government on the creation of a larger body to deal with questions of the air, and the formation of a separate Air Service. That Lord Curzon was only voicing the government's clear intention is apparent from a speech which had been made in the House of Commons a few days earlier by Mr. Bonar Law, who said:

> The right way to get an Air Ministry—and I think an Air Ministry may come out of it—is to make some arrangement of this kind, to let it grow, and gradually absorb more and more the work of the Air Services. That is the proposal. . . . More and more the new body will have allocated to it all the duties, so far as they can be performed, of an Air Ministry. That is the object of the proposal.

The minutes of the subsequent meetings of the Air Board reveal many difficulties and divergences of opinion. In July 1916 the Board put forward to the Ministry of Munitions a demand for absolute priority for steel, machine tools, and labour, for aeronautical work. Mr. Lloyd George, the Minister, replied with a suggestion that the supply branches of the two air services should be amalgamated under his Ministry. This idea had already been put forward, when the formation of the Air Board was under discussion, by Mr. Weir at that time Director of Munitions in Scotland. He had argued:

> To facilitate rapid action, it appears better to take the fullest advantage of present organisations rather than to create entirely new and independent ones, especially on a question bound up with conditions of industry. . . . It is submitted that the Ministry of Munitions undoubtedly possesses more of the qualifications and powers necessary for an ideal War Supply Department than can be possessed or granted by law to any new department still to be created.

Mr. Weir went on to propose that design as well as supply should be taken over by the Ministry of Munitions. But Mr. Lloyd George's suggestion, on these lines, was rejected by the Admiralty, the War Office, and the Air Board. The Ministry of Munitions had been established in the first place as the recognised supply department for the War Office, and the Admiralty was, in consequence, doubtful whether naval air requirements, if supply were passed to the Ministry, would receive the effective treatment accorded to the War Office. There was, too, the old difficulty that the Admiralty was apprehensive of divided relations between the user and the producer.

So, things remained as before. The Ministry of Munitions had found it essential to control the resources of the country in material and labour. This fact brought the Air Board into inevitable conflict with the Ministry, and the Board's authority in argument was not strengthened by the knowledge that it offered a divided front.

Meanwhile the public dissatisfaction that had resulted in the formation of the Air Board had led also to an investigation into the administration and command of the Royal Flying Corps. Many charges, in Parliament and in the Press, had been levelled against the officials and officers responsible for the Flying Corps, and the government appointed a committee, under the chairmanship of the Hon. Mr. Justice Bailhache, to adjudicate upon these charges.

The committee took evidence on twenty-two days between the 18th of May and the 1st of August 1916, and their investigations, which entailed the preparation of a mass of documented evidence as well as the examination of technical and flying personnel, threw a great strain on the Royal Flying Corps staff both at home and in the field. The committee drew up two reports, an Interim Report, dated the 3rd of August 1916, and a final report dated the 17th of November 1916. The reports refuted all the more serious charges and expressed the admiration of the committee for the wonderful growth of the service, an admiration which was increased, they said, when they remembered that:

> All the work necessary to bring it into its present state of efficiency has been done while bearing the heavy burdens of rendering such services as the Army required of it in the Field.

On the question of supply, however, the committee were more critical and, in their November report, definitely proposed that there should be one Equipment Department for both the naval and military air services.

This proposal had been forestalled by Lord Curzon. As president of the Board he had come up against a blank wall time and again. Notably, in August 1916, he suddenly learned that the Admiralty, ignoring the Air Board, had sought and received Treasury sanction for a programme of expenditure on seaplanes, aeroplanes, and engines, amounting in value to nearly three million pounds. He summoned a special meeting of the Board and pointed out that the Admiralty action was against the terms of reference which laid upon the Air Board the duty of co-ordinating the supply of material and of preventing competition between the two services. The naval representatives on the Board were not empowered to offer either explanation or defence, and a formal note of protest was sent to the Admiralty. The reply made it clear that the Admiralty view was that the matter was not one which rightly came within the province of the Air Board. The Admiralty, indeed, was not prepared to have its air policy controlled by the Board, indirectly, through the instrumentality of the Treasury.

By October 1916 there was an open breach between the two departments. On the 23rd Lord Curzon presented a long Report to the Prime Minister and to the War Committee. This paper, he stated, had been prepared in consultation with his civilian colleagues, but no part in its production had been played by the representatives on the Board of the service departments. The Report, written in plain and forceful language, was, in effect, an indictment of the Admiralty's attitude towards the Board.

> We are not prepared at this moment, while the war is still proceeding, and in the face of the dislocation that might be caused, to advocate the amalgamation of the two Services into a single Imperial Service, or the creation of an Air Ministry which shall assume supreme responsibility for the administration of such a service. Should the Board be in existence at the end of the war, it will be prepared to formulate a plan for the creation of an Air Ministry, which appears to be the only solution of the problem of the Air Service of the future, having regard both to its Imperial aspects and to the great expansion that may be expected, not on the Naval and Military side alone, but in respect of commercial and other developments.

The Report therefore recommended that the existing Supply Departments for both services should be unified and placed under the Air Board, which would be charged with the whole responsibility for supply, design, inspection, and finance, and further recommended that the administration of the Royal Naval Air Service at the Admiralty should no longer be divided among the various Sea Lords but made self-contained as was the administration of the Royal Flying Corps at the War Office. The officer who presides over the Naval Air Service should, said the Report, be made a member of the Board of Admiralty with authority and powers similar to those enjoyed by Sir David Henderson at the War Office.

On the 24th of October 1916, the day following this Report,

a leading article appeared in *The Times* which expressed, fairly and clearly, the general public feeling on the same subject. *The Times* said:

> Those who are best qualified to judge of the working of the Board, are unanimous that there has as yet been no real solution of the ancient rivalry between its naval and its military representatives. . . . We need to fix our eyes, not on the unquestioned superiority of our airmen in these closing months of the great battle on the Somme, but on the situation as it may stand in the spring of next year. Undoubtedly the main defect in our organisation is the weakness of the Air Board. Its powers were dependent from the outset on the readiness of its individual members under an independent chairman, to work together for common ends. It was never invested with such authority as was instantly assumed, for instance, by the Ministry of Munitions; and it was for that reason—not, as our critics supposed, from any ridiculous notion of directing air strategy from Whitehall—that we pressed for the creation of a Minister of the Air. . . . We should like to see Lord Curzon, who should know his subject by this time, insist at once upon fuller powers and abandon all his other work in order to exercise them. . . .

The Report of the Air Board drew a trenchant reply from Mr. Balfour, the First Lord in a memorandum to the Cabinet:

> There is one underlying fact, which is consistently ignored through all the thirty pages of the Air Board's Report—the fact that the Admiralty, and not the Air Board, is responsible for the conduct of the Royal Naval Air Service. The Air Board's criticism, therefore, of the constitution of the Admiralty (with which it seems to have but an imperfect acquaintance) is based upon a misconception I do not propose to discuss in this paper the constitution of the Admiralty. It was created some generations before the Air Board, and its framers had not the wit to foresee that it would someday be required to carry out its duties in subordination to another department. . . .
>
> In the Air Board's Report a proposal is made which, if carried out, would hand over to that body the whole design and provision of aeronautic material. The easy task of criticism would then be exchanged for the difficult labour of administration. . . .
>
> I do not dogmatically deny, however, that the time may come—perhaps, indeed, has already come—when a single Air Supply

> Department may be desirable. But, when such a department is established, I hope it will not be on the model of an Air Board with extended powers. The relation between a fighting department and a supply department should resemble that which now exists between the War Office and the Munitions Department. The department which supplies should do nothing but supply; it should neither determine the amount and character of the things supplied, nor the uses to which they should be put.
> The Air Board are not likely to content themselves with so modest a role . . . the Admiralty . . . would view with the greatest misgiving a system under which they would have to use aeroplanes and seaplanes whose numbers and design were determined for them by an independent and (I suppose I must now add) a hostile department—a department which would have the right to criticise, the power to embarrass, but no direct responsibility for military or naval action.

Mr. Balfour wrote in the white-heat of conviction, but he expressed misgivings which were profoundly felt by the Board of Admiralty whose sole concern was the efficient discharge of their grave responsibilities. Lord Curzon and those who associated themselves with his views were no less convinced and no less patriotic. Each looked at the problem from a national standpoint, and that the resultant conclusions were so divergent and so forcefully held, is indicative of the difficulties with which the subject bristled.

There was another problem which pressed for settlement and one which affected the question of supplies. This was the long-range bombing policy of the Naval Air Service. At the time the Air Board rendered their report to the Cabinet, Colonel Barés, representing the French Air Service, was on a visit to England. He attended meetings at the Admiralty on the 22nd of October 1916 and at the Air Board on the following day, and he pleaded the great importance of bombing operations against German towns and the advisability of concentrating British engine orders in France on two types—Hispano-Suiza and Clerget. He suggested that the British naval and military air services and the French and Russian air services should combine to place orders for these engines. The Admiralty considered that such co-operation offered many advantages and a memorandum was put before the Air Board suggesting that:

> It should be definitely laid down that the navy should keep an

effective force of at least 200 bombers in France (to include Dunkirk).

If this policy were approved the Admiralty considered that 1,000 engines of each type would not be excessive for the Royal Naval Air Service alone.

Sir David Henderson strenuously resisted this proposal. He did not agree with Colonel Barés' views on the results which long-distance bombing would achieve and he asked that all available aeronautic material should be allotted afresh, irrespective of the origin of the orders placed under the 'present competitive methods'. The Admiralty proposal also drew a strong letter of protest from Sir Douglas Haig on the 1st of November 1916. He stated his opinion that the views attributed to Colonel Barés were unsound in theory and should not be accepted in practice.

He protested, emphatically, in the interests of the Empire, against any interference by the naval authorities with the British land forces such as the projected force of naval bombing aeroplanes would involve. Unless his air requirements were first adequately met, the provision of aeroplanes by the naval authorities for work on the fronts of the French and Belgian armies amounted, he said, 'to a very serious interference with the British land forces, and may compromise the success of my operations'. It was not that Sir Douglas Haig was lukewarm towards the idea of bombing German military centres. His view, which he often stated, was that until he had sufficient aeroplanes to ensure adequate air co-operation in his operations, the bombing of Germany was in the nature of a luxury.

Once that co-operation was assured, then the bombing of Germany became a necessity.

Meanwhile, until the government pronounced on this thorny question, steps were taken to place orders for 8,000 Hispano-Suiza engines in France (the raw material to be supplied by Great Britain), on the understanding that the engines would form part of a general pool.

No decisions had been reached when Sir Douglas Haig's letter of the 20th of November 1916 arrived asking for the twenty extra fighting squadrons. The matter was anxiously discussed at a meeting of the Air Board on the 11th of December which Major-General Trenchard attended. He made it clear that the new military squadrons promised for the coming winter would not be enough and that there would, in addition, be an insufficient supply of spares. He suggested it was essential that there should be a stocktaking of the air resources of the whole nation and that, in the meantime, he would like to get from the navy four fully-equipped squadrons. He was not discussing the question of policy, he said, about whether it would have been better to have the whole air force at the front military. We were now in a position where it was obligatory for the army to obtain everything that the navy could afford to lend. He also asked, in addition to four complete naval squadrons, for one hundred Rolls-Royce and fifty Hispano engines which would ensure the equipment of six further squadrons (2 D.H.4, 2 Bristol Fighter, and 2 Spad).

The Air Board put the matter before the Admiralty, expressing the hope that the navy would find it possible, 'at this moment of great emergency', to come to the assistance of the army. The Admiralty thereupon agreed to place four additional squadrons at the disposal of the Flying Corps. They could, however, only surrender fifty-five of the hundred Rolls-Royce engines asked for (twenty-five 250 horse-power and thirty 190 horse-power) and they proposed, further, that instead of giving up fifty Hispano engines, they should surrender to the Flying Corps sixty complete Spad aeroplanes from their contract of one hundred and twenty then in course of fulfilment.

These proposals were gladly accepted. (By a further agreement, in February 1917, the army were to have the complete programme of naval Spads in exchange for all army Sopwith Triplanes.) They entailed considerable reductions in the naval air stations at home. The Eastchurch War Flight was abolished and that at Manston reduced by one-third. Ultimately, also, it was found compulsory to disband No. 3 Naval (Bombing) Wing at Luxeuil. Three of the four naval fighting squadrons had joined the Royal Flying Corps by the end of March 1917, and the fourth arrived in the middle of May.

Meanwhile, at the end of November 1916, the War Committee had debated the questions of aircraft supply and of the Air Board's powers, and a number of conclusions had been drafted. Before they were finally approved, however, there was a change of government, Mr. Lloyd George succeeding Mr. Asquith as Prime Minister on the 7th of December. One of Mr. Lloyd George's first acts was the formation of a War Cabinet which superseded the larger War Committee. Lord Curzon addressed a note to the War Cabinet on the 19th of December 1916 calling attention to the outstanding problems of air policy and supply. He made it clear that there was no possibility of meeting Sir Douglas Haig's demand for twenty extra fighting squadrons from

Royal Flying Corps resources, and he stated that it was indispensable that stock should be taken of all material to be produced for both air services during the next few months.

At a War Cabinet meeting on the 22nd of December 1916 it was decided that the powers of the Air Board should be widened. It was laid down that:

> (1) The Air Board should continue to fulfil the functions allotted to it, devoting special attention to the question of the proper allocation of the aerial resources of the country whenever conflict of competition arose as between the Admiralty and War Office.
> (2) A Fifth Sea Lord should be added to the Board of Admiralty in order to represent that Department on the Air Board with a status and authority of the Director-General of Military Aeronautics.
> (3) A representative of the Ministry of Munitions should be added to the Air Board.
> (4) The design and supply of aircraft should be transferred from the Admiralty and War Office to the Ministry of Munitions.

Before this decision of the War Cabinet was recorded, clauses relating to the new Air Board had been inserted in the New Ministries and Secretaries Act then in course of passage through the House of Commons. In this Act, which became law on the 22nd of December 1916, it was stated that:

> The President of the New Board shall be deemed to be a Minister appointed under this Act and the Air Board a Ministry established under this Act.

Section 7 of the Act said the Air Board was formed for the purpose of organising and maintaining the supply of aircraft in the national interest in connexion with the present war, and Section 8 of the Act that:

> The Air Board shall in relation to aircraft have such powers and duties of any Government Department or Authority, whether conferred by Statute or otherwise, as His Majesty may by Order in Council transfer to the Board, or authorise the Board to exercise or perform concurrently with or in consultation with the government department or authority concerned.

Lord Cowdray was appointed President of the new Board, which held its first meeting on the 3rd of January 1917. It was left to the President to report to the Cabinet what the definite duties and responsibilities of the Board should be. One of the first modifications of the War Cabinet's proposals of the 22nd of December 1916 was an agreement that the Air Board, and not the Ministry of Munitions, should be responsible for design. All the departments concerned agreed to the proposal that the Board should select the designs of aeroplanes and seaplanes with their engines and accessories. The Board was further to decide the numbers to be ordered and their allocation between the two services, while the Ministry of Munitions undertook production and inspection during manufacture.

The officers and staff previously engaged at the Admiralty and War Office on design and supply and on the Board of Invention and Research were lent for service with the Air Board or Ministry of Munitions. As, at this time, a great number of the engines and aircraft on order were of Government design, the Royal Aircraft Factory at Farnborough, where the designs were prepared, was taken over by the Ministry of Munitions.

The constitution of the Air Board was defined by an Order in Council dated the 6th of February 1917, which made no mention of the specific powers to be transferred to the Board from other departments.

★★★★★★

On February the 7th the composition of the Board was announced as follows: President, the Rt. Hon. Viscount Cowdray; Parliamentary Secretary, Major J. L. Baird, M.P., C.M.G., D.S.O.; Fifth Sea Lord of the Admiralty, Commodore Godfrey Paine, C.B.; Director-General of Military Aeronautics, Lieutenant-General Sir David Henderson, K.C.B.; Controller of Aeronautical Supplies, Mr. William Weir; Controller of Petrol Engines, Mr. Percy Martin; Secretary, Sir Paul Harvey, K.C.M.G., C.B.; Assistant Secretary, Mr. H. W. W. McAnally.

★★★★★★

The separation of design from supply and the division of responsibilities between the Cowdray Air Board and the Ministry of Munitions would, possibly, have made the Board unworkable, but for a happy chance. At the beginning of January 1917, the Hotel Cecil was acquired to house all the various departments connected with the Board, including the representatives on the Board of the Ministry of

Munitions (Mr. William Weir and Mr. Percy Martin) and the military and naval air executives. (Mr. William Weir, shortly afterwards knighted and created a Baron in June 1918, was Secretary of State for Air from 27th April 1918 until December 1918.) This meant that the closest possible liaison was secured between the Cowdray Air Board, the Aeronautical Supply Department of the Ministry of Munitions, and the air executives of the army and navy.

The Board, as constituted, became, in effect, a Ministry of Supply, and as such it was eminently successful. It eliminated competition between the two air services and, in co-ordination with the Ministry of Munitions, laid the foundations for an enormous increase in the production of aeroplanes and engines. Indeed, the two departments, working in close co-operation, overcame a host of difficulties and solved the supply problem for the remainder of the war.

★★★★★★

> Total deliveries of aeroplanes increased from 6,633 in 1916 to 14,832 in 1917, and 30,782 in 1918. For complete figures of war aircraft and engine output and of their allocation to various theatres of war see Appendices 7 and 8.

★★★★★★

It was, however, some time before the energetic measures taken by this strangely composite but highly successful organisation could bear fruit and, in spite of the assistance rendered by the Royal Naval Air Service, the supply position for the Royal Flying Corps in France in the early part of 1917 was acute. In the middle of January 1917, when the Nivelle offensive plans were discussed, Sir Douglas Haig told the War Cabinet that the Royal Flying Corps would not be fully ready for an offensive by the 1st of April.

By the middle of February 1917, the air situation was even worse than he had feared, and he again directed the attention of the War Cabinet to the seriousness of the position. He pointed out that there had, through the winter, been continual postponements of the arrival of new squadrons and of aeroplanes for replacement. By the beginning of March 1917 there would be a shortage of from four to seven fighting squadrons below what was promised and seven to ten below what he had asked for, and a further shortage of two new-type corps squadrons. Also, five squadrons, scheduled for re-equipment, would remain unconverted. The commander-in-chief wrote:

> Our fighting machines, will almost certainly be inferior in

number and quite certainly in performance to those of the enemy. In view, therefore, of the marked increase in the number and efficiency of the German aeroplanes, it appears that we cannot expect to gain supremacy in the air in April, and it is even possible that it may pass to the enemy. The seriousness of this situation cannot be overrated, and its possible effect on the results of our operations will no doubt be fully realised by the War Cabinet.

In the event, as will be told, Sir Douglas Haig's fears were only too well founded, and the Royal Flying Corps in France had to pay, in heavy losses, for the muddled direction of the supply problem at home before the formation of the Cowdray Air Board. Actually, on the 9th of April 1917 the number of squadrons with the Expeditionary Force was no more than 50, including the four attached naval squadrons. Of these 21 were corps squadrons, 27 were fighting squadrons, and 2 were bombing squadrons (for types and strength see Appendix 12).

★★★★★★

At the end of October 1916 there were in France, with the Flying Corps, 34 squadrons, plus No. 8 (Naval) Squadron. Between October 1916 and 9th April 1917 further squadrons arrived as follows: No. 52 (R.E.8) 16th November; No. 57 (F.E.2d) 16th December; No. 54 (Sopwith 'Pup') 24th December; No. 53 (B.E.2) 1st January 1917; No. 43 (Sopwith two-seater) 17th January; No. 35 (Armstrong-Whitworth, Beardmore) 24th January; No. 59 (R.E.8) 23rd February; No. 66 (Sopwith 'Pup') 6th March; No. 55 (D.H.4) 6th March; No. 48 (Bristol Fighter) 8th March; No. 100 (F.E.2b for night bombing), nucleus, 24th March; No. 56 (S.E.5) 8th April.

Naval squadrons attached R.F.C.: No. 3 (Sopwith 'Pup')—(to relieve No. 8) 1st February 1917 and No. 1 (Sopwith Triplane) 15th February; No. 6 (Nieuport Scout) 15th March; No. 8 (Sopwith Triplane) re-attached, 28th March.

★★★★★★

Recruitment and Training (Royal Flying Corps)

At the beginning of the war the Royal Flying Corps was severely handicapped by the War Office policy, which was based on the assumption that the war would probably be of short duration. When Lord Kitchener took control this view was changed, but in the meanwhile the plans had been framed so that almost the whole available strength of the Flying Corps was put into the field in the four squadrons which were sent to France. To make the squadrons up to strength for overseas, pilots were taken from the Reserve and from the Central Flying School and mechanics from the School, the Depot, and from the nucleus of No. 6 Squadron. The Central Flying School was also depleted of aeroplanes. In other words, there was a clean sweep which almost paralysed development at home in the early stages.

At Farnborough there were a number of partly-trained pilots and a few aeroplanes considered useless for work overseas. From these resources No. 1 Reserve Aeroplane Squadron was created and the further training of pilots begun. To make up the deficiencies in mechanics the Military Aeronautics Directorate, without waiting for Treasury sanction, began the enlistment of civilian mechanics at the same rates as those authorised for the Army Service Corps, and thus brought together a nucleus of experienced men who were to form a backbone of the squadrons created in 1915. Seven civilian pilots employed at the Hendon aerodrome were enlisted in the Royal Flying Corps.

The outstanding factors in the creation of new squadrons were the vision and backing of Lord Kitchener, the Secretary of State for War. The day after the original squadrons left for overseas Lord Kitchener sent for Lieutenant-Colonel Brancker and told him he would require large numbers of new squadrons to co-operate with the new armies which he proposed to create. This verbal assurance strengthened the Military Aeronautics Directorate and enabled them to push boldly ahead with plans for expansion.

Down to December 1914 certain new squadrons and additions of personnel were sanctioned, as asked for, but on the 19th of December Lieutenant-Colonel Brancker outlined a policy of development which contemplated thirty squadrons in the field and a probable five in reserve. This estimate, as the Chief of the Imperial General Staff (Sir James Wolfe Murray) minuted, was 'an endeavour to forecast our requirements for some distance ahead'. But it did not look ahead far enough for Lord Kitchener. When the papers reached him on the 21st of December 1914 he gave his approval in these words:

> A.D.M.A. ought to be prepared to double this.

Those few words lifted the whole subject to a different plane. They came as a tonic and an incentive to the directing staff of the Flying Corps, created an atmosphere in the War Office favourable to a generous consideration of the air service demands, and, of even greater importance, swept away the uncertainty and petty obstruction which must have arisen from the need of obtaining sanction for increases step by step. Furthermore, Lord Kitchener continued to maintain a keen personal interest in the development of the new squadrons and, for some months, had an almost daily talk on progress with Lieutenant-Colonel Brancker.

It has been said that a beginning in the training of new pilots was made by the creation at Farnborough of No. 1 Reserve Squadron. At the same time, it was urgently represented to the Expeditionary Force that expert pilots must be sent home from France to act as instructors if development was to be begun on the right lines. Eventually, at the end of September 1914, Major C. A. H. Longcroft and a few other pilots came back from France to take over new squadrons and to act as instructors, and they gave the first impetus to fresh development and expansion.

Aerodromes, left untenanted when the original squadrons went to France, were available at Netheravon, Gosport, Montrose, and Dover.

******

> Montrose, owing to its great distance from London and France, was handed over to the Quartermaster-General for other army requirements. It is a commentary on current ideas of the probable duration of the war, that when No. 2 Squadron left Montrose for France, notices were posted on various doors, bearing the words, 'Not to be opened until we come back'.

******

But many others would be needed and the existing civil aerodromes at Brooklands and Hounslow were taken over by the War Office in August 1914, and, in September, Shoreham and Joyce Green were acquired. Officers were sent round the countryside to reconnoitre for other suitable sites and, as a result, land at Norwich, Castle Bromwich, Beaulieu, Catterick, and Northolt was taken up.

The policy adopted, with the object of providing pilots and mechanics to replace casualties in the field and to produce a nucleus of new squadrons, was to set up as many reserve squadrons as possible charged with the duty of training pilots *ab initio* and of organising the nucleus of service squadrons. In the early stages, before the instructors in the reserve squadrons were judged experienced enough to assess the qualifications of their pupils, newly trained pilots were sent to the Central Flying School to pass their final tests.

Reference has been made to the recruitment of expert mechanics on special rates of pay. The numbers so enlisted, immediately following the dispatch of the Expeditionary Force, sufficed to satisfy all urgent demands created by the early expansion at home. Meanwhile a scheme of recruitment on the peace rates of pay was laid down and the numbers each month regulated.

Unfortunately, in the early stages of development, many experienced mechanics who came forward could not be absorbed by the Royal Flying Corps. No efficient system existed in the army whereby recruits were allotted to work for which they were best suited, and large numbers of the most expert mechanics who, inspired by patriotism, enlisted freely were dissipated into line regiments, and the majority of them were lost to the technical services for ever. An effective control of these men at this period would have been richly rewarded later when they could have been transferred to the ranks of the rapidly growing air service.

With the decentralisation of the Flying Corps into Wings, which took place in November 1914, the units in England were reorganised. The Military Wing was abolished and the Reserve Squadrons at Farnborough and Brooklands (Nos. 1 and 2), together with the Depot, the Aircraft Park, and the Record Office, were grouped to form the Administrative Wing under Lieutenant-Colonel E. B. Ashmore, and the Fourth Wing was created at Netheravon under Lieutenant-Colonel J. F. A. Higgins to comprise Nos. 1 and 7 Squadrons.

Up to the middle of 1916 no very great difficulties in the recruitment of mechanics arose. It was more frequently necessary temporarily to stop recruiting than to devise means for hastening it. The Regent Street Polytechnic and its Director of Education, Major Robert Mitchell, deserve mention in connexion with the supply and technical training of men for the Royal Flying Corps. Even when recruiting was temporarily closed, men who possessed the trade certificate of this institution found a ready entry into the Flying Corps.

They proved to be of such a good standard of intelligence and efficiency that, in the spring of 1916, the Polytechnic was formally asked by the War Office to undertake the responsibility for the special recruitment of tradesmen for the air service, an offer of out-of-pocket expenses at the rate of one shilling per head (afterwards reduced to ninepence per head) being made, payable for every man accepted and graded as 1st or 2nd Class Air Mechanic. The words 'out-of-pocket' are euphemistic as the men, apart from being recruited under an organisation developed by the Polytechnic, received also a specialised training. The Polytechnic organisation became well known throughout the whole of the United Kingdom. Its representatives in all the industrial centres were in personal touch with men in the requisite trades in a way impossible to officers acting for the Directorate of Recruiting. Major Robert Mitchell, writing to the War Office in March 1917, said:

> The work entailed involves a considerable amount of trouble and expense, especially in connexion with the examination of candidates for the wireless. Very careful selection is made, and a number of those sent forward are men who have passed public examinations including the London Matriculation and the B.Sc. . . . During the last two months some 3,000 recruits have been sent forward. . . . We have to interview a great many more than we select.

In the middle of December 1915, the Royal Flying Corps had established a testing school at the Duke of York's headquarters, Chelsea, where men were put through a test in the trade for which they wished to enter. If successful, they were given a certificate which they presented at the recruiting depot in Whitehall as authority to enlist. By the beginning of January 1916 other testing centres, for men wishing to enlist in Scotland, had been established in Glasgow, Dundee, and Edinburgh, as well as in a number of smaller centres in England.

The recruitment of men proceeded with comparative smoothness until the middle of 1916. Then, in June, came Sir Douglas Haig's request that the number of Royal Flying Corps squadrons in France should be increased to fifty-six by the spring of 1917. He said:

> I fully realise that any demands for this large number of squadrons involves the provision of a very large number of pilots and observers. The importance of this service is, however, so great, that I consider it essential that the necessary personnel should be found, even at the expense of a reduction in other directions.

The Adjutant-General at the War Office (Lieutenant General Sir C. F. N. Macready) was perturbed, he minuted:

> If the R.F.C. are to be given precedence, we shall probably collapse in some other direction. At present we are short of artificers for the guns and for Army Service Corps. I am trying to come to an arrangement with Ministry of Munitions to get artificers, but have not much hope until I bring the matter before

> the War Committee to decide if the authorised establishment of the army is, or is not, to have precedence over Munitions claims. As regards R.F.C, if the C.I.G.S. decides that it is to have precedence I will give effect to it, but I am satisfied that this will cause loss of gun power at the front.

The only source of supply of artificers at this time, it was stated, was the front, where they were being combed out from the infantry and other non-technical units, but the numbers were not expected to be large.

In the result it was decided that provisional sanction should be given for one-half the proposed expansion, and that the whole subject should be reviewed again in October 1916. On the 17th of October Sir David Henderson raised the question again, seeking authority for the remainder of the programme. But Sir Nevil Macready could hold out small hopes, he replied:

> Seeing that it is not in my power to produce the men you require, this being dependent on factors over which I have no control, I cannot do more than say that as men, skilled and unskilled, become available I will do my best to provide what is necessary for the completion of your programme.

Meanwhile Sir Douglas Haig was anxious. On the 1st of November 1916, he requested the War Office to tell him whether his proposals for the expansion of the Royal Flying Corps were approved. He was answered on the 15th of November that the expansion to fifty-six squadrons was approved and would be carried out as it was found possible to allot rank and file in the required numbers.

Next day, the 16th, the commander-in-chief made his application for twenty extra fighting squadrons and, on receipt of this, the Director of Air Organisation (Brigadier-General W. S. Brancker), in a comprehensive minute, reviewed the full implications of this demand. The completion of the existing programme still required 10,200 men, he said, and the additional twenty squadrons, together with an essential expansion of reserve squadrons, would require a further 13,560 men. The existing approved programme was for eighty-six service squadrons, for all theatres of war, and for sixty reserve squadrons. This estimate of sixty reserve squadrons to create and maintain eighty-six service squadrons had proved too low.

Under very favourable conditions, it had only just been possible to replace the wastage in pilots during the Somme battle. It had to be expected that casualties would become proportionately heavier as air fighting increased, and for the same reason it was essential that a higher future standard should be exacted from pupils before qualification, with a consequent slowing down of the output of trained pilots. The Director of Air Organisation, therefore, asked that sanction should be obtained at once for thirty-five additional training-squadrons as well as for the twenty extra fighting squadrons. Sir David Henderson pressed the matter to a decision, and at an Army Council meeting on the 12th of December 1916 the expansion of the Royal Flying Corps to 106 service squadrons and 95 reserve squadrons was formally approved. The latter number was increased, at the beginning of January 1917, by two squadrons specially sanctioned for the training of night-flying pilots for home and overseas.

To get the men necessary to fulfil this expanded programme, energetic measures were undertaken. All unskilled men attached to the squadrons in France, who were deemed fit to qualify for a skilled trade, were gradually replaced by men of a lower medical grading and sent to England for training. Recruitment of suitable skilled and unskilled labour in the Dominions was intensified. Qualified tradesmen were combed out from the infantry and other combatant units and transferred to the air service. A closer scrutiny of men engaged in munition and other protected industries was undertaken, and great numbers of these were released, more especially as women became qualified to replace them.

There was, furthermore, a steady stream of recruits into the Flying Corps as men were called to the colours under the system of conscription. A suggestion, put forward by the Director of Air Organisation in his minute already referred to, was also adopted and was to bear unlooked-for fruits. His suggestion was that some of the new reserve squadrons might be raised and maintained in Canada. Training aeroplanes, he thought, could be built in America, and possibly in Canada, and the raising of squadrons in the latter country would save the shipping of material across the Atlantic. In the result it was decided that twenty reserve squadrons should be formed in Canada, and a small Royal Flying Corps party left for Toronto early in January 1917. From this modest beginning a great training organisation grew up which constituted an ever-expanding source of supply of highly trained pilots for the western front.

All these various measures arose out of Sir Douglas Haig's requests made before 1916 had ended. They were not to bear their full fruits until 1918. It is not too much to say that the whole development of the Royal Flying Corps in France and the direction of the air war down to the armistice, were conditioned by the practical foresight of Major-General Trenchard and of Sir Douglas Haig as outlined in their programmes of 1916.

Before the war both branches of the air service made use of the Central Flying School for the training of pilots. But the School, like every other air activity, was kept short of money, and, although the course was cut down from the six months considered essential for really satisfactory training to three months to enable double the number of pupils to be taken, the School could not fully supply the demands of the two services. In the short time during which the course lasted some attempt was made to teach general military subjects, but in the main the School staff could do little more than teach the elements of handling an aeroplane in the air, landings, and simple cross-country flying. As the School could not train all the pilots required by the Flying Corps a number of pupils had to be taught in the squadrons.

In August 1914 Netheravon was taken over as an annexe to the Central Flying School for the preliminary training of officers, and reserve aeroplane squadrons were formed to give initial training to officers and men and to provide the nuclei of service squadrons. Thus, at the end of 1914, in addition to the Central Flying School, there was No. 1 Reserve Aeroplane Squadron at Farnborough, No. 2 at Brooklands, (Brooklands aerodrome had been taken over from the British and Colonial Aeroplane Company in August 1914), and No. 3 at Netheravon (from 13th January 1915).

******

> The annexe to the Central Flying School at Netheravon was closed down in October 1914 and reopened as an instructional establishment by No. 3 Reserve Aeroplane Squadron on the 13th of January 1915.

******

The advanced training of all pilots was carried out whenever possible at the Central Flying School, but when no vacancies existed, pilots from the reserve squadrons completed their training in the service squadrons. (The service squadrons in England at the beginning of 1915 were Nos. 1, 7, and 8.)

It was soon clear that the Central Flying School could not cope with the number of pupils sent forward for instruction, and in January 1915 each service squadron at home was called upon to give a complete course of training to pilots and personnel required for the creation of one new service squadron. The nuclei of new squadrons were also, as before, to be formed in each of the Reserve Squadrons, which were to continue to give preliminary training to pilots and technical instruction to men. At the beginning of January 1915, the three reserve squadrons and the three service squadrons were, between them, preparing to form six new squadrons (Nos. 10, 11, 12, 13, 14, and 15). By May 1915 it was obvious that the existing arrangements for training pilots were still inadequate, especially in view of a proposal to increase the number of pilots with the squadrons in France from twelve to fifteen. The reserve squadrons were therefore given the task of providing advanced as well as preliminary training to a limited number of pilots.

******

> In December 1915 the arrangement whereby elementary and advanced training to pilots was given in the same units, was modified, and certain Reserve Aeroplane Squadrons were set apart for preliminary training only.

******

In the autumn of 1915 specialisation in training began. A War Office letter in September 1915 said:

> The importance of a thorough knowledge of the Lewis gun, and of training in firing from an aeroplane, is daily becoming more evident.

At the end of September, therefore, a Flying Corps school for instruction in the Lewis gun was opened at Dover. The school was moved at the end of November to Hythe, which offered better facilities. (The school was known as the 'Machine Gun School, R.F.C until September 1916 when it became 'The School of Aerial Gunnery, Royal Flying Corps'.) Officers and men who were trained at the school went back to their squadrons, and as part of their duties were required to give instruction in the Lewis gun.

The next attempt at specialisation was the beginning of modest instruction in air fighting. A War Office letter of November 1915, to the officer commanding the II Brigade, says:

> I am directed to inform you, hat as the 'number of combats in the air is constantly increasing it 'has been decided that pilots and observers under instruction at home should be trained, as

far as practicable, in fighting in the air.

******

The II Brigade was formed in England by Brigadier-General J. F. A. Higgins in August 1915. The II Brigade was disbanded in England on the 15th of January 1916 (it was re-formed in France on the 10th of February 1916), and its place taken by the VI Brigade, formed on the same day.

******

Graduated pilots, the letter suggested, should be instructed by being opposed to an experienced flight commander. In the same month training in night flying, for specially selected officers, was added to the work of the squadrons.

In November also, a Flying Corps training centre for men was opened at the Curragh in Ireland and a School of Instruction for officers at Reading. The latter was an innovation, as the School was to be a depot from which vacancies in the reserve squadrons could be filled. Officers who were candidates for the Royal Flying Corps were sent to Reading for instruction in engines and the rigging of aeroplanes, and in map reading, reconnaissance, co-operation between the Flying Corps and other arms, signalling, and organisation. The Reading School was formed on the 1st of December 1915, its equipment at the opening being two old Martinsyde aeroplanes and one fifty horse-power Gnome engine.

******

A school, on similar lines, was opened at Christ Church, Oxford, in April 1916. By this time, it was stated that the two schools were to be regarded as preparatory schools supplying all other training establishments in the United Kingdom. They were known as 'Schools of Instruction' until October 1916, when their nomenclature was changed to 'Schools of Military Aeronautics'.

******

About the same time a special wireless school was formed at Brooklands for the instruction of observers and wireless officers.

The position at the end of 1915 was that eighteen reserve squadrons were in existence and eight service squadrons had been formed and were assisting in the training. There were, additionally, the Central Flying School, and the Schools of Instruction at Reading, Hythe, and Brooklands. There were, however, a few squadrons about to be formed, and early in January 1916 the number of service squadrons in England had increased to thirteen, while the number of reserve squadrons remained the same.

In the early part of 1916 Major-General Trenchard had many times to complain that the pilots sent as reinforcements to France from England were insufficiently trained. This was due in part to bad weather interfering with training and in part also to a shortage of instructors. Pilots were required at the front quickly and in great numbers, and the existing training resources were strained to meet the demand. Had the need in the field been less pressing many pilots who went overseas would have been kept back for further instruction.

On the 16th of February 1916, Brigadier-General J. M. Salmond returned from France to command the V Brigade at home, an appointment which put him at the head of the training organisation in England. From now onwards training was put on a sound basis and expansion was rapid. (On the 9th of March 1916 Brigadier-General Salmond took command of the VI Brigade, which proceeded to absorb the V Brigade. In July 1916, the VI Brigade became the Training Brigade and, in August 1917, the Training Division.) To raise the standard of pilots passing out from the schools and squadrons in England, new qualification tests were drawn up on the 23rd of March 1916. These stated:

(1) The pilot must have spent at least 15 hours in the air solo.
(2) He must have flown a service aeroplane satisfactorily.
(3) He must have carried out a cross-country flight of at least 60 miles successfully. During this flight he must land at two outside landing places under the supervision of an officer of the R.F.C.
(4) He will climb to 6,000 feet and remain at that height for at least 15 minutes, after which he will land with his engine stopped, the aeroplane first touching the ground within a circular mark of 50 yards diameter. This test can be combined with (3) if proper supervision can be arranged.
(5) He will make two landings in the dark assisted by flares.

Officers qualifying in the above tests were to be given, during the time they remained with the squadrons at home, every opportunity to gain further air experience. They were to be made to fly in bad weather on all possible occasions and to practise landing, bomb-dropping, righting in the air, night flying, and flying in formation.

In May the importance of practice in fighting and in night flying was further emphasised. Pilots, said a War Office order, were to be encouraged in trick flying, and to be given every opportunity to practise fighting manoeuvres. It was intimated that a certain proficiency in this direction would shortly be required from pilots before graduation.

When the Training Brigade was formed from the VI Brigade, in July 1916, the reserve squadrons were reorganised and definitely divided into two categories sufficiently indicated by their new names, Elementary Training Squadrons and Higher Training Squadrons.

A step forward in the training for fighting in the air was the result of an ingenious invention introduced in the summer of 1916. This was the Hythe Gun Camera, built in the form of a Lewis gun, which responded to the action of firing by taking photographs which told the pupil approximately where his shots would have hit. The pupil took a sight on an aeroplane and, when he judged he was on his target, pressed the trigger which caused a photograph to be taken. The action of pulling back the cocking handle of the gun changed the film so that the practice could be continued until the spool of films was finished. The films, when developed, showed a series of concentric circles and, if the aiming were approximately accurate, a photograph of the target aeroplane.

As the air speed of the aeroplane was known, it was a simple matter to calculate the degree of accuracy of the aiming, and to analyse the type of error. The Gun Camera, which was adopted by all the Allied flying services, could be used from the ground against aeroplanes landing and getting off, and in the air against other aeroplanes in all the manoeuvres of aerial combat, and it formed in effect a continuous education in the art of aerial gunnery. In addition to training with the Hythe Gun Camera, actual firing practice was given in the Training Brigade against dummy aeroplanes moored in reservoirs, lakes, or in the sea, and against small balloons in the air.

In December 1916 new regulations under which a pilot would be required to qualify were drawn up. The number of hours solo was now increased from fifteen to twenty for qualification, and up to twenty-eight, according to type of aeroplane, before a pilot could be considered fit for duty overseas. Before a pilot was allowed to wear 'wings' he was required to pass auxiliary tests in gunnery, artillery observation, bomb-dropping, and photography.

In February 1916 an Officers' Cadet Battalion had been formed at Denham to train selected men from the infantry. In October the battalion became the 'Cadet Wing, Royal Flying Corps', and it was laid down in this month that all candidates for admission to the Flying Corps, other than commissioned officers, would be required to pass through the Cadet Wing. An exception was made for candidates, specially qualified, for appointment as assistant Equipment Officers who could be commissioned direct.

In July 1916 the School at Reading (which at that time had 300 officers under instruction) was expanded to give training to men in fitting and rigging. A jam works at Coley Park was taken over and equipped to give instruction to 1,000 men at a time. The object of the course, which first lasted for five weeks (later increased to eight), was to produce mechanics with a general knowledge of fitting or rigging and special knowledge of one type of engine or aeroplane. In August 1916 a subsidiary school was set up in Edinburgh for the training of skilled squadron fitters. In September further steps were taken to meet the deficiency in skilled fitters and turners by placing 400 men at a time under instruction at Polytechnic Institutes. A headquarters was established at the Regent Street Polytechnic (known as the School of Preliminary Technical Training) which was officially made responsible for the administration of all similar centres throughout the country.

By the summer of 1916 the number of military balloon sections had grown considerably. The Kite Balloon Training Depot, which had been established in March 1915, was reorganised, and two subsidiary schools were opened at Larkhill and Lydd at the end of July 1916. In December the home balloon units were grouped to form a Kite Balloon Training Wing.

Some attempt was made in this same period to regularize the training of observers. From the beginning of the war selected officers, many of them from infantry and artillery units, had been sent to the home reserve and service squadrons for training. In 1914 little more than reconnaissance practice was given to observers under training, but during 1915 other subjects were added. It was not, however, until August 1915 that qualification tests for observers were laid down. Even then they were not looked upon as being hard and fast, but were drafted to procure a similar general standard of proficiency among observers throughout the Flying Corps.

The observer, before being posted overseas, was now required to know the Lewis gun thoroughly, to be proficient in the use of the Flying Corps Camera, to be able to send and receive wireless messages, to know the methods of co-operation between aeroplanes and artillery, and to have had some practice in the air in ranging batteries or in reconnaissance. After the formation of the school at Reading, officers who were attached to the Flying Corps as observers on probation were sent there for a course whenever vacancies were available, while others went to the Wireless School at Brooklands (three weeks), and to squadrons mobilizing for overseas. As many as could be accommodated were given a three-weeks' course at the School of Aerial Gunnery at Hythe. In September 1916 the Wireless School at Brooklands, hitherto under the direct orders of the War Office, was placed under the Training Brigade.

The Wireless Test Flight was transferred from Brooklands to Joyce Green where its experimental work continued to be controlled by the War Office, and Brooklands, now charged with wireless, artillery co-operation, and machine-gun work, became the 'Wireless and Observers School'. The general idea now was that corps observers should be completely trained at Brooklands and army observers at Hythe. It was not, however, until the middle of 1917 that this demarcation was definitely followed.

Equipment officers, usually recruited from candidates skilled in a particular branch of engineering, were given a general course, from July 1916, at the School at Reading, whence they passed for special instruction to Brooklands (wireless), or to the Northern or Southern Aircraft Depots (engines, rigging, or mechanical transport). In September 1916 the training of equipment officers was made more comprehensive. The Reading course was increased to eight weeks, following which a further six weeks' course was given in the Training Brigade (for training in squadron duties), the Aircraft Depots (for Aircraft Depot or Aircraft Park duties), or at the Royal Aircraft Factory (for instruction in engine repairs).

Men were trained at Farnborough in general service matters, in wireless, and in photography, and at Coley Park, Reading, in fitting and rigging. As has been told, the Polytechnic Institutes of the country also assisted in the training of men. Tribute must be paid to the staff at Marconi House, and to other civilian wireless and cable schools, to whose co-operation the wireless organisation of the Royal Flying Corps was indebted.

Specialised instruction to men was given at the most suitable stations. Armourers, for example, were trained at the School of Aerial Gunnery at Hythe.

The general position at the end of 1916 may be thus summarised. There was no shortage of officers either for training as pilots or observers or for technical duties, and there was every prospect that officers could be supplied, with a fair training, to meet all the demands that might be made in the ensuing year. With men it was different. There was a serious shortage of skilled and unskilled men likely to make efficient mechanics. The setting up of the school at Coley Park, Reading, had done much to alleviate the serious shortage of skilled fitters and riggers and was to do more in the future, but the position could not be remedied until suitable candidates, in far greater numbers, were coming forward. The measures taken to get these men have already been outlined, but while those measures were being organised, the shortage of skilled mechanics persisted.

It may be well here to re-state the various factors which retarded the early development of the Royal Flying Corps. They were:

(1) The pre-war starvation of the Royal Flying Corps, which resulted in a home aircraft industry of minute proportions and small experience.
(2) Our entire dependence on the French in the early days of the war for engines and our lesser dependence for aeroplanes.
(3) Our pre-war dependence on Germany for magnetos.
(4) The competitive system of supply between the naval and military air services and a consequent muddled direction of supply sources at home and abroad.
(5) The confusion which arose from the difficulty of defining the relative duties of the Royal Naval Air Service and of the Royal Flying Corps.
(6) The initial war mistake of sending all available Royal Flying Corps aeroplanes and personnel to France, which handicapped early training and expansion at home.
(7) The early enlistment of skilled mechanics in infantry and other combatant regiments and the consequent permanent loss of much expert service to the Royal Flying Corps.

We have seen how these factors delayed expansion and re-equipment, and we shall see in the following chapters what were the effects on the early operations in France in 1917.

Chapter 5

The Western Front in the Winter of 1916-17

Operations and Developments

As the Somme battle was drawing to a close the Commanders-in-Chief of the British and French armies and representatives of the other Allied nations met at Chantilly to discuss plans for the offensive in 1917. They had similarly met at the end of 1915 to talk over the 1916 campaign, and had then decided that July was the likeliest month for the main effort. But the Germans had forestalled them by opening the Verdun offensive in February, 1916, and this had necessitated a modification of the Allied plans. The enemy was to be given no such opportunity to wrest the initiative in 1917.

The Chantilly Conference decided that the pressure on the Western front must be maintained throughout the winter and that the Allied armies should prepare for an offensive on the various fronts to be launched in the middle of February 1917. The British part in this offensive was to be, initially, an attack on the enemy salient created as a result of the Somme advance between the Scarpe and the Ancre. The salient was to be pinched out by simultaneous attacks on each shoulder, the Fifth Army operating on the Ancre front and the Third Army from the north-west about Arras. As a preliminary, to secure the left flank of the advance on the south bank of the Scarpe, the capture of Vimy Ridge was planned, the task being allotted to the First Army.

This was to be the beginning. But Sir Douglas Haig had also a task elsewhere along the front that might be expected to tax his utmost resources. The German submarine war was causing the gravest disquiet. Allied, and more particularly British, shipping was being sunk at an increasing and alarming rate. At the Admiralty, indeed, a conviction was growing that so long as the enemy retained the Belgian coast and with it the increasingly important submarine bases of Bruges, Ostend, and Zeebrugge, the submarine menace, already severe, might easily become a vital danger. It was therefore decided that the main purpose of the British campaign in 1917 must be the clearance of the Flanders coast; and Sir Douglas Haig intended, after weakening the enemy by the spring offensive at Arras, to transfer his main summer operations to Flanders. It was his hope that he would be able to develop this offensive to follow quickly on the completion of the spring campaign and that the enemy would be dealt a hard blow in the north before he realised the southern attack was ended.

Coincident with the Arras offensive, there was to be an attack between the Oise and the Somme by the French northern group of armies and, a fortnight later, the main French offensive was to be launched on the Aisne.

But, once again, the Chantilly plans were not to come to fruition. On the 12th of December 1916, the French Government was reorganised under the premiership of M. Briand, and a new French Commander-in-Chief, General Nivelle, was appointed.

******

General Joffre, relieved of his command, was promoted Marshal of France, and appointed technical military adviser to the French War Cabinet. General H. Lyautey, who became Minister of War soon after, successfully claimed that no such appointment was foreseen in the Constitution and that the Minister of War was, by law, the adviser of the Government. Marshal Joffre's appointment thus became a sinecure.

******

General Nivelle had little faith in the efficacy of movement by steady stages to limited objectives. Instead he envisaged a complete and decisive break-through by means of a rapid and smashing blow delivered with the maximum strength. The new commander-in-chief therefore proposed that the British army and the French northern group of armies should be used to pin the enemy forces on a wide front while he delivered a breakthrough assault on the Aisne. The rupture which he held must follow, would be exploited to the full and with rapidity, and to this end he would require a large mass of manoeuvre. The decisive attack on the Aisne would be delivered by two armies of three corps each with a third army acting as the mass of manoeuvre to exploit the initial victory which was to be achieved in twenty-four or, at the most, forty-eight hours. But General Nivelle could only effect his concentration by withdrawing large forces from the line, and he therefore appealed to the British Commander-in-Chief, on the 21st of December 1916, to take over from the French the line between the Somme and the Oise.

Sir Douglas Haig felt unable to accede to these demands in full, but he agreed to extend his front south of the Somme to the Amiens-Villers-Bretonneux cross-roads, the extension to be completed by the beginning of February 1917. This proposal did not satisfy General Nivelle who appealed to his government, which in turn appealed to the newly constituted British War Cabinet. In the result a conference was held in London on the 15th and 16th of January 1917 at which General Nivelle, in the presence of Sir Douglas Haig and of Sir William Robertson, the Chief of the Imperial General Staff, unfolded his plans to the British Ministers with brilliant and convincing advocacy. It became clear that there was to be no repetition, on a wider scale, of the long drawn out Somme battle, but one sharp and overwhelming rupture.

The plan, so powerfully and so lucidly presented, was accepted by the War Cabinet mainly on the grounds that the French had the larger army, and their country was occupied by an invader and that therefore they must have the final decision. It was agreed that Sir Douglas Haig should be given two additional divisions from England and that he should relieve the French as far south as the Roye-Amiens road by the 1st of March. It was further agreed that the decisive offensive should begin not later than April the 1st, (Sir Douglas Haig expressed the view at this conference that the Royal Flying Corps could not be ready for an offensive by the 1st of April), and that if, within reasonable time, the offensive did not produce the results hoped for, it was to be ended by mutual agreement in order that the main British effort might be transferred to Flanders in accordance with the original Chantilly plans.

★★★★★★

> At a further conference at Calais, held on the 27th of February 1917, Sir Douglas Haig was informed of the British War Cabinet's decision that, for the period of the forthcoming operations, General Nivelle would be in complete command, and he was instructed to conform to the French Commander-in-Chief's strategic direction until the offensive terminated.

★★★★★★

The extension thus decided upon was completed by the 26th of February 1917, by which time the British were responsible for one hundred and ten miles of exceptionally active front. The role of the British Army, now subsidiary to that of the French, was to attract and hold as great a force of the enemy as possible, particularly on the Arras front, before the French Aisne offensive opened. British preparations were therefore pushed ahead for spring operations on the Ancre by the Fifth Army, at Arras by the Third Army, and at Vimy Ridge by the First Army.

Such were the new plans. The German command, however, had no intention of maintaining their great salient intact until such time as the Allies were ready to assault it. Towards the end of February 1917, they began an evacuation of the sector stretching from Arras to Noyon, devastating the whole area with ruthless thoroughness as they fell quietly back.

It will be recalled that air reconnaissances in November 1916 had discovered the beginnings of a formidable defensive line far back behind the Somme area. (Vol. 2.) From the time the early digging was discovered, air reconnaissances kept watch on its progress and periodical photographs were taken. The completed line, henceforward identified by the British as the Hindenburg Line, branched off from the original defences near Arras, ran south-eastwards for twelve miles to Quéant, and passed thence west of Cambrai towards St. Quentin.

While this line was being perfected throughout the winter, the British kept up a steady pressure which took them quietly forward on the Somme front. But before the end of February 1917 there came a number of indications that an enemy withdrawal over a wide front was contemplated. From the 17th of February onwards, prisoners spoke of it. It became known also that advanced wireless stations and batteries were moving back. From the 16th to the 24th of February whatever German movements there were, were hidden in mist. Rain made many British aerodromes waterlogged, and even had pilots been able to go up they would have seen nothing of the fog-shrouded German area.

But in a bright interval in the afternoon of the 25th of February six Sopwith 'Pups' of No. 54 Squadron got through to the Hindenburg Line and their pilots brought back news of great fires burning in dumps and villages as they passed on their way. This information threw light on a statement made by a prisoner, captured on the previous day, that orders had been issued for the German troops to fall back, by successive stages, to the Hindenburg Line. On the 26th of February a reconnaissance by No. 18 Squadron of the Hindenburg Line reported on the elaborate strength of this system of defences and revealed that many new battery positions had been constructed in its vicinity. Furthermore, the intermediate trench systems between the existing German front line and the Hindenburg Line had been strengthened by a number of small forts and strong points. By the end of February, the British command had accepted the contemplated withdrawal, but the date and the time to be taken between the successive stages were still unknown. During the first two weeks of March the number of fires and explosions reported from the air rapidly mounted, the majority of them being in villages in a zone extending eight miles east of the German front line. On the 5th of March air observers reported that the enemy artillery was using only one gun per battery, from which the army intelligence staff concluded that the remaining guns had already been withdrawn. On the 14th of March, German guns were registering the enemy trenches in St. Pierre Vaast Wood and German dug-outs were seen blazing.

On the same day the full plans of the German evacuation fell into our hands. They were picked up in a dug-out in Loupart Wood and revealed the successive stages by which the withdrawal to the Hindenburg Line was to be made and gave details of the rear-guard defence to be fought by detachments with strong machine-gun support. The stages of the further retirement, shown as planned to begin on the 11th of March, were to the Bapaume-Rocquigny line, thence to the Beugny-Ytres line, and finally to the Hindenburg Line. Now that the full enemy plan was revealed, a general British advance was ordered to begin on the 17th of March 1917 from the south of Arras to the Roye Road. Before the work of the squadrons of the Royal Flying Corps in this advance and the subsequent air operations can be described, it will be necessary to go back over the preceding winter months and review the growth and tactical development of the air service.

Air Lessons of the Somme Battles

The operations fought out on the Somme taught some minor lessons in the tactical employment of aircraft and confirmed the basic soundness of the air offensive policy. They led also, among many officers holding high military command, to a change of attitude on the value of air power, a change which found expression in proposals that the control of the corps squadrons should pass to the Artillery.

The first proposal had been put forward by Sir Henry Rawlinson, the Fourth Army Commander, in a letter to General Headquarters on the 29th of October 1916, in which he submitted that all artillery squadrons should be placed, except for purely technical matters, under the direct orders of the Corps Artillery Commanders he said:

> To ensure perfection, we require:
> (1) Experience on the part of the artillery in matters of organisation and executive. This is very important and is being dealt with.
> (2) The observers must be highly skilled. Aeroplane observation for artillery purposes is skilled work of a very high order. With an unskilled observer the best trained and best equipped battery is useless. The large percentage of effective shoots carried out with aeroplane observation have been the work of a few men.
> (3) The number of observers and machines must be adequate for the tasks to be undertaken. Aeroplane artillery observation is trying work, the amount which one observer can do in a day is strictly limited, casualties are not uncommon, and the observers require rest from time to time.
> (4) Intimate relations must exist between the artillery units and the Flying Corps units working in combination.

He also urged that steps should be taken to increase the number and quality of aeroplane observers and that, if necessary, officers should be taken from the Corps artillery and trained for air work.

Major-General Trenchard, in a memorandum of the 1st of November 1916, outlined the difficulties which stood in the way of the Fourth Army Commander's proposals. He said:

> Artillery work is not the entire duty of the Corps Squadron, which is also charged with contact patrol work, trench reconnaissance, and trench photography. Nor are Corps Squadrons at present equipped with machines of a suitable type to do all the work required by the artillery, such as photography at a distance behind the lines which must be done by fighting machines. If machines working with them were to be handed over to the artillery, smaller squadrons consisting of artillery machines and those doing other work respectively would be necessary, and small squadrons are extravagant both of personnel and material. Again, technical matters cannot be divorced from tactical employment. A large part of the artillery work is technical, *e.g.* wire-

less, use of machine-gun, etc. . . . The batteries detailed to work with aerial observation change even more often than do the observers, and it is this which has often prevented the best results in the past. A more detailed knowledge of each other's work and methods, especially among the higher commanders, would effect great improvement. The Fourth Army appear to be under a misapprehension. By far the largest part of the work of ranging batteries is and must be done by the pilot and not by the observer, since the pilot only is able to place his machine exactly as he requires it at any moment to give him the view he desires. The observer's principal duty is watching for, and reporting, other hostile batteries which open fire, and keeping a look-out for hostile aircraft. . . . More artillery officers would be welcome, but they must form part of, and live with, the squadron, and must be trained as pilots, or they will lose most of their value. The actual observation of the fall of rounds is the easiest part of artillery work and can be quickly learnt by anyone with good eyesight. Skill in the technical work, knowledge of methods employed, careful recording of results and their use are the essentials of good artillery work, and these can be learnt nowhere else but in the squadron.

The number of machines which can work on any length of front at the same time is limited by technical difficulties of observation and communication, but it is seldom that the resources of a Corps Squadron as at present constituted are fully employed. The relations between squadron commanders, pilots and observers, and the batteries with which they work, are generally speaking intimate under present conditions, provided batteries are not constantly changed. It is in the higher ranks that more intimate relations and mutual knowledge are required. . . .

On the 13th of November General Sir H. S. Home, Commanding the First Army, submitted a proposal almost identical with that of Sir Henry Rawlinson and, in his letter, after stating that:

The operations on the Somme had proved that tactical success is largely dependent on superiority in artillery and supremacy in the air, (gave his opinion that) until the direction and control of artillery fire from the air is placed in the hands of the artillery we shall not gain full advantage from our superiority in guns and ammunition.

Many discussions took place at General Headquarters, and, in the result the Commander-in-Chief, than whom the air service had no more whole-hearted supporter, decided that aeroplane work for the artillery must continue to be a Royal Flying Corps responsibility, and that such shortcomings as there were in the co-operation between the two arms must be overcome by closer liaison.

There was, however, a measure of agreement that the time was approaching when the Balloon Sections could form part of the artillery command. Major-General J. F. N. Birch, the artillery adviser at General Headquarters, proposed, as a preliminary step, that artillery officers should be selected for immediate training as balloon observers. His proposal was approved and, at the end of November 1916, it was arranged that one artillery officer should be attached to each of the twenty-two balloon sections then existing. This was not to entail an increase in the establishment of four officers to each section; a Royal Flying Corps officer from each section was to be sent home to help in the formation and training of new sections.

★★★★★★

> The proposal to make the Balloon Sections a part of the Royal Artillery was never put into force. In February 1918, however, the number of artillery officers detached for duty with the sections was increased by fifty *per cent*.

★★★★★★

At the same time to facilitate an anticipated expansion of the balloon service in the spring of 1917, changes in organisation and nomenclature were made. On the 20th of November 1916, a Balloon Wing was incorporated in each of the Royal Flying Corps Brigades with the armies. The Balloon Wing was to comprise a headquarters and a varying number of companies (each of two sections providing one balloon) on the scale of one Balloon Company to each corps in the army.

Although from the end of the Somme battle onwards, improvements in the methods of aircraft co-operation with the artillery were made only in matters of detail, these improvements were important. In particular, considerable advance was made in the wireless communication. Before the Somme one wireless aeroplane for every 2,000 yards of trench line was the maximum that could be employed without the wireless signals clashing, but by the spring of 1917 it was possible to increase the number of wireless observers to one for every 1,000 yards or, in other words, to double the number of aircraft that could help the artillery on any given section of the front at the same time.

This improvement was due, in part, to wireless technical developments and, in part also, to better organisation. Air signals were still further cut down and advantage was taken of the directional qualities of wireless. Experience in the Third Wing, during the early part of the Somme battle, had made it clear that wireless reception was at its best at artillery ground stations, and that the air observer's signals came in most strongly when the aeroplane was flying *towards* the battery with its aerial parallel, or in line with, the ground aerial. It was therefore laid down that the aerials at the artillery ground stations should be so placed that their line of direction bisected the arc of fire of the guns and the method of flying and signalling when targets were being ranged was standardised as follows:

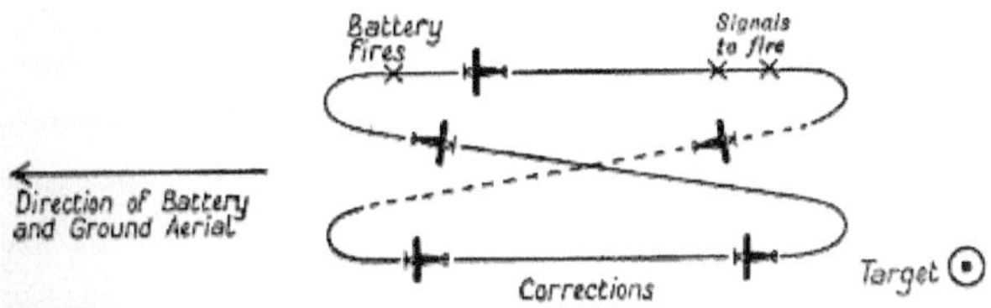

From this it will be seen that the observer sent his signal calling for fire as he turned his back on the target and flew towards the battery. When the battery fired, the aeroplane was headed diagonally towards the target to enable the observer to mark the burst of the shell, and the corrections were sent after the aeroplane had again turned towards the battery. It was found that this method, apart from the fact that it was simple and rapid, made it unnecessary for the aeroplane to return close to the ground station before the wireless signals were made—a practice which had always hitherto increased the possibilities of wireless jamming.

A further improvement was the setting up of an organisation for the systematic analysis of every instance of failure in the co-operation. An advanced squadron wireless unit, known as the 'Central Wireless Station', was established in each corps area, at or near the head-quarters of the Corps Heavy Artillery. The central wireless stations were equipped with several aerials and listened to the wireless progress of all shoots. If the communication between the aeroplane and the battery broke down the observer could call up the central wireless station, which was well forward and therefore less subject to jamming, and learn, by ground signal, the cause of the trouble. If necessary the central station could, by telephone to the battery commander, act as a medium between the aeroplane and the battery and carry on the shoot.

The central wireless station also formed an advanced store for the rapid dispatch of wireless spares to the battery ground stations and housed the expert staff whose duty it was to inspect and supervise those stations. This system was first introduced by Lieutenant-Colonel E. R. Ludlow-Hewitt in the Third (Corps) Wing in August 1916 and was adopted by the remaining corps wings in the spring of 1917.

★★★★★★

> At a Corps Wing Commanders' Conference on the 12th of February 1917, Lieutenant-Colonel Ludlow-Hewitt supplied full details of the working of the central wireless station in his Wing to all other Corps Wing Commanders.

★★★★★★

Changes had also been made in the numbers and establishments of wireless stations. Up to August 1916 the number of wireless operators had been based on the number of Flying Corps squadrons. Each corps squadron was allowed thirty receiving stations and thirty operators, and each army two-seater squadron twenty stations and twenty operators. But this allowance took no account of the fluctuating number of artillery units served by each squadron, nor did the approved establishment allow of any reliefs for the operators. Experience had shown that, for efficient service, at least two operators were required at each station.

Major-General Trenchard had sought approval therefore, on the 11th of August 1916, for a new wireless organisation based, not on the number of squadrons, but on the number of artillery units each squadron had to serve, as follows:

(1) Two operators and one station for each heavy or siege battery, and for each counter-battery group headquarters and each corps headquarters.
(2) Ten operators and five stations for each Divisional Artillery.
(3) Two operators and one station for each Corps Wing and six operators and two stations for each Corps Squadron.
(4) A pool of operators and wireless sets at each Aircraft Depot.

He further proposed that the Royal Flying Corps wireless stations with the artillery units should be permanently allotted and should accompany the batteries whenever they moved. These recommendations had received War Office approval on the 14th of September

1916 and the new wireless organisation had been brought into force in the field five days later.

These changes and improvements in the wireless communication and organisation are matters of detail, but they had wide effects. As it was now possible to employ twice as many wireless aeroplanes on a given length of front, it was first contemplated that the number of corps squadrons in France would have to be doubled, but Major-General Trenchard showed that it would be more economical in personnel, especially of squadron and flight commanders, and certainly not less efficient, if, instead of increasing the number of squadrons, the number of aeroplanes in each corps squadron was raised from eighteen to twenty-four, and his proposal embodying this was approved by the Army Council on the 27th of March 1917.

******

When the Army Council approved this increase, they hoped that B.E. aeroplanes made surplus by the proposed re-equipment of five corps squadrons with R.E.8 aeroplanes could be used to bring the remaining B.E. squadrons in France up to the increased establishment. But delays occurred in the R.E.8 replacement programme and, on the 26th of April, the War Office informed Sir Douglas Haig that it would be impossible to provide for a permanent increase of corps squadron establishments during 1917.

******

Meanwhile steps had been taken to expand those corps squadrons which would be active in the area of the 1917 spring offensive. When this offensive opened, four squadrons in the main area of operations had been increased to twenty-four aeroplanes and one to twenty-one, while north and south of the main sector three squadrons had been increased to twenty-one aeroplanes.

******

No. 16 Squadron was increased to twenty-four aeroplanes by taking three each from Nos. 5 and 10 Squadrons. No. 5 also lost three to bring No. 2 Squadron up to twenty-one aeroplanes. Nos. 8, 12, and 13 Squadrons were increased to twenty-four aeroplanes by taking nine from R.F.C. H.Q. Reserve, five from the Home Defence Wing, and four from the II Brigade—Squadrons Nos. 6 (1), 42 (1), and 53 (2). No. 59 Squadron (R.E.8's) was increased to twenty-one by keeping the similarly equipped No. 21 Squadron down to fifteen. Finally, Nos. 7 and 9 Squadrons were also increased to twenty-one aeroplanes by taking a further six from R.F.C. H.Q. Reserve.

******

The improvements which took place in artillery cooperation as a result of the Somme battle were not confined to equipment and organisation. The experiences of the battle were embodied in a revised pamphlet, 'Co-operation of Aircraft with Artillery', (S.S.131.) issued by the General Staff in December 1916. The broad principles in this paper remained in force to the end of the war although it was revised from time to time to incorporate minor modifications. (The general state of the development of aircraft co-operation with the artillery is shown in a memorandum issued by the Artillery Adviser at G.H.Q. in April 1917, reprinted as Appendix 9.)

One modification, made in April 1917, had reference to the 'Zone Call'. Occasional confusion had been caused, when this call was used, because batteries sometimes took in calls meant for an adjacent army corps. The reason was that the original call gave no indication of the map sheet to which the call referred. From the 1st of April 1917, the four subsidiary squares, into which each lettered square of the 1/40,000 map was divided, were lettered A, B, C, D and W, X, Y, Z on alternate sheets from north to south.

A development of the winter period, which bore indirectly on aircraft co-operation with artillery, but also had wider significance, was the setting up of a special intelligence system for the Royal Flying Corps. It had been realised, during the Somme offensive, that full advantage was not taken of the great mass of information collected, or assimilated, by pilots and observers. It was not enough that reconnaissance reports and air photographs should be passed on to the army units. Every officer who flew over the lines, no matter on what duty, might be able to tell something valuable. It was essential also that all information should be rapidly collated, interpreted, and communicated. Major-General Trenchard proposed therefore, in October 1916, that Intelligence Sections should be established in certain squadrons and wings where the Intelligence Officer could be in intimate touch with the flying and photographic personnel.

******

The idea of Squadron Intelligence Sections had been partly anticipated by some of the Squadrons in the Third Wing, in which, early in the Somme battle, enthusiastic air observers organised, and voluntarily made themselves responsible for, the collation and dissemination of information.

******

The experience of the French had shown that the opportunities for question and discussion which an Intelligence Section enjoyed through living with the flying officers were essential to the efficiency of the intelligence system. The proposal was approved and was embodied in instructions issued to Armies in December 1916. Major-General Trenchard would have preferred that the intelligence units should form part of the Royal Flying Corps, but G.H.Q. ruled that they must remain under the Army Intelligence Chief. The new Branch Intelligence Sections were set up at the headquarters of each corps squadron and of each army wing.

******

> Each Section consisted of one Intelligence Corps Officer, two draughtsmen with duplicator, one clerk with typewriter, and an orderly.
> On the 5th of April 1917 the War Office approved the appointment of an additional G.S.O. 2 at R.F.C. H.Q. for the sole duty of examining and disseminating information.

******

Their duties were thus defined:

> (1) To interrogate every observer and ensure that full advantage be taken of such information as he might possess,
> (2) To disseminate to all concerned with the least possible delay information obtained by the Royal Flying Corps which required immediate action,
> (3) To examine and, where necessary, to mark all photographs and to issue both photographs and sketch maps illustrating the photographs.

Although the sections formed part of the Army or Corps Intelligence they were placed under the direct orders of the officer commanding the wing or squadron who could, at his discretion, disseminate information. This meant, in effect, that anything likely to be of urgent tactical importance could be passed to the troops concerned direct and with the minimum of delay.

The changes in the contact patrol organisation, embodied in amended instructions issued in December 1916, were of a minor nature. Wireless, as a method of communicating the positions of our own troops, was given up. It was held to be too dangerous as informative to the enemy and, in practice, it had rarely been used. The use of wireless by contact patrol observers was now restricted to sending targets to the artillery under the zone call system. These targets were not to include enemy batteries, normally dealt with by the air artillery observers, but were to be confined to such targets as '*minenwerfers*', machine-guns, and strong points holding up the advance, to troops massing for counter-attack, or to immediate reserves.

The use of mirrors, displayed on the backs of the advancing infantry, was also discarded. There were instances, in the early days of the Somme battle, when mirrors had given satisfactory results, but there were so many objects on a battlefield reflecting light that this device proved too unreliable. The method which had given the best results, namely, the lighting of flares, was now to be the sole means by which the attacking infantry were to signal their progress, and the information so obtained was to be passed back to the head-quarters of the corps or divisions by message-bag dropped from the air, followed by a personal report when the observer landed.

Battalion and Brigade headquarters communicated with the aeroplane by signal panel or by lamp. This had proved satisfactory provided the signals were displayed only when asked for or when the air observer was obviously in a position to see them. These headquarters had sometimes wished to send instructions incorporating the positions of troops or targets on their front. The existing method was to flash out, on the panel or lamp, the coordinates of the positions, but, in practice, confusion had sometimes resulted as long messages and, in particular, a series of numerals, proved difficult to read from the air. Under the amended instructions, such positions were to be indicated by the clock-code method. The sender was to be considered in the centre of the clock and the twelve hour to point due north.

★★★★★★

> On the 14th of November 1916, the headquarters of the 20th Australian Infantry Battalion had displayed their ground sheets from the moment they established their new centre. The sheets were observed, in due course, by an enemy observer and the headquarters were promptly shelled and had to be evacuated.

★★★★★★

Air fighting during the Somme battle, as has been said, taught a number of lessons about the tactical employment of offensive formations. These lessons were incorporated in a memorandum drawn up by Flying Corps headquarters in January 1917, (issued by the General Staff, March 1917, see Appendix 11), in which it was emphasized that certain fundamental principles of land and sea fighting are equally applicable to fighting in the air. Among these are concentration, mutual co-operation and support, and a system of command whereby the number of units under each commander is limited to what he can directly and effectively control.

Experience had shown that fighters of performance superior to the majority of the enemy fighters could successfully patrol alone or in pairs, but that flying in formation was essential where this superiority was absent or not definitely marked. Fighting, however, even between formations had, up to this time, always tended to develop into a series of more or less independent individual combats. It was realised that the striking power of a unit would be enhanced by greater cohesion and an attempt was made to evolve a fighting formation that would have this cohesion but would also be flexible. It was laid down that such a formation would be made up of a number of units of two or three aeroplanes under a sub-leader. These units, so far as possible, were to be permanent organisations to give pilots that instinctive rapidity in action that comes of experience, knowledge of each other's methods, and community of doctrine.

A formation, it was stated, would not normally exceed three units, but if greater strength was required separate formations could be employed in such a way that, while they acted independently, they could also be mutually supporting. The important feature of this new grouping was that the fighting unit was now two or three aeroplanes. Each pilot was to select, and concentrate on, a single aeroplane of the enemy formation, but pilots were instructed to keep cohesion by fighting inward towards the leader. Actual tactics, once the issue was joined, varied according to the type of aeroplane and to the personal characteristics of individual pilots. The rules laid down for the guidance of fighting pilots did not aim at rigidity nor did they envisage any standardization of method.

Commanders and formation leaders were given a wide discretion, and nothing which could be avoided was done to cramp their initiative. (The tactics of fighting in single-seaters at this time are outlined in a pamphlet, 'Notes on Aeroplane Fighting in Single-Seater Scouts,' issued by the General Staff in November 1916, and reprinted as Appendix 10.) It was not long since opinion was sceptical on the feasibility of individual pilots fighting one another in the air. But now, with the definite recognition of the fact that the air fighting unit was not one but a number of aeroplanes, the day of the individual pilot flying alone on a roving commission was drawing to its end. There were to be many other pilots of outstanding fighting qualities, but they were to achieve their successes as formation leaders.

Reconnaissance formations were similarly organised into groups each under its own sub-leader. If an escort of single-seater fighters was also provided it was found preferable to keep the two types of aeroplane separate, each under an independent leader, with the fighters above the reconnaissance formation in a position which gave a good view and freedom of manoeuvre. The duties of the fighters were to attack and break up an approaching hostile formation, to prevent the concentration of superior force on any part of the reconnaissance formation, and to assist any aeroplanes which might be compelled to drop out through engine trouble or other cause.

Bombing formations at this time were provided, in addition to escorting fighters, with a local escort for protection if the enemy got through to close quarters. Some of the bombers, notably the B.E.'s, were virtually without defence. Had all bombing formations been composed of aircraft capable of giving an account of themselves in a fight, many of the escorting aeroplanes could have been dispensed with. B.E. aeroplanes which carried out bombing raids were usually given a close escort of six F.E.2b's and an offensive escort of six single-seater fighters. When, near the objective, the bombing pilots got into formation of line ahead to drop their bombs, the escorting pilots circled above ready to swoop on enemy fighters which might attempt to interfere.

As a result of the more aggressive attitude of the German airmen, it became necessary to enlist the help of the army wireless interception stations (known as 'Compass Stations') towards the quick location of enemy aeroplanes working along the British front. An elaborate scheme of co-operation was drawn up in October 1916. Trained observers at the compass stations were to communicate, by wireless, the bearing of enemy aeroplanes, as indicated by their signals or by ground observation, to army wing headquarters. When fighting aeroplanes came to be fitted with receiving sets, these messages from the compass stations, it was stated, would go to the aeroplanes direct, but meanwhile the wing head-quarters would inform the fighting squadrons by telephone and order special action if this was considered necessary. It was not, however, planned, except in the event of a big enemy air attack, to send up fighting aeroplanes specially. As far as possible German aircraft on the British side of the line were to be dealt with by pilots already in the air, and, until such time as fighting aircraft were fitted with wireless receiving apparatus, forward ground stations, on a direct telephone line from the compass stations, were established in each army area to signal to pilots. This they did by laying out ground strips indicative of the areas in which enemy aeroplanes were reported.

******

Pilots had maps divided into sectors, numbered on the enemy side of the lines and lettered on the British. The ground station signals included the number of enemy aeroplanes working and, when they crossed the lines, their direction of flight. The scheme was put into operation in November 1916.

******

Air Fighting in the Winter of 1916-17

How necessary this new organisation was, is proved by the fact that in December 1916, and in the early months of 1917, air fighting, on the few fine days there were, took place almost entirely within a mile or so on either side of the front line trenches. It was now the German practice to patrol the area of the trenches, and it is illustrative of the change in the air position that of the twenty-seven Flying Corps aeroplanes destroyed in December 1916, seventeen fell in the British lines, many of them while doing tactical work for the army corps. The enemy was most active in the Arras area, where the British spring offensive was to be staged, and his fighting formations, led by Richthofen, were conspicuous.

To indicate the supremacy of the German aeroplanes and the success of their leader an example may be quoted. On the 20th of December 1916 an offensive formation of six D.H.2's of No. 29 Squadron was attacked by Richthofen at the head of his group of five Albatros fighters. One of the D.H.2's fell in the German lines with a dead pilot, and of the others four in a damaged condition were forced down, one landing in the trenches and three on the Squadron aerodrome.

The D.H.2's, however, were not at the same disadvantage against formations other than those led by Richthofen or by one or two other prominent leaders. It was noticeable, in much of the fighting at this period, that, probably owing to lack of experience, many of the German pilots did not get the best out of their superior aeroplanes, and their dominance was to that extent discounted. Furthermore, there was one British aeroplane which could stand up to the best of the German fighters. This was the Sopwith 'Pup' with which No. 54 Squadron and No. 8 (Naval) Squadron were equipped. In his report of a combat with a pilot (Flight Lieutenant A. S. Todd) of the latter squadron on the 4th of January 1917, Richthofen says:

> One of the English planes (Sopwith one-seater) attacked us and we saw immediately that the enemy plane was superior to ours. Only because we were 'three against one, we detected the enemy's weak points. I managed to get behind him and shot him down.

In January 1917, although the fighting still took place over the trenches and even well into the British lines, the enemy formations were, on the whole, out-fought. The enemy airmen continued the activity into the night by the low-bombing of aerodromes and other objectives with occasional success. A bomb which hit a hangar of No. 16 Squadron at Bruay in the early hours of the nth of January destroyed four aeroplanes and wounded three men.

In one of the many fights, over the area of the trenches, on the 7th of January 1917, an F.E.2d of No. 20 Squadron was set on fire at 9,000 feet over Ploegsteert Wood. The pilot, Sergeant T. Mottershead, enveloped in flames, dived to make a landing, his observer, Lieutenant W. E. Gower, spraying him with a fire extinguisher as the aeroplane went down. Sergeant Mottershead made a good attempt at landing, but his aeroplane collapsed and threw the observer clear, but pinned the pilot in the burning wreckage. The observer again tried to check the flames with the extinguisher, but without success. Sergeant Mottershead, who died of his injuries, was posthumously awarded the Victoria Cross.

With improved weather in March 1917 came wider activity indicative of the fierceness of the impending air struggle. The main centre of action shifted from the Arras area to the front of the First Army, where the I Brigade of the Royal Flying Corps had to meet an onslaught that surpassed all previous experience. The pressure became so great that, on the 19th of March, the III and V Brigades were ordered to maintain offensive patrols in the neighbourhood of Douai where the I Brigade was most hard pressed. Elsewhere along the British front the Arras sector still remained the most active. Numerous enemy formations, made up of six or eight aeroplanes, patrolled the lines in readiness to pounce on unprotected corps aeroplanes or on reconnaissance and photographic formations. To counter these tactics close escorts of two fighters were, in the more dangerous areas, provided for each aeroplane working for the artillery and, in addition, there were line patrols by groups of from four to seven fighters from the Army Wing and offensive patrols specially sent out to intercept the enemy formations. Even so, twenty-five per cent, of the casualties during the month were aeroplanes doing tactical work for the corps; and in many other instances, where aeroplanes so working escaped when attacked, the escorting aeroplanes themselves fell victims. (One hundred and twenty Flying Corps aeroplanes were shot down in March, fifty-nine in the British and sixty-one in the German lines.)

Two examples of the trend of the fighting may be quoted from the records of the I Brigade. On the 9th of March an offensive patrol of nine F.E.8's of No. 40 Squadron was suddenly dived on by an enemy formation led by Richthofen. In the fight which ensued, lasting half an hour, four of the F.E.'s were shot down and four sent down to be landed in a damaged condition. The pilot in the last aeroplane of the F.E. formation was wounded and his aeroplane caught fire before he could land. The pilot jumped clear before the impact. The only visible damage inflicted on the enemy fighters was one aeroplane shot down and apparently destroyed.

★★★★★★

> This aeroplane, piloted by Richthofen, was not destroyed. An account of the fight is given by Richthofen in *The Red Air Fighter*. (This book is republished by Leonaur in *Richthofen & Böelcke in Their Own Words* along with *An Aviator's Field Book* by Oswald Böelcke.) He had a narrow escape. His petrol tank was pierced by a bullet, the petrol pouring into his cockpit, and his engine was hit in many places, but he made a successful forced landing in a small field. Another pilot of the German formation was slightly wounded.

★★★★★★

The second example is the experience of three F.E. 2b pilots of No. 25 Squadron who were engaged on a line patrol in protection of B.E. artillery aeroplanes on the 28th of March. A formation of five Halberstadt fighters attacked and were engaged by the F.E. pilots while the B.E.'s were getting clear. As a result one of the F.E.'s was shot down in the German lines and the other two, with damaged engines, in the British lines.

Major-General Trenchard was in a position of difficulty and anxiety. He had to look forward to enormous demands preliminary to, and concurrently with, the Arras offensive. What the outcome of that offensive would be no man could know, but it was clear that the fighting both on the ground and in the air would be of unprecedented intensity.

That air co-operation was essential to the success of the coming offensive was no longer questioned. That this co-operation must be bitterly paid for, at least in the early stages of the offensive, there was now no doubt. But would it be possible, on an effective scale, at all? The answer to that question would depend, in a degree, on elements outside Major-General Trenchard's control, chiefly on the extent to which the enemy air service was reinforced and on the early arrival of his own new fighting squadrons. But what he could, and must, do, before the offensive began, was to conserve to the utmost the forces he had. This was a matter of difficulty.

An army of inferior strength may fall back behind strong defensive positions and there get breathing space for reorganisation. Not so an air force. The enemy air service must be effectively and continuously countered. An enemy who is not kept busy in the air can, with the utmost freedom, use his energy to devastate the vitals of the army's communications. The general instructed his brigade commanders to avoid the risk of large casualties. He also decided that, to secure the advantages of surprise once the air offensive began, the employment of squadrons equipped with the new-type aeroplanes, such as the Bristol Fighter and the D.H.4, should be restricted, and that, further, the squadrons of the head-quarters Ninth Wing should not be used until five days before the battle opened. It was found impossible to keep strictly to the latter arrangement, but, during March, the activity of the Ninth Wing was kept at the minimum.

There were instances when distant air work, judged by the army as imperative, had to be undertaken and the risk of heavy loss accepted. The German withdrawal to the Hindenburg Line in the middle of March necessitated reconnaissances in search of defence systems east of that line and demanded that a close watch should be kept for indications of further withdrawals. These distant reconnaissance flights, made by the Ninth Wing in the latter part of March, suffered severely. On the 24th of the month six Sopwith two-seaters of No. 70 Squadron, on their way to Valenciennes, were attacked by the enemy in superior strength and lost two of their number while the remainder, badly shot about, got back with difficulty. The same reconnaissance was again attempted next morning by a similar formation. This time worse befell. One pilot, who turned back over Cambrai with engine trouble, survived; the remainder were shot down.

Thus, in this unsuccessful attempt at one reconnaissance, the squadron lost fourteen officers killed or missing and seven aeroplanes. On the other hand, a reconnaissance formation occasionally went its way unmolested. While the Sopwiths of No. 70 Squadron were being shot down on the morning of the 25th of March, a formation of No. 57 Squadron (eight F.E.2d's—a more formidable type of aeroplane than the Sopwith), elsewhere in the air, successfully reconnoitred as far as Le Cateau and got back to the lines before they met with opposition, which they shook off.

The Advance to the Hindenburg Line

It has been told how air reports and other indications revealed the German retirement to the Hindenburg Line and how a general Allied advance from Arras to Roye was ordered to begin on the 17th of March 1917, to conform with the German movements. For two weeks the British Fourth and Fifth armies moved steadily forward. The air co-operation over this brief period is of interest because for the first time since the early days of the war conditions approximated to open warfare. But it was open warfare of a special kind. There was no question of a long-prepared pursuit of a demoralised enemy.

The German armies went back with deliberation and in accordance with a detailed plan. With a ruthlessness that exceeded their military needs they laid waste the countryside as they went. They fell back on established defensive systems from which they could, at their wish, develop a counter-stroke at any moment. The British armies, on the other hand, left prepared positions further and further behind them and they were required to rebuild every link in their communications as they advanced. In these circumstances the policy adopted was to move forward from one line of resistance to another to ensure that there was always a roughly prepared defensive line on which the troops could accept battle if the necessity arose.

It also assured the food and ammunition supply, as each forward step was made only after the communications to the next line of resistance were opened. Thus, cavalry and infantry outposts kept touch with the enemy while, in their rear, the main body of the infantry moved to successive lines which were at once put into a state of defence.

It was with the advanced parties that most of the tactical work of the Flying Corps squadrons was done. There was no determined air opposition to this work. The German command knew that the Allied offensive could not be developed from the area the German troops were evacuating, that it must come at Arras and in the Champagne. On the 3rd of March the Germans captured an important Staff memorandum of General Nivelle which fully revealed the French commander-in-chief's strategy. Furthermore, the Allied preparations at Arras and on the Aisne were open to the surveillance of the German airmen. Great enemy concentrations, including air squadrons, were made in these areas to meet the approaching menace and there was, in consequence, no effective attempt to dispute the work of the Royal Flying Corps in the area of the Hindenburg Line.

The British air concentration was also in progress behind the Arras—Vimy front, but although Major-General Trenchard was in no position to divert air squadrons to harass the German retreat, he instructed his Brigade Commanders to exploit the position to the full with their available means. They were told that the essentials of the situation were:

> (*a*) To keep the enemy, in immediate contact with our own troops, under constant observation, so as to obtain the earliest possible indication of any withdrawal.
> (*b*) In the event of a withdrawal, to harass the enemy's retiring troops by every means in their power.
> (*c*) To push out reconnaissances to a distance whenever the weather permitted to search for new trench systems east of the Hindenburg Line, and for any indication of a withdrawal east of that line, such as burning villages, road and rail movements, new aerodromes, &c.

General Headquarters had laid down in September 1916, that in the event of rapid movement:

> (1) The Army Wing, and squadrons of the Corps Wing not allotted to leading Corps, would be moved under Army arrangements, moving normally only when Army headquarters moved.
> (2) Squadrons of the Corps Wing allotted to the leading Corps were to keep as close to the Corps headquarters as possible and move under the orders of the Corps.

★★★★★★

On the 30th of November 1916 G.H.Q. instructions stated that squadrons attached to corps were under the orders of the corps commander and that for all artillery and contact patrol work and for close reconnaissance or photography in the corps area, they would receive their orders from the corps direct. Brigade and wing commanders were only to be responsible for the methods employed to carry out the corps orders.

★★★★★★

It was held that even if the advance was rapid it would not be necessary for squadrons to move every day and that the use of temporary landing grounds would often meet the situation.

On the 21st of March 1917 brigades were instructed that although some corps headquarters had already moved and that others were about to move the military situation was not sufficiently clear to warrant the moving of aerodromes. Instead, advanced landing grounds were to be selected near the corps headquarters and portable hangars erected for the daytime protection of the aeroplanes. Wherever possible aeroplanes were to be flown back at night to their squadron aerodromes.

As the British Fourth and Fifth armies were concerned in the advance, the air work fell to the IV and V Brigades.

Squadrons of the IV Brigade worked with the Corps of the Fourth Army as follows: No. 34 with the III, No. 7 with the IV, No. 9 with the XIV, and No. 52 with the XV. In the Fifth Army area No. 15 Squadron worked with the V Corps and Nos. 3 and 4 Squadrons with the I Anzac Corps.

A feature of the tactical air work in the forward movement was the attachment of squadrons, or flights, to divisions. In the I Anzac Corps No. 4 Squadron was directly attached to the left forward Australian division and No. 3 to the right. No. 15 Squadron, more particularly for contact patrols, co-operated with the 7th Division, and, in addition, provided two aeroplanes for work with the Lucknow Cavalry Brigade. Similarly, in the Fourth Army area, No. 7 Squadron reported to the 32nd Division and, when the advance was well under way, No. 52 Squadron provided one aeroplane for contact patrol work for the 8th and 20th Divisions.

The air co-operation with the cavalry provided the chief features of interest. The 5th and 4th Cavalry Divisions were detached from the Cavalry Corps and placed under the orders of the Fourth and Fifth Army commanders for the advance. (The Lucknow Cavalry Brigade was already with the Fifth Army.) The task of the cavalry was to keep touch with and to harass the enemy. Cavalry may be checked by many and various obstacles, and a careful study from the air of the ground over which the cavalry were to operate was important. Further, advancing cavalry, even more than advancing infantry, are liable to lose touch with the rearward commands and the value, therefore, of aircraft as a connecting link is enhanced.

The latest instructions applicable to aircraft co-operation with cavalry were those issued in September 1916, when No. 18 Squadron had been attached to the Cavalry Corps for the Somme battle. But the expectations which had prompted this attachment had been doomed to disappointment, and there had been no opportunity to test the efficacy of the arrangements under battle conditions. For the advance to the Hindenburg Line, orders for the co-operation with the cavalry, incorporating these earlier instructions, were issued as follows. Aeroplanes were to be detached from their squadrons, during the daylight hours, to work under the direct orders of the Cavalry Divisional commanders.

The air observers were to be given definite limits for reconnaissance and were to be asked to report on a clearly-defined area, answer specific questions, or follow a stated course, and to drop their information by message bag on the report centre of the formation ordering the reconnaissance, and to follow this up, on landing, by a personal report to the headquarters of the formation. A code of signals was issued by which the ground stations could give the pilot and observer further instructions, within narrow limits, when they were in the air. The air observers were to watch for artillery targets during these cavalry operations, notably:

(1) Fleeting targets such as troops on the move or massed in the open behind cover.
(2) Troops in trenches, guns in the open or under cover, and fortified houses or strong points which might be holding up the advance.

When a suitable target was seen observers were to call for fire, under the zone call system, and give general observations of the results. For targets under heading (2), where deliberate ranging might be essential, preliminary arrangements were to be made beforehand, whenever possible, with specified batteries. For close liaison, and to advise the cavalry commanders on the uses and limitations of aircraft, a wing commander was attached to the staff of the Cavalry Corps and a junior Flying Corps officer to the head-quarters of each of the Cavalry Divisions. These liaison officers were also responsible for the selection and preparation of temporary landing grounds, for the provision and operation of the ground signals to aircraft, and for the emergency supply of petrol and oil carried by the Cavalry Divisions. In addition to the liaison officers, the equipment and personnel for two wireless stations, and a rigger and a fitter with a light tender to deal rapidly with minor repair work, were attached to each Cavalry Division.

The main air co-operation with the cavalry was done by No. 9 Squadron, working with the 5th Cavalry Division (Fourth Army), and by No. 15 Squadron working with the Lucknow Cavalry Brigade (Fifth Army). Air observers had no difficulty in following and communicating the movements of the cavalry and of the advanced guards of the British infantry, but the air reports, particularly on the Fourth Army front, were often robbed of their full value because, after the first few days, ground communications were found, with few exceptions, to be swift and reliable. The German artillery fire was small, so that telephone lines were not much interfered with and the forward cavalry were able to keep touch with divisional commands by mounted orderlies.

Thus, owing to the special nature of the advance, this aspect of air work lost some of its usefulness, but the event proved that the organisation was sound and that the airmen could be relied upon to provide a connecting link when all other methods had failed. There were, indeed, a number of instances, on both army fronts, when aeroplanes were used to carry messages from forward units to corps headquarters, and when urgent corps operation orders were similarly carried in the opposite direction. On the Fifth Army front, also, there were times when the first news of the progress of the forward troops came from the air. On the whole, however, this role of aircraft was complementary.

On the other hand, air observers had difficulty in locating and in estimating, with any degree of accuracy, enemy movements. They caught occasional glimpses of isolated German groups, but so well were the German movements concealed that observers might often have missed them were it not that the enemy troops seldom let pass an opportunity to fire on the aeroplanes. Pilots therefore flew low over the area of the German retirement with the special object of drawing fire and so enabling their observers to plot the villages and strong points which were still occupied by rear-guards. Most of the information about the rear-guard positions was elicited in this way, but it was seldom possible to estimate their strength. When small German patrols of cavalry or infantry were met in the open, pilots went down to attack them with machine-gun fire or with bombs. On the 18th of March, for example, snipers who were holding up a cavalry patrol were dispersed in this way, but such attacks from the air were episodes and had little influence on the ground operations. In air co-operation with the artillery there were some failures. In his report on the Fourth Army advance, Sir Henry Rawlinson stated:

> Provision had been made for wireless stations to be taken forward, but units were slow in establishing them or neglected to do so altogether. On some occasions, therefore, opportunities for acting upon information derived by aeroplane observation and of inflicting losses on the Germans were missed.

★★★★★

> Instructions issued in December 1916 stated: 'Wireless officers are primarily responsible that stations are properly erected, but artillery commanders must make themselves acquainted with the correct method and assist the wireless officer in this matter.' It was, further, the responsibility of the artillery commanders that operators and receiving equipment accompanied the 'firing battery' in any movement and that one wireless operator was always on duty wherever there was a possibility of an aeroplane working with his station.

★★★★★

This breakdown in the artillery wireless organisation led to a G.H.Q. memorandum on the 7th of April 1917 which laid stress on the importance of the forward disposition and rapid setting up of the wireless stations. By that time, however, the opportunity was lost; nor was it, for long, to recur.

It may thus be generally stated that the tactical work of the aeroplanes in the advance was confined to occasional message carrying; and to reconnaissance of the German area to discover what villages and positions were manned from time to time and what was the condition of the country (for example, what cross-roads, culverts, &c. had been mined and destroyed, or bridges blown up); and, finally, to spasmodic co-operation with the artillery.

The more distant air work, by the army wings of the Fourth and Fifth Brigades, was directed to reconnaissance of the Hindenburg Line and of the area eastwards of it, and to photography of the new defence systems. A novel feature was the use of single-seater fighters to assist in these duties. (Reconnaissances were made by No. 23 Squadron—Spads, and by No. 32 Squadron—D.H.2's. Other reconnaissances were made by F.E.2D formations of No. 18 Squadron.) These distant reconnaissances made it clear that there was no intention to continue the retirement beyond the Hindenburg Line. There was no organised defensive line east of it, but there were, on the contrary, many new dumps and new aerodromes and other general indications that the Hindenburg Line was planned to constitute a great defensive barrier. Photography of the Hindenburg Line proceeded systematically, notably by F.E.2b's of No. 22 Squadron escorted by Sopwith 'Pups' of No. 54 Squadron.

BATTLE C

DISPOSITION OF ROY
(WITH FIRST AND

9th April,

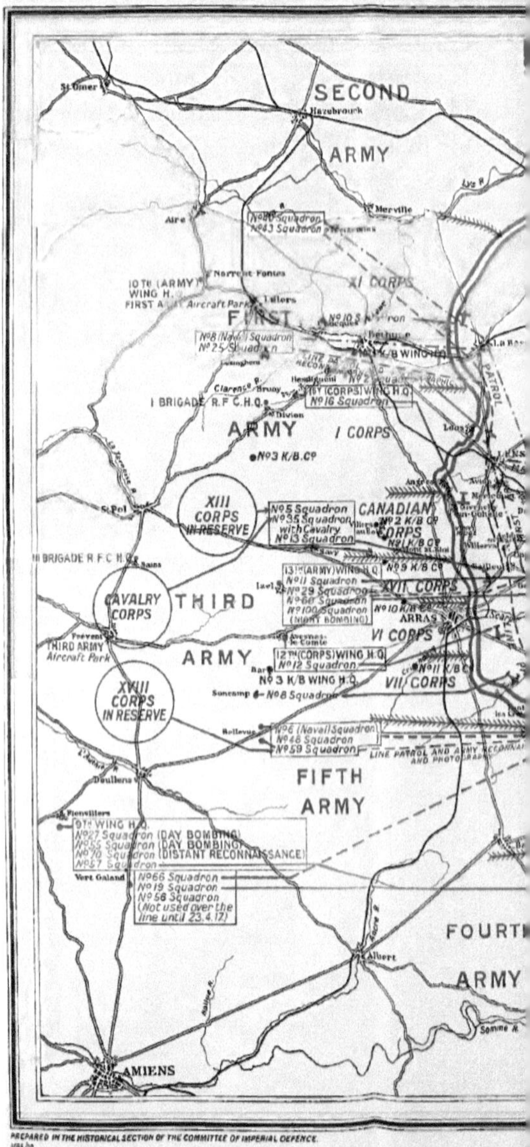

PREPARED IN THE HISTORICAL SECTION OF THE COMMITTEE OF IMPERIAL DEFENCE.

MILES 10 9 8 7 6 5 4 3 2 1 0

ARRAS

FLYING CORPS
IRD ARMIES)

17.

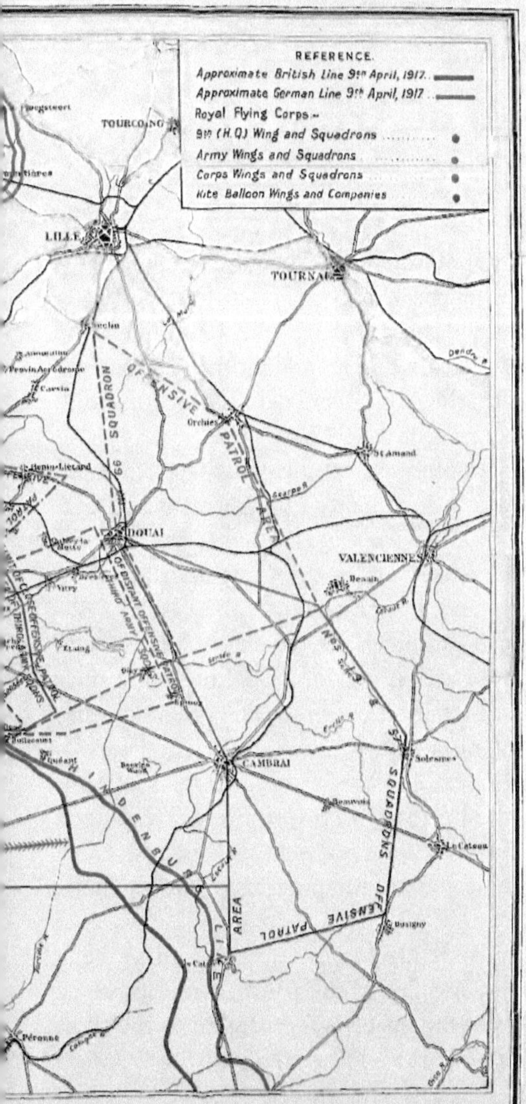

Chapter 6

The Battles of Arras, 1917

It has been told how the appointment of General Nivelle in December 1916 to the command of the armies of France led to changes in the original plans for the Allies' spring offensive in 1917. The British operations at Arras, subsidiary to, and dependent for their strategic results on, the French attacks on the Aisne, were destined to constitute the main British effort in the first half of 1917.

The full plans for the Nivelle offensive on the Aisne were revealed to the enemy by captured French documents. The Germans had ample time to interpolate an additional army in the line at the place of attack and to combine the defences under the Crown Prince. The Nivelle offensive was a failure and, in consequence, the battle of Arras was a limited victory which produced no definite strategic result. Though far less costly, it was an action on the model of the Somme battle, a stage in the process of attrition by which the enemy armies were gradually weakened in morale and military efficiency. It was, within its limits, a successful operation. So far as concerns the work of the Royal Flying Corps the period is rich in interest. The Flying Corps was superior to the German air service along the active front numerically, but inferior technically, and the progress of the air fighting teaches a number of lessons.

The British front of attack extended from Givenchy-en-Gohelle in the north to a point near Croisilles in the south. The capture of Vimy Ridge, the key position in the north, was entrusted to the right of the First Army (the Canadian Corps reinforced by the 5th Division and by heavy artillery of the I Corps), and the attack on the remainder of the front, to the Third Army (XVII, VI, and VII Corps with the XVIII Corps in reserve).

The main air work in co-operation with the First Army fell to No.

16 Squadron attached to the Canadian Corps, and to a less extent to No. 2 Squadron with the I Corps. The remaining squadrons of the First (Corps) Wing working for the First Army were Nos. 5 and 10.

The strength of the Army Wing—the Tenth—working with the First Army was four squadrons: No. 8 (Naval) equipped with Sopwith Triplanes; No. 40 (Nieuport Scouts); No. 25 (F.E.2b's and d's); and No. 43 (Sopwith 1½ Strutters). The single-seater fighters of the first two squadrons were detailed for offensive patrols and for attacks on kite-balloons, and the two-seaters of Nos. 25 and 43 Squadrons were to provide line patrols in protection of artillery aeroplanes, and to undertake long and medium distance reconnaissance and photography, and medium distance offensive patrol work.

In the Third Army area the four squadrons of the Twelfth (Corps) Wing were allotted for artillery co-operation, photography up to a distance of 4,000 yards behind the German front line, close reconnaissance, and contact patrol work, as follows:

XVII Corps—No. 13 Squadron.

VI Corps—No. 12 Squadron.

VII Corps—No. 8 Squadron.

XVIII Corps (in reserve)—No. 59 Squadron.

With the Cavalry Corps which had also been placed in the Third Army Area was No. 35 Squadron.

With the Thirteenth (Army) Wing, in the Third Army area, were five squadrons: No. 6 Naval (Nieuport Scouts); Nos. 29 and 60 (Nieuport Scouts); No. 11 (F.E.2b's); and No. 48 (Bristol Fighters). The first three (single-seater fighters) were to be used for offensive patrols and (except No. 6 Naval) for attacks on kite balloons. The role of No. 11 Squadron was reconnaissance, photography, and night bombing. No. 48 was to be used as a fighter-reconnaissance squadron.

The air concentration for the battle was completed by the headquarters Ninth Wing comprising seven squadrons; No. 19 (Spads); No. 27 (Martinsyde Scouts); No. 55 (D.H.4's); No. 56 (S.E.5's, not used over the lines until the 23rd of April 1917); No. 57 (F.E.2d's); No. 66 (Sopwith 'Pups') and No. 70 (Sopwith two-seaters). In addition, No. 100 Squadron (F.E.2b's) was under direct orders from headquarters for night bombing.

The total strength of the Royal Flying Corps along the whole front of the First and Third Armies was, for the opening of the Battle of Arras, twenty-five squadrons, (Excluding No. 56 Squadron. See Appendix 12.) representing 365 serviceable aeroplanes of which a third were single-seater fighters. (The number on the charge of these squadrons on the 9th was approximately 465; 100 aeroplanes were temporarily unserviceable.) Opposed to these two British armies was the German Sixth Army with an air strength of eighteen reconnaissance and artillery flights, five fighter flights, and seven protection flights, comprising a total of 195 aeroplanes, nearly one-half of which were equipped for fighting.

******

If we take a wider area the figures are still more favourable to the Royal Flying Corps. On the opening day of the battle, April 9th, there were forty-one squadrons with the four British armies (the First, Third, Fifth, and Fourth) along the front stretching approximately between Lille and Peronne. They had, on charge, on this day, 754 aeroplanes of which 385 were single-seater fighters or fighter-reconnaissance aircraft. With the two German Armies—the Sixth and First—opposed to them were 264 aeroplanes of which 114 were single-seater fighters or protection aeroplanes. The main German air concentration on this day was opposite the French on the Aisne where the German Seventh and Third armies had 480 aeroplanes, nearly half of which were fighters. Particulars of the strengths of the German air units are supplied by the *Reichsarchiv*, Potsdam.

******

The Air Offensive

The air offensive opened along the whole British front on the 4th of April 1917, five days before the infantry action began. The object of this offensive, which was part of the general battle plan, was to force the enemy airmen away from the immediate battle area so as to ensure the greatest measure of freedom to the corps aeroplanes. Close protection for these was only to be provided, exceptionally, when they were engaged at unusual distances across the lines.

As had often happened before, the beginning of the air offensive was marked by low clouds and rain, but the fighting was intense and the losses severe. On the five days from the 4th to the 8th of April, seventy-five British aeroplanes fell in action with a loss in flying personnel of 105 (nineteen killed, thirteen wounded, and seventy-three missing). In addition, there was an abnormally high number of flying accidents in which, in the same brief period, fifty-six aeroplanes were wrecked and struck off the strength of the squadrons. These heavy losses by accidents were due in part to insufficiency of training which had been speeded up to danger point, and in part also to the strain imposed on pilots who had to meet in the air an enemy equipped, with few exceptions, with superior fighting aeroplanes.

The enemy pilots were now getting the full benefit from their better aeroplanes. Their confidence was high and there were occasions when a single enemy fighter attacked British formations. The hesitancy, possibly due to lack of experience, with which some of the Albatros and Halberstadt pilots had handled their fighters earlier in the year had now disappeared. The de Havilland (D.H.2) pilots had often hitherto fought them with success, but from the beginning of April 1917 the D.H.2's were outclassed.

'The hostile scouts with their superior speed and good handling were able throughout the fight to prevent the pilot from getting a single shot at any one of them', is a typical sentence from the combat reports of the de Havilland pilots. Indeed, this disadvantage was common to all the pusher-type fighting aeroplanes, (IV Brigade orders on the 3rd of April stated that F.E.2d aeroplanes were no longer to be used by themselves on offensive patrols.) with the possible exception of the 250 horse-power Rolls-Royce F.E.2d. About this time, however, No. 57 Squadron, equipped with this aeroplane, suffered heavy casualties.

On the 6th of April, five aeroplanes of this squadron, on offensive patrol, were all shot down by a formation of enemy two-seaters. Nor did the Bristol Fighter, from which so much was hoped and which was indeed to justify expectations, begin well. On the 5th of April a formation of six Bristols of No. 48 Squadron, led by Captain W. Leefe Robinson, V.C., had made a first offensive patrol. Near Douai, they met Richthofen at the head of five Albatros Scouts (D. III). Action was joined in which other German fighters intervened. Two of the Bristols fell to the machine-guns of Richthofen and two others to junior members of his squadron. The remaining two Bristols got back, one of them much shot about.

★★★★★★

Captain Leefe Robinson, V.C., was one of the missing pilots. His engine had been shot out of action, forcing him to land. He suffered from his imprisonment and fell an easy victim to influenza when he returned to England on the 14th of December 1918, dying on the 31st of December.

★★★★★★

During the fighting two of the enemy aeroplanes went down, apparently out of control, but they were not seen to crash. In his report of the encounter Richthofen stated that his own aeroplane was unquestionably superior to the Bristol Fighter both in speed and climbing powers.

This adverse beginning of the service career of the Bristol Fighter deserves examination. The testimony of Richthofen, that the new British aeroplane was not to be feared, spread throughout the German air service and gave the enemy fighters that confidence in the superiority of their craft which acts as a great moral asset during combat. In fact, Richthofen was misled. There was little that was wrong with the aeroplane itself. There were some minor technical defects, but the initial failures were due chiefly to the erroneous belief that the Bristol Fighter was structurally weak, and to mistaken fighting tactics. The small technical defects of the engine and of the machine-gun mechanism were soon remedied. The view from the pilot's cockpit, particularly important in a fighting aeroplane where rapidity of manoeuvre is essential, was improved. But it required some little experience before the basic reasons for the failure were appreciated.

The critical nature of the air situation in France had led to No. 48 Squadron being put into the line before the pilots and observers had had time to get thoroughly used to their aeroplanes. Many accidents, during training manoeuvres in England, had given the Bristol a bad reputation, and the belief existed that, owing to inherent structural weaknesses, it could not safely be thrown about during flight. The pilots knew, or quickly realised, that no aeroplane in the fighting line, thus handicapped, could live in the air, and as they acquired experience in the handling of their craft they undertook every type of manoeuvre until they had finally proved that the Bristol Fighter had the strength to respond to every demand made on it.

The mistake in tactics was revealed after a few combats. This mistake was in the idea that the observer, or machine-gunner, in the rear seat, was the important firing unit, with the result that pilots, in the early encounters, continuously manoeuvred to get their rear gunners into firing position. But pilots came to realise that the offensive weapon was the front gun under their own control and in the line of their movements, and that the rear gun was protective. When these various defects were remedied, that is within a few weeks of its first patrol, the Bristol Fighter came into its own, and its contribution to the offensive strength of the Royal Flying Corps will be apparent as this history progresses.

The Nieuports of No. 60 Squadron which operated over the area north-east of Arras, much frequented by Richthofen's formation, suffered severely. The Albatros and Halberstadt single-seaters had the superior performance. In addition, the Nieuport, until modified on suggestions put forward by No. 2 Aeroplane Supply Depot, proved structurally weak in the air with the result that pilots were cramped in manoeuvring. Its armament was a Lewis gun, and pilots were further handicapped by the necessity of changing the drums of ammunition. The enemy fighters had twin synchronised machine-guns which gave them a double volume of continuous fire.

In the four days before the Battle of Arras opened, No. 60 Squadron, although its pilots were among the best in the service, suffered losses wholly disproportionate to those they inflicted. An example of their experience was a fight with five Albatros Scouts led by Richthofen on the 7th of April. The Nieuport formation of six pilots was outmanoeuvred and could fire few shots, none of them effective. Two Nieuports fell in the German lines and, of the others, only one got back undamaged. (One of the Nieuports, which, although damaged, got safely back to its aerodrome, was claimed by Richthofen as his 37th victim.)

The critical nature of the air position was considerably relieved by the Sopwith 'Pup' and the Sopwith Triplane. These two single-seater aeroplanes, the former of which had first been used by the Naval Air Service at Dunkirk in May 1916, and the latter in June 1916, were as good as the best of the German fighters. No. 3 (Naval) Squadron south of the main battle area, whose 'Pups' were involved in some of the fiercest of the fighting before the battle of Arras, suffered no casualty in action. On the other hand, the losses they inflicted were such as to cause the enemy pilots to avoid them in the air whenever they could. On the 6th of April five Sopwith 'Pups', led by Flight Commander T. C. Vernon, while escorting a bombing formation of B.E.'s, attacked four Halberstadts which were manoeuvring to dive on the bombers. All four Halberstadts were shot down, two of them in Bourlon Wood, and the bombing raid was completed without further interference. There were similar victories, but they were exceptional and the air offensive was maintained at a heavy cost.

It has been explained in a previous volume how the period of the Fokker predominance, from the autumn of 1915 to the spring of 1916, brought about formation flying, and it was there stated that the change in tactics which the Fokker necessitated was, in effect, equivalent to a shrinkage in the Flying Corps strength. (Vol. 2.) It was the same in this new period of German air predominance. Reconnaissance formations had to be given disproportionately large fighting escorts. The photography of enemy positions at any appreciable distance beyond the lines required many aeroplanes. Fifteen aeroplanes in fighting support of three operating cameras was common. Bombing had to be curtailed. Twelve fighters—six two-seaters as close escort and six single-seaters in formation above—were sent out with a bombing formation of six B.E. aeroplanes.

Pilots were too much in demand for more urgent duties to allow of bombing on a scale comparable with that undertaken as an integral part of the air offensive waged during the Somme battles. Thus, the numerical superiority of the Royal Flying Corps was greatly discounted. Furthermore, the German fighting pilots, at this time, owing to their fewer losses—a result of the economic use by the enemy of his air strength—had had longer flying experience than the average British pilot. In addition, their superior aircraft gave them the tactical initiative in combat. They could fight or not as they wished and they could break off a combat at any moment. If a German formation found itself in inferior strength the enemy pilots could, at their will, open their throttles and disappear.

The British airmen had to stand and fight no matter how unfavourable their tactical position might be. And they had to contend with the prevailing westerly winds which often caused the fight to drift far away from the British aerodromes. Many British aeroplanes, crippled in combat, which might otherwise have reached their own lines, were lost because they could not fight against the adverse winds. These two periods of German predominance have demonstrated that in assessing the fighting strength of an air force, speed, climbing power, height, gun-power, and a wide view from the pilot's cockpit, outweigh every other consideration, and that an air offensive will not ensure local superiority against a determined and skilful enemy numerically weaker, but better equipped. (When urging the speeding up of the production of efficient fighters, Major-General Trenchard had often used the phrase 'the war in the air will be won at home'.

The spirit of the Royal Flying Corps personnel in these days of adversity was not weakened. This is no empty statement. It has been claimed that it was insistence on the policy of the air offensive which helped to keep up the morale of the pilots and observers. Let us examine this contention. Every pilot along the front knew that the Flying Corps could maintain an offensive only at the expense of heavy casualties. That these casualties would exceed those inflicted on the enemy was accepted. Suppose the Royal Flying Corps, admitting the enemy's temporary superiority, had fallen back on the defensive; what would have been the result? This defensive policy had been tried by the German air service at Verdun and again during the Somme battles and had proved disastrous. The morale of the enemy airmen had been sapped and their service discredited in the eyes of the German Army.

Furthermore, defensive flying had offered no sort of defence either to the airmen or to the ground formations below them. Towards the end of the Somme battles, it is true, the *Jagdstaffeln* had confined their fighting for the most part to the German side of the lines and had, under the leadership of Böelcke, brought about a change in the air position. But the *Jagdstaffeln* had then been equipped with aeroplanes superior to anything flying against them and they could have fought with advantage anywhere. The policy which kept the German fighting pilots over their own troops resulted in a curtailment of the distant work of the Royal Flying Corps, but it meant that the German airmen co-operating with the armies were denied the only kind of protection that would have enabled them adequately to fulfil their essential duties.

The lessons of Verdun and of the Somme had been correctly read by the Royal Flying Corps command and had formed a subject for debate on many a squadron aerodrome. That the spirit of the German air service would revive and that the enemy would then turn and attempt to do to us as we had done to him had been foreseen. The Royal Flying Corps was in no way taken by surprise by the German air superiority at Arras. That this superiority could best be met by offence and not by defence was the opinion of the majority of Flying Corps officers.

An air service which confines its flying to its own territory may save aeroplanes forced down damaged, but the armies suffer. Their positions are open to reconnaissance and to attack by the enemy airmen. The morale of the troops is adversely affected by the attention of the hostile aeroplanes. The artillery of the army whose air service is flying defensively is inadequately registered, the opposing defences are not photographed, and there may be no close reconnaissance. But an inferior air service which maintains the initiative of the offensive may force the enemy to fight over his own territory, and no matter how strenuously the enemy fights he cannot prevent some part of the reconnaissance, photography, and other work being accomplished. It came to this then. Air co-operation was judged essential to the success of the British offensive at Arras.

That cooperation might be assured only by aggressive tactics, and the cost, though it must be high, was not to be counted. Pilots and observers went into the battle sustained by the knowledge that they were helping the men on the ground. Their record for some weeks was a monotonous tale of loss. But they came through a dark period of their history with their morale unimpaired. The enemy deserves and will receive full credit for the qualities that went to his mastery, but he, in his turn, has not failed to pay tribute to the spirit that never accepted defeat.

The aircraft bombing programme, operated under the direct orders of Royal Flying Corps head-quarters, was put into effect, concurrently with the bombardment, on the 5th of April. The bombing offensive was planned with the idea of compelling the enemy to withdraw anti-aircraft guns and aeroplanes from the front line area. The I, II, IV, and V Brigades had each been instructed to set aside six B.E. aeroplanes to work from their own aerodromes, on medium distance bombing, under orders from the G.O.C. Royal Flying Corps. The long-distance raids were made by the squadrons of the headquarters Ninth Wing. For special night bombing No. 100 Squadron in the Third Army area was also under headquarters orders.

Places attacked on the 5th of April 1917 included the engine depot at Hirson, Don Station, and the railway junctions at St. Quentin and Marcoing. With darkness came the first night raid by No. 100 Squadron made on Douai aerodrome which housed the unit commanded by Richthofen. Twice during the night, the aerodrome was attacked and there was evidence that four hangars were destroyed at a cost of one F.E.2b which failed to return. A night attack on Provin aerodrome was made by No. 10 Squadron.

On the 6th of April bombing was resumed. Three Martinsydes of No. 27 Squadron were met over Ath railway junction, their objective, by Halberstadt Scouts, and all three were shot down. At the same time six Martinsydes of the squadron bombed Aulnoye, this time with greater success, all bombs being dropped on the objective. A similar formation of D.H.4's of No. 55 Squadron bombed the sidings at Valenciennes, and a feature of their attack was the ease with which the de Havillands out-manoeuvred and out-distanced enemy fighters which endeavoured to intercept them. Nearer the lines dumps, billets, villages, and railway objectives were attacked successfully.

On the 7th of April, though clouds and rain stopped distant bombing, Provin aerodrome was attacked twice, morning and evening, and Mouveaux aerodrome once. Twice during the night raids were made on the railway station and aerodrome at Douai by No. 100 Squadron. In the first of the two attacks, by nine F.E.2b's, a hit was claimed on a shed in the station yard and three hangars were wrecked and a group of buildings on the aerodrome damaged. On the second attempt, during which one F.E.2b was compelled to land in the enemy lines, a further hangar on the aerodrome was destroyed. A feature of these two raids on Douai was the attacking of ground targets by F.E.2b's armed with pom-pom guns. (Two F.E.2b's armed with 1-pounder pom-poms, were received by No. 100 Squadron from England on the 7th of April for use by night against special ground targets.) During the same night raids on the aerodromes at Provin and Wervicq and on stations and trains were made by the various brigades.

On the 8th of April the weather improved and the distant bombing was resumed. Aulnoye engine sheds were attacked by six Martinsydes of No. 27 Squadron and an ammunition dump at Valenciennes by six D.H.4's of No. 55 Squadron. An attempted attack on Crown Prince Rupprecht's headquarters near Mons by four D.H.4's of No. 55 Squadron, met with disaster. Two of the de Havillands were shot down on the way back from their objective, and a third by anti-aircraft fire near the trenches.

The bombing formations of the brigades usually consisted of six B.E.'s or F.E.2b's escorted by a separate formation of six or more fighters. In the IV Brigade the raids were made by combined formations of six B.E.'s from one of the corps squadrons, six F.E.2b's from the army squadron, and six Sopwith 'Pups'. The B.E.'s flew in two lines, three abreast, the F.E.'s were slightly above and behind, and the fighter escort further behind and from 1,000 to 2,000 feet above the rear bombing formation. The long-distance raids by the headquarters Ninth Wing were supported by the offensive patrols although, except for the D.H.4's, whose raiding was carried out from high altitudes, close escorts for the bombing formations were also occasionally provided.

An attempted offensive against the enemy kite balloons, which opened on the 5th of April, met with small success. The aeroplanes engaged on this work were Nieuport single-seaters of Nos. 1, 29, 40, and 60 Squadrons, and Sopwith 'Pups' of No. 54 Squadron. The ammunition used was chiefly Buckingham Tracer. The pilots found extreme difficulty in pushing the attacks home owing to the rapidity with which the balloons were hauled down. During the four days to the opening of the offensive, that is to say up to and including the 8th of April, five hostile balloons were destroyed at the cost of a similar number of Flying Corps aeroplanes. The balloons were often attacked at heights under 200 feet, and all the attacking aeroplanes met with severe machine-gun and rifle fire.

The First Phase

Three weeks before the battle was timed to open the corps squadrons had begun an intensive programme of flying in connexion with the systematic registration of the enemy positions and the destruction of his barbed wire defences. This preliminary work led up to the main opening bombardment, against Vimy Ridge on the 2nd of April and, along the Third Army front, on the 4th of April. The general progress of the bombardment was recorded by frequent air photography. Many new enemy battery positions were found, but it was seldom possible for the air observers to range batteries on the new positions at the time of discovery, and they were marked down for destruction in the further artillery-programmes before the opening attack or for neutralization on the opening day. There was, in addition, continuous close reconnaissance of the enemy defence systems, which reported the detailed effect of the bombardment on the trenches and on the wire.

Sunday the 8th of April 1917 had been a day of fine weather, but, in the evening, the wind changed and rain and snow squalls set in. At 5.30 a.m. on the 9th of April, Easter Monday, when the general attack was begun, there was a drizzle of thin snow and visibility was low. The plan of attack allowed for a series of comparatively short advances, the capture of each successive objective being timed in accordance with a pre-arranged programme. Under this programme contact patrol aeroplanes were to fly over the front and call for flares a few minutes after the time allowed for the capture of each line.

Between 6.0 and 6.30 a.m., aeroplanes of Nos. 12, 13, and 16 Squadrons were flying over the fronts of the Third and First Armies calling to the infantry by Klaxon horn and by Very light. (Three of these contact patrol aeroplanes were lost. The pilot and observer in one of them, wounded and shot down in enemy territory, were found in a dug-out in Givenchy when that place was captured by the 4th Division on the 13th of April.) Over much of the area the snow was at times blinding, but the air observers were able to report that the whole of the first objective, except on the extreme left, had been reached.

At 7.30 a.m. the infantry advance to the second objective was begun, but stronger German resistance was encountered, and at 8.15 a.m., for which hour its capture had been timed, strong enemy parties were still holding out here and there. Flares along this line were lighted in response to calls from the air observers, and the points of the enemy resistance were made plain. By noon the whole line had been taken except south of the Scarpe where the enemy held tenaciously to the Railway Triangle. At 2.0 p.m. this position fell before the attacks of the 15th Division which then moved forward, capturing many guns in Battery Valley on the way, to the German third line. Elsewhere, by the evening, this third line had been entered. The general progress of the advance throughout the afternoon and evening was reported from the air, often by direct observation owing to the paucity of lighted flares, but, as it happened, the ground communications were well maintained and the air reports were confirmatory and supplementary.

The greater part of the air work for the artillery throughout the day was concerned with the locations of active enemy batteries, whose positions were notified to the artillery by the zone call. The British neutralization fire, as a result of the air reports, is described in the artillery war diaries as being exceptionally effective, and the enemy fire throughout the day was said to be 'feeble', so that many batteries were enabled to turn from counterbattery work and engage infantry targets.

Owing to the adverse weather—a south-westerly gale, was blowing at high altitudes—the bombing programme for the opening day was abandoned and the offensive patrols curtailed. What patrols there were were mostly over the battle front, where the Bristol Fighters of No. 48 Squadron had many successful combats. The only distant patrols of the day—to Cambrai by No. 6 (Naval) Squadron—accounted for two enemy single-seaters, shot down out of control.

Between the German third line of defence and the incomplete Drocourt-Quéant Switch line there was no prepared position. A breach of the Drocourt line, which covered Douai and Cambrai, might have yielded important strategic results. It was, however, never reached. The sodden ground made the task of bringing up guns and ammunition laborious, and a well-organised enemy mobile machine-gun defence made an advance by the cavalry impossible. The battle, therefore, now resolved itself into a methodical completion of the capture of the third line.

At dawn on the 10th—a day of wild weather—contact aeroplanes were over the front calling for flares so that the limits of the British advance might be plotted. The flare positions were marked on maps which were dropped at the forward report centres of the various corps whence the information was telephoned to the corps headquarters. Contact patrols continued at intervals throughout the day, more particularly from noon when the infantry and tank advance was resumed and its progress reported. Tactical reconnaissances from a low height (200-300 feet) were made by Nieuports of No. 60 Squadron, a novel task for these single-seater fighters.

During the contact patrol work many attacks with machine-gun fire were made on detachments of German infantry. The air artillery observers were handicapped by poor visibility and intermittent snow, but a number of active batteries were reported and engaged and some important trench targets were ranged. Four artillery and contact aeroplanes, forced down by snowstorms, were wrecked, one was shot down by bullets, and two others, whose pilots had been wounded by fire from the ground, were wrecked on landing.

The main feature of the ground operations on the nth of April was the capture of Monchy-le-Preux, a key position, on the ridge of a small plateau, of the country between the Scarpe and the Sensée. Air observers of No. 12 Squadron watched the infantry, with the assistance of tanks and followed by cavalry, assault the position at 5.0 a.m. They were witnesses of the heavy fighting which followed, and it was not until 9.0 a.m. that they were able to report that the infantry had gone through and that the cavalry had entered the village.

The weather had improved slightly and the enemy air service was more active. Between 10.0 a.m. and 1.0 p.m. patrols by formations of single-seater fighters, in which Richthofen's unit was prominent, interfered seriously with the work of the corps aeroplanes. Three, of No. 13 Squadron, were shot down and wrecked and two others badly shot about, and, elsewhere along the active front, four other corps aeroplanes were destroyed. An early offensive patrol of four Bristol Fighters of No. 48 Squadron fought an equal formation of Albatros Scouts about 8.30 a.m. and sent two of the enemy down. When this fight ended one of the Bristols returned with machine-gun trouble and, shortly afterwards, the remaining three were involved in a second fight with four Albatros Scouts. All three Bristols were shot down in the enemy lines, two of the officers being killed and the remaining four taken prisoners.

In spite of the enemy activity on the 11th of April, the photography of a section of the Drocourt-Quéant line by three R.E.8's of No. 59 Squadron met with only slight opposition. A bombing attack on Cambrai led to much fighting which was illustrative of the defensive weakness of a formation including B.E. aeroplanes incapable of putting up a fight. There were five B.E.'s of No. 4 Squadron with an escort of Sopwith 'Pups' of No. 3 (Naval) Squadron and Spads of No. 23 Squadron. On the way to the objective an Albatros two-seater which unhesitatingly attacked was sent down in flames by a pilot of No. 3 (Naval) Squadron. Over Cambrai, Albatros and Halberstadt fighters flew into the bombers, and a stern fight ensued. Two enemy aeroplanes were shot down by naval pilots, but two of the B.E.'s and a Spad were lost. A naval pilot, Flight Sub-Lieutenant J. S. T. Fall, who became detached from the fight in the early stages, reported as follows:

> When B.E.'s were attacked at Cambrai I attacked H.A. head on at about 8,000 feet. I saw many tracers go into his engine as we closed on one another, I half looped to one side of him, and then the H.A. dived with a large trail of blue smoke. I dived after him down to about 4,000 feet and fired about fifty rounds when he went down absolutely out of control. I watched him spinning down to about 1,000 feet, the trail of smoke increasing. I was immediately attacked by three more Albatros which drove me down to about 200 feet. We were firing at one another whenever possible, when at last I got into a good position and I attacked one from above and from the right. I closed on him, turning in behind him and got so close to him that the pilot's head filled the small ring in the Aldis sight.
>
> I saw three tracers actually go into the pilot's head; the H.A. then simply heeled over and spun into the ground. The other two machines cleared off. I saw two other H.A. spinning down out of control and while fighting saw two B.E.'s being attacked by H.A. Having lost sight of all the other machines and being so low, I decided to fly home at about that height (200 feet). A company of German cavalry going east along a small road halted and fired on me; also, several machine guns opened fire. After flying west for about five minutes I was again attacked by a Halberstadt single-seater and as he closed on me I rocked my machine until he was within fifty yards. I side-looped over

him and fired a short burst at him. He seemed to clear off, and then attacked me again; these operations were repeated several times with a slight variation in the way I looped over him, until within about five minutes of crossing the lines (flying against a strong wind), when he was about 150 yards behind me, I looped straight over him and coming out of the loop I dived at him and fired a good long burst. I saw nearly all the tracers go into the pilot's back, just on the edge of the cockpit. He immediately dived straight into the ground.

I then went over German trenches filled with soldiers, and I was fired on by machine-gun, rifles, and small field guns, in or out of range. There was a lot of small artillery firing and many shells bursting in and about the German trenches, somewhere in the vicinity of the Cambrai-Arras Road. I saw many small companies of infantry and cavalry of about ten to fifty in each going east along small roads. I noticed no convoys or movement of artillery. I landed at the first aerodrome I saw, No. 35 Squadron, R.F.C. My machine was badly shot about.'

On the 12th of April, another day of snow blizzards, when the infantry improved their positions on each flank of the battle-field, there was little air work. Some successful photographic reconnaissances were made between the storms, and one of them, on the Fifth Army front, led to severe fighting. Four F.E.2b's of No. 25 Squadron were taking their photographs, under the protection of four Sopwith 'Pups' of No. 3 (Naval) Squadron, when six enemy single-seater fighters attacked. Two of the F.E.2b's and one of the Sopwiths were lost and four of the hostile fighters were shot down by the Sopwiths, apparently out of control.

Air reconnaissances in the late afternoon of the 12th reported fires and explosions in the area commanded as a result of the consolidation of the capture ofVimy ridge. It seemed clear that the enemy was about to withdraw from positions he no longer found tenable, and next morning, the 13th, orders were given that patrols, well supported, were to push forward with vigour. Air observers came back throughout the morning and afternoon with news of further widespread fires and explosions as far back as Lens.

Troops of the I Corps and Canadian Corps advanced their lines during the day through Angres, Givenchy-en-Gohelle, Vimy, Willerval, and Bailleul, while the cooperating air squadrons, dogged by German fighting formations, gave their attention to ranging the heavy batteries from their new positions.

The 13th of April was the first reasonably fine day since the opening of the battle and the first on which a full day's air work was possible. The Flying Corps offensive patrols, maintained throughout the day well over the lines, had very few encounters with enemy airmen who flew, at lower heights, nearer the battle front with the double object of protecting their own corps aeroplanes—especially in the neighbourhood of the German retirement in the Vimy area—and of interfering with the work of ours. Here they came into contact with the Flying Corps line patrols, particularly with those provided by F.E.2b's of No. 11 Squadron and by Nieuports of No. 29 Squadron. One Nieuport, three F.E.2b's, and two corps aeroplanes were shot down in this fighting, but no losses to the enemy were reported.

The improved weather provided the opportunity for a renewal of the bombing. A dump at Wervicq was attacked in the morning by No. 20 Squadron (eight 112 lb. bombs), and the aerodrome at Mouveaux by the same squadron in the evening (fourteen 112 lb. bombs). On the morning raid the F.E.2d's flew alone, but in the evening were escorted by six Nieuport single-seaters. The attacks, however, were carried out without incident, as was a raid on Busigny railway station by No. 22 Squadron (six F.E.'s escorted by six Sopwith 'Pups') during which thirty-three 20-lb. bombs were dropped. Not so an evening massed bombing attack on Henin-Liètard, a German detraining station behind the Arras-Lens front, in which thirty-eight aeroplanes took part.

The operation was carried out by twelve Martinsydes of No. 27 Squadron (escorted by five Spads of No. 19 Squadron and six Sopwith 'Pups' of No. 66 Squadron) and by nine F.E.2d's of No. 25 Squadron (escorted by six Nieuports of No. 40 Squadron). The Martinsydes dropped six 230-lb. and seven 112-lb. and the F.E.2d's forty-two 20-lb. bombs on the target. The bombing had ended and the escorting Nieuports had left to make a direct return when Richthofen appeared with his fighting formation. The bombers, unaware that the Nieuports had gone, mistook the Richthofen formation for the Nieuports and the F.E.2d's were taken by surprise when the German fighters dived. A sharp encounter ensued in which three of the F.E.2d's were lost and one German single-seater was shot down.

One of the Martinsydes was also shot down on the return journey. This was Richthofen's second and lesser triumph of the day. He had, in the morning, inflicted severe loss on No. 59 Squadron in circumstances that merit attention. Six R.E.8's of this squadron had set out at 8.15 a.m. to obtain photographs of the Drocourt-Quéant Switch line. Two of the R.E.8's carried cameras and the remaining four were acting as a close escort. The section of line they were required to photograph stretched from Quiéry-la-Motte to Etaing, that is, in proximity to the Douai aerodrome, where was massed a great part of the German air fighting strength, including Richthofen's unit. Photographic reconnaissance, unlike other forms of air activity, entails careful flying along the whole line of the objective. This was clearly an instance which called for a strong fighting escort, which might have been provided by Sopwith Triplanes of No. 1 (Naval) Squadron, fifteen of which were, at the time, engaged on a line patrol of the Arras area.

It was thought, however, that the R.E.8's would be adequately protected by offensive patrols of the Ninth Wing and of the Thirteenth Wing, which were timed to cover the area during the flight of the R.E.8's. The offensive patrols would possibly have proved adequate had they been made as they were planned. The Ninth Wing patrol was to consist of six F.E.2d's and three Spads. The Spads, however, started twenty minutes late. The F.E.2d's, which went over alone, lost formation and, in desultory fighting, two were shot down. The Bristol Fighters of the Thirteenth Wing saw nothing of the R.E.8's. In the result, the six reconnaissance aeroplanes had been isolated by a formation of six single-seaters led by Richthofen. The unequal fight was a brief one and the six R.E.8's were shot down, all the pilots and observers, except two, being killed. (Richthofen's unit of six aeroplanes claimed on this day thirteen British aeroplanes.)

A word is due here on the technical qualities of the R.E.8, an aeroplane which, for long, had something of an evil reputation. It was designed by the Royal Aircraft Factory to meet specifications (put forward by Flying Corps headquarters in France in the autumn of 1915), for a standard corps reconnaissance and artillery aeroplane, capable of self-defence, which could supersede the B.E.2c. The R.E.8 was fitted with a 150 horse-power Royal Aircraft Factory engine and had a Vickers synchronised gun for the pilot and a Lewis gun on a Scarff ring mounting for the observer in the rear seat. The aeroplane, once the design was approved, was made under contract by a number of motor-car manufacturers and by the Coventry Ordnance Works. Misfortune dogged production from the beginning. Shortages in the supplies of raw material led to delays, and then, when the R.E.8 began to come forward in quantities, weaknesses were revealed which had not been disclosed when the original aeroplane of the type had been put through its tests. The early R.E.8's, especially in the hands of new pilots, had a marked tendency to spin, and there were fatal accidents, at home and overseas, before this tendency was checked by adjustments in the design. If a bad landing threw the aeroplane on its nose there was almost a certainty of fire. The engine was pushed back into the emergency and main petrol tanks, so that the whole of the spirit flowed over the engine, and in the fires which resulted, many pilots and observers perished.

The evil reputation of the R.E.8 spread throughout the Royal Flying Corps. Nothing is so calculated to sap a pilot's morale as a lack of confidence in the flying capabilities of his aeroplane. Lord Cowdray, the President of the Air Board, took up the matter with energy. Under the direction of the deputy-controller of the technical department of the Board, a series of investigations and trials of the aeroplane were undertaken, and so numerous were the modifications in the design that the R.E.8 emerged almost as a new type. It outlived its bad reputation and survived to the end of the war as the standard aeroplane for the corps squadrons in France.

******

At the Armistice, November 11th 1918, the corps squadrons in France were equipped as follows: R.E.8's, fifteen squadrons; Armstrong-Whitworth-Beardmore, five squadrons; and Bristol Fighter, five Special Flights, one to each of the five Corps Wings.

******

Following the loss of the unescorted R.E.8's, the task of photographing the Drocourt line was allotted next day, a April the 14th, to a stronger formation, consisting of six F.E.2b's of No. 11 Squadron with four Nieuport single-seaters of No. 29 Squadron as escort. The reconnaissance was also timed to take place when the routine offensive patrols of Nos. 19 and 60 Squadrons would, normally, be in the area. The photography formation was attacked over Vitry by Halberstadt and Albatros Scouts, but the escorting Nieuports and the F.E.2b's fought so effectively that all the F.E.2b's got safely home, although without their photographs. One of the German fighters and one of the Nieuports were shot down, and a dead observer was brought back by one of the F.E. pilots. The offensive formation of No. 60 Squadron, consisting of five Nieuports, which was patrolling the area covered by the photographic reconnaissance, became involved in a fight with

Richthofen's unit. The Nieuports had begun an attack on two German two-seaters, near Douai, when Richthofen appeared and four of the Nieuports were shot down. The fifth pilot spun away and made a safe return.

Meanwhile German air reinforcements had arrived in the Arras sector. These were four reconnaissance and artillery flights, one protection flight, and two single-seater fighter Flights. Of these reinforcements, one fighter Flight and two reconnaissance Flights came from the German First Army and the remainder from the Army Detachment 'A' in the area south of Metz. The three German Army Detachments holding the line from south of Verdun to the Swiss frontier yielded four out of nine fighter flights and three out of four protection flights to the German armies along the remainder of the front, and it is a point of interest that this transfer of fighting strength coincided with the disbandment of No. 3 Naval (Bombing) Wing at Luxeuil which had, during the spring, carried out bombing operations in conjunction with the French Air Service.

******

The Protection Flights (normal strength six two-seater aeroplanes) had the nominal task of providing constant close escorts for the artillery and reconnaissance aeroplanes. They were, however, mainly used for machine-gun attacks on front-line troops.

The German First Army was withdrawn from the Bapaume-Péronne area on the 12th of April when the German line was shortened as a result of the retreat to the Hindenburg Line. The German First Army was re-formed, in the area of the French offensive, south of the Aisne, on the 16th of April, by taking in the left flank of the German Seventh and the right flank of the German Third Armies.

The last day raid by the Wing—except for a retaliatory raid on Freiburg on the 14th of April—was made on the 26th of March. The help in men and aeroplanes, given by the Admiralty to the Royal Flying Corps, made the retention of the Wing impossible, and what remained of it was withdrawn in the middle of May to complete the equipment of No. 10 (Naval) Squadron for service with the Royal Flying Corps.

******

It had become clear from a reconnaissance made by No. 16 Squadron on the morning of the 14th of April, that the enemy intended to halt his retirement along the line Avion-Mericourt-Oppy. This line, which would protect Lens from the south and also form a barrier to our eastward progress, was so far removed from the eastern slopes of Vimy Ridge as to deprive that position of many of its advantages as an observation centre. It was decided not to attack the Avion-Mericourt-Oppy Line until the Canadian Corps had had time to bring its guns forward. Farther south, on this day, enemy counterattacks developed, notably at Monchy-le-Preux held by the VI Corps. Small parties of German infantry penetrated the eastern defences of the village, but, by the evening, the attacks had been repulsed. In this fighting the aeroplanes of No. 12 Squadron played a notable part. From six in the morning until eight in the evening the squadron was flying continuously over the battlefield, and the squadron reports contributed much to the repulse of the enemy attack which had been delivered with determination.

The 14th of April marked the end of the first phase of the operations. The British gains had been substantial in guns, prisoners, and ground. The line had been advanced four miles and the dominating features which were the immediate objectives of the offensive had been conquered. On Monday the 16th of April the great French offensive was to begin, and it was important that the British pressure should be maintained, but the object of that pressure was to distract the enemy from the Aisne front rather than win special objectives. Before, however, active operations could be resumed on the Arras front, communications had to be re-established and artillery brought forward.

The weather, during the opening phase, had severely restricted air work, but what had been possible had shown that a change of tactics was desirable. The offensive patrols had too often passed without incident, and it seemed clear that the enemy had, at least temporarily, ceased to fly at great heights. A memorandum, issued from the Royal Flying Corps headquarters on the 15th of April, stated:

'The enemy seems for the moment to have given up, to a certain extent, his method of depending entirely upon height, and his machines and formations are undoubtedly slipping underneath our high patrols without being seen by them. His tactics are of course rendered easier by the cloud layer which, even on fine days, has extended of late somewhere between 5,000 and 7,000 feet. By coming up through or underneath these clouds his machines have on several occasions attacked our photographic and artillery machines unseen by our scouts although large numbers of the latter have been in the area at the time. High patrols must be maintained, otherwise the enemy will undoubtedly adopt his former tactics once again, but they often miss an opportunity through being too high. It must be remembered that the conditions which favour this form of attack by the enemy apply equally in our own case, and that low patrols working under or through the clouds should obtain many opportunities of acting by surprise. While therefore the G.O.C. is very strongly opposed to anything in the nature of a local escort of scouts, he would like brigadiers to consider carefully the advisability of working some of 'their patrols at or about the height at which the corps machines are working, with high patrols up at the same time.'

It is possible now to throw more light on the German tactics. The enemy was on the defensive and, under instructions from the Supreme Army Command, the majority of single-seater fighters were sent up only when the Royal Flying Corps was most active. Special air protection officers (*Luftschutz Offiziere*) were stationed well forward to watch and report on the movements of the Royal Flying Corps aeroplanes. On their reports the air commanders at the various corps headquarters (*Grufl*) judged the opportunities most favourable for bringing the fighting aeroplanes into action. (Particulars supplied for this history by the *Reichsarchiv*, Potsdam.)

The Second Phase

On Monday the 16th of April the main French attack opened, but its success, as has been said, fell far short of what had been promised, and the renewal of the British operations at Arras, with the object of diverting German strength from the Aisne heights, became a matter of some urgency.

The weather on the 16th was favourable for flying and many artillery targets were registered, and the Drocourt-Quéant line was extensively photographed by F.E.2b's of No. 11 Squadron. In view of past experience when the photographing of this line had been attempted, strong precautions were taken to deal with enemy opposition. In addition to a close escort of four Nieuport single-seaters, offensive formations of Nos. 48, 60, and 1 (Naval) Squadrons were ordered to patrol the area while the photographs were being procured.

The Bristol Fighters of No. 48 Squadron and the Sopwith Triplanes of No. 1 (Naval) Squadron flew for twenty-five minutes over the German aerodrome at Douai, but they were not challenged and their patrol as well as the photographic reconnaissance passed off without incident. The offensive formation of No. 60 Squadron, however, consisting of six Nieuports, had met with severe fighting on its outward journey. As the formation crossed the lines, near Monchy, the leader saw a corps aeroplane to the north attacked by four German fighters, and went to the help of the B.E. The German pilots turned to meet the Nieuports and shot four of them down with a loss of one aeroplane to themselves.

For the next four days little useful flying was possible and the artillery preparations were so retarded that it became necessary to postpone the resumption of the offensive—planned for the 21st of April—for two days. On the evening of the 20th the weather showed signs of improvement and some leeway was made up in the programme of air and artillery co-operation.

On the 21st of April the preliminary bombardment began in improved weather which made possible a full day's air co-operation. Trench junctions were registered, batteries were located and engaged, and wire entanglements were destroyed. Next day the air activity on both sides increased. The day opened with Royal Flying Corps attacks on enemy kite balloons along the whole front which brought retaliatory attacks on British balloons. Two German balloons on the front of the Third Army and one in front of the Second Army were destroyed and three British balloons were shot down in flames. Four other German balloons which received direct hits emitted smoke, but did not catch fire and they were hauled to safety, the observers in each instance making parachute descents.

While the balloon attacks were being made there were, over the active battle front, in an area roughly twenty miles long by six miles deep, seven patrolling formations of single-seater fighters, and line patrols by three formations of two-seaters. These formations totalled fifty fighting aircraft, and there were similar numbers operating at other periods throughout the day, but the fighting in which they engaged was comparatively light. For the most part the enemy fighters were content to play a game of hide and seek. They dived away east on being attacked, following which manoeuvre they regained height and returned to the lines, seeking their opportunity to slip in and make sudden surprise attacks on the corps aeroplanes which were repeatedly engaged throughout the day and were often forced down.

Two attempts by No. 11 Squadron to reconnoitre and photograph the Drocourt-Quéant switch line failed. In neither instance was a close escort provided and the protection afforded by offensive patrols in the area was ineffective. The first attempt, a reconnaissance in the morning by six F.E.2b's, was thwarted by two Albatros fighters and the F.E.2b formation was forced to turn back with two wounded observers. A similar formation set out in the afternoon and was taking photographs when Richthofen's flight appeared. The F.E.2b's turned for home, but they were fiercely assailed. One was shot down in enemy territory, and, of the others, four, damaged in the fight or with wounded personnel, were wrecked on landing.

******

In the missing aeroplane the observer was killed and the pilot taken prisoner. In those which returned one observer was mortally wounded, and two pilots and three observers wounded. The pilot, Lieutenant C. A. Parker, who brought back the mortally wounded observer, had a remarkable journey. His observer, shot when the fight began, fell across the side of the F.E.2b. The pilot had to hold on to him when he attempted to land the aeroplane in which most of the controls had been shot away. He came down just clear of the front line trenches, the aeroplane bursting into flames before it touched the ground. As the pilot was carrying his observer clear, the F.E.2b was blown to pieces by a direct hit from a heavy shell.

******

The enormous advantage possessed by the superior fighting aeroplane when confidently handled, as was continuously demonstrated by Richthofen and his pilots, was also well brought out by the experience of two Sopwith Triplane pilots of No. 1 (Naval) Squadron. After indecisive encounters with German two-seaters the Sopwith pilots (Flight Commander R. S. Dallas and Flight Sub-Lieutenant T. G. Culling) met an enemy formation of fourteen two-seaters and single-seater fighters. The German pilots were flying towards the lines at 16,000 feet on a mission that appeared to be of some importance, but they were frustrated by the Sopwiths which fought the Germans for forty-five minutes, kept their formation split up, shot three of them down (one fell in flames and one crashed), and left the remainder only when the German pilots had retreated, individually and at a low height, far to the eastward. The triplanes had the superior speed and climbing powers, and the two pilots were enabled to keep up a continuous series of attacks. They each chose an enemy aeroplane, made a short dive, put in a rapid burst of fire, regained height on a climbing turn, and then repeated their diving attacks.

An evening bombing attack on the aerodrome at Cambrai on the 22nd of April met: with opposition. The bombs (twenty-four 20 lb. and twelve incendiaries) were carried by six F.E.2b's of No. 18 Squadron escorted by five Spads of No. 23 Squadron and six Sopwith 'Pups' of No. 3 (Naval) Squadron. Soon after the bombs had been dropped, the formation was attacked by four enemy single-seaters, but the Sopwiths had little difficulty in driving them off and escorted the bombers safely home. Meanwhile the Spads, which had lost the main formation, were involved with another group of Albatros fighters which the leader of the Spad formation mistook for British aeroplanes and climbed to join. The Albatros pilots dived on the Spads, shot two of them down in the German lines, and wounded the pilot in a third which crashed in the British lines. In the fighting, which was severe, some of the enemy aeroplanes were driven down, but none was observed to crash.

A prominent pilot of Richthofen's unit, Lieutenant Schafer, had a narrow escape on this evening. He was flying alone near Monchy when he saw a B.E. of No. 12 Squadron, low down, working for the artillery. He attacked the B.E. to within 150 feet from the ground when he gave up and turned away, but he was not quick enough to avoid machine-gunners of the 15th Division who shot his engine out of action and forced him down in No Man's Land. Machine-gun and artillery fire was opened on the enemy aeroplane, but Schafer, unhurt, escaped to the cover of a shell-hole, and, when darkness came, crawled to the German front-line trenches. He returned to his aerodrome and, flying a new aeroplane, took his revenge on No. 12 Squadron in the afternoon of the 23rd of April when he destroyed one of their artillery aeroplanes in the same area.

The infantry attacks along the fronts of the First and Third Armies on the 23rd of April were begun at 4.45 a.m. from Gavrelle to Croisilles. Throughout the day fighting was continuous, and the enemy, who was in strength, delivered strong counter-attacks so that the line fluctuated. (R.E.8's of No. 59 Squadron patrolled in pairs over the advanced troops to locate, report, and attack enemy reinforcements. Their duty foreshadowed the counter-attack patrols which were brought into general use in May 1917.) The contact patrols by the various corps squadrons failed to elucidate the progress of the battle owing to a lack of response to the repeated requests of the air observers for the lighting of flares. Pilots flew a few hundred feet above the battlefield (two aeroplanes were shot down from the ground), but direct observation revealed only isolated bodies of infantry, and the contact patrol reports were of small value. The Third Army Commander, in the evening, informed his corps commanders:

> R.F.C. report flares hardly used by infantry again today. This makes effective artillery support almost impossible. Attention of all ranks is to be called to the importance of lighting flares when called for.

The infantry were desperately occupied in fighting, and there were many enemy aeroplanes patrolling the area of the battlefield throughout the day—a fact which probably added to the reluctance of the forward troops to reveal their positions by lighting flares. The enemy formations, usually of two or three aeroplanes, made many attacks on the corps aeroplanes and repeatedly interrupted their work. The harassing tactics of the enemy fighters succeeded in spite of the presence of great numbers of Royal Flying Corps fighting formations. Close offensive patrols by the Ninth Wing and by the Army Wings of the I and III Brigades were maintained in the area bounded by Lens-Hen-in-Liètard-Bullecourt-Sains, and the battle-line itself was patrolled by two-seater fighters. At any time during the day, in the above area, there were from forty to fifty patrolling single-seaters and Bristol Fighters, with another twenty two-seater fighters along the line.

******

> During the initial infantry advance, up to 8.0 a.m. there were forty-eight single-seater fighters patrolling the area made up of fifteen Sopwith triplanes (No. I Naval Squadron), five Sopwith triplanes (No. 8 Naval Squadron), seven S.E.5's of No. 56. seven Spads of No. 19, eight Nieuports of No. 29, and six Nieuports of No. 60 Squadron. On line patrol were six Sopwiths of No. 43 Squadron, six F.E.'s of No. 57, six F.E.'s of No. 25, four Armstrong Whitworths of No. 35, and two R.E.8's of No. 59 Squadron.

******

There were many encounters which attracted additional formations from either side and developed into 'dog-fights' of long duration, but the enemy showed a fair measure of caution and the decisive combats were, in view of the numbers engaged, few.

A combined reconnaissance and bombing operation in the morning by squadrons of the Ninth Wing was supported by distant offensive patrols of Sopwith 'Pups' (No. 66 Squadron) and Spads (No. 19 Squadron). This operation, which was successful, is of some tactical interest. Nine Sopwith two-seaters of No. 70 Squadron set out at 5.55 a.m. to photograph and report on inundations along the Mons-Condé canal. They were ordered to cross the trenches north of the active battle area outward, and south of it on the homeward journey. Close behind the Sopwiths followed five Martinsydes of No. 27 Squadron and four D.H.4's of No. 55 Squadron with 112-lb. bombs. The bombers were to keep to the path of the Sopwith formation as far as St. Amand, when the Martinsydes were to diverge to bomb the sugar factory at Lecelles, and the D.H.4's to turn south to attack the station at Valenciennes.

On the homeward journey the bombing formations were to proceed by way of Haspres and Beauvois, joining, over the latter place, the homeward line taken by the reconnoitring Sopwiths. Protection on the outward journey was to be provided by six Sopwith 'Pups' of No. 66 Squadron which were to accompany the nine two-seater Sopwiths as far as the line Cysoing-Orchies and wait there until the two bombing formations had passed. For the return journey a similar number of Sopwith 'Pups' of No. 66 Squadron, together with three Spads of No. 19 Squadron, were to await, east of Cambrai, the arrival of the reconnaissance and bombing formations and then escort them home. Except that on the outward journey four of the six escorting Sopwith 'Pups' were forced to turn back with engine or machine-gun trouble, the whole operation passed off according to plan; no enemy opposition was encountered, and all aeroplanes returned safely.

No. 55 Squadron was less fortunate in the afternoon, when eight D.H.4's set out to make an independent attack on the ammunition depot at Boué, north-east of Etreux. Two of the de Havillands crashed before the lines were reached, but the remaining six got through to their objective and dropped twelve 112-lb bombs. On the return journey they were sharply attacked by seven single-seater fighters, and, before the attackers were shaken off, one de Havilland pilot had been killed and three observers wounded.

Other notable bombing during the day was on villages north and south of the Arras-Douai road by No. 27 Squadron and by Nos. 10 and 25 Squadrons of the I Brigade. Trains and stations on the lines radiating from Douai were made the targets for night attacks by the F.E.2b's of No. 100 Squadron.

An attempted bombing attack on Epinoy led to a 'dogfight' which may be quoted as typical of the mass fighting throughout the day. The bombers—six F.E.2b's of No. 18 Squadron with an escort of five Sopwith 'Pups' of No. 3 (Naval) Squadron—were on their way to Epinoy at 5.30 p.m. when they were attacked by two formations of Halberstadt and Albatros fighters. The fight became so intense that the F.E.'s were compelled to turn back. One F.E. pilot was wounded, but the Sopwiths covered the retreat of the F.E.'s and all made a safe return. Many of the German single-seaters were driven down by the Sopwiths, two of them out of control.

As soon as the F.E.'s were clear of the line, the Sopwith pilots turned to engage the enemy again, and, with other British and German formations joining, the fight became general and lasted until after 7.0 p.m. Sopwith triplanes of No. 1 (Naval) Squadron, Bristol Fighters of No. 48, Nieuports of No. 60, and Sopwith 'Pups' of No. 66 Squadron were all involved. Several enemy fighters were forced down, apparently damaged, and one of them was seen to catch fire near the ground. Two Sopwiths were badly shot about, but made safe landings, and there were no other British casualties. The fight lasted until the enemy pilots, probably through petrol shortage, withdrew. One feature of the fighting was the superiority of the Bristol Fighter, now improved in minor details and confidently handled by its pilots. The Bristols were frequently outnumbered, but it was found they could more than hold their own against the best enemy fighters.

As a contrast to the mass fighting, Captain Albert Ball of No. 56 Squadron, and Captain W. A. Bishop of No. 60 Squadron, flew alone on roving commissions and had successful encounters. (See *Winged Warfare* by William A. Bishop also published by Leonaur). Captain Ball's tactics, when he attacked a two-seater in which the observer sat behind, were to dive from the half-rear until the German observer had got his gun in position in that direction, and then to swerve suddenly, pass to the opposite side, and fire at close range from below before the observer had time to swing his gun round.

Flying a Nieuport in the morning of the 23rd of April, Ball attacked two German two-seaters and shot one down to crash upside down. Later in the morning, in an S.E.5, he was over Cambrai at 13,000 feet, when he saw a formation of five Albatros fighters. He gave chase, came up with them over Selvigny, dived unhesitatingly at the nearest and sent it down in flames. The remainder put many bullets into Ball's aeroplane before he made good his escape. On his homeward journey he attacked, and forced to land, another two-seater.

Captain Bishop, in a Nieuport, forced down a two-seater near Vitry and kept up his attack after the enemy aeroplane had landed. He climbed again and, at 6,000 feet, found another Nieuport under attack from three Albatros fighters. He took one of the enemy pilots by surprise, put in a burst at close range, and watched the Albatros spin down and crash.

On the 24th of April the ground operations were continued. They were of a local character and included the repulse of many German counter-attacks. In the air, intense activity was maintained. An attack on the enemy kite balloons along the whole front was defeated by the rapidity with which the balloons were hauled down. Only two German balloons were destroyed—one by No. 60 Squadron and the other by No. 29 Squadron.

A combined reconnaissance and bombing operation, similar in conception to that carried out on the 23rd, was partly successful. The distant reconnaissance—to Le Quesnoy and Landrecies—by No. 70 Squadron could not be completed owing to low clouds. The formation, of nine Sopwith two-seaters, together with its escort of six Sopwith 'Pups' of No. 66 Squadron, was attacked over Solesmes. One of the two-seater Sopwiths was shot down in flames and one of the escorting pilots was forced to land and was made prisoner. Three of the German fighters were driven down, two of them apparently out of control. The bombing formations, which followed, fared better.

Five Martinsydes of No. 27 Squadron each dropped one 230-lb. bomb in the neighbourhood of the sheds at Ath Station. The three escorting Spads had a brief indecisive encounter with two Albatros two-seaters on the outward journey, but there was no other opposition. Meanwhile seven Martinsydes of the same squadron bombed Hirson station and reported hits on the engine sheds and on a moving train, which was derailed. This formation, which met with no opposition, lost direction on the homeward journey and the pilots landed at various places in Normandy.

Close behind the Martinsydes which flew to Hirson, there followed six D.H.4's of No. 55 Squadron with bombs for the German aerodrome at Valenciennes. One of the D.H.4's turned back with engine failure, but the remainder, although attacked before they reached their objective, persisted and dropped forty-nine 20-lb. bombs over the aerodrome, but had no opportunity to observe the results. There were repeated attacks by Albatros fighters which continued their attacks to the neighbourhood of the Flying Corps aerodrome at Fienvillers, where one of the D.H.4's was shot down with a dead pilot and a wounded observer.

Once again, the offensive and the line patrols had few decisive combats. The S.E.5's of No. 56 Squadron figured in many encounters, but gun trouble compelled pilots to give up most of the fights.

★★★★★★

These S.E.5's were fitted with the new Constantinesco gear, which was at first not properly understood. Mr. George Constantinesco, the Roumanian inventor of wave transmission of power, began, in May 1916, experimental work with a gear designed to fire a machine-gun by means of impulses transmitted through a column of liquid contained under pressure in a pipe. He was helped, unofficially, by Major C. C. Colley, R.A., of the Munitions Inventions Department, and the first gear was successfully demonstrated on a B.E.2C in August 1916. A great advantage of the 'C.C.' Gear, as it was called, apart from its revolutionary advance on gears operated mechanically, was its adaptability to any type of engine.

When the Constantinesco Gear had come through its 'teething' troubles, it was an outstanding success. It became, and still remains, the standard gear for British service aircraft. The first squadron to arrive in France, whose aeroplanes were fitted with the Constantinesco gear, was No. 55 (D.H.4) Squadron, on the 6th March 1917. No. 48 (Bristol Fighter), similarly fitted, arrived on the 8th of March and No. 56 (S.E.5) on the 8th of April. 6,000 of the gears were issued during the period March to December 1917 and 20,000 from January to October 1918.

★★★★★★

The three Naval squadrons, Nos. 1, 3, and 8, were continuously engaged, but were given few opportunities to drive home their attacks. The sight of a Sopwith triplane formation, in particular, induced the enemy pilots to dive out of range.

When they stayed to fight they handled their Albatros fighters with great skill and showed up to special advantage against mixed British formations. In one encounter, in the afternoon of the 24th, five enemy single-seaters, probably from Richthofen's unit, survived attacks from formations of British fighters to the number of twenty (including Sopwith triplanes, S.E.5's, Nieuports, F.E.2b's, and a Spad). When the Albatros pilots had tired of the fight, they broke off the combat and dived away east unscathed.

By this time the limited progress of the initial French attacks on the Aisne had produced acute discouragement in the French Army and among the French people. The French operations had resulted in gains in territory, guns, and prisoners, and the cost had not been disproportionately high, but the French people had been led to expect too much. There followed changes in the high command, but, notwithstanding, the offensive had necessarily to be continued until, at least, the initial gains had been consolidated.

★★★★★★

> On the 29th of April 1917 (the Minister of War now being a civilian—M. Painlevé in place of General H. Lyautey) the post of Chief of the General Staff at the French Ministry of War was revived and the appointment given to General Petain, an exponent of the steady tactics of the Somme battle. General Nivelle was invited to resign, refused, and, on the 15th of May, was replaced by General Pétain. General Foch thereupon was selected to succeed General Pétain as Chief of the General Staff in Paris.

★★★★★★

To assist the French, Sir Douglas Haig decided to continue his operations at Arras. Movements of troops, guns, &c, required to complete the preparations for the British Flanders offensive, were postponed. Instead, preparations were made for a repetition of the attacks on the Arras front. The first of these attacks was delivered on the 28th of April on a front of eight miles north of Monchy-le-Preux.

From the 25th to the 28th the main duty of the corps squadrons was co-operation with the artillery. Clouds were low during these days and the offensive patrols were drawn in closer to the lines, where they could afford direct protection to the corps aeroplanes. There were many combats, but the presence of the fighting formations ensured a measure of temporary dominance over a restricted front line area.

At 4.25 a.m. on the 28th of April the infantry attack was renewed, and, after a day of severe fighting, the enemy was driven from his trenches along a two-mile front at Arleux-en-Gohelle, and ground was won at Oppy and on the slopes of Greenland Hill. The early advance, marked by flares, was reported by contact patrol observers, but as the German counter-attacks developed, the lighting of flares almost ceased and little of the further progress could be reported from the air. The enemy fighting pilots concentrated their energies on the corps aeroplanes, and of the twelve Flying Corps aeroplanes destroyed or damaged during the day, ten were B.E.'s engaged on tactical work.

The attacking pilots were aided by low clouds which they used to cover their approach. Bombing attacks on Busigny Station (four 230-lb. bombs), and on the dump at Bohain Station (eight 112-lb. bombs), met with no opposition.

Next day, April the 29th, when the weather improved, air fighting was intense. A conflict in the morning began with an attack by six grey Albatros fighters on an offensive patrol of three S.E.5's of No. 56 Squadron. The S.E.'s were severely tested, but survived. After the attack had been in progress some time, it was seen by a formation of five F.E.2d's of No. 57 Squadron which dived to join in. One of the F.E.'s was shot down, the pilot and observer being made prisoners, and one of the Albatros fighters was destroyed, the pilot falling from his aeroplane as it went down out of control.

The German formation broke away and shortly afterwards joined Richthofen's flight of six red Albatros fighters. The combined group was sighted from above by Major H. D. Harvey-Kelly who had with him two other Spads of No. 19 Squadron. Major Harvey-Kelly promptly led his Spads down in a dive, but the odds were too great and, after a fierce encounter, all three Spads were shot down. Major Harvey-Kelly, badly wounded, was taken prisoner, and he died of his wounds a few days later. His loss was severely felt. He had flown to France in August 1914 with No. 2 Squadron, and was the first Flying Corps pilot to land on French soil. His high spirits and serene temper, which no odds or adversity affected, had been a moral asset to his squadron and to his service.

The desperate plight of the Spads had been seen from a distance by a formation of six Sopwith triplanes of No. 1 (Naval) Squadron. The triplanes went down at once but were too late to save the Spads. For twenty minutes the Sopwiths fought the enemy single-seaters and sent three of them down out of control, one of which was seen to crash. The German formations split up and followed the Sopwiths back to the lines. Captain W. A. Bishop, who was with an escort to a photographic reconnaissance of No. 11 Squadron, seeing one of the enemy fighters passing below him, dived and attacked, and shot it down in flames.

While these combats were taking place, extensive fighting was also in progress near Cambrai, involving ten Sopwith 'Pups' of No. 3 (Naval) Squadron which were acting as escort to an F.E. reconnaissance formation of No. 18 Squadron. The British aeroplanes were challenged by eleven enemy fighters and the Sopwith formation was quickly broken up. In the individual fighting which followed, two enemy aeroplanes were destroyed, and the Sopwiths succeeded in escorting the F.E.'s safely back to the lines. The Sopwith pilots then turned to re-engage the enemy and fought, without further decisive results, until their petrol was finished.

Richthofen was again prominent in the afternoon. Leading his formation of six red single-seaters, he attacked, at 4.0 p.m., a reconnaissance formation of four F.E.2b's of No. 18 Squadron, of which only one got back undamaged. The F.E.'s, although outnumbered and out-manoeuvred, fought well and sent one of Richthofen's pilots down in flames. Two of the F.E.'s, one with a wounded, and the other with a dead, observer, landed clear of the trenches, and the third was shot down by Richthofen (his fiftieth victim) who says, in his combat report:

> After a long fight, during which the adversary defended himself admirably, I managed to put myself behind him. After 300 shots the enemy aeroplane caught fire. The aeroplane burnt to pieces in the air and the occupants fell out.

Richthofen was again leading his flight along the Third Army front about 6.30 p.m., when he came upon two B.E.'s of No. 12 Squadron. He and his brother Lothar, left their formation and attacked the B.E.'s, one of which fell in flames, and the other, with a dying pilot and a wounded observer, crashed within the British lines. Six triplanes of No. 8 (Naval) Squadron came up with the enemy formation soon after the attack on the B.E.'s. The triplanes dived and were promptly joined by five other triplanes of the same squadron and by a Nieuport pilot of No. 60 Squadron. The Nieuport pilot was attacking an enemy single-seater when Richthofen dived from behind and shot him down in flames. This was the German leader's fifth personal success of the day. Shortly afterwards, one of the German fighters was shot down in a combined attack by two of the Sopwiths, and crashed on its aerodrome, and one of the Sopwiths was lost. The remainder returned safely.

Escorted bombing attacks on Bohain station by No. 27 Squadron (six 230-lb. bombs), and on Valenciennes by No. 55 Squadron (ten 112-lb. bombs) passed off successfully without appreciable opposition, as did a photographic reconnaissance by nine Sopwith two-seaters of No. 70 Squadron.

The 30th of April was notable for a change in German air fighting tactics. The fighter flights attached to the Arras Corps at Douai (3rd, 4th, 11th, and 33rd) were combined to form one group which could, as occasion demanded, operate as a massed fighting formation. This group, which made its first sweep on the morning of the 30th, was promptly named by us 'Richthofen's Circus', although, in fact, the first fighting squadron under Richthofen was not formed until June. The original idea seems, to have arisen from a desire to link up a number of fighting formations for occasional combined sweeps, whereas Richthofen's circus proper was a homogeneous squadron which operated under the German leader's personal command.

The new group numbering twenty single-seaters, in two formations, set out from the Douai aerodrome in the morning of the 30th. Their first encounter was with seven F.E.2d's of a line patrol of No. 57 Squadron and three Sopwith triplanes of No. 8 (Naval) Squadron. Two of the F.E.'s were shot down in the German lines and a third, with a wounded pilot and a dying observer, crashed in the British area. The triplanes succeeded after a bitter fight, during which several German fighters were driven down, in extricating the four remaining F.E.'s. The enemy group then turned away, joined a number of two-seaters, and, shortly afterwards, came up with a formation of six Bristol Fighters on their way, escorted by five Sopwith triplanes, to reconnoitre a reported trench system east of Douai.

There followed a continuous fight for twenty minutes in which three S.E.5's of No. 56 Squadron joined. Two of the enemy aeroplanes were shot down and seen to crash and one S.E.5 went down in flames, but in the end the Bristol Fighters had to abandon their reconnaissance attempt and, with their Sopwith escort, fight their way home. The enemy group, now numbering fifteen, turned south, followed by two of the Sopwith triplanes, and found a photographic formation of eight F.E.2b's of No. 18 Squadron. The enemy fighters attacked and the two Sopwiths joined in the fighting which lasted half an hour. Two of the F.E.'s were shot down, but the remainder, with the help of the Sopwiths, fought their way back.

While this German fighting group was making a general sweep behind the battle area, smaller fighting formations, at lower heights, patrolled the battle front. The Royal Flying Corps line patrols had also been strengthened. The activity of the German artillery aeroplanes had been increasing from day to day, and attacks with machine-gun fire, by low flying two-seater aeroplanes, on the British front line trenches, were becoming a feature of the battle. In consequence, single-seater fighters (Nieuports of Nos. 29 and 60 Squadrons and Spads of No. 19 Squadron), had been given the duty of making line patrols at low heights. Throughout the 30th, therefore,' there were continuous encounters over the front line area. Five British corps aeroplanes were destroyed, but none of the many encounters between the Flying Corps fighters and the German two-seaters was decisive.

Bombing attacks on the enemy aerodrome at Epinoy went unchallenged. In two day raids on the aerodrome four 112-lb. and sixty-four 20-lb. bombs were dropped and some direct hits reported, and further bombs were dropped during the night.

The month of April 1917 had ended. In no other month throughout the war was the Royal Flying Corps so hard pressed, nor were the casualties suffered so heavy. From May onward a change came over the air position. On the 1st of May Freiherr von Richthofen returned to Germany on leave and his departure coincided with a slackening of the German effort. The fighting formations which he led, and the others on the Arras front which were closely associated with him, had had long practice on a type of aeroplane which was still supreme, and their practice had had opportunity to flower, during the Arras battle, in one great effort.

It was, perhaps, asking too much of human nature that the same pilots should go on with their fighting spirit unimpaired. Many of them must have been tired in body and mind. The pilots and observers of the Royal Flying Corps had, perhaps, more cause to be tired, for they had fought no less strenuously and had suffered severe casualties. But there were factors which were now to tell in their favour. They had struggled on, throughout April, without thought of defeat. They had stood up to the enemy no matter what the odds. They were, therefore, immediately ready to profit from any reaction, no matter how slight, in the fighting spirit of the German pilots. They had, also, old scores to pay off. And they had learnt much. The pilots of the fighting squadrons equipped with the new type aeroplanes, the S.E.5, the Bristol Fighter, the D.H.4, and the Sopwith 'Pup', had gained confidence and experience in handling their craft, and the squadron mechanics had come to understand the new engines and equipment.

There was, from May onwards, a marked diminution of engine and gun trouble which, throughout April, had been a source of irritation to many pilots and had too often led to the breaking-off of a combat. Furthermore, the new German tactics of grouping the fighters, while it had the apparent effect of concentrating the striking power of the fighting unit, had also the further effect of localising the German effort. In a word, the sky appeared to be clearer. Had the German group formation been a true fighting unit, at this time, the enemy air service might have dominated the air. But it was not such a unit, because it lacked the cohesion which can come only of sound tactics and long practice. It was, indeed, little more than a collection of individuals who tended, when issue was joined, to split up and so dissipate the striking power which is the measure of success in formation fighting. What helped further towards the elimination of casualties was the strengthening of all Royal Flying Corps reconnaissance and bombing formations, and of the line patrols, during the periods, in the morning and evening, when the enemy fighters proved most active over the battle area.

From the beginning of May, therefore, the casualties to the corps aeroplanes dropped appreciably, and the air fighting was pushed away from the lines towards the German back areas.

On the 1st and 2nd of May there was a brief lull in the infantry attack for re-organisation and for artillery preparation. The weather was good and the corps aeroplanes were up all day co-operating with the heavy and siege batteries. A well-planned attack on the enemy kite balloons on the 2nd of May, which made full use of the element of surprise, met with success. The rapidity with which the German balloons were hauled down on the approach of aeroplanes had hitherto made decisive attacks difficult or impossible.

Lieutenant-Colonel W. R. Freeman, the officer commanding the Tenth Wing, worked out a plan according to which the artillery were to put down a special barrage on the German trenches while Nieuport pilots of No. 40 Squadron passed over at a height of fifty feet to attack the balloons before they could be hauled down. It seemed likely that the Nieuports would reach the neighbourhood of their targets unseen, but to ensure a surprise approach, the pilots, in practice flying, gained experience in taking advantage of the cover offered by trees, houses, and undulations of the ground. This form of flying, known as 'hedge-hopping' or 'contour-chasing', was later developed in connexion with aeroplane machine-gun attacks on infantry and other ground targets.

At 9.0 a.m. on the 2nd of May the artillery barrage was put down and six Nieuport pilots left the ground. Their attack came as a complete surprise. Eight balloons were caught at heights up to 2,000 feet and four of them were destroyed and the remainder damaged. All the attacking pilots returned safely, but with many bullet holes in their aeroplanes from rifle and machine-gun fire.

On the 1st of May seventy-six 20-lb. bombs had been dropped by twelve Martinsydes of No. 27 Squadron on the aerodrome at Epinoy. On the 2nd bombing was concentrated against the enemy rail communications. No. 55 Squadron attacked Valenciennes station with ten 112-lb. bombs and No. 27 Squadron dropped twelve of the same weight on Orchies station. During the night of the 2nd/3rd of May the bombing attacks were continued by No. 100 Squadron on Valenciennes, Somain, and Goulée. (No. 100 Squadron, operating temporarily from Bailleul, had made two night attacks on April 30th/May 1st, on the St. Sauveur station at Lille and on trains on the Lille-Seclin line.) In addition, day and night attacks were made by all brigades on important targets within the army reconnaissance areas.

On the evening of the 2nd of May there was a clash in the air east of Arras which involved forty fighting aeroplanes of which twenty-five were British. The enemy pilots were gradually driven east to Douai, but the majority of the many individual combats were indecisive. Many German aeroplanes were driven down, one fell in flames, and another, shot down by Captain A. Ball, was followed by him to the ground and seen to crash. There were no British losses.

The British infantry attack, which opened at 3.45 a.m. on the 3rd of May, extended for sixteen miles along the fronts of the First, Third, and Fifth Armies. The objective of the Fifth Army was a formidable section of the Hindenburg Line near Bullecourt. Along the whole front the troops broke into the enemy positions, but their success was short-lived. The enemy had recently adopted new counter-attack tactics drawn up under Ludendorff's supervision in the winter of 1916 and based on the lessons learned during the Somme battles. These tactics, known as the 'elastic defence' (which, incidentally, had been previously used by the French and also by the British 4th Division) allowed for a light holding of the front-line system while the majority of the troops remained in support to the rear, ready and organised to deliver rapid counter-attacks.

It was calculated that such attacks, made before the British troops had time to reorganise or consolidate, would ensure the recovery of any ground initially lost. These calculations were well founded. That the counter-attack was an integral part of the German scheme of defence had already been made clear, and orders had been issued to armies, on the 1st of May, that aeroplanes were to be specially detailed for counter-attack patrol duties. They were to fly, low down, from dawn to darkness, behind the captured positions, and the air observers were to concentrate their attention on preparations for counter-attacks and make immediate reports to the artillery. During the 3rd of May, however, bombardment and counter-bombardment, attack and counter-attack, made chaos of the battlefield, and the air observers could seldom give definite information.

There was an exception in the morning when observers of No. 43 Squadron reported enemy troops massing in the trenches for a counter-attack on the XIII Corps. Five Sopwith two-seaters of the same squadron were sent out to attack the enemy, which they did, with machine-gun fire, from between 50 and 300 feet. Other low-flying attacks on isolated bodies of troops were made by the same squadron in the afternoon. There was little air fighting throughout the day, and over the active front there were no Flying Corps casualties.

Bombing attacks on the 3rd of May, which were spread over a wide area, met with no opposition. Don station was twice attacked by No. 27 Squadron, strongly escorted, and a total of twelve 230-lb. bombs dropped. No. 55 Squadron dropped eight 112-lb. bombs on Busigny Junction in the morning, and in the evening, in combination with No. 27 Squadron, attacked Brebières junction with eleven 112-lb. and forty-two 20-lb. bombs. For the Brebières attack the bombers (six from each squadron) were escorted by fifteen single-seater fighters. Bombing on the front of the V Brigade was concentrated on the enemy ammunition dump at Iwuy.

One of the first pilots to attack was rewarded with a red glow which appeared in the centre of the dump, and when later pilots arrived they found the dump ablaze. They added their bombs, and by the time the last pilot came upon the scene the whole dump was in flames. He therefore went on to Eswars aerodrome, north of Cambrai, and dropped his load there. The bombing along the whole front was kept up during the night and was aimed chiefly at trains and railway junctions. Three trains, attacked from fifty feet by pilots of No. 100 Squadron, were hit and damaged, and direct hits by an officer of No. 16 Squadron were made on hangars on Tourmignies aerodrome.

On the 4th of May the fine weather continued, the German pilots were more active, and the Flying Corps bombing and reconnaissance formations met with sterner resistance. An unescorted photographic reconnaissance by nine Sopwiths of No. 70 Squadron to Tournai was surrounded and attacked by groups of enemy single-seaters at the moment when the plates were being exposed. A number of photographs were procured and new aerodromes located before the Sopwiths were compelled to turn back. The Sopwith formation had to fight the whole way home. One aeroplane, with a riddled petrol tank, had to land in the German lines, and in another an observer was killed. Three enemy single-seaters were driven down, one of them out of control. A photographic reconnaissance by six D.H.4's to Valenciennes was more successful. One German single-seater pilot attacked the formation, but he was driven down after a brief encounter. Two independent bombing formations, which had for objectives the German aerodromes at Eswars and La Brayelle, were strongly supported, and the escorting fighters had no difficulty in driving off small enemy formations which attacked.

There was a lull on the 5th. To give pilots a rest no bombing or reconnaissance flying was ordered and the offensive patrols were curtailed. Captain Ball had a successful encounter in the evening. Flying alone in an S.E.5 he sighted two German single-seaters coming from the direction of Cambrai. He allowed them to approach the tail of his aeroplane and then did a rapid turn and attacked one of them, at close range, from underneath. This one fell out of control and Ball manoeuvred for position to attack the second. The two shortly approached head on. This was a position which Ball welcomed and one which he had often exploited successfully. It was his experience that if he held his course firmly, the enemy pilot would at the last moment, swerve away to avoid a collision.

This brief moment, when the enemy pilot lost the cover given by his engine, usually sufficed for Ball to finish his opponent. If not, he was ready for a rapid climbing turn and dive which would put his enemy at a disadvantage. In this instance the two approached, almost to the point of collision, when the German aeroplane began to fall out of control. The engine of the S.E.5 had been hit and Ball was covered in oil, but he went down low to look at his victims before making his return. The two German aeroplanes lay on the ground within a few hundred yards of one another, completely wrecked.

On the morning of the 7th of May, the Nieuport pilots of No. 40 Squadron set out to repeat their low-flying success against the enemy kite balloons. The attack was carried out on the same principle as that made by the squadron on the 2nd of May. An artillery barrage was put down on the enemy trenches and the six Nieuports crossed the lines at heights under fifty feet, the pilots taking every advantage of cover afforded by ground objects. To distract attention from the Nieuports, a formation of twelve Sopwith triplanes flew above them, high up, and to give them close protection four other Nieuports patrolled immediately over them. Seven German balloons were destroyed in flames. One of the Nieuports was shot down in enemy territory, but the others, although hit many times, recrossed the lines safely. One of them, however, was wrecked in a forced landing.

Two German aerodromes were photographed by nine Sopwiths of No. 70 Squadron, strongly escorted, and the aerodrome at Abscon was bombed by No. 55 Squadron (sixty 20-lb. bombs). There was no opposition in either instance, although the Sopwith formation was followed home, at a respectful distance, by groups of enemy fighters.

In an endeavour to catch the German aeroplanes during their periods of greatest activity, patrols by eighteen fighters of the Ninth Wing were ordered to be in the neighbourhood of the German aerodrome at Douai in the morning and in the evening of the 7th of May. One of these patrols in the evening had severe fighting. The aeroplanes chiefly involved were ten S.E.5's of No. 56 Squadron. Of six Spads of No. 19 Squadron, which were patrolling in conjunction with the S.E.5's, only one joined in the fighting, which was confused by rain and poor visibility, and took place through layers of cloud. The remaining Spad pilots lost touch with one another and saw nothing of the combats.

In this fighting Captain Albert Ball was killed. The ten S.E.5's, flying in three layers, met, near Cambrai, a group of red Albatros fighters similarly disposed in layers. A general engagement followed in which two of the enemy aeroplanes were shot down. After a time, the S.E.5 pilots lost touch and one of them, Captain H. Meintjes, flew off alone in the direction of Lens where he found and had a close-range combat with a single red Albatros. During this fight, Captain Meintjes was hit in the wrist and he thereupon dived steeply and made his escape.

Another detached group of four S.E. pilots, headed by Captain C. M. Crowe, had made for Vitry and had shot down an enemy single-seater fighter apparently flying alone. Almost immediately, however, other German fighters had attacked from above and had destroyed one of the S.E.'s, had wounded the pilot in another (who succeeded in landing near a Canadian hospital), and had so damaged a third S.E. that the pilot only got back with great difficulty to make a forced landing. Captain Crowe had thereupon flown back to the pre-arranged rendezvous point above Arras and there rejoined Captain Ball and the remaining three pilots. The five closed formation and resumed their patrol towards Vitry and Lens, and shortly became involved with four red single-seaters. Rain was now falling and, hampered by the clouds and the poor visibility, the five S.E.5's became split up soon after the engagement began, and three of them shortly returned home.

Captain Ball and Captain Crowe, however, although out of touch with one another, continued to patrol independently until 8.0 p.m. when they met over Fresnoy and flew thence in company. After a time, Captain Ball was seen to fire two Very lights, following which he dived on a single red fighter near Loos. Captain Crowe dived also and a Spad of No. 19 Squadron joined in. All three British pilots attacked the enemy single-seater in turn and then Ball and the German pilot disappeared, still fighting, into a cloud bank. Captain Crowe followed, but when he came through the clouds he could see nothing of either the British or German aeroplanes. He therefore returned.

Captain Ball, whose body was recovered by French civilians from the wreckage of his aeroplane, was buried by the enemy at Annoeullin. It is impossible to say definitely how he came by his death. The German authorities stated that he fell in a fight with Richthofen's younger brother Lothar, who was himself forced to land with his petrol tanks smashed by bullets. Although there seems little doubt that Captain Ball's last fight was with Lothar von Richthofen—a worthy opponent—there is some evidence that his S.E. 5 was also hit by anti-aircraft gun fire. He was posthumously awarded the Victoria Cross.

Albert Ball, who was modest and gentle and without aggressiveness in his ordinary nature, is revealed in his many score of combats as the embodiment of the offensive spirit. He made use of any advantage, as of cloud or sun, which came his way, but he relied above all on the surprise that comes of daring. He would, single-handed, fly straight into a formation, throw it into confusion, shoot one or two opponents down, and be away before the others had time to recover. The moral effect of such tactics cannot be over-estimated.

It may be argued that, in his long immunity in such fights against odds, there was an element of luck. The truth is he had the qualities of genius. He was a clever pilot and a dead shot, but he was also an uncannily quick thinker. He judged the risks, measured himself against them, and proceeded to enforce his will with all his rare qualities in perfect co-ordination. He was credited officially with forty-one enemy aeroplanes destroyed, but his total was probably higher. There were a few pilots who exceeded these figures, but there was none who achieved his successes with such calculated indifference to the odds against him. In the ranks of the great fighting pilots of the war Albert Ball yields place to none.

RAILWA
N.E. FRANCE AN

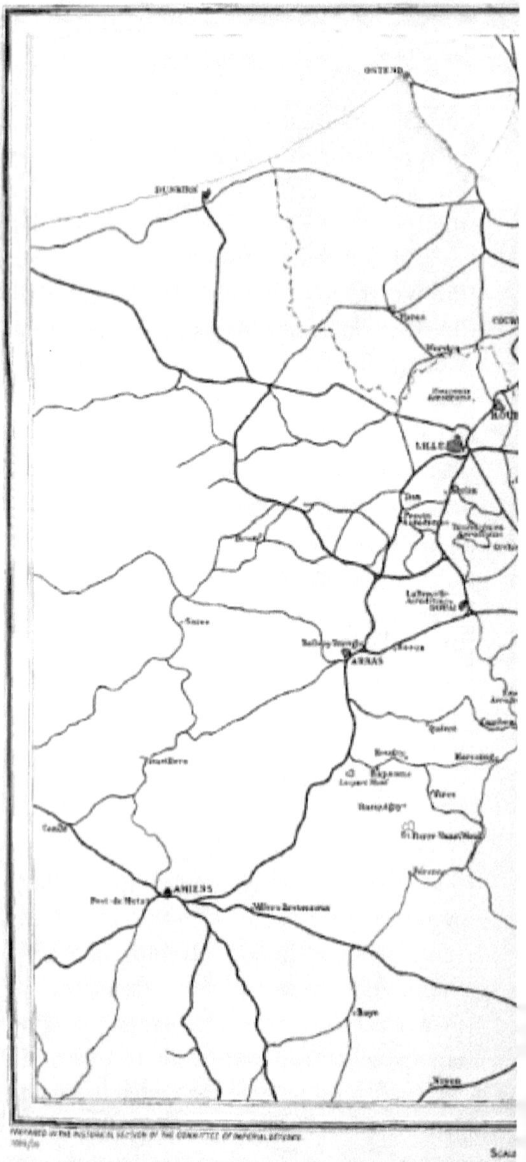

PREPARED IN THE HISTORICAL SECTION OF THE COMMITTEE OF IMPERIAL DEFENCE

SCAL

Y MAP

D S.W. BELGUIM

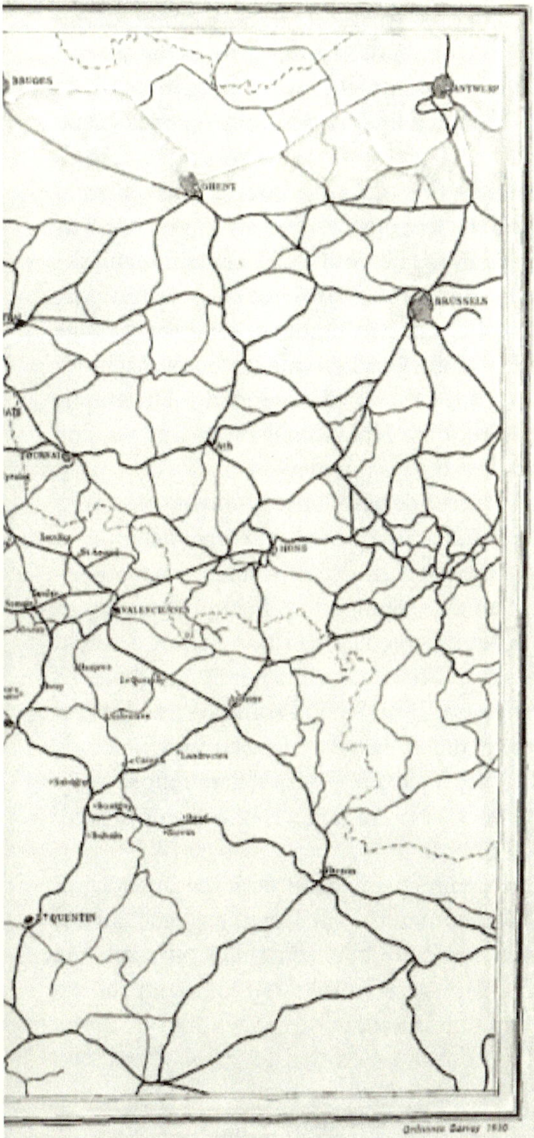

On the 9th of May Major-General Trenchard put forward his proposals for the redistribution of the Royal Flying Corps squadrons for the summer offensive in Flanders. The proposals were approved and the movements begun. This is not to say that the operations at Arras ceased. There were notable attacks at Bullecourt, by which the village was finally captured on the 17th of May. And there were minor attacks in which fighting aircraft, for the first time, directly assisted the assaulting battalions. The first occasion was on the evening of the 11th of May when the Third Army captured enemy positions on both banks of the Scarpe.

On the left bank of the river the attacking troops, who left their trenches at 7.30 p.m. behind a creeping barrage, were preceded by two flights of aeroplanes—one of F.E.2b's of No. 11 Squadron and the other of Nieuports of No. 60 Squadron. The aeroplanes were under the control of one pilot who led the two flights beyond the barrage and then dived to engage the waiting German infantry with machine-gun fire. Several of the pilots, after they had expended their ammunition, returned to their aerodromes, replenished their supplies, and went back to the battle to repeat the manoeuvre.

When the barrage finally lifted, detachments of enemy troops in shell holes in the open were similarly attacked. The co-operation of the aeroplanes was reported by the Third Army staff to have been particularly effective. The infantry, keeping close behind the barrage, made rapid progress, and Roeux cemetery and the chemical works near Roeux station were taken together with some hundreds of prisoners. During the advance north of Roeux some of the forward troops mistook their objective and deviated to the south, whereby a gap was left in the line. This was discovered from a flare report made by a contact aeroplane observer of No. 13 Squadron, and troops were promptly sent forward to fill the gap.

Nos. 11 and 60 Squadrons again co-operated with the infantry on the morning of the 20th of May when the VII Corps began an assault on the sector of the Hindenburg Line between Bullecourt and the British front line west of Fontaine-lez-Croisilles. At 5.15 a.m., as the attacking waves of infantry were leaving their trenches, six Nieuports of No. 60 and seven F.E.2b's of No. 11 crossed to a line about two miles on the enemy side of the barrage, where they dived to within a hundred feet or so of the ground and attacked detachments of German infantry and gun crews. In addition to machine-gun fire each F.E.2b attacked with two 20-lb. bombs.

Desultory fighting on the Arras front continued into June, but by this time the centre of interest had shifted to the north where the great Flanders offensive had opened.

Appendices

APPENDIX I

GERMAN NAVAL AIRSHIPS 1911–1918

Type & No.	Completed at:	Date Commissioned.	Capacity (Cu. Ft.)	Length (Ft.)	Diameter (Ft.)	Engines (Maybach) No.	Engines (Maybach) H.P.	Engines (Maybach) Total H.P.	Speed (M.P.H.)	Ceiling. (Ft.)	Remarks.
Zeppelin L.1	Friedrichshafen	7.10.12	793,600	518·2	48·9	3	170	510	29	10,500	Lost in storm off Heligoland, 9.9.1913.
L.2	”	9.9.13	953,600	518·2	54·4	4	180	720	47	9,500	Caught fire in flight near Johannisthal, 17.10.1913.
L.3	”	11.5.14									Wrecked in forced landing off Fanö Island, Denmark, 17.2.1915.
L.4	”	18.8.14									Wrecked in forced landing at Blaavands Huk, Denmark, 17.2.1915.
L.5	”	24.9.14									Damaged by gunfire, and wrecked in forced landing at Plungiany, Russia, 6.8.1915.
L.6	”	3.11.14	793,600	518·2	48·9	3	210	630	53	9,300	Burnt in shed at Fuhlsbüttel, Germany, 19.9.1916.
L.7	”	22.11.14									Destroyed by gunfire by British naval forces near List, off Schleswig coast, 4.5.1916.
L.8	”	19.12.14									Damaged by gunfire near Nieuport on 4.3.1915, and wrecked at Tirlemont, Belgium, 5.3.1915.
L.9	”	8.3.15	879,500	529·4	52·5	3	210	630	36	10,200	Burnt in shed at Fuhlsbüttel, Germany, 16.9.1916.
L.10	”	13.5.15									Destroyed by lightning near Cuxhaven, Germany, 3.9.1915.
L.11	Löwenthal	7.6.15									Deleted, broken up at Hage, Germany, 5.4.1917.
L.12	Friedrichshafen	21.6.15									Damaged by gunfire while raiding England 10.8.1915, towed into Ostend and dismantled.
L.13	”	23.7.15									Deleted, broken up at Hage,

L.14	Löwenthal	9.8.15									Destroyed at Nordholz, 23.6.1919.
L.15	,,	9.9.15	1,126,700	536·4	61·35	4	240	960	61	12,800	Hit by gunfire from Purfleet and foundered in mouth of Thames, 31.3.1916.
L.16	Friedrichshafen	23.9.15									Wrecked on landing at Nordholz, Germany, 19.10.1917.
L.17	,,	20.10.15									Burnt in shed at Tondern, Germany, 28.12.1916.
L.18	Löwenthal	3.11.15									Burnt in shed at Tondern, Germany, 17.11.1915.
L.19	Friedrichshafen	27.11.15									Foundered in North Sea 2.2.1916, after raiding England.
L.20	,,	21.12.15									Driven by storm to Norway and foundered near Stavanger, 3.5.1916, after raiding Scotland.
L.21	Löwenthal	10.1.16									Destroyed by British aircraft off Lowestoft, 28.11.1916.
L.22	,,	3.3.16	1,264,400	585·5	61·35	4	240	960	59	13,800	Destroyed by British aircraft off Terschelling Island, Holland, 14.5.1917.
L.23	Potsdam	16.4.16									Destroyed by British aircraft off Lyngvig, Denmark, 21.8.1917.
L.24	,,	20.5.16									Burnt in shed at Tondern, Germany, 28.12.1916.
L.25	,,	14.11.15	1,126,700	536·4	61·35	4	240	960	61	12,800	Old L.Z.88 reconstructed, renamed L.25 and recommissioned 19.1.1917. Deleted and broken up at Potsdam, Germany, 15.9.1917.
L.30	Friedrichshafen	30.5.16									Broken up and delivered to Belgium in August 1920.
L.31	Löwenthal	17.7.16									Destroyed by British aircraft at Potters Bar, 1.10.1916.
L.32	Friedrichshafen	8.8.16									Destroyed by British aircraft at Billericay, Essex, 24.9.1916.
L.33	,,	2.9.16									Damaged by gunfire and forced to land at Little Wigborough, Essex, 24.9.1916.
L.34	Löwenthal	27.9.16									Destroyed by British aircraft at Hartlepool, Co. Durham, 27.11.1916.
L.35	Friedrichshafen	18.10.16									Deleted, broken up at Jüterbog, Germany, in October 1918.

L.36	"	7.11.16	1,949,600	649·4	78·4	6	240	1,440	64	17,700	Wrecked in fog near Rethen, Germany, 7.2.1917.
L.37	Staaken	27.11.16									Broken up and delivered to Japan in August 1920.
L.38	Löwenthal	26.11.16									Wrecked in a storm near Seemuppen, Russia, during a raid, 29.12.1916.
L.39	Friedrichshafen	18.12.16									Destroyed by gunfire at Compiègne, France, 17.3.1917, after raiding England.
L.40	"	7.2.17									Wrecked on landing at Neuenwald, Germany, 17.6.1917.
L.41	Staaken	30.1.17									Training ship; put out of commission at Nordholz, Germany, 11.6.1918.
L.42	Friedrichshafen	28.3.17									Training ship; put out of commission 19.11.1918. Destroyed by Germans at Nordholz, 23.6.1919.
L.43	"	15.3.17	1,960,000	644·7	78·4	5	240	1,200	62	21,000	Destroyed by British aircraft off Vlieland Island, Holland, 14.6.1917.
L.44	Löwenthal	5.4.17	1,970,800	644·7	78·4	5	240	1,200	65	22,000	Destroyed by gunfire near Lunéville, France, 20.10.1917, after raiding England.
L.45	Staaken	7.4.17	1,949,600	649·4	78·4	6	240	1,440	64	17,700	Destroyed by crew after forced landing at Sisteron, France, 20.10.1917, after raiding England.
L.46	Friedrichshafen	1.5.17	1,970,800	644·7	78·4	5	240	1,200	65	22,000	Burnt in shed at Ahlhorn, Germany, 5.1.1918.
L.47	Staaken	4.5.17	1,949,600	649·4	78·4	6	240	1,440	64	17,700	Burnt in shed at Ahlhorn, Germany, 5.1.1918.
L.48	Friedrichshafen	23.5.17									Destroyed by British aircraft at Theberton, Suffolk, 17.6.1917.
L.49	Löwenthal	15.6.17	1,970,800	644·7	78·4	5	240	1,200	67	23,000	Forced landing near Bourbonne-les-Bains, France, 20.10.1917, after raiding England, 19.10.1917.
L.50	Staaken	13.6.17	1,949,600	649·4	78·4	6	240	1,440	64	17,700	Forced landing near Bourbonne-les-Bains, France, 20.10.1917 after raiding England. The ship

											and apparently foundered in the Mediterranean Sea.
L.51	Friedrichshafen	26.7.17									Burnt in shed at Ahlhorn, Germany, 5.1.1918.
L.52	Staaken	24.7.17	1,970,800	644·7	78·4	5	240	1,200	67	23,000	Destroyed by Germans at Wittmund, Germany, 23.6.1920.
L.53	Friedrichshafen	21.8.17	1,977,900	644·7	78·4	5	290	1,450	71	24,000	Destroyed by British aircraft off Terschelling Island, Holland, 11.8.1918.
L.54	Staaken	20.8.17	1,970,800	644·7	78·4	5	240	1,200	67	23,000	Destroyed by British aircraft in shed at Tondern, Germany, 19.7.1918.
L.55	Löwenthal	8.9.17									Wrecked at Tiefenort, Germany, 20.10.1917, after raiding England.
L.56	Staaken	28.9.17	1,977,900	644·7	78·4	5	290	1,450	71	24,000	Destroyed by Germans at Wittmund, Germany, 23.6.1920.
L.57	Friedrichshafen	25.9.17	2,419,400	743·1	78·4	5	240	1,200	67	26,900	Burnt at Jüterbog, Germany, 7.10.1917.
L.58	"	4.11.17	1,977,900	644·7	78·4	5	290	1,450	71	24,000	Burnt in shed at Ahlhorn, Germany, 5.1.1918.
L.59	Staaken	3.11.17	2,419,400	743·1	78·4	5	240	1,200	67	26,900	Burnt over Straits of Otranto 7.4.1918.
L.60	"	2.4.18									Destroyed by British aircraft in shed at Tondern, Germany, 19.7.1918.
L.61	Friedrichshafen	19.12.17									Delivered to Italy, August 1920.
L.62	Löwenthal	29.1.18	1,977,900	644·7	78·4	5	290	1,450	71	24,000	Destroyed by British Aircraft off Heligoland, 10.5.1918.
L.63	Friedrichshafen	10.3.18									Destroyed by Germans at Nordholz, Germany, 23.6.1920.
L.64	Staaken	13.3.18									Delivered to England, July 1920.
L.65	Löwenthal	3.5.18									Destroyed by Germans at Nordholz, Germany, 23.6.1920.
L.70	Friedrichshafen	8.7.18									Destroyed by British aircraft off Wells-next-the-Sea, Norfolk, 5.8.1918.
L.71	"	10.8.18	2,196,900	693·9	78·4	7	290	2,030	81	23,000	Delivered to England, 30.6.1920.
L.72	Construction stopped at Armistice										Delivered to France, 11.6.1920.

Schütte-Lanz (all of wood construction)											
S.L.3	Mannheim	20.2.15									Crashed in Baltic off Windau, Russia, and burnt by crew, 1.5.1916.
			1,147,575	513	64	4	210	840	50	7,900	
S.L.4	"	16.6.15									Wrecked in shed by storm at Seddin, Germany, 11.12.1915.
S.L.6	"	10.10.15	1,239,380	534	64	4	210	840	58	8,500	Exploded in the air near Seddin, Germany, 18.11.1915.
S.L.8	"	20.6.16									Broken up 18.12.1917.
S.L.9	"	31.5.16									Disappeared in a storm *en route* from Seerappen to Seddin, Germany, 23.3.1917.
			1,370,000	571	65	4	240	960	58	11,500	
S.L.12	Königswusterhausen	15.11.16									Wrecked on landing at Ahlhorn, Germany, 28.12.1916.
S.L.14	Mannheim	24.8.16									Wrecked on landing, 18.5.1917.
S.L.20	"	11.9.17									Burnt in shed at Ahlhorn, Germany, 5.1.1918.
S.L.22	"	12.6.18	1,989,700	651	74	5	240	1,200	63	16,400	Broken up in summer of 1920, and delivered to Allies.
Non-Rigid Airships.											
P.L.6		1.9.14	282,500			2	110	220	33		The two engines were Nürnberg A.G. type. The *P.L.* 6 was broken up, 27.12.1914.
P.L.19		18.9.14	363,700			2	180	360	48		Destroyed by gunfire at Libau, Russia, 25.1.1915.
P.L.25		23.3.15	473,150			2	210	420	44		Broken up, 28.12.1915.

Early in the war the military airships M. IV, *Viktoria Luise* and *Sachsen* were taken over by the Navy. The following Military Airships were also employed on Naval duties: L.Z.87 (May to August 1916); L.Z.88 (May to September 1916); L.Z.98 (May to September 1917); L.Z.111 (May to July 1917); L.Z.113 (August to December 1917); L.Z.120 (May to August 1917). For technical details of these ships see Military Airships, Appendix II

APPENDIX II

GERMAN MILITARY AIRSHIPS, 1906–18

Type & No.	*Completed at.*	*Date Commissioned.*	*Capacity (cub. ft.)*	*Length (ft.)*	*Diameter (ft.)*	*Engines D = Daimler, M = Maybach.* No.	H.P.	Total H.P.	*Speed in (M.P.H.)*	*Ceiling. (ft.)*	*Remarks.*
Zeppelin Z.I	Manzell	9.10.06	399,000	419·8	38·4	2	85D	170	27	3,600	Reconstructed, March 1909, broken up, February 1913.
Z.II	"	26.5.08	529,800	446·1	42·6	2	105D	210	30	4,100	Wrecked, April 1910.
Ersatz Z.II	Friedrichshafen	2.10.11	628,700	459·2	45·9	3	150M	450	47	4,600	Deleted, broken up in Summer of 1914.
Viktoria Luise	"	1911–12	659,700	485·4	45·9	3	150M	450	47		Handed over to the Navy. Wrecked in June 1915.
Z.III	"	25.4.12	628,700	459·2	45·9	3	150M	450	47	4,600	Deleted, broken up in Summer of 1914.
Hansa	"	1912	659,700	485·4	47·2	3	180M	540	50		Deleted, broken up in Summer of 1916.
Ersatz Z.I	"	16.1.13									Wrecked in March 1913.
Z.IV	"	14.3.13									Deleted, broken up in Spring of 1917.
Ersatz E.Z.I	"	6.6.13	690,300	459·2	48·9	3	180M	540	48	5,900	Wrecked in June 1914.
Z.V.	"	8.7.13									Damaged by gunfire in Poland and wrecked, August 1914.
Sachsen	"	1913	688,000	462·5	48·5	3	180M	540	47		Handed over to the Navy. Broken up in Spring of 1916.
Z.VI	"	10.11.13	737,100	485·4	48·9	3	180M	540	46	9,800	Damaged by gunfire over Liège, Belgium, and crashed at Cologne, Germany, 6.8.1914.
Z.VII	"	8.1.14									Damaged by gunfire and wrecked in the Argonne, France, August 1914.
Z.VIII	"	21.2.14	782,000	511·7	48·9	3	180M	540	45	9,200	Brought down by gunfire at Badonviller, France, 23.8.1914.

Z.IX	"	29.7.14									Bombed and destroyed in shed at Düsseldorf, by British aircraft, 8.10.1914.
Z.X	"	13.10.14									Damaged by gunfire while raiding Paris, and crashed at St. Quentin, 21.3.1915.
Z.XI	Potsdam	11.11.14									Wrecked and burnt when leaving shed at Posen, Prussia, 20.5.1915.
L.Z.34	"	6.1.15	793,600	518·2	48·9	3	210M	630	53	9,300	Damaged by gunfire while raiding Kovno; crashed and burnt in forced landing in East Prussia, 21.5.1915.
L.Z.35	Friedrichshafen	11.1.15									Damaged by gunfire near Poperinghe during raid; crashed at Thielt, Belgium, 13.4.1915.
L.Z.37	Potsdam	28.2.15									Destroyed by British aircraft near Ghent, after raiding Calais, 7.6.1915.
Z.XII	Frankfurt	14.12.14	883,000	528·7	52·5	3	210M	630	50	11,800	Deleted, broken up at Jüterbog, Germany, 8.8.1917.
L.Z.38	Friedrichshafen	3.4.15	1,126,700	536·4	61·35	4	240M	960	61	12,800	Destroyed by British aircraft in shed at Evere, Belgium, 7.6.1915.
L.Z.39	"	24.4.15	879,500	529·4	52·5	3	210M	630	36	10,200	Destroyed after attacking Kovno, Russia, December 1915.
L.Z.72	Potsdam	15.6.15									Deleted, broken up at Jüterbog, Germany, 16.2.1917.
L.Z.74	Friedrichshafen	8.7.15									Wrecked near Mézières, France, 8.10.1915.
L.Z.77	"	24.8.15									Brought down by gunfire at Revigny, France, 21.2.1916.
L.Z.79	Potsdam	2.8.15									Damaged by gunfire while raiding Paris, and wrecked near Ath, Belgium, 30.1.1916.
L.Z.81	Friedrichshafen	7.10.15									Damaged by gunfire while raiding Bucharest, and wrecked in forced landing near Tir-

L.Z.85	Potsdam	12.9.15	1,126,700	536·4	61·35	4	240M	960	61	12,800	Brought down by gunfire at Salonika, 5.5.1916.
L.Z.86	"	10.10.15									Wrecked in landing at Temesvar, Hungary, 4.9.1916.
L.Z.87	Friedrichshafen	6.12.15									Deleted, broken up at Jüterbog, Germany, 28.7.1917.
L.Z.88	Potsdam	14.11.15									Renamed L.25. (See Appendix I).
L.Z.90	"	1.1.16									Blown away from Wittmund, Germany, and lost at sea, 7.11.1916.
L.Z.93	"	23.2.16									Deleted, broken up at Trèves, Germany, in Summer of 1917.
L.Z.95	Friedrichshafen	31.1.16									Hit by gunfire in Champagne, and wrecked at Namur, 22.2.1916.
L.Z.97	"	4.4.16									Deleted, broken up at Jüterbog, 5.7.1917.
L.Z.98	"	28.4.16									Deleted, broken up at Schneidemühl, Prussia, in August 1917.
L.Z.101	Potsdam	29.6.16	1,264,400	585·5	61·35	4	240M	960	59	13,800	Deleted, broken up at Jüterbog, in September 1917.
L.Z.103	"	8.8.16									Deleted, broken up at Königsberg, in August 1917.
L.Z.107	"	16.10.16									Deleted, broken up at Darmstadt, in July 1917.
L.Z.111	"	20.12.16									Deleted, broken up at Dresden, 10.8.1917.
L.Z.113	Staaken	22.2.17	1,949,600	649·4	78·4	6	240M	1,440	64	17,700	Delivered to Allies.
L.Z.120	Friedrichshafen	31.1.17									Delivered to Allies.
Schütte-Lanz (of wood construction)											
S.L.2	Mannheim-Rheinau	1914	882,750	472	60	4	180M	720	54	6,200	Wrecked near Luckenwalde Germany, 10.1.1916.
S.L.5	Darmstadt	June 1915	1,147,575	513	64	4	210M	840	50	7,900	Wrecked near Giessen, Germany, 5.7.1915.
S.L.7	Mannheim-	Sept. 1915	1,239,380	534	64	4	210M	840	58	8,500	Dismantled, 6.3.1917.

S.L.10	"	Aug. 1916								Wrecked in the Black Sea, 27.7.1916, after attacking Sevastopol.
S.L.11	Leipzig	Aug. 1916								Destroyed by British aircraft at Cuffley, Middlesex, 3.9.1916.
S.L.13	"	Oct. 1916	1,370,000	571	65	4	240M	960	58	11,500	Wrecked by collapse of shed at Leipzig, 8.2.1917.
S.L.15	Mannheim-Rheinau	Dec. 1916								Deleted, 25.4.1917.
S.L.16	Leipzig	Jan. 1917								Deleted, 7.4.1917.
S.L.17	Zeesen, Königswusterhausen	1.3.17								Deleted, 25.4.1917.
S.L.21		Nov. 1917	1,989,700	651	74	5	240M	1,200	63	16,400	Deleted, February 1918.
Non-Rigid Airships										
M IV	Tegel	7.9.13	688,550	400	43·6	3	160 (Koerting)	480	50		Handed over to the Navy 24.11.1914. Broken up, 3.11.1915.
P IV	Bitterfeld	1913	388,100	314·8	49·2	2	180M	360	46		Dismantled, 24.3.1916.

APPENDIX III

STATISTICS OF GERMAN AIR RAIDS ON GREAT BRITAIN, 1914–16

TABLE A. AIRSHIP RAIDS

Date.	*Number of Enemy Airships which*		*Locality (in general where bombs were dropped).*	*Bombs dropped.*				*Casualties.*				*Total Estimated Monetary damage.*	*Number of aircraft which ascended in Great Britain.*	*Casualties to defence aircraft.*	*Remarks.*	*Sec. pp.*
				Number.		*Weight.*		*Total.*		*In London (M.P.D.)*						
	Started.	*Crossed British Coast.*		*Total.*	*On London (M.P.D.)*	*Total in lb.*	*On London (M.P.D.)*	*Killed.*	*Injured.*	*Killed.*	*Injured.*					
1915																
19th/20th Jan.	3	2	Norfolk, Snettisham, King's Lynn, Yarmouth.	24	..	2,155	..	4	16	..	..	£7,740	..	..	..	90–1
14th Apr.	1	1	Northumberland, Tyneside.	31	..	1,602	..	..	2	..	..	£55	2	..	..	94–5
15th/16th Apr.	3	3	Essex, East Suffolk.	78	..	3,065	..	..	1	..	..	£6,498	1	Slight damage to floats.	..	95–6
29th/30th Apr.	1	1	Suffolk, Ipswich.	76	..	2,928	..	..	..	..	..	£9,010	..	..	..	97
10th May	1	1	Southend.	124 (Between 90 and 120 incendiary.)	..	3,757	..	1	2	..	..	£5,301	11	..	..	97–8
17th May	1	1	Kent, Ramsgate.	53	..	1,797	..	2	1	..	..	£1,600	1	..	..	98–9
26th May	1	1	Southend.	70 (47 incendiary, 23 grenades.)	..	1,412	..	3	3	..	..	£947	5	Two damaged on landing.	..	99
31st May/1st June	2	1	East London.	120 (90 incendiary, 30 grenades.)	120	2,636	2,636	7	35	7	35	£18,596	9	One crashed. (Pilot killed, observer injured.)	..	99–100
4th/5th June	2	2	Kent, East Riding.	23	..	1,547	..	..	8	..	..	£8,740	8	..	..	101–2
6th/7th June	4	1	East Riding, Hull, Grimsby.	61	..	2,762	..	24	40	..	..	£44,795	..	..	The Military Zeppelins L.Z.37 and L.Z.38 which turned back were destroyed, the former by Flt. Sub.-Lieut. R. A. J. Warneford, over St. Amand, near Ghent, the latter by bombs in her shed at Evere.	102–4
15th June	2	1	Northumberland, Tyneside.	53	..	3,536	..	18	72	..	..	£41,760	2	..	..	104–5
9th/10th Aug.	5	4	East Riding, Goole, Lowestoft, Dover, Eastchurch.	79	..	5,980	..	17	21	..	..	£11,992	19	Two crashed on landing; one damaged on landing. (One pilot killed.)	L.12 bombed and damaged at Ostend by pilots from Dunkirk.	109–12

12th/13th Aug.	4	2	East Suffolk, Woodbridge, Essex, Parkstone.	47	..	2,791		7	23	..	..	£3,649	4	One badly damaged, one slightly damaged on landing.	..	113–14
17th/18th Aug.	4	2	Kent, Essex, London (M.P.D.).	107	43	6,188	2,762	10	48	10	48	£30,750	6	One blown up by its own bombs. (Pilot slightly injured.)	..	114–15
7th/8th Sept.	3	3	East Suffolk, London (City).	97	45	5,746	2,736	18	38	18	38	£9,616	2	One wrecked on landing.	..	115–17
8th/9th Sept.	4	3	North Riding, Norfolk, London (City)	152	70	8,895	3,730	26	94	22	87	£534,287	Six, and one seaplane from trawler about 40 miles east of Yarmouth.	One damaged and one blown up by bombs on landing. (One pilot killed.)	..	118–21
11th/12th Sept.	1	1	Essex, Epping.	60 (52 incendiary.)	..	2,320	..	..	..	..	..	Nil	2	..	..	124
12th/13th Sept.	1	1	Essex, East Suffolk.	31	..	2,680	..	..	..	..	..	£508	1	..	..	124–5
13th/14th Sept.	3	1	East Suffolk.	46	..	3,122	..	..	..	..	..	£2	..	..	..	125–6
13th/14th Oct.	5	5	Norfolk, Suffolk, Home Counties, London (City).	189	81	13,672	5,635	71	128	47	102	£80,020	5	Two wrecked on landing.	..	129–32
1916																
31st Jan./1st Feb.	9	9	The Midlands.	379	..	27,459	..	70	113	..	..	£53,832	22	Seven damaged on landing and one wrecked. (Three pilots injured.)	..	135–44
5th/6th Mar.	3	3	East Riding, Hull, Lincolnshire, Leicestershire, Rutland, Kent.	111	..	6,961	..	18	52	..	..	£25,005	1	..	..	184–7
31st Mar./1st Apr.	9	6	Lincolnshire, Suffolk, Ipswich, Essex.	223	..	16,188	..	48	64	..	..	£19,431	21	One crashed, one slightly damaged. (One pilot killed.)	L.15 brought down by gunfire.	189–95
1st/2nd Apr.	2	1	County Durham, Sunderland, North Riding, Middlesbrough.	34	..	3,176	..	22	130	..	..	£25,568	4	..	..	195–6
2nd/3rd Apr.	6	5	Scotland, Leith, Edinburgh, Northumberland, East Suffolk, Essex, Waltham Abbey, London (M.P.D.)	280	90	16,354	4,559	13	24	..	..	£73,113	12	One wrecked; one blown up by bombs on landing; one damaged, and two slightly damaged. (One pilot injured.)	..	196–200
3rd/4th Apr.	2	1	Norfolk.	13	..	1,105	..	..	..	..	..	Nil	1	..	..	200
5th/6th Apr.	3	2	Yorkshire, Hull, County Durham.	83	..	5,856	..	1	9	..	..	£7,983	5	Two crashed. One damaged. (One pilot killed.)	..	201–2
24th/25th Apr.	7	6	Norfolk, Lincolnshire, Cambridgeshire, Suffolk.	107	..	9,006	..	1	1	..	..	£6,412	15	..	..	203–5
25th/26th Apr.	5	4	East Suffolk, Essex, Romford, Kent, London (M.P.D.).	115	15	6,752	1,657	..	1	..	1	£568	13	Two crashed on landing.	..	207–9
26th Apr.	1	1	Kent.	3	..	331	..	..	..	..	..	Nil	8	..	..	209
2nd/3rd May	9	8	Yorkshire, York, Northumberland	148	..	12,292	..	9	30	..	..	£12,030	6	..	..	209–13

			Scotland.													
28th/29th July	10	6	East Riding, Lincolnshire, Norfolk.	69	..	4,696	..	..	..	..	..	£257	1	..	..	213–14
31st July/1st Aug.	10	5	Kent, Ramsgate, Norfolk, Suffolk, Cambridge, Isle of Ely, Lincolnshire.	103	..	7,569	..	..	..	..	..	£139	12	One crashed. (Pilot seriously injured.)	..	215
2nd/3rd Aug.	6	6	Norfolk, East Suffolk, Kent.	137	..	11,492	..	..	1	..	..	£796	22	..	..	216–17
8th/9th Aug.	11	9	Norfolk, Yorkshire, Hull, County Durham, Northumberland, Scotland, Roxburghshire.	173	..	12,736	..	10	16	..	..	£13,196	1	..	..	217–19
23rd/24th Aug.	1	1	East Suffolk.	34	..	2,513	..	..	..	..	..	£3	..	..	..	219
24th/25th Aug.	12	4	East Suffolk, Essex, Kent, London.	103	44	13,195	7,388	9	40	9	40	£130,203	15	Two crashed on landing.	..	219–22
2nd/3rd Sept.	16	14	East Riding, Lincolnshire, Boston, Nottinghamshire, Norfolk, Isle of Ely, Cambridgeshire, Huntingdonshire, Suffolk, Essex, Hertfordshire, Bedfordshire, Kent, London, (M.P.D.).	463	60	34,420	4,559	4	12	..	..	£21,072	14 (One pilot made three ascents.)	Three wrecked. (One pilot slightly injured.)	S.L.11 destroyed by Lieut. W. Leefe Robinson.	221–25
23rd/24th Sept.	12	9	East Riding, Lincolnshire, Notting-	371	101	38,790	10,276	40	130	37	124	£135,068	23	One slightly damaged. (One pilot killed and one slightly injured.)	L.32 destroyed by 2nd Lieut. F. Sowrey, R.F.C.	226–31

TABLE B. AEROPLANE AND SEAPLANE RAIDS

Date.	Number of Enemy: Aero-planes.	Number of Enemy: Sea-planes.	By Day or Night. D = Day. N = Night.	*Locality. (In general where bombs were dropped.)*	Bombs dropped: Number.	Bombs dropped: Weight in lb.	Casualties: Killed.	Casualties: Injured.	Total Estimated Monetary damage.	Number of aircraft which ascended in Great Britain.	Remarks.	See pp.
1914												
24th Dec.	1	..	D.	Dover.	1	22	..	..	£40	2	..	89
25th Dec.	..	1	D.	Thames up to Erith.	2 (on Cliffe, Kent).	44	..	..	..	6	..	"
1915												
21st Feb.	..	1	N.	Essex, Braintree, Coggeshall, Colchester.	4	64	..	..	£30	..	..	150
16th Apr.	1	..	D.	Kent, Faversham, Sittingbourne.	10	162	..	..	..	13	..	150–1
3rd July	1	1	D.	East Suffolk.	No bombs dropped on land.	..	..	..	..	9	..	151
13th Sept.	..	1	D.	Margate.	10	221	2	6	£500	2	..	"
1916												
9th Jan.	1	..	D.	Dover.	No bombs dropped.	..	..	..	..	6	..	"
22nd/23rd Jan.	1	..	N.	Dover.	9	188	1	6	£1,591	..	..	"
23rd Jan.	..	2	D.	Dover, Folkestone.	5	110	..	..	..	6	..	"
24th Jan.	..	1	D.	Dover, Folkestone.	No bombs dropped.	..	..	..	..	4	..	151–2
9th Feb.	..	2	D.	Broadstairs, Ramsgate.	13	287	..	3	£305	18	..	248
20th Feb.	..	4	D.	Walmer, Lowestoft.	25	552	1	1	£1,168	26	..	248–9
1st Mar.	..	1	N.	Broadstairs, Margate.	7	154	1	..	£497	..	..	249
19th Mar.	..	4	D.	Dover, Deal, Margate, Ramsgate.	48	1,060	14	26	£3,809	31	2 enemy seaplanes shot down by aircraft.	"
23rd Apr.	1	..	D.	Dover.	No bombs dropped.	..	..	..	..	7	..	"
24th Apr.	1	..	D.	Dover.	No bombs dropped.	..	..	..	..	15	..	"
3rd May	1	..	D.	Deal.	9	200	..	4	£720	12	..	"
20th May	5	..	N.	Kent, Dover.	59	1,304	1	2	£960	4	1 enemy aeroplane was shot down by a Naval pilot from Dunkirk.	"
9th July	1	..	D.	Thanet.	No bombs dropped.	..	..	..	..	17	..	"
9th/10th July	1	..	N.	Dover.	7	154	..	..	£48	..	..	"
12th Aug.	1	..	D.	Dover.	4	88	..	7	..	10	..	"
22nd Sept.	1	..	D.	Dover.	7	154	..	..	£5	10	1 defence aircraft damaged on landing.	"
22nd Oct.	1	..	D.	Sheerness.	4	88	..	..	£20	9	1 enemy aeroplane was shot down by a Naval pilot from Dunkirk.	249–5
23rd Oct.	1	..	D.	Margate.	3	66	..	2	£229	13	..	250
28th Nov.	1	..	D.	London.	6	132	..	10	£1,585	17	German pilot was forced to land near Boulogne with engine trouble.	"

App. IIIb

APPENDIX IV

AIR RAID STATISTICS FOR THE COUNTY OF LONDON, 1915–16

Date.	District Principally Affected.	Air-ships.	Aero-planes.	Number of Bombs dropped. Incendiary.	Explosive.	Total Weight in lb.	Casualties Killed.	Injured.	Fires Caused.	Casualties Dealt with by London Ambulance Service.	Buildings Destroyed.	Seriously Damaged.	Estimated Monetary Damage.
1915													
31st May/1st June	Stoke Newington, Hoxton, Whitechapel, Islington, Kingsland and Hackney.	1	..	87	25	2,300	7	32	41	..	1	4	£18,396
7th/8th Sept.	Woolwich, Millwall, and New Cross.	2	..	27	18	2,736	18	38	8	11			£7,809
8th/9th Sept.	Bloomsbury, Holborn, Farringdon Street, Wood Street, Bishopsgate Street, Shoreditch.	1	..	45	13	3,232	22	87	29	3	30	39	£530,787
13th/14th Oct.	Holborn, Strand, Minories, Woolwich.	2	..	39	24	3,730	38	87	13	8	2	20	£50,250
1916													
24th/25th Aug.	Millwall, Deptford, Blackheath, Greenwich, Plumstead, and Eltham.	1	..	8	36	6,562	9	40	6	3	8	42	£130,000
23rd/24th Sept.	Streatham, Brixton, Kennington, Bow, Hackney, and Bromley.	2	..	46	27	6,353	26	73	30	13	14	47	£64,662
28th Nov.	Eaton Sq., Brompton Road, and Victoria.	..	1	..	6	133	..	10	..	..	..	..	£1,585
Seven Raids				252	149	25,046	120	367	127	38	55	152	£803,489

Appendix 5

Summary of the War Development of Tracer, Incendiary, and Explosive Ammunition

(1) S.P.K. Mark VII.T.

Before the war it had been recognised that the Air Services could make use of small arms ammunition with a tracing effect, and some preliminary work on tracer bullets had been done at the Royal Laboratory, Woolwich. There was, on the outbreak of war, a design ready to meet the demands of the Royal Flying Corps, and the bullet was at once introduced into the Service. It proved unsatisfactory. The length of the trace was insufficient and, owing to difficulties of manufacture, rejections for inaccuracy were many, and the percentage of 'blinds' and 'prematures' was high.

On account of the pressure of work at the Royal Laboratory, further experiments on the tracer bullet were dropped and, early in 1916, the Ministry of Munitions took over part of the premises of Messrs. Aerators as an experimental factory. Working on the assumption that the failure of the bullet was due to the tracing composition used, experiments with new compositions were made and, in June, a mixture of one part magnesium to eight parts of barium peroxide was found to give good results. Extensive trials took place with the new bullet at the Musketry School at Hythe, and the consequent reports stated that it was 'easily the best yet tested at 'this School; it gives a clear, bright light which can be easily observed'. The bullet was therefore approved for issue to the Royal Flying Corps in July 1916. From its appearance and its place of origin it was first known as 'Sparklet', but later became known as S.P.K. Mark VILT.

(2) S.P.G. Mark VII.G.

The bullet described in (1) was superseded about June 1917 by a new type bullet, the product of the Royal Laboratory working in cooperation with Dr. S. Smiles, F.R.S., of University College, London. The new bullet, known as the S.P.G. Mark VII.G., was also used by France, the United States, and Italy.

(3) Buckingham 0.303" Bullet.

Mr. J. F. Buckingham, the proprietor of an engineering works in Coventry, foresaw, at the beginning of the war, the value of incendiary projectiles as anti-Zeppelin ammunition. After many preliminary experiments, he decided to use phosphorus as a basis for his incendiary composition, and he took out his first patent in January 1915. In April 1915, at a demonstration before officers of the Royal Naval Air Service, his 0.45" incendiary bullets set fire to balloons at 400 yards range. With Admiralty encouragement he further improved his 0.45" bullet, and, transferring his experiments to the 0.303", which could be fired from any machine gun, he produced a number of trial bullets which were sent to the Admiralty in October 1915. An order from the Admiralty was placed at once, and deliveries to the Royal Naval Air Service began in December 1915.

Then came a demand for Buckingham ammunition from the Royal Flying Corps, and the first order on their behalf was placed by the Ministry of Munitions at the end of April 1916. In June 1916 Mr. Buckingham further improved his bullet, which, in Mark VII form, and later with a flattened nose, was used for the rest of the war. The flat-nosed bullet resulted from experiments made in France. The pointed type made only a small tear in the fabric of a balloon, and this did not allow enough gas to escape for ignition. The flat-nosed bullet, it was pointed out, could punch a circular hole and give a free escape of gas. The flattening of the nose, however, affected the accuracy of the bullet; the tracing was sometimes poor, and in many instances the ammunition collapsed before leaving the barrel of the rifle or gun. Further improvements were made, but finality was not reached when the war ended. The Buckingham bullet was also used by France and the United States, the full war-time deliveries amounting to some 26,000,000 rounds.

(4) The Brock Bullet.

At the beginning of 1915 it was wrongly believed that the exhaust gases from the motors of the Zeppelins were led between the outer and inner fabrics of the airships to produce a layer of inert gas as a protection against incendiary ammunition. It was this belief which induced Commander F. A. Brock—at that time in charge of the Intelligence Section of the Air Department at the Admiralty—to experiment with a bullet which would explode between the first and second fabrics in such a way that the hydrogen could connect with the outside air. At official trials in October 1915, a balloon was set on fire by Brock ammunition fired from a Lewis gun. The range in these trials was short, but the sensitive nose of the bullet was improved until it was effective up to a range of 800 yards. All the initial cost of experiment and manufacture was borne by Commander Brock. In May 1916 an order for half a million of the Brock Zeppelin bullets was placed with Messrs. C. T. Brock & Co., Ltd., of Sutton. The firm did the filling only, complete cartridges with special bullets being supplied to them. The firm experienced difficulties in manufacture, but the order was completed by December 1916, after which manufacture of the bullet was suspended. The Brock bullet was superseded early in 1917 in the Royal Flying Corps, but it remained in use throughout the war in the Royal Naval Air Service for anti-Zeppelin work over the North Sea.

(5) P.S.A. Bullet.

Mr. John Pomeroy, an engineer, first submitted an explosive bullet to the War Office in August 1914. He received small encouragement and left for his home in Australia, where he demonstrated his invention before the military authorities. After further trials in America he returned to England in June 1915, and again attempted to interest the War Office, but without success. In December 1915, however, the Munitions Inventions Department took up the Pomeroy invention, carried out trials, and in May 1916 gave an order for half a million rounds. The bullet was introduced into the Service under the name of P.S.A. While in its experimental stage it was seen by representatives of the Royal Flying Corps, who asked for supplies.

When the bullet came to be manufactured in quantities it was found that premature explosions occurred owing to the composition being nipped between the core and the envelope. To avoid this a copper tube called the 'war-head' was inserted to cover the joint, and the incendiary composition was placed in this tube. Trials in July 1916 gave good results, and the Pomeroy bullet was generally approved in the following month. It was found that the bullet would not detonate except at high striking velocities, nor on a fabric containing rubber. The Munitions Inventions Department undertook further experimental work and, towards the end of 1916, a new design was evolved which made the bullet more sensitive. The new design, known as P.S.A. Mark II, was approved in February 1917 and superseded the original P.S.A. bullet. The use of this type of ammunition was confined to Royal Flying Corps home defence units, and supplies were always ahead of requirements.

(6) R.T.S. Bullet.

None of the existing special bullets was considered entirely satisfactory, and research for better designs continued. In July 1917 a new bullet, known as the R.T.S., was produced by Sir Richard Threlfall. It was both incendiary and explosive and was extremely sensitive. As secrecy in manufacture was essential, the Ministry of Munitions decided to build a special factory for the filling of the ammunition and to carry it on as a national factory with Mr. J. F. Buckingham as manager. The first experimental bullets were produced in November 1917, and by March 1918 the factory was in full working order. Production increased rapidly during 1918, and by June a weekly delivery of 200,000 bullets was being made. Up to September 1918 the bullet was used only in England, against raiding aeroplanes, where it proved so effective that its use overseas was sanctioned. It was never used to any great extent in the field. Experimental work on this bullet, and on a variant known as R.T.T., which contained high explosive instead of the R.T.S. incendiary composition, continued to the Armistice.

Appendix 6

The Royal Aircraft Factory

Table A

Statement of Duties

(From a paper prepared by the Superintendent, Lieutenant-Colonel Mervyn O' Gorman, for the Burbidge Committee (Sir Richard W. Burbidge, Bt., Chairman) set up by the War Office in March 1916.)

(1) To make experimental constructions of all sorts—aeroplanes, engines, kites, balloons, armaments, bombs, instruments, and sundries—on the full scale, and verifying, criticizing, and making suggestions to guide the model research work of the N.P.L. and Advisory Committee.

(2) To get out from these experiments designs suitable for reproduction by R.A.F. and private firms.

(3) To set a standard of workmanship, design, performance of aeroplanes, kites, balloons, &c, as well as armaments, bombs, bomb-sights, gun-mountings, camera fittings, wireless apparatus, protective dopes and pigments, &c.

(4) To make aeroplane designs conform to the War requirements by incorporating in the designs the armaments and equipment needed for military purposes.

(5) To manufacture spares of all kinds.

(6) To assist the trade and industry of aircraft making—

(*a*) by introducing standardization of parts and sub-parts;

(*b*) by manufacturing such pieces as are for some reason or another holding up or delaying these private makers;

(*c*) by teaching their employees how to make parts which are novel to them—propellers, special castings, special tools, taps, &c, Raf wires, dope, varnish, pigments, air-speed instruments, mariners' compasses, &c;

(*d*) by providing them with full working drawings.

(7) To assist in keeping the government free from the pressure of monopoly prices, by working out its costs and the costs of aeroplanes

and sundries; and in the event of a monopoly being formed, breaking the monopoly by manufacturing against the monopolists, and finding designs which meet the same technical result which can be put up to public tender.

(8) To effect repairs. (Repairs generally cannot be quoted for by private firms, owing to the complexity of quoting, involving dismemberment of the broken aircraft or engine.)

(9) Consulting Engineering work: To assist the War Office by producing specifications for tenders for all classes of material, producing drawings and blue prints in enormous quantities, preparing catalogues, index numbers for ordering spares, instructions for using appliances, &c.

(10) To supervise the technical routine of contracts for new R.A.F. designs.

(11) To conduct metallurgical and chemical operations on new substances, and to test specimens of all sorts.

(12) To report on inventions and devices.

(13) Incidental to the urgent expansion of work, it has been necessary to design engine testing plant, chemical production plant, and to effect unusually large amounts of upkeep and other work in adapting buildings—design of aeroplane shops of unprecedented size, &c.

TABLE B. AEROPLANES BUILT AT THE FACTORY, 1911–18.

YEAR	TYPE																																TOTAL.
	A.E.3.	*B.E.1.*	*B.E.2.*	*B.E.3 & 4.*	*B.E.5 & 6.*	*B.E.7.*	*B.E.8.*	*B.S.1.*	*C.E.1.*	*F.E.2.*	*F.E.2a.*	*F.E.2b.*	*F.E.2c.*	*F.E.2d.*	*F.E.3.*	*F.E.4.*	*F.E.6.*	*F.E.8.*	*F.E.9.*	*Hydro 17.*	*Handley Page.*	*N.E.1.*	*R.E.1.*	*R.E.3.*	*R.E.5.*	*R.E.8.*	*S.E.1.*	*S.E.2.*	*S.E.4.*	*S.E.4a.*	*S.E.5.*	*Target.*	*Vickers 'Vimy'.*	
1911	..	..	..	..	..	..	..	..	..	1	..	..	..	..	..	..	..	..	..	..	..	..	..	..	..	..	1	..	..	..	..	..	..	2
1912	..	1	1	2	2	..	2	..	..	..	..	..	..	..	..	..	..	..	..	..	..	..	..	..	..	..	..	..	..	..	..	..	..	8
1913	..	..	5	..	..	1	1	1	..	..	..	..	..	..	1	..	..	..	..	1	..	..	2	1	..	..	..	1	..	..	..	..	..	14
1914	..	..	..	..	..	..	..	..	..	..	..	..	..	..	..	..	1	..	..	..	..	..	..	..	22	..	..	..	1	..	..	..	..	24
1915	..	..	..	..	..	..	..	..	..	..	12	11	..	..	..	..	..	2	..	..	..	..	..	..	2	..	..	..	..	4	..	..	..	31
1916	..	..	..	..	..	..	..	..	..	..	..	36	2	74	..	2	..	..	..	..	..	..	..	..	..	39	..	..	..	..	2	..	..	155
1917	..	..	..	..	..	..	..	..	1	..	..	..	..	11	..	..	..	..	3	..	..	4	..	..	..	6	..	..	..	..	132	6	..	163
1918	3	..	..	..	..	..	..	..	1	..	..	..	..	..	..	..	..	..	..	..	24	2	..	..	..	..	..	..	..	..	104	..	2	136
TOTAL	3	1	6	2	2	1	3	1	2	1	12	47	2	85	1	2	1	2	3	1	24	6	2	1	24	45	1	1	1	4	238	6	2	533

APPENDIX VII

OUTPUT OF AIRCRAFT AND ENGINES, AUGUST 1914–DECEMBER 1918, BY QUARTERS

TABLE A. AEROPLANES, SEAPLANES, AND FLYING-BOATS

NOTE: The statistics in Tables A and B are extracted from a Ministry of Munitions of War paper, *Review of Munitions Output*, 1914–1918. For 'Home' the figures up to May 1917 represent the numbers 'Handed to Services'. From June 1917 to December 1918 they represent 'Passed Inspection'. For other than British manufacture the figures represent 'Handed to Services'.

	1914.		*1915.*				*1916.*				*1917.*				*1918.*				
	Aug. & Sept.	*4th Qtr.*	*1st Qtr.*	*2nd Qtr.*	*3rd Qtr.*	*4th Qtr.*	*1st Qtr.*	*2nd Qtr.*	*3rd Qtr.*	*4th Qtr.*	*1st Qtr.*	*2nd Qtr.*	*3rd Qtr.*	*4th Qtr.*	*1st Qtr.*	*2nd Qtr.*	*3rd Qtr.*	*4th Qtr.*	*Total.*
AEROPLANES—																			
Single-Seater—																			
Home—																			
Bristol Scout	1	11	1	33	23	66	58	74	87	17	11	2	..	..	..	..	..	..	384
Martinsyde Scout	..	11	15	20	19	4	28	32	44	48	63	51	3	..	..	..	..	..	338
Sopwith Scout	..	4	15	17	..	..	..	..	10	54	159	262	208	344	500	68	133	32	1,806
S.E.5	..	..	..	..	..	..	..	..	..	..	16	51	157	604	1,040	1,423	1,230	684	5,205
Sopwith Camel	..	..	..	..	..	..	..	..	..	..	..	135	471	719	1,069	1,194	1,272	630	5,490
Sopwith Dolphin	..	..	..	..	..	..	..	..	..	..	..	..	..	121	355	519	314	223	1,532
Sopwith Snipe	..	..	..	..	..	..	..	..	..	..	..	..	..	..	..	..	161	336	497
Other Types	..	3	3	..	1	7	18	39	101	96	120	337	469	339	132	23	26	117	1,831
Total—Home	1	29	34	70	43	77	104	145	242	215	369	838	1,308	2,127	3,096	3,227	3,136	2,022	17,083
Abroad—																			
France—All types	..	..	..	2	22	43	26	68	23	56	155	258	128	46	38	1	..	..	866
Total Single-Seaters	1	29	34	72	65	120	130	213	265	271	524	1,096	1,436	2,173	3,134	3,228	3,136	2,022	17,949

Home—																			
Avro	5	3	26	34	48	102	79	88	126	150	263	220	277	370	766	949	1,810	1,713	7,029
B.E.2a, b, c, and d	10	8	37	80	216	377	355	321	191	127	21	8	13	14	15	..	..	..	1,793
F.E.2b	..	..	..	5	5	22	69	139	171	165	173	286	235	127	15	140	185	202	1,939
R.E.8	..	..	..	..	..	..	..	..	3	55	271	492	535	314	592	731	626	458	4,077
Bristol Fighter	..	..	..	..	..	..	..	..	..	12	40	80	138	207	346	543	749	986	3,101
D.H.4	..	..	..	..	..	..	..	..	..	..	58	130	233	427	352	70	76	103	1,449
D.H.6	..	..	..	..	..	..	..	..	..	..	..	37	123	452	1,099	432	96	43	2,282
D.H.9	..	..	..	..	..	..	..	..	..	..	..	..	..	5	331	1,156	1,052	660	3,204
D.H.9a	..	..	..	..	..	..	..	..	..	..	..	..	..	..	..	18	288	579	885
Other Types	30	47	76	120	134	141	264	565	1,049	1,024	1,185	1,050	668	585	473	431	338	298	8,478
Total—Home	45	58	139	239	403	642	767	1,113	1,540	1,533	2,011	2,303	2,222	2,501	3,989	4,470	5,220	5,042	34,237
Abroad—																			
All types—																			
France	1	3	31	129	105	105	114	78	108	186	115	72	39	41	5	35	24	..	1,191
U.S.A.	..	..	6	31	100	73	109	122	9	11	57	138	5	..	..	..	..	..	661
Italy	..	..	..	..	..	..	..	..	..	..	..	..	..	..	6	..	..	..	6
Total Two-Seaters	46	61	176	399	608	820	990	1,313	1,657	1,730	2,183	2,513	2,266	2,542	4,000	4,505	5,244	5,042	36,095
Experimental, &c.—																			
Home	33	27	6	5	15	8	14	10	8	14	17	12	9	19	14	36	13	9	269
France	2	1	2	8	4	..	2	..	5	..	1	5	..	6	1	..	..	1	38
Total Experimental	35	28	8	13	19	8	16	10	13	14	18	17	9	25	15	36	13	10	307
Twin-Engine Bombers—																			
Home	..	..	..	..	..	..	1	1	4	5	5	14	9	2	5	101	165	120	432
Four-Engine Bombers (Handley Page 'V' type)—																			
Home	..	..	..	..	..	..	..	..	..	..	..	..	..	..	..	..	..	6	6
Total { Home	79	114	179	314	461	727	886	1,269	1,794	1,767	2,402	3,167	3,548	4,649	7,104	7,834	8,534	7,199	52,027
Total { Abroad	3	4	39	170	231	221	251	268	145	253	328	473	172	93	50	36	24	1	2,762
Grand Total—Aeroplanes	82	118	218	484	692	948	1,137	1,537	1,939	2,020	2,730	3,640	3,720	4,742	7,154	7,870	8,558	7,200	54,789

SEAPLANES AND SHIP AERO-PLANES—																			
Home	19	33	34	58	77	81	178	131	70	51	56	144	316	394	257	230	238	211	2,578
Abroad (France)	..	..	..	..	6	6	..	..	..	..	..	..	..	..	2	..	..	..	14
Total Seaplanes, &c.	19	33	34	58	83	87	178	131	70	51	56	144	316	394	259	230	238	211	2,592
FLYING-BOATS—																			
Home	..	..	..	..	2	..	2	..	..	1	2	16	28	26	60	126	112	113	488
Abroad—																			
France	..	..	..	..	12	9	17	4	..	..	11	1	12	..	..	..	..	..	66
U.S.A.	1	3	4	1	28	21	..	..	..	..	2	10	4	31	25	12	32	31	205
Italy	..	..	..	..	..	..	..	..	..	..	..	..	4	..	..	..	..	..	4
Total Flying-Boats	1	3	4	1	42	30	19	4	..	1	15	27	48	57	85	138	144	144	763

TABLE B. AERO ENGINES

NOTE: For 'Home' the figures up to May 1917 represent the numbers 'Handed to Services'. From June 1917 to December 1918 they represent 'Passed Test'. For other than British Manufacture the figures represent 'Handed to Services'. With the exception of French engines, deliveries do not include spares.

	1914.		1915.				1916.				1917.				1918.				
	Aug. & Sept.	*4th Qtr.*	*1st Qtr.*	*2nd Qtr.*	*3rd Qtr.*	*4th Qtr.*	*1st Qtr.*	*2nd Qtr.*	*3rd Qtr.*	*4th Qtr.*	*1st Qtr.*	*2nd Qtr.*	*3rd Qtr.*	*4th Qtr.*	*1st Qtr.*	*2nd Qtr.*	*3rd Qtr.*	*4th Qtr.*	*Total.*
Stationary Water-cooled—																			
Home—																			
160 h.p. Beardmore	..	..	..	..	..	..	2	43	124	148	146	162	211	414	378	394	306	228	2,556
190–220 h.p. Rolls-Royce 'Falcon'	..	..	..	..	..	..	..	..	5	33	74	191	161	210	274	234	224	226	1,632
150–180 h.p. Hispano-Suiza	..	..	..	..	..	..	..	..	..	..	49	33	19	123	301	452	468	408	1,853
250 h.p. B.H.P.	..	..	..	..	..	..	..	..	..	..	..	6	70	241	798	948	1,243	1,076	4,382
200 h.p. Sunbeam 'Arab'	..	..	..	..	..	..	..	..	..	..	..	4	8	69	138	212	334	430	1,195
Other Types	16	35	57	124	189	175	311	223	351	260	481	752	784	737	560	587	669	742	7,053
Total Home	16	35	57	124	189	175	313	266	480	441	750	1,148	1,253	1,794	2,449	2,827	3,244	3,110	18,671

Abroad—																			
France																			
200 h.p. Hispano-Suiza	..	..	..	..	..	..	..	..	..	..	..	110	290	588	1,083	1,209	773	309	4,362
Other Types	..	4	6	27	31	19	59	70	22	27	32	101	12	148	24	20	33	293	928
U.S.A.—																			
90 h.p. Curtiss	..	..	..	..	13	15	34	36	34	40	92	218	226	270	836	395	..	..	2,209
400 h.p. Liberty	..	..	..	..	..	..	..	..	..	..	..	..	..	..	..	80	540	454	1,074
200 h.p. Sunbeam 'Arab'	..	..	..	..	..	..	..	..	..	..	..	..	..	..	..	1	2	113	116
Italy—																			
250–300 h.p. F.I.A.T.	..	..	..	..	..	..	..	..	..	..	..	..	..	253	58	..	299	..	610
500 h.p. F.I.A.T.	..	..	..	..	..	..	..	..	..	..	..	..	..	..	6	..	..	..	6
160 h.p. Isotta	..	..	..	..	..	..	..	..	..	..	..	..	4	..	2	..	..	..	6
Total Abroad	..	4	6	27	44	34	93	106	56	67	124	429	532	1,259	2,009	1,705	1,647	1,169	9,311
Total Stationary Water-cooled	16	39	63	151	233	209	406	372	536	508	874	1,577	1,785	3,053	4,458	4,532	4,891	4,279	27,982
Stationary Air-cooled—																			
Home—																			
90 h.p. R.A.F.	..	..	1	76	138	241	297	270	296	226	333	199	274	278	210	105	30	..	2,974
80 h.p. Renault	..	..	..	..	..	16	86	66	79	52	9	80	124	174	275	431	397	227	2,016
140 h.p. R.A.F.4a	..	..	..	..	..	2	40	237	239	238	440	443	458	337	637	456	80	1	3,608
300 h.p. A.B.C. Dragonfly	..	..	..	..	..	..	..	..	..	..	..	..	..	..	..	3	7	13	23
Other Types	..	13	97	77	93	79	74	41	55	43	29	43	47	20	32	13	5	14	775
Total Home	..	13	98	153	231	338	497	614	669	559	811	765	903	809	1,154	1,008	519	255	9,396

APPENDIX VIII

DISTRIBUTION OF AEROPLANES TO SERVICE AND TRAINING UNITS OF THE ROYAL FLYING CORPS AND ROYAL AIR FORCE, AUGUST 1914–OCTOBER 31st 1918

	T.U. 1914.	T.U. 1915.	T.U. 1916.	T.U. 1917.	T.U. 1918.	H.D. 1915.	H.D. 1916.	H.D. 1917.	H.D. 1918.	E.F. 1914.	E.F. 1915.	E.F. 1916.	E.F. 1917.	E.F. 1918.	I.F. 1918.	14th Wing 1917.	14th Wing 1918.	M.E.B. 1915.	M.E.B. 1916.	M.E.B. 1917.	M.E.B. 1918.	5th Group 1918.	Med. 1918.	Total.
Avro	9	100	366	766	3,530	..	..	11	263	9	..	..	..	..	..	..	..	15	25	66	286	..	..	5,416
A.W. Quadruplane	..	..	1	..	..	..	..	..	..	..	..	..	..	..	..	..	..	..	..	..	..	..	..	1
A.W.	..	4	80	275	247	..	1	7	..	..	..	17	213	547	..	..	..	..	24	35	146	..	..	1,596
B.E.	..	..	..	..	..	..	..	..	..	4	..	..	..	..	..	..	..	..	..	..	..	..	..	4
B.E.2	2	..	..	..	..	..	..	..	..	30	..	..	..	..	..	..	..	..	..	..	..	..	..	32
B.E.2a	1	5	1	..	..	..	..	..	..	6	1	..	..	..	..	..	..	..	1	..	..	..	..	15
B.E.2b	5	..	33	26	..	..	..	1	..	8	10	1	..	..	..	..	..	..	1	..	..	..	..	85
B.E.2c	..	92	143	58	1	20	114	1	1	..	218	263	6	..	..	..	..	24	171	5	..	..	..	1,117
B.E.2d	..	5	19	25	5	..	1	..	..	..	..	136	..	..	..	..	..	..	..	..	..	..	..	191
B.E.8	8	4	..	..	..	..	..	..	..	5	5	..	..	..	..	..	..	..	..	..	..	..	..	22
B.E.8a	..	29	9	..	..	..	..	..	..	..	..	..	..	..	..	..	..	..	..	..	..	..	..	38
B.E.9	..	..	..	..	..	..	..	..	..	..	1	..	..	..	..	..	..	..	..	..	..	..	..	1
B.E.2e	..	..	44	565	304	..	33	126	1	..	..	223	278	2	..	..	..	..	29	171	25	..	..	1,801
B.E.12 & 12a	..	..	88	51	31	..	21	44	36	..	..	118	10	2	..	..	..	..	11	44	12	..	..	468
B.E.12b	..	..	..	1	2	..	..	12	24	..	..	..	..	..	..	..	..	..	..	..	..	..	..	39
Blackburn Twin	..	..	..	..	11	..	..	..	..	..	..	..	..	..	..	..	..	..	..	..	..	..	..	11
Bristol Tractor	10	..	..	..	..	..	..	..	..	..	..	..	..	..	..	..	..	..	..	..	..	..	..	10
Bristol Scout	..	10	69	33	3	..	7	2	..	2	27	45	6	..	..	..	..	..	26	6	..	..	..	236
Bristol (Mono)	..	..	1	2	39	..	..	..	..	..	..	..	1	..	..	..	..	..	..	17	18	..	..	78
Bristol Fighter	..	..	2	112	455	..	..	2	113	..	..	..	308	626	..	..	68	..	..	17	51	..	..	1,754
Bleriot	13	41	16	2	..	..	..	..	..	23	9	..	..	..	..	..	..	..	..	..	..	..	..	104
B.A.T.	..	..	..	..	1	..	..	..	..	..	..	..	..	..	..	..	..	..	..	..	..	..	..	1
Box Kite	3	..	..	..	..	..	..	..	..	..	..	..	..	..	..	..	..	..	..	..	..	..	..	3
Caudron	..	44	10	..	38	..	..	..	..	..	9	..	..	..	..	..	..	2	6	..	..	..	..	109
Curtiss J.N.	..	32	74	51	..	..	..	..	..	..	..	..	..	..	..	..	..	..	4	..	..	..	..	161
De Hav.1	..	5	37	1	..	..	..	24	..	..	..	..	..	..	..	..	..	..	6	..	..	..	..	73
De Hav.2	..	..	53	44	3	..	..	2	..	..	..	222	43	1	..	..	..	..	1	31	..	..	..	400
De Hav.4	..	..	1	146	181	..	..	1	..	..	..	1	340	323	91	..	..	..	..	5	13	67	1	1,170
De Hav.5	..	..	..	131	11	..	..	..	..	..	..	1	340	..	..	..	..	..	..	..	..	..	..	483
De Hav.6	..	..	..	342	1,189	..	..	..	71	..	..	..	..	..	..	..	..	..	..	27	125	..	..	1,754
De Hav.9	..	..	..	..	956	..	..	..	..	..	..	..	..	789	144	..	..	..	..	..	92	52	133	2,166
De Hav.9a	..	..	..	..	113	..	..	..	..	..	..	..	..	70	89	..	..	..	..	..	..	..	..	272
De Hav.10	..	..	..	..	..	..	..	..	1	..	..	..	..	..	2	..	..	..	..	..	..	..	..	3
F.E.2b	..	..	86	114	177	..	8	117	88	1	18	315	269	378	17	..	..	..	..	..	..	24	..	1,612
F.E.2d	..	..	14	23	3	..	..	23	2	..	..	67	116	..	..	..	..	..	..	..	..	..	..	248
F.E.4	..	..	1	..	..	..	..	..	..	..	..	..	..	..	..	..	..	..	..	..	..	..	..	1
F.E.8	..	..	25	8	..	..	..	2	..	..	..	103	44	..	..	..	..	..	..	..	..	..	..	182
F.E.9	..	..	..	..	..	..	..	1	..	..	..	..	..	..	..	..	..	..	..	..	..	..	..	1
Grahame White	..	..	23	27	..	..	..	..	..	..	..	..	..	..	..	..	..	..	..	..	..	..	..	50
Handley Page	..	..	..	..	96	..	..	..	..	..	..	..	..	71	103	..	..	..	..	..	2	18	..	290
H. Farman	11	26	113	76	..	..	..	25	..	28	3	..	..	..	..	..	..	..	22	33	..	..	..	337
M. Farman	25	147	361	446	15	..	..	..	..	15	13	..	..	..	..	..	..	5	45	12	..	..	..	1,084
Martinsyde Scout	4	46	37	70	3	..	..	1	..	..	4	83	50	..	..	..	..	4	23	41	..	..	..	366
Martinsyde F.3	..	..	..	..	..	..	..	..	4	..	..	..	..	..	..	..	..	..	..	..	..	..	..	4
Morane	3	14	43	29	..	..	..	..	..	3	92	223	96	..	..	..	..	..	..	..	..	..	..	503
[illegible]	[illegible]	[illegible]	[illegible]	[illegible]	[illegible]	[illegible]	[illegible]	[illegible]	[illegible]	[illegible]	[illegible]	[illegible]	[illegible]	[illegible]	[illegible]	[illegible]	[illegible]	[illegible]	[illegible]	[illegible]	[illegible]	[illegible]	[illegible]	109

R.E.7	..	2	91	54	..	..	..	19	..	..	14	32	9	3	..	..	..	..	..	..	..	..	..	224
R.E.8	..	..	9	319	867	..	..	5	14	..	..	18	1,114	1,025	..	37	68	..	..	172	155	..	..	3,803
R.T.1	..	..	..	1	1	..	..	..	..	..	..	..	1	..	..	..	..	..	..	..	..	..	..	3
Sopwith Bomber	..	..	..	71	1	..	..	3	..	..	..	..	..	1	..	..	..	..	..	13	..	..	..	89
Sopwith Camel	..	..	..	235	944	..	..	61	316	..	..	..	471	1,645	24	60	158	..	..	..	57	145	72	4,188
Sopwith Dolphin	..	..	..	9	205	..	..	..	7	..	..	..	19	381	..	..	..	..	..	..	..	..	..	621
Sopwith Salamander	..	..	..	..	2	..	..	..	..	..	..	..	..	3	..	..	..	..	..	..	..	..	..	5
Sopwith Snipe	..	..	..	..	45	..	..	..	1	..	..	..	..	95	2	..	..	..	..	..	..	..	..	143
Sopwith 2-str.	..	..	44	104	57	..	8	48	..	..	..	135	211	..	..	..	..	..	..	..	..	..	..	607
Sopwith Triplane	..	..	..	..	1	..	..	..	1	..	..	..	..	..	..	..	..	..	..	..	..	..	..	2
Sopwith Scout	4	1	12	383	428	..	..	62	11	3	1	17	197	2	..	..	1	..	..	10	69	..	..	1,201
S.E.2	..	..	..	..	..	..	..	..	..	1	..	..	..	..	..	..	..	..	..	..	..	..	..	1
S.E.5 & 5a	..	..	..	105	623	..	..	14	60	..	..	1	335	1,663	..	..	..	..	..	34	138	..	..	2,973
Spad	..	..	..	60	40	..	..	..	..	..	..	11	202	37	..	..	..	..	..	16	3	..	..	369
Vickers F.B.9	..	..	..	50	..	..	..	..	..	..	..	..	..	..	..	..	..	..	..	..	..	..	..	50
Vickers F.B.12c	..	..	..	..	..	..	..	1	..	..	..	..	..	..	..	..	..	..	..	..	..	..	..	1
Vickers F.B.14	..	..	..	..	..	..	..	6	..	..	..	..	..	..	..	..	..	..	..	..	..	..	..	6
Vickers F.B.16	..	..	..	1	..	..	..	..	..	..	..	..	..	..	..	..	..	..	..	..	..	..	..	1
Vickers F.B.19	..	..	4	8	..	..	1	5	..	..	..	6	..	..	..	..	..	..	..	12	..	..	..	36
Vickers F.B.26	..	..	..	..	..	..	..	..	1	..	..	..	..	..	..	..	..	..	..	..	..	..	..	1
Vickers Vimy	..	..	..	..	..	..	..	..	..	..	..	..	..	..	1	..	..	..	..	..	..	..	..	1
Vickers Box Kite	3	..	..	..	..	..	..	..	..	..	..	..	..	..	..	..	..	..	..	..	..	..	..	3
Vickers Fighter	6	44	77	4	..	..	..	..	..	..	60	49	..	..	..	..	..	..	..	1	..	..	..	241
Voisin	..	5	21	2	..	..	..	..	..	..	16	..	..	..	..	..	..	..	..	..	..	..	..	44
Totals	111	660	2,019	4,859	10,629	20	194	627	1,015	144	507	2,320	4,965	7,672	473	97	295	50	395	787	1,241	306	206	39,592

Abbreviations:

T.U. = Training Units. (Includes Grand Fleet and Anti-Submarine.)
H.D. = Home Defence.
E.F. = Expeditionary Force, France.
I.F. = Independent Force.
14th Wing = Expeditionary Force, Italy.
5th Group = Dover–Dunkirk Command.
M.E.B. = Middle East Brigade.
Med. = Mediterranean.

Note. The statistics above do not include Royal Naval Air Service units before the formation of the Royal Air Force, April 1918. The figures given for the years 1914 and 1915 should be accepted with reserve. All figures include aeroplanes delivered to units in France direct from the French manufacturers.

APPENDIX 9

Aerial Co-Operation During the Artillery Bombardment and the Infantry Attack (April 1917)

(Memorandum prepared by R.F.C. H.Q., and issued to the Second Army by the Artillery Advisor at G.H.Q.)

1. The following notes regarding the possibilities and limitations of aerial co-operation during the artillery bombardment and infantry attack are issued for the information of commanders concerned in the preparation of plans for an offensive.

2. The work required of aeroplanes prior to and during the bombardment and during the infantry attack comprises:

(*a*) Observation of fire for batteries engaged on counter-battery work.
(*b*) Observation of fire for batteries bombarding the trenches and cutting wire.
(*c*) Trench reconnaissance and contact patrol work.
(*a*) and (*b*) include any ranging required previous to the bombardment, and (*a*), (*b*), and (*c*) include photography.

3. Squadrons R.F.C. are organised in three Flights, and it much facilitates the work of the R.F.C. if this organisation is borne in mind when making the plan and allotting the aerial work. Each Flight consists of from six to eight machines under a Flight Commander, and the best results will be obtained if Flights are normally employed either wholly on counterbattery work or wholly on trench bombardment and reconnaissance. More machines will usually be required for counter-battery work than for trench bombardment.

4. The number of aeroplanes which can work at the same time on a corps front is limited by:

(*a*) The strength of the squadron.
(*b*) The length of the front.

As regards (*a*), at least four machines or, on a long summer day, five are required to keep one in the air throughout the hours of daylight.

Further, although damaged machines can usually be replaced in a few hours, allowance must always be made for a certain number of the squadron's machines being temporarily unserviceable through minor defects which can be remedied in the squadron.

As regards (*b*), the length of the front governs the number of machines using wireless which can be employed at the same time. Provided that observers are highly trained in signalling, that wireless operators are very efficient, and that all the personnel concerned have carried out much previous practice together, it may be possible for as many as one machine per 1,000 yards of front to work simultaneously, but any attempt to employ more than this will inevitably cause failure. If the above conditions are not fulfilled, it is far better to employ fewer machines than to risk a breakdown.

5. Successful co-operation for counter-battery work demands:

(*a*) A suitable allotment of artillery and ammunition.
(*b*) A suitable organisation of the artillery allotted.
(*c*) A time-table which will admit of efficient observation.

(*a*) The allotment of the available artillery and ammunition to counterbattery and other work is a matter for the commander concerned, but if best results are to be obtained it is essential that as far as possible the artillery allotted to counter-battery work during the bombardment should remain unchanged and that sufficient time for methodical destructive fire should be allowed. A limited number of batteries so allotted, which will enable fire for destruction with efficient aerial observation as well as neutralizing fire to be carried on continuously, will give far better results than a large number of batteries allotted for limited periods. Under this latter system fire cannot be observed with any accuracy, if at all, owing:

(1) to the limitation in the number of machines which can be employed at one time (see para. 4 (*b*) above):
(2) to the smoke and dust raised when a large number of batteries are being engaged simultaneously, and to the confusion caused by rounds wide of their own target falling near that of another battery. At the same time the employment of ground and instrumental observation must never be overlooked.

(*b*) It is impossible to maintain the necessary close touch between the artillery and the R.F.C. if the personnel of the latter have many artillery commanders to deal with or vice versa. Aerial co-operation will therefore be rendered easier if the artillery is normally organised in counter-battery groups and trench bombardment groups, and not in mixed groups employed on both duties. Artillery commanders will then have to deal only with counter-battery Flights or trench Flights as the case may be, and not with both.

(*c*) The necessity for a suitable time-table in the case of counter-battery work is obvious from the considerations discussed in para. 5 (*a*) above. The number of batteries on which fire for destruction can be carried out efficiently at any one time depends, apart from the question of the number of batteries available to engage them:

(1) on the number of machines available:
(2) on the distance apart of the hostile batteries.

As regards (1), if two Flights of the squadron are employed on counterbattery work, the maximum number of machines which can be kept in the air will be four, and three will be more usual. In addition to observing fire for destruction these machines will have to carry out the necessary photography and report by zone call all active hostile batteries other than those actually being engaged. This latter duty can be done by the machines observing fire for destruction in the intervals between rounds, but when possible it is better to detail one of the available machines specially for the work; this machine can then be made responsible for the whole of the Corps counter-battery area. The limitations imposed by wireless are explained in para. 4 (*b*) above. It must be remembered that machines of the trench Flight will be using wireless at the same time. Experienced pilots and observers can observe fire on two hostile batteries at once, but only in very exceptional cases on more than two. Provided suitable targets are selected, balloons can assist the aeroplanes in counter-battery work.

As regards (2), any attempt to observe fire for destruction simultaneously on two hostile batteries which are situated so close to one another as to run the risk of rounds falling wide of one battery aimed at being mistaken for those fired at the other battery, will only lead to confusion.

It follows that the programme of counter-battery work with aerial observation requires the most careful co-ordination if successful results are to be obtained. This is primarily the duty of the Staff Officer for counterbattery work to the G.O.C. R.A. of the Corps who must review the programme for the ensuing day each evening with the Squadron Commander and Balloon Company Commander or their representatives.

6. Successful co-operation between the batteries allotted to trench bombardment and wire cutting and the R.F.C., both prior to and during menu the bombardment, needs perhaps even more careful and detailed prearrangement than in the case of counter-battery work. In framing a plan, the following points must be borne in mind:

(*a*) Aerial observation should not be asked for on any target which can be equally well observed from the ground.
(*b*) Little or no aerial observation on the enemy's nearer trench systems is possible during the actual bombardment.

If failures and delays are to be avoided and accurate shooting ensured, attention must be paid to the following points:

(1) The selection from photographs, whenever possible in consultation with the observer, of suitable and clearly defined points on which to range or to fire for effect as the case may be.
(2) The numbering of these points in the order in which it is intended to engage them. Care must be taken to avoid any possible confusion with the numbers allotted to active hostile batteries.
(3) Fire by other batteries in the near vicinity of the ranging-point must be stopped during the process.

The work may be arranged in several ways:

(*a*) One gun of each battery may be ranged on several points.
(*b*) All guns of each battery may be ranged on different points.
(*c*) All guns of each battery may be ranged on the same point.

As a guide it may be assumed that an experienced observer can range a battery on eight to twelve points during a flight in any of the above ways, always provided the programme is carefully compiled with due attention to the points enumerated above.

7. Very little aerial observation of trench destruction is possible once the general bombardment has been commenced, and one machine per Corps front will usually be sufficient for any work which can be usefully done by an aeroplane at this stage.

If observation is required on any points of particular importance, no one point must be allotted to more than one battery. The observer and each battery must be provided with maps and time-tables showing the tasks and the calls and positions of the batteries concerned. At the time arranged for observation on each point, a few single rounds of battery fire should be fired, the observer giving mean point of impact corrections. Subsequently the observer can watch the general effect of the fire and, if it is inaccurate, call up the battery concerned and range it afresh.

8. The arrangements for observing the fire of batteries engaged on wire-cutting are similar to those required in the case of trench bombardment, but, where it is a question of cutting lanes, by a careful arrangement of times and tasks more aerial observation is possible and consequently more machines may be usefully employed if available.

9. Trench reconnaissance and contact patrol work are best done by the Flight charged with the observation of trench bombardment, owing to the intimate acquaintance of pilots and observers with the trench system. In the case of back lines situated in the counter-battery area, however, any bombardment or wire-cutting required can be suitably observed by machines of the counter-battery Flight. The Flight carrying out the observation is also responsible for photographing the results of bombardments. These duties throw a great deal of work on the trench Flight, and the most careful allotment of machines to the various duties is therefore necessary to obtain the best results. It may be repeated that the number of machines of counter-battery and trench Flights combined which can observe artillery fire is limited both by the number of machines available and the necessity of avoiding jamming of wireless signals.

10. During the infantry attack the principal duty of the trench Flight will be contact-patrol work, while counter-battery work will largely consist of neutralisation with a view to keeping down the fire of as many of the enemy's guns as possible. Since contact-patrol machines use wireless to a limited extent only, the number of counter-battery machines can be somewhat increased. A proportion are best employed on calling for neutralization of active batteries by means of the zone call. The remainder working with specially detailed batteries of heavy howitzers can observe fire for the destruction of hostile batteries whose fire continues in spite of our neutralising fire. Balloons can be usefully employed during this period in keeping the Counter-Battery Staff informed as to the activity of the enemy's batteries.

11. It will be seen from the above notes that a successful artillery plan necessitates a thorough knowledge and most careful consideration of the powers and limitations of both the artillery and the R.F.C.

Artillery commanders must therefore always arrange for the Corps

Wing, Corps Squadron, and Balloon Company Commanders to attend conferences at which the targets are discussed and decided upon, and must fully consider the effect of all proposals on the possibility or otherwise of aerial observation. Co-operation must be worked out to the minutest detail, but the plan must foresee and allow for the contingency of aerial observation being impossible, dependent as it is and must always be on the weather.

April 1917.

Appendix 10

Notes on Aeroplane Fighting in Single-Seater Scouts (November 1916)

Our single-seater scouts have now taken part in a sufficient number of engagements to enable us to deduce, from observed facts, some principles governing the use of these machines.

The present notes merely aim at stating these principles and the means of applying them.

1. Characteristics of the Single-seater Scout.

1. The single-seater scout is fast, very easily handled, a good climber, and capable, owing to its qualities of penetration through the air and the stoutness of its build, of diving with great speed on an adversary.

2. Its armament consists of a machine gun, whose axis of fire is directed forward and in a fixed position in relation to the machine. Sometimes a second gun is carried; its axis of fire is parallel to that of the other gun.

Thus equipped, the machine is best fitted for attack. For defence it chiefly relies on its speed and power of manoeuvre.

3. Its field of view upwards and downwards is only fairly good; constant attention and much practice are required to keep other machines concerned, friendly or enemy, in sight during the movements of an engagement.

2. Qualifications of Single-seater Scout Pilots.

1. None but specially selected pilots are capable of flying these machines.

2. A high standard of physical fitness is essential. The heart, lungs, and ears are subject to great strain, for pilots, in the course of their flights and fights are called upon not only to climb very high (15,000 feet or over), but also to undergo great, sudden and frequent changes of altitude. Eyesight, too, must be excellent; otherwise the enemy's machines will escape, and the pilots themselves will be open to surprise, or may attack friendly machines, a mistake that is easily made.

3. Pilots must give constant attention to increasing their skill not

only as pilots, but also as machine gunners, and to keeping their machines and guns in fighting trim.

4. Important as are self-control and courage in action, an attack to be successful must be thoroughly thought out.

5. The chief characteristic, however, of a fighting pilot is a fixed determination to bring down the greatest possible number of adversaries.

3. Fighting Tactics of the Single-seater.

1. As a general principle a single-seater should never cruise alone, and an attack by an isolated single-seater should be the exception.

2. If the pilot, instead of confining his attention to the sky, allows it to be diverted to examining the ground, he may be easily surprised. A single-seater pilot should make a point of collecting useful information in his flights, and for this he will, as a rule, have many opportunities, for it is only rarely that the enemy aviation will be so active that it will claim his entire attention.

3. The principle on which the isolated single-seater fights is surprise, which is only made possible by keen observation, coolness, patience, and experience. Surprise, moreover, is daily becoming more difficult, as enemy machines are now often warned of the presence of our scouts by observers from the ground who fire very visible, generally on the dangerous side, smoke balls that are very easily seen.

4. If the enemy are numerous, chance of surprise is small, and the attack not only will be deprived of this element of success, but also will lack the impulse which springs from the consciousness of superiority of force.

5. The Germans now put up barrages at different levels, and often wait to catch our scouts when they are manoeuvring prior to attacking the enemy's machines.

6. In frequent cases isolated scouts will be called upon to fight singlehanded, *e.g.*:

(1) When enemy machines have penetrated our lines, for every enemy machine which crosses our lines must be destroyed *at any price.*

(2) When for some reason or other a formation has been broken up and its elements have failed to join other formations.

4. Scout *v.* Scout.

1. The fight of scout *v.* scout is a struggle either to obtain position

behind the enemy's machine in prolongation of its axis or, if he is faster in manoeuvring, to prevent him obtaining a favourable position for firing. The manoeuvre for position often takes a very long time without either machine being able to fire at the other.

5. SCOUT *v.* SINGLE-, DOUBLE-, OR MULTI-SEATER MACHINE.

1. Principle. Act by surprise; when this is not possible, manoeuvre so that the enemy cannot direct his fire properly.

To carry this principle into effect it is essential:

(1) To observe the adversary,
(2) To approach without being seen, and
(3) To give the enemy no opportunity for adjusting his fire.

2. Observe the Adversary. Very often the adversary has a mission to fulfil, *e.g.* ranging, photography. The time to attack is when he is engaged in carrying this mission out, For instance, a hostile machine is seen to approach the line in uncertain evolutions. Generally, on such occasions he begins by observing the sky. Eventually, reassured by his inspection, he makes up his mind to fly across the lines and to undertake his mission. It is when thus occupied that he is open to surprise.

Again, a machine may be seen cruising, apparently without any special mission that requires his undivided attention to the ground. On such occasions it is often better to watch him for some time from afar until his attention slackens and his evolutions become less regular. Then is the time to effect a surprise.

3. Approach without being seen. As a general rule, place yourself between your adversary and the sun; then, according to the height of the sun, dive on him or make your attack on his own level.

If there is no sun, an opportunity of surprising him often arises in the course of his evolutions, by getting behind him, in prolongation of his axis or slightly below it. Such a form of attack is especially applicable when manoeuvring in enemy country, for then the hostile observer is not so much on the alert, and, in order to shelter from the wind, is likely not to put his head over the fuselage to keep watch. If he observes at all, it is only the air above him.

When a scout is far over the enemy's lines and sees a hostile machine rise from the aerodrome, climb for height, and make for the line, with its probable intention of carrying out a reconnaissance—indications of which are his high altitude and clearly marked direction—a chance of surprise is offered, provided the scout follows the hostile machine close and in the same vertical plane, but on a slightly lower level, where he will be hidden by the tail-piece of the hostile machine from the enemy's crew. When within some half-dozen kilometres of the lines the enemy will cruise for a brief period to see that the air is clear; he will then go straight to his objective. This is the time for attack, for both pilot and observer, reassured by their observations, will be keeping a look-out forward.

In cloudy weather, as an aeroplane then forms but a thin and barely visible line, it is generally an advantage to approach the enemy on his own level. In such weather scouts must be very active, for then the Germans venture much more readily over our lines than in sunny weather, even though the time is favourable for a surprise by our scouts.

4. Do not let the enemy adjust his fire. If the enemy attempts to fire, do not fire yourself, and do not make for him in a straight line, for a cool gunner firing at a machine making straight for him has the greatest chances of hitting it and bringing it down.

Make for your opponent in a zigzag course which obliges him to change the aim of his gun from side to side. Keep also a little above him, and as you approach get ready to start firing; then when about 100 yards off, and the conditions are favourable, e.g. when the enemy gun is still pointed to port, and you yourself have turned and are already slightly on the starboard side, charge straight at him, firing a rapid burst. The shots should be fired at about 50 yards from the target.

Under these conditions 15 to 50 rounds can be fired, after which you must swerve so as to avoid a collision.

If the enemy is not brought down, sheer off quickly to the rear by a sudden turn or loop; be very careful to keep tacking, with sharp turns, and avoid losing height.

As soon as you are again in position repeat the attack in the same manner. In these attacks it is needless to make any correction of aim on account of the relative speed of the machines, as the courses of the two machines are parallel during the firing and the distance is small.

Some pilots, instead of charging the enemy after this method, approach him within 100 yards in one of his blind sectors, and then by a sudden loop get into a position to shoot him from behind. This manoeuvre requires a great knowledge of the German machines and plenty of training, for it must be carried out with extreme precision. It cannot be recommended for general adoption.

In any case single-handed attacks by single-seaters require a coolness, a gift of observation, a familiarity with the gun, and a skill in manoeuvring which are possessed only by first-class pilots.

Naturally the attack of two double-seaters by a single-seater requires very special qualities of judgement, for it must be very accurately timed. The problem is comparatively simple when the group of enemy machines is within our lines, the machine farthest from the line must then be vigorously attacked.

6. Battle Teams.

1. The normal battle unit is a group of two machines; a third machine may join them if needs be.

The constitution of such units is a matter which requires the particular attention of a Squadron Commander.

2. An essential condition of success is that a team be homogeneous; consequently, the machines must be of the same type or at any rate equivalent in speed and capacity of manoeuvre. But above all the two pilots of a team must have mutual trust in one another's courage, skill, and judgement. A single-seater squadron should, therefore, be composed of none but first-class pilots.

7. Co-ordination of Movements in a Team.

1. The team always manoeuvres in accord. One of the two pilots is appointed before the flight to take the lead, the other co-ordinates his movements to those of the guide's. As a principle the machines never fly more than 400 yards apart, the one in the rear slightly higher and in echelon. Normally the two machines fly at low speed.

2. If the leading pilot sees his comrade suddenly move away by a sudden increase of speed, a change of course, a climb or dive, he must follow in order to find out the cause of this evolution—*e. g.* attack by enemy aeroplane, heavy A.A. fire—and it is only after the reason no longer exists that he resumes his part as guide.

3. Except in cases of urgency, no movement that would break up the team should be made by either machine without first signalling 'attention' to its comrade; the signal for this purpose will be a violent and continuous lateral swinging of the machine. To ensure that the signal is seen, the machine which makes it must put itself in a position where it can be seen by its comrade; the latter will repeat the signal as soon as it is seen.

8. Attack on an isolated German Machine by a Team of two Scouts.

1. In this case surprise is not essential. Faced by a combined converging attack the enemy is likely to lose his nerve. While he is engaged with one machine he is attacked and driven down by the other.

2. Two methods are recommended:

(1) The attack on both sides. The two scouts first obtain a position above the enemy, and, if possible, with the sun behind them. They then increase the distance between them to 600 to 800 yards, following at the same time the movements of the enemy. They next increase their speed and dive on him simultaneously. At 100 to 50 yards from him they open fire. When the German prepares to fire at one of the attackers the latter closes on him, carefully tacking to avoid a straight course, but remaining on the side from which his attack started; meanwhile the other scout closes in and fires at leisure. This manoeuvre requires a very high measure of co-operation between the two pilots, for it is absolutely necessary for them to approach simultaneously so that the enemy cannot shoot one first and then turn on the other.

(2) The attack on a vertical line. One of the machines dives into a position 150 yards behind the enemy in the blind angle of its tail piece and opens fire at this range if sure of his aim; his comrade dives in the same vertical plane, keeping 100 yards higher than the first, and fires point blank. The enemy's defence will generally consist in an attempt to circle round the lower scout and shoot him in the process. The scout must manoeuvre so as to keep behind all the time. While the German thus tries to shoot the lower scout the upper one has ample opportunity to sweep down on him and shoot him point blank. Very often the lower scout will not even need to open fire at all. This manoeuvre is one of the easiest to co-ordinate well.

9. Attack of two Enemy Machines by a Team of Scouts.

1. This attack resolves itself into two distinct duels of scout versus scout, each scout diving on one of the adversaries. It would appear at first sight that such attacks can be executed only by pilots of exceptional capacity; but in practice it will be found that the German team breaks up under the threat of attack. The two scouts must then converge at once on the hindmost machine.

2. It often happens that, of the two enemy machines, one is entrusted with a mission—*e. g.* ranging or photography—while the other simply protects the first. In this case the protecting machine usually

stays within its lines to cover the retreat of the other, which goes out alone to the point necessitated by his mission.

The scouts must of course attack the protecting machine while the other is busy, and then settle the latter's account. With these objects close observation of the doings of the enemy is essential.

10. Engagement of several Teams of two Scouts.

1. If the scouts are equal in number to the enemy machines, the teams attack each team for itself, as explained above. As often as not, however, the Germans scatter before such an attack; some take to flight and the scouts must then co-ordinate their movements so as to concentrate their efforts on the machines lagging behind.

2. If the scouts are in superior numbers, the teams which are in the less favourable positions for an attack owing to distance, bad position of the sun, &c, must attract to themselves the enemy's attention and, while watching the fight, be ready to help any of our machines in a difficulty, or to intervene if an opportunity offers. A careful watch must be kept for hostile reinforcements which might turn up unperceived and attack the scouts while they manoeuvre. In short, the surplus teams form a reserve and a guard.

3. If a group of German machines, instead of scattering, makes a stand before the attack of a group of scouts, it becomes necessary, according to the circumstances, either to engage in a fight to the last or to force the enemy to scatter by means of turning movements on the part of the surplus teams. In any case, any faint-hearted demonstration, particularly if far behind the German lines, must be avoided.

11. How to Manoeuvre One or More Groups of Teams.

1. The number of teams that can manoeuvre properly together is three (i.e. six machines). A group of scouts beyond that number is difficult to handle, and it is better to form several groups working independently. One of the team Commanders is Group Commander; the other Commanders conform to his movements after having been warned by the signal 'attention'.

2. From one group to another the only means of signalling is by flares. Each Group Commander should therefore be provided with a signalling pistol. The signals by flare should be settled beforehand. No general code can now be laid down.

12. Departure and Assembling of Groups.

1. As a principle the two machines of a team leave the aerodrome

together and land together. They go straight to the starting-point. The group, on the contrary, meets at a starting-point chosen above the lines, for there would be a waste of time if all the machines were to leave the same aerodrome together.

2. When two or more groups have to carry out flights simultaneously, they must have different starting-points and must fly at different altitudes between 7,500 and 15,000 feet.

13. Rallying-points of Groups.

A group of scouts is almost always scattered after a fight. Immediately after the engagement it goes to its starting-point to re-form; and this is also its rallying-point.

Issued by the General Staff.
November 1916.

Appendix 11

Fighting in the Air (March 1917)
General

1. The Necessity of Fighting.

The uses of aeroplanes in war are many, but the efficient performance of their missions in every case depends on their ability to gain and maintain a position from which they can see the enemy's dispositions and movements. Cavalry on the ground have to fight and defeat the enemy's cavalry before they can gain information, and in the same way aerial fighting is usually necessary to enable aeroplanes to perform their other duties. Artillery co-operation, photography, and similar work can only be successful if the enemy are prevented as far as possible from interfering with the machines engaged on these duties, and such work by hostile machines can only be prevented by interference on our part. The moral effect of a successful cavalry action is very great, equally so is that of successful fighting in the air. This is due to the fact that in many cases the combat is actually seen from the ground, while the results of successful fighting, even when not visible, are apparent to all.

The moral effect produced by an aeroplane is also out of all proportion to the material damage which it can inflict, which in itself is considerable, and the mere presence of a hostile machine above them inspires those on the ground with exaggerated forebodings of what it is capable of doing. On the other hand, the moral effect on our own troops of aerial ascendancy is most marked, and the sight of numbers of our machines continually at work over the enemy has as good an effect as the presence of hostile machines above us has bad.

2. Similarity to Fighting on Land and Sea.

To seek out and destroy the enemy's forces must be the guiding principle of our tactics in the air, just as it is on land and at sea. The battle-ground must be of our own choosing and not of the enemy's, and victory in the fight, to be complete, must bring other important results in its train. These results can only be achieved by gaining and keeping the ascendancy in the air. The more complete the ascendancy, the more far reaching will be the results.

The struggle for superiority takes the form, as in other fighting, of a series of combats, and it is by the moral and material effect of success in such combats that ascendancy over the enemy is gained.

3. Necessity of Offensive Action.

Offensive tactics are essential in aerial fighting for the following reasons:

(1) To gain the ascendancy alluded to above.

(2) Because the field of action of aeroplanes is over and in rear of the hostile forces, and we must therefore attack in order to enable our machines to accomplish their missions and prevent those of the enemy from accomplishing theirs.

(3) Because the aeroplane is essentially a weapon of attack and not of defence. Fighting on land and sea takes place in two dimensions, but in the air, we have to reckon with all three. Manoeuvring room is therefore unlimited, and no number of aeroplanes acting on the defensive will prevent a determined pilot from reaching his objective.

4. Factors of Success.

The success of offensive tactics in the air depends on exactly the same factors as on land and sea. The principal of these are:

(1) A choice of objectives which will play on the enemy's fears and force him to act on the defensive,
(2) Surprise.
(3) The power of manoeuvre,
(4) Effective use of weapons.

5. Choice of Objectives.

An aerial offensive is conducted by means of:

1. Offensive patrols whose sole mission is to find and defeat the enemy's aeroplanes. The farther such patrols penetrate behind the hostile front the greater will be the moral effect of the success they gain, and the more they will interrupt the work of the enemy's machines, while enabling ours to accomplish their missions without interference.

2. By the attack with bombs and machine gun fire of the enemy's troops, transport, billets, railway stations, rolling stock and moving trains, ammunition dumps, &c. In this case, again, such raids may be

expected to produce their maximum effect when undertaken against distant objectives, since they may cause the enemy to withdraw artillery and aeroplanes from the front for the protection of the locality attacked. They are also, however, of great use on the immediate front in connexion with operations on the ground.

Every patrol or raid should therefore be sent out with a definite mission, the successful performance of which will not only help us to gain aerial ascendancy by the destruction of hostile aircraft, but will also either tend to induce the enemy to act on the defensive in the air, or further the course of operations on the ground.

6. Surprise.

Surprise has always been one of the most potent factors of success in war, and although it might at first sight appear that surprise is not possible in the air, in reality this is by no means the case. It must be remembered that the aeroplane is working in three dimensions, that the pilot's view must always be more or less obstructed by the wings and body of his machine, and that consequently it is often an easy matter for a single machine, or even a pair of machines to approach unseen, especially if between the hostile aeroplane and the sun. Fighting by single machines is, however, rapidly becoming the exception (see paras. 15 and 16), and surprise is more difficult of attainment by machines flying in formation.

Even when in view, however, surprise is possible to a pilot who is thoroughly at home in the air, and can place his machine by a steep dive, a sharp turn, or the like, in an unexpected position on the enemy's blind side or under his tail.

7. Power of Manoeuvre.

Individual skill in manoeuvre favours surprise as pointed out above. Individual and collective power of manoeuvre are essential if flying in formation is to be successful or even possible. They can only be obtained by constant practice.

The following points must always be borne in mind:

(1) Pilots and observers must know the fuel capacity of their machine, and its speed at all heights.

(2) The direction and strength of the wind must be studied before leaving the ground and during flight. This study is most important since wind limits the range of action, as machines when fighting are bound to drift down wind.

(3) To guard against surprise, direction must be varied frequently unless making for a definite point, and a good look out must always be kept in every direction.

(4) Every advantage must be taken of the natural conditions, such as clouds, sun, and haze, in order to achieve surprise.

(5) The types of hostile aeroplanes must be carefully studied, so that the performance and tactics of each, its blind side and the best way to attack it, can be worked out. Some machines have a machine-gun mounted to fire downwards and backwards through the bottom of the fuselage.

(6) Height means speed, since it is easier to overhaul a hostile machine on a dive. If a hostile machine seeks safety by diving, it is bound to flatten out eventually and may, therefore, be overtaken by a machine from above, if the latter dives in front of it. The hostile machine must be watched all the time in case it turns.

(7) The engine must always be kept well in hand in a dive. If it is allowed to choke the opportunity will be lost.

8. Effective Use of Weapons.

The offensive weapons in use in aeroplanes are machine and Lewis guns and bombs. Machine and Lewis guns in the air, as on the ground, are very powerful weapons of offence, owing to the volume of fire they are capable of producing. Their effective use in the air demands even more skill and practice than on the ground and is dependent on:

(1) Absolute familiarity with the mechanism of the gun so that jams can be rectified in the air.

(2) A high degree of skill in manipulation and accuracy in aim, both on the ground and in flight,

(3) Constant study of the conditions affecting their use in an aeroplane, and continual practice under those conditions. Skill and accuracy in bombing in the same way can only be acquired by continual practice and careful study of the conditions which govern the correct setting and use of bomb sights. Such practice is best obtained by the use of the camera obscura and must be carried out from varying altitudes up to 10,000 feet, from which height bombs will often have to be dropped on service.

Types of Fighting Machines

9. Existing Types.

The machines at present in use for offensive purposes may be divided into three main classes:

(1) Fighters (*a*) single-seater, (*b*) two-seater,
(2) Fighter reconnaissance,
(3) Bombers.

10. Fighters.

(*a*) Single-seaters are fast, easy to manoeuvre, good climbers, and capable of diving steeply on an adversary from a height.

Their armament consists of one or more machine-or Lewis guns, whose axis of fire is directed forward and in some types in a fixed position in relation to the path of the machine.

Single-seater fighters are essentially adapted for offensive action and surprise. In defence they are dependent on their handiness, speed, and power of manoeuvre. They have no advantage over an enemy single-seater as regards armament and are at a disadvantage in this respect when opposed to a two-seater, and, therefore, the moment they cease to attack are in a position of inferiority, and must break off the combat, temporarily at any rate, until they have regained a favourable position. On the other hand, provided they are superior in speed and climb to their adversary, they can attack superior numbers with impunity, since they can break off the combat at will, in case of necessity.

(*b*) Two-seater fighters have, in addition, a machine-gun for the observer, on a mounting designed to give as wide an arc of fire as possible, especially to the flanks and rear. Their front gun or guns remain, however, their principal armament.

The two-seater is superior in armament to the single-seater, since it is capable of all round fire, but is generally somewhat inferior in speed, climb, and power of manoeuvre. It has greater powers of sustaining a prolonged combat, being less vulnerable to attacks from flanks and rear, but as in the case of single-seaters its chief strength lies in attack.

11. Fighter Reconnaissance Machines.

The first duty of these machines is to gain information. They do not go out with intent to fight, but must be capable of doing so, since fighting will often be necessary to enable the required information to be obtained. Those at present in use are two-seaters, the pilot flying the machine and the observer carrying out the reconnaissance. They are seldom called upon to act alone, but fly in formation, one or more machines carrying out the reconnaissance, while the remainder act as escort on the same principle as an escort on the ground. That is to say, they do not seek an engagement, but fight if necessary to enable the reconnaissance machines to do their work. They approximate to the two-seater fighter type.

12. Bombing Machines.

Bombing machines may be single-seater or two-seater. Two-seaters are preferable, provided they can carry the necessary weight, as they can, in case of necessity, undertake their own protection even when loaded. Their requirements as regards armament are similar to those of fighter reconnaissance machines. Single-seaters usually require an escort.

Formation Flying

13. Evolution of Formation Flying.

The development of aerial fighting has shown that certain fundamental maxims which govern fighting on land and sea are equally applicable in the air. Among these are concentration, mutual co-operation and support, and a well organised system of command under which no individual has more than a limited number of units under his immediate control. The adoption of formation flying has followed as an inevitable result.

Any mission which has fighting for its object, or for the accomplishment of which fighting may normally be expected, must usually, therefore, be carried out by a number of machines, the number depending on the amount of opposition likely to be encountered.

Flying in formation is, therefore, necessary in the case of:

(1) Offensive patrols;

(2) Reconnaissances, including photography, and their escorts;

(3) Bomb raids and their escorts; and is the normal method of carrying out these duties.

14. Principles Common to all Formations.

The formations adopted vary in accordance with the mission and with the type of machine. Certain principles are, however, common to all formation flying.

(1) A leader must be appointed, and a sub-leader in case the leader has to leave the formation for any reason, *e.g.* engine trouble. The machines of leaders and sub-leaders must be clearly marked. Streamers attached to different parts of the machine are suitable.

(2) The leader cannot control efficiently more than a certain num-

ber of machines. If, therefore, this number is exceeded, the mission must be carried out by two formations acting in concert, but each with its own leader.

(3) An air rendezvous must be appointed, and the leader must see pilots and observers before leaving the ground and explain his intentions to them. Machines of each group (see following paragraphs) should leave the ground together and should arrive at the rendezvous in the correct formation of their group. When all machines have reached the rendezvous, the leader fires a signal light, indicating that formation is to be picked up at once. He should then fly straight for a short time, as slowly as possible, while his observer, if he has one, reports on the formation. If one or more machines are rather far behind, the leader should turn to the right or left, after he or his observer has given a signal that he is going to do so.

Thus, the machine behind will be enabled to cut a corner and close up. When the leader is satisfied with the formation, he fires a light signifying that he is ready to start. The actual signal to start can be given either by the leader or from the ground; in the latter case the officer on the ground, who is responsible for the despatch of the group, will also be responsible for deciding when the proper formation has been adopted. It is usually best for the signal to be given from the ground. The decision as to the suitability or otherwise of the weather conditions will rest with the leader of the formation. A suitable code of signals for formation flying is given in Appendix A. Signal lights must be fired upwards by the leader, otherwise machines in the rear may have difficulty in seeing them.

(4) Pilots must clearly understand how the formation is to re-form after a fight. Definite instructions by the leader on the point are essential. A rendezvous over a pre-arranged spot has been found suitable, in the case of a small area. In the case of a large area two or more spots may be previously designated, the rendezvous to take place over the nearest. It must be realised that prearrangements may be found unsuitable, and in every case each machine must rejoin the leader at the earliest possible moment. To rendezvous successfully after a fight needs continual practice,

(5) Formations must not open out under anti-aircraft gun-fire. It has been found by experience that fire is usually less effective against a well closed up group of machines than when directed on a single machine. To open out is to give the enemy the chance, for which he is waiting, of attacking the machines of the formation singly. N.B.

Experiments are being carried out with wireless telephones, lamps, Very's lights, &c., with a view to evolving a suitable system of signalling between machines in the air as an aid to formation flying. A code of signals which has been used successfully by the leader of two-seater formations is given in Appendix B.

15. Offensive Patrols.

The sole duty of offensive patrols is to drive down and destroy hostile aeroplanes, and they should not be given other missions to perform, such as reconnaissances, which will restrict their fighting activities. In the face of opposition of any strength, offensive patrols usually have to fly in formation in order to obtain the advantage of mutual support, but the formations adopted can be governed solely by the requirements of offensive fighting. Single-seater scouts, or even two-seaters, if superior in speed and climb to the great majority of the enemy's machines, may be able to patrol very successfully alone or in pairs, taking advantage of their power of manoeuvre and acting largely by surprise, but in the case of machines which do not enjoy any marked superiority formation flying is essential.

Fighting in the air, however, even when many machines are involved on each side, tends to resolve itself into a number of more or less independent combats, and it has been found advisable to organise a purely fighting formation accordingly. Such a formation can consist of six to nine machines, organised in groups of two or three machines each, every group having its own subleader, the senior of whom takes command of the formation. A deputy leader should also be designated, in case the leader falls out for any reason. As far as possible, the groups should be permanent organisations, in order that the pilots may acquire that mutual confidence and knowledge of each other's tactics and methods which is essential for successful fighting. It must be impressed on pilots that the group is the fighting unit and not the individual (see paragraph 16).

Normally a formation should consist of not more than three groups, and if greater strength is required, separate formations should be employed, acting independently, but in such a way as to be mutually supporting.

A fighting formation should consist of machines of one type, but single- and two-seater machines can be combined if of similar performance. A suitable flying formation with groups of three machines is in column of groups, with flank machines echeloned slightly back, the whole formation being in vertical echelon, the rear group being the highest, and consisting of two-seaters in the case of a mixed formation of machines of equal performance.

Fast single-seaters if combined with two-seaters should fly above them, circling so as to obtain a good view all round.

A similar flying formation in the case of groups of two machines is in line of groups, the two machines of each group flying one behind the other, the rear machine at a higher altitude. The flank groups should not be echeloned back, as in this position they will be unable to see the centre group.

Fighting Tactics

16. Offensive Tactics.

Fighting tactics vary with the type of machine, and with the powers and favourite methods of individual pilots.

(1) Single-seaters. Although as a principle single-seaters should not act alone, yet in many cases isolated scouts will be called upon to fight single-handed, *e.g.*, when a formation has become split up during a combat and a machine fails to rejoin its formation. Again, selected pilots on the fastest types of single-seaters may be usefully employed on a roving commission, which will enable them to make the greatest use of surprise tactics.

In every case the safety of an isolated scout lies in attack, by surprise if possible, approaching either from the direction of the sun, or from the enemy's blind side. When surprise is impossible, advantage must be taken of the handiness and manoeuvring power of the scout to prevent the enemy from taking careful aim by approaching him in a zigzag course, and never in a straight line, since a machine attacking in a straight line offers a comparatively easy target. When within about 100 yards the zigzag course must be abandoned, and the moment when the enemy is in the act of shifting his aim should if possible be chosen. He can then be attacked in a straight line with a burst of rapid fire, or it may be possible to place oneself below him and fire at him more or less vertically at almost point-blank range.

To open fire at long range is to give the advantage to the enemy, since it is necessary to fly straight to bring fire to bear, and an easy mark is thus offered.

When it is necessary to swerve to avoid a collision or to break off the combat temporarily to change a drum or rectify a jam, this should be done by a sudden turn or climb, care being taken subsequently to avoid flying straight or losing height. When ready, a favourable position must be regained by manoeuvre before renewing the attack.

If surprised in an unfavourable position it is by no means easy to shake off the adversary. If time permits it should be the invariable rule to turn and attack before he comes to close quarters. If, however, he succeeds in doing so the best chance lies in a side-slip, or a fall out of control. A turn will expose the broad side of the machine to his fire, while to dive straight away is to court disaster.

Surprise can often be attained by carefully watching the adversary, preferably from behind. An especially favourable opportunity for surprise occurs in the case of an hostile machine crossing our front on some special mission, for once the hostile observer has satisfied himself that the air is clear, he will give his principal attention to his work. The enemy will often choose cloudy weather for such missions, and this gives special chances of surprise to a skilful pilot, working with intelligence. In such weather it must be remembered that it is often of advantage to approach the hostile machine on his own level, when the planes form but a thin line which is difficult to see.

In the case of single-seaters acting in pairs or in groups of three, surprise will be more difficult, and success must be sought in close co-operation, and in boldness of attack. If the enemy is inferior in numbers an opportunity will occur for a converging attack by two machines against one; but the attacks must be simultaneous, so that the enemy cannot engage the machines singly.

Another method is to attack echeloned in height, the lower machine diving and attacking the enemy from behind, while the upper machine waits an opportunity to swoop down on him when he turns to engage the machine that attacked first. The latter method is preferable in the case of two single-seaters, since if both machines attack on the same level, they run the risk of being themselves surprised from above. For this reason, groups are, generally speaking, better composed of three machines than of two. An attack of equal numbers will usually resolve itself into a series of individual duels. In attacking superior numbers success lies in the destruction of the enemy's moral by excessive boldness.

Decoy tactics are sometimes successful. One or more machines attempt to draw the enemy on to attack, while others fly high above them, ready to surprise the enemy should he seize the apparent opportunity. Watch must be kept for similar tactics on the part of the enemy.

When fighting in formations of one or more groups, the fighting unit should be the group, each selecting its own objective and acting as described above. The groups will often become separated, but every effort should be made to retain cohesion within the groups, by fighting inwards towards the leader. If the enemy machines scatter, attention should be concentrated on those lagging behind; and, if they dive and are followed down, at least one group should remain at a height as a protection from surprise.

The dangerous quarter in the case of a formation of single-seaters is the rear, and care must always be taken to keep a constant watch behind and above.

Fighting in formation with single-seaters is a most difficult operation and demands constant study and practice, the highest degree of skill on the part of the individual pilots, mutual confidence between them, and intimate knowledge of each other's methods.

(2) Two-seaters. The principles of fighting in two-seaters are similar to the above, but in the actual combat they are able to rely more on their power of all round fire and less on quickness of manoeuvre. The fighting tactics adopted should, therefore, be such as to favour the development of fire.

The single-seater when no longer able to approach its adversary, temporarily loses all power of offence and has to manoeuvre to regain a favourable position. The two-seater, on the other hand, can develop fire from its rear gun, after passing its adversary or on the turn. This, however, only applies partially in the case of pusher types, whose fire power to the rear is comparatively feeble.

A two-seater like a single-seater must, however, never dive straight away from an adversary, as even though it can fire to the rear the advantage is all with the machine which is following.

Formations of two-seaters are less liable to surprise from the rear, since the observers of the rear machines can face in that direction and keep a constant look out. Mutual fire support is also easier in their case, in view of their all-round fire. They are, therefore, as already pointed out, better able to sustain a protracted battle. The essence of successful fighting in two-seaters lies in the closest co-operation between pilot and observer. They must study their fighting tactics together, and each must know what the other will do in every possible situation.

17. Reconnaissances.

In reconnaissance the whole object is to protect the reconnaissance machine or machines and enable them to complete their work. Opposition will usually take one of two forms. The enemy's scouts may employ guerilla tactics, hanging on the flanks and rear of the formation, ready to cut off stragglers, or attacking from several directions simultaneously; or else the formation may be attacked by a hostile formation. A suitable type of two-seater fighter reconnaissance machine will often be able to deal with either class of opposition without assistance. The machines must fly in close formation, keep off enemy scouts which employ guerilla tactics, by long-range fire, and be ready to attack a hostile formation if the enemy's opposition takes that form.

Reconnaissance formations, like fighting formations, can be organised in groups, each with its sub-leader, but as the object is to secure the safety of the reconnaissance machine, the whole formation must keep together and act as one.

If scouts are used in combination with two-seater machines on a reconnaissance, it is usually preferable to keep the two types of machines as distinct formations, each under a separate leader. The two-seaters act as described, and the scouts fly above them in such a position as to obtain the best view of them and the greatest freedom of manoeuvre in any direction. Their role is:

(1) To break up an opposing formation.
(2) To prevent the concentration of superior force on any part of the reconnaissance formation.
(3 To assist any machine which loses formation through engine or any other trouble.

A suitable formation in the case of six two-seater machines has been found to be two lines of three, the flankers in the front being slightly higher than the centre (reconnaissance) machine, and the three machines in rear slightly higher again. The intervals between the machines should not be more than 100 yards, and the distance of the rear rank from the front should be sufficient only to admit of a good view being obtained of the leading machines.

The pace must be slow, otherwise the rear machines are bound to straggle. Machines must therefore fly throttled down. Sharp turns by the leader also lead to straggling; a signal, therefore, should always be given before turning and a minute or two allowed, if possible, after giving the signal before the turn is commenced, in order to give the machines on the outer flank time to gain ground.

18. Bomb Raids.

A bomb raid in the air may be compared to a convoy on the ground, and similar measures are required for its protection, namely, an escort designed to act offensively and keep the enemy at a distance, and, in addition, an escort keeping with the raid for the local protection of bombing machines, should the enemy succeed in getting to close quarters.

The duty of the bombing machines is to get to their objective and to drop their bombs on it, and the duty of the escort is to enable them to do so, and only to fight in the execution of their duty. The bombing machines, like a convoy, must keep in close formation. Any tendency to straggle or to open out under anti-aircraft fire will render the task of the escort impossible. When near their objective the machines must get into a formation of line ahead in order to drop their bombs, but a rallying point must always be chosen beforehand where they will collect and resume flying formation as soon as their bombs have been released.

An escort to a bombing raid may be suitably composed of single-seater and two-seater fighters, the latter being disposed round the bombing machines so as to protect them, especially on the flanks and rear, while the single-seaters fly above the formation.

The single-seaters constitute the offensive portion of the escort, and can be reinforced, if necessary, by some of the two-seaters, but a portion of the latter must invariably remain with the bombing machines as local escort.

Bombing machines, two-seaters and single-seaters, will each require their own leader. The leader of the bombing machines should take command of the whole when flying as one formation.

The secret of success in bombing operations is the most careful prearrangement, so that everyone knows exactly what he has to do.

When a very large raid is contemplated, it will often be best to carry out the attack by two separate formations, since there is a limit to the number of machines which can be controlled efficiently by a single leader. Eight to ten bombing machines are normally the maximum.

The departures of the two formations from their respective rendezvous, if they are to make a single raid should be so arranged as to enable them to give one another mutual support in case of a heavy hostile attack. The rendezvous should not be too close together, ten to fifteen miles apart is a suitable distance. Departures from the rendezvous should be timed so that the first formation is leaving the objective as the second approaches, and the leaders should watch each other's signals. As soon as the bombing machines of the first formation have re-crossed the lines, their escort should turn back and assist the second formation, which is likely to bear the brunt of any hostile attack.

While the bombs are being dropped, the escort should circle round above the bombing machines, protecting them from attack from above and ready to dive on to any hostile machine that may interfere with them.

When bombs have to be dropped from a low altitude, as in the case of an attack on trains, a portion of the escort should be specially told off for the protection of the bombing machines.

The above is merely a suggested method of carrying out a raid on a fairly large scale. Raids will often be carried out by a single type of machine, some carrying bombs and others acting as escort, and the formation adopted will vary with the number and type of machine available, the distance of the objective, and the opposition expected. The principles in every case, however, remain the same.

Gunnery

19. Importance of Gunnery.

The first essential of successful fighting in the air is the highest possible degree of skill in flying the machine, the second is a thorough knowledge of the gun and proficiency in its use. The manipulation of a gun in the air, especially in single-seater machines, is a very much more difficult matter than on the ground. Changing drums, for instance, though simple on the ground is by no means easy when flying.

Every pilot and observer who is called upon to use a machine-gun must have such an intimate knowledge of its mechanism as to know instinctively what is wrong when a stoppage occurs, and, as far as the type of machine allows, must be able to rectify defects while flying. This demands constant study and practice both on the ground and in the air.

Aerial gunnery is complicated by the fact that both gun and target are moving at variable speeds and on variable courses. Accurate shooting on the ground from a fixed gun at a fixed target is the first step in training; subsequently constant practice on the ground both when stationary and when moving, at fixed and moving targets is essential. Finally, every opportunity must be taken of practice in the air under the conditions of a combat.

20. Use of Sights and Tracer Ammunition.

Except at point-blank range, it is essential to use the sights if accurate fire is to be obtained, and constant practice is needed with the sights provided. The aim can be checked with absolute accuracy by means of the gun camera, and combats in the air during which the camera is used, are a most valuable form of training.

Tracer ammunition is of considerable assistance but must be used in conjunction with the sights and not in place of them. Not more than one bullet in three should be a tracer, otherwise the trace tends to become obscured. Too much reliance must not be placed on tracer ammunition at anything beyond short range. The principle should be to trust to the tracer at short ranges, but at medium ranges to rely almost entirely on the sights.

21. Fire Tactics.

Opportunities in the air are almost invariably fleeting, and consequently the most must be made of them when they occur. Fire should therefore be reserved until a really favourable target is presented and should then be in rapid bursts. Fire should only be opened at ranges over 300 yards when the object is to prevent hostile machines coming to close quarters, as in the case of an escort to a reconnaissance machine and should not be opened at ranges over 500 yards under any circumstances. In offensive fighting the longer fire can be reserved and the shorter the range, the greater the probability of decisive result.

For an observer in a two-seater machine, however, a range of from 200 to 300 yards is suitable, since it enables full advantage to be taken of the sight. Fire may be opened at longer range when meeting a hostile machine than when overhauling it, otherwise there will be no time to get in more than a very few rounds owing to the speed with which the machines are approaching one another. Pilots and observers must accustom themselves to judging the range by the apparent size of the hostile aeroplane and the clearness with which its detail can be seen. This needs constant practice.

A reserve of ammunition should be kept for the return journey when fighting far over the lines.

Manoeuvre is an integral part of fire tactics, and every endeavour must be made to manoeuvre in such a way as to create favourable opportunities for one's own fire and deny such opportunities to the enemy.

Issued by the General Staff. March 1917.

		Code of Light Signals to be used in Formation Flying.
Colour.	*Fired by.*	*Indicates.*
Red	Leader in conjunction with K strips and red light from ground.	Leave the rendezvous. Leader fires a light to indicate he is ready to leave the rendezvous. The formation leaves on this signal or awaits an order from the ground consisting of a K and a red light.
White.	Leader or from the ground in conjunction with N in strips.	Return to your aerodrome. Expedition abandoned. This signal applies E. or W. of the line. If fired E. of the line it also indicates 'Keep formation till line is crossed'.
Red.	Any member of formation.	'I am being attacked and need assistance.'
Red.	Leader.	Rally to continue operation—(attack having been dispersed).
Green.	Any member of expedition (including leader).	'I am forced to return to my aerodrome.' This signal if fired by the leader does not imply that the expedition is abandoned. The leadership must be taken up by the deputy leader.

Appendix B

Lamp Signals for Use of Leader of Two-Seater Formations

The following code letters are painted on the machine where visible to the observer and within reach of the pilot's hand. When the leader wishes to give an order, he places his finger on the letters required, which the observer then sends to the machines concerned with the lamp. The order can be acknowledged by the lamp or by a 'waggle' of the machine if lamps are not carried. Single-seaters working with two-seaters can take such messages.

Code

(A) When working as an escort on raids:
T T T T . . . Means throttle back and hang back.
E E E E . . . Means open throttle and close up.

(B) When working as a single group, from group leader to his two machines:
N N N N . . . Bunch—close up.
A A A A . . . Scatter—open out.

(C) When working as an offensive patrol of two groups, from patrol leader to group leader of rear group:
1. SR SR SR . . . Swing round to the right.
2. SQ SQ SQ . . . Swing round to the left.
3. GN GN GN . . . Groups bunch.

Note.—Signals 1 and 2 are used when it is required to separate the two groups for interception.
Signal 3 to collect the groups into one patrol.

APPENDIX XII

ORDER OF BATTLE OF THE ROYAL FLYING CORPS ON 9th APRIL 1917 (ARRAS)

General Officer Commanding: Major-General H. M. Trenchard, C.B., D.S.O., A.D.C.

ST. ANDRÉ-AUX-BOIS.

Ninth Head-quarters Wing.
(Lieut.-Col. C. L. N. Newall.)

FIENVILLERS.

No. 19 Squadron.	*No. 27 Squadron.*	*No. 55 Squadron.*	*No. 56 Squadron.*[2]	*No. 57 Squadron.*	*No. 66 Squadron.*	*No. 70 Squadron.*
(Maj. H. D. Harvey-Kelly, D.S.O.)	(Maj. S. Smith, D.S.O.)	(Maj. J. E. A. Baldwin.)	(Maj. R. G. Blomfield.)	(Maj. L. A. Pattinson, M.C.)	(Maj. O. T. Boyd, M.C.)	(Maj. A. W. Tedder.)
VERT GALAND.	FIENVILLERS.	FIENVILLERS.	VERT GALAND.	FIENVILLERS.	VERT GALAND.	FIENVILLERS.
18 Spads.[2]	18 Martinsyde Scouts.[1]	18 D.H.4's.[1]	13 S.E.5's.	19 F.E.2d's.	18 Sopwith 'Pups'.	18 Sopwith 2-seaters.

[1] Establishment figures. It is impossible, for these squadrons, to give the actual numbers of aeroplanes on charge.

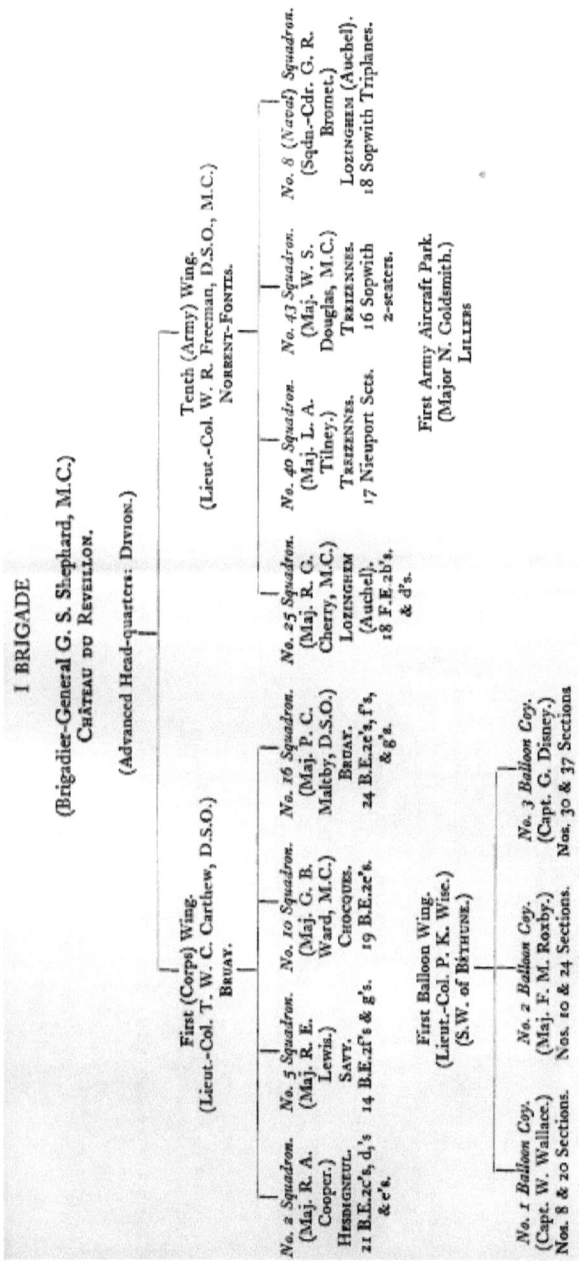

I BRIGADE

(Brigadier-General G. S. Shephard, M.C.)
Château du Reveillon.

(Advanced Head-quarters: Divion.)

First (Corps) Wing.
(Lieut.-Col. T. W. C. Carthew, D.S.O.)
Bruay.

- *No. 2 Squadron.* (Maj. R. A. Cooper.) Hesdigneul. 21 B.E.2c's, d,'s & e's.
- *No. 5 Squadron.* (Maj. R. E. Lewis.) Savy. 14 B.E.2f's & g's.
- *No. 10 Squadron.* (Maj. G. B. Ward, M.C.) Chocques. 19 B.E.2e's.
- *No. 16 Squadron.* (Maj. P. C. Maltby, D.S.O.) Bruay. 24 B.E.2e's, f's, & g's.

Tenth (Army) Wing.
(Lieut.-Col. W. R. Freeman, D.S.O., M.C.)
Norrent-Fontes.

- *No. 25 Squadron.* (Maj. R. G. Cherry, M.C.) Lozinghem (Auchel). 18 F.E.2b's. & d's.
- *No. 40 Squadron.* (Maj. L. A. Tilney.) Treizennes. 17 Nieuport Scts.
- *No. 43 Squadron.* (Maj. W. S. Douglas, M.C.) Treizennes. 16 Sopwith 2-seaters.
- *No. 8 (Naval) Squadron.* (Sqdn.-Cdr. G. R. Bromet.) Lozinghem (Auchel). 18 Sopwith Triplanes.

First Balloon Wing.
(Lieut.-Col. P. K. Wise.)
(S.W. of Béthune.)

- *No. 1 Balloon Coy.* (Capt. W. Wallace.) Nos. 8 & 20 Sections.
- *No. 2 Balloon Coy.* (Maj. F. M. Roxby.) Nos. 10 & 24 Sections.
- *No. 3 Balloon Coy.* (Capt. G. Disney.) Nos. 30 & 37 Sections

First Army Aircraft Park.
(Major N. Goldsmith.)
Lillers

II BRIGADE

(Brigadier-General T. I. Webb-Bowen.)

(Oxelaere) Cassel.

Second (Corps) Wing.
(Lieut.-Col. C. F. de S. Murphy, D.S.O., M.C.)
Eecke.

- *No. 6 Sqdn.* (Maj. A. S. Barratt, M.C.) Abeele. R.E.8's. B.E.2d's. B.E.2e's (17).
- *No. 21 Sqdn.* (Maj. P. E. L. Gethin.) Droglandt. 15 R.E.8's.
- *No. 42 Sqdn.* (Maj. J. L. Kinnear, M.C.) Bailleul. B.E.2e's. R.E.8's (17).
- *No. 46 Sqdn.* (Maj. P. Babington, M.C.) Droglandt. 14 Nieuport 2-seaters.
- *No. 53 Sqdn.* (Maj. C. S. Wynne-Eyton.) Bailleul. 16 B.E.2e's

Eleventh (Army) Wing.
(Lieut.-Col. G. B. Stopford.
St. Sylvestre.

- *No. 1 Sqdn.* (Maj. G. C. St. P. de Dombasle.) Bailleul. 18 Nieuport Scts.
- *No. 20 Sqdn.* (Maj. W. H. C. Mansfield, D.S.O.) Boisdinghem. 18 F.E.2d's.
- *No. 41 Sqdn.* (Maj. J. H. A. Landon.) Abeele. 18 F.E.8's.
- *No. 45 Sqdn.* (Maj. W. R. Read, M.C.) St. Marie-Cappel. 16 Sopwith 2-seaters.

Second Balloon Wing.
(Lieut.-Col. W. F. MacNeece, D.S.O.)
Mont Rouge.

- *No. 5 Balloon Coy.* (Maj. C. H. Stringer.) Nos. 2 & 25 Sections.
- *No. 6 Balloon Coy.* (Capt. H. P. L. Higman.) Nos. 9 & 32 Sections.
- *No. 7 Balloon Coy.* (Capt. F. X. Russell.) No. 15 Section.
- *No. 8 Balloon Coy.* (Capt. H. M. Meyler, M.C.) No. 23 Section.

Second Army Aircraft Park.
(Major H. Lee.)
Hazebrouck.

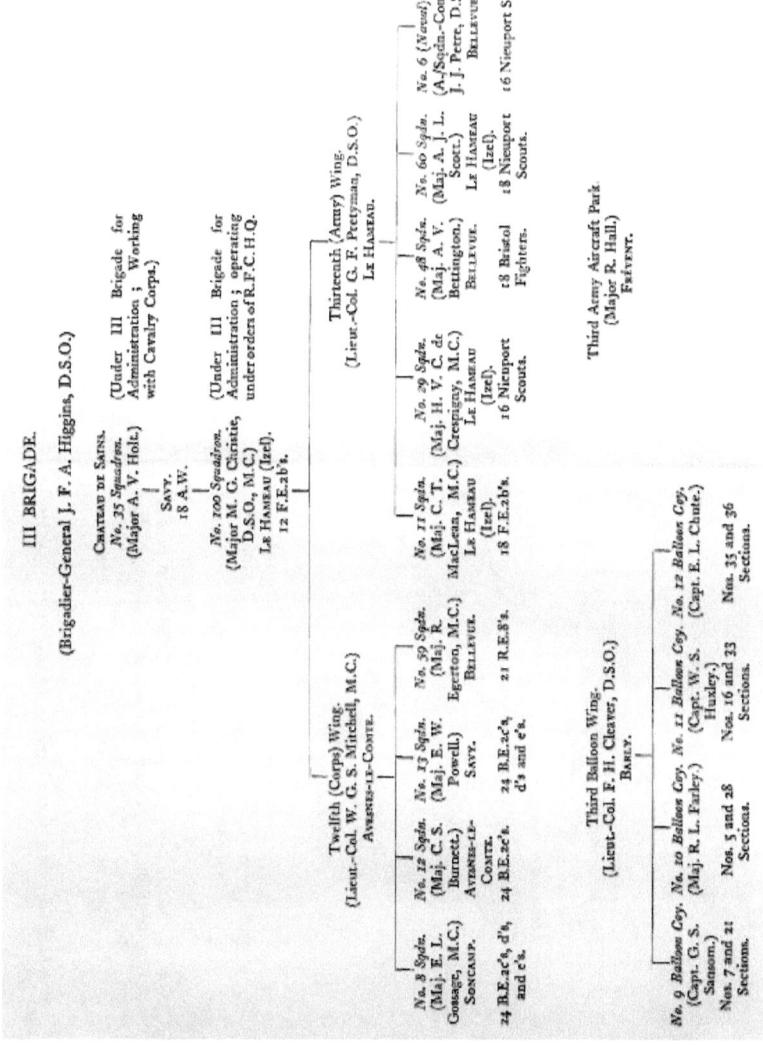

III BRIGADE.

(Brigadier-General J. F. A. Higgins, D.S.O.)

CHATEAU DE SAINS.

No. 35 Squadron. (Major A. V. Holt.) (Under III Brigade for Administration; Working with Cavalry Corps.)

SAVY.
18 A.W.

No. 100 Squadron. (Major M. G. Christie, D.S.O., M.C.) LE HAMEAU (Izel). 12 F.E.2b's. (Under III Brigade for Administration; operating under orders of R.F.C. H.Q.

Twelfth (Corps) Wing.
(Lieut.-Col. W. G. S. Mitchell, M.C.)
AVESNES-LE-COMTE.

- *No. 8 Sqdn.* (Maj. E. L. Gossage, M.C.) SONCAMP. 24 B.E.2c's, d's, and e's.
- *No. 12 Sqdn.* (Maj. C. S. Burnett.) AVESNES-LE-COMTE. 24 B.E.2e's.
- *No. 13 Sqdn.* (Maj. E. W. Powell.) SAVY. 24 B.E.2c's, d's and e's.
- *No. 59 Sqdn.* (Maj. R. Egerton, M.C.) BELLEVUE. 21 R.E.8's.

Thirteenth (Army) Wing.
(Lieut.-Col. G. F. Pretyman, D.S.O.)
LE HAMEAU.

- *No. 11 Sqdn.* (Maj. C. T. MacLean, M.C.) LE HAMEAU (Izel). 18 F.E.2b's.
- *No. 29 Sqdn.* (Maj. H. V. C. de Crespigny, M.C.) LE HAMEAU (Izel). 16 Nieuport Scouts.
- *No. 48 Sqdn.* (Maj. A. V. Bettington.) BELLEVUE. 18 Bristol Fighters.
- *No. 60 Sqdn.* (Maj. A. J. L. Scott.) LE HAMEAU (Izel). 18 Nieuport Scouts.
- *No. 6 (Naval) Sqdn.* (A./Sqdn.-Commr. J. J. Petre, D.S.C.) BELLEVUE. 16 Nieuport Scouts.

Third Balloon Wing.
(Lieut.-Col. F. H. Cleaver, D.S.O.)
BARLY.

- *No. 9 Balloon Coy.* (Capt. G. S. Sansom.) Nos. 7 and 21 Sections.
- *No. 10 Balloon Coy.* (Maj. R. L. Farley.) Nos. 5 and 28 Sections.
- *No. 11 Balloon Coy.* (Capt. W. S. Huxley.) Nos. 16 and 33 Sections.
- *No. 12 Balloon Coy.* (Capt. E. L. Chute.) Nos. 35 and 36 Sections.

Third Army Aircraft Park.
(Major R. Hall.)
FRÉVENT.

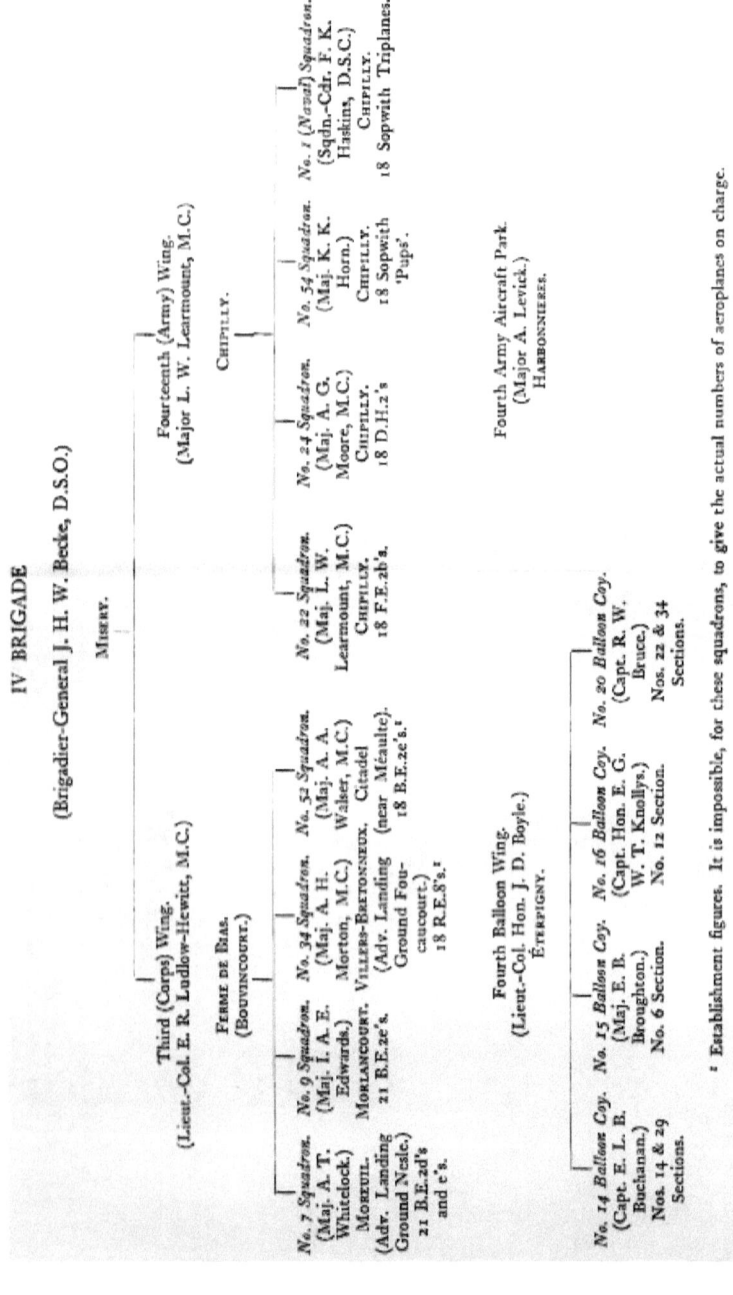

IV BRIGADE

(Brigadier-General J. H. W. Becke, D.S.O.)

MISERY.

Third (Corps) Wing.
(Lieut.-Col. E. R. Ludlow-Hewitt, M.C.)

FERME DE BIAS.
(BOUVINCOURT.)

No. 7 Squadron. (Maj. A. T. Whitelock.) MOREUIL. (Adv. Landing Ground Nesle.) 21 B.E.2d's and e's.

No. 9 Squadron. (Maj. I. A. E. Edwards.) MORLANCOURT. 21 B.E.2e's.

No. 34 Squadron. (Maj. A. H. Morton, M.C.) VILLERS-BRETONNEUX. (Adv. Landing Ground Foucaucourt.) 18 R.E.8's.[1]

No. 52 Squadron. (Maj. A. A. Walser, M.C.) Citadel (near Méaulte). 18 B.E.2e's.[1]

Fourteenth (Army) Wing.
(Major L. W. Learmount, M.C.)

CHIPILLY.

No. 22 Squadron. (Maj. L. W. Learmount, M.C.) CHIPILLY. 18 F.E.2b's.

No. 24 Squadron. (Maj. A. G. Moore, M.C.) CHIPILLY. 18 D.H.2's

No. 54 Squadron. (Maj. K. K. Horn.) CHIPILLY. 18 Sopwith 'Pups'.

No. 1 (Naval) Squadron. (Sqdn.-Cdr. F. K. Haskins, D.S.C.) CHIPILLY. 18 Sopwith Triplanes.

Fourth Balloon Wing.
(Lieut.-Col. Hon. J. D. Boyle.)
ÉTERPIGNY.

No. 14 Balloon Coy. (Capt. E. L. B. Buchanan.) Nos. 14 & 29 Sections.

No. 15 Balloon Coy. (Maj. E. B. Broughton.) No. 6 Section.

No. 16 Balloon Coy. (Capt. Hon. E. G. W. T. Knollys.) No. 12 Section.

No. 20 Balloon Coy. (Capt. R. W. Bruce.) Nos. 22 & 34 Sections.

Fourth Army Aircraft Park.
(Major A. Levick.)
HARBONNIERES.

[1] Establishment figures. It is impossible, for these squadrons, to give the actual numbers of aeroplanes on charge.

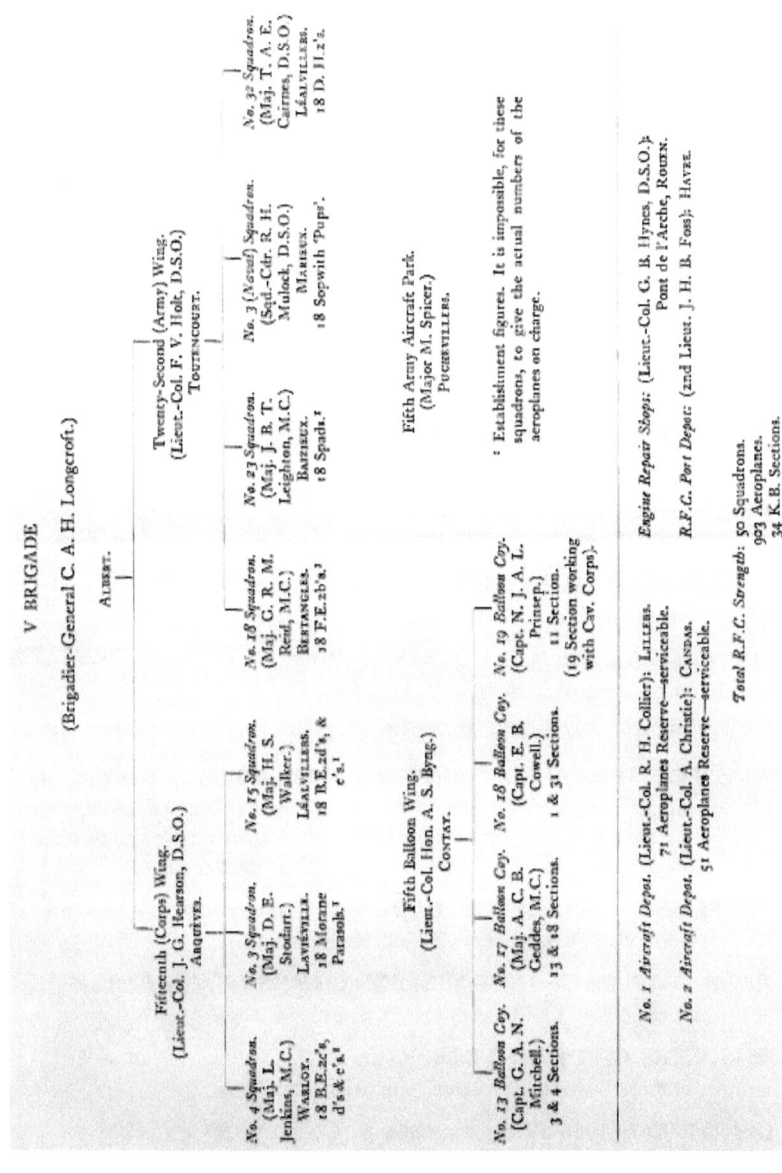

V BRIGADE

(Brigadier-General C. A. H. Longcroft.)

ALBERT.

Fifteenth (Corps) Wing.
(Lieut.-Col. J. G. Hearson, D.S.O.)
ANQUÈVES.

- *No. 4 Squadron.* (Maj. L. Jenkins, M.C.) WARLOY. 18 B.E.2c's, d's & e's.[1]
- *No. 3 Squadron.* (Maj. D. E. Stodart.) LAVIÉVILLE. 18 Morane Parasols.[1]
- *No. 15 Squadron.* (Maj. H. S. Walker.) LÉALVILLERS. 18 B.E.2d's, & e's.[1]

Twenty-Second (Army) Wing.
(Lieut.-Col. F. V. Holt, D.S.O.)
TOUTENCOURT.

- *No. 18 Squadron.* (Maj. G. R. M. Reid, M.C.) BERTANGLES. 18 F.E.2b's.[1]
- *No. 23 Squadron.* (Maj. J. B. T. Leighton, M.C.) BAIZIEUX. 18 Spads.[1]
- *No. 3 (Naval) Squadron.* (Sqd.-Cdr. R. H. Mulock, D.S.O.) MARIEUX. 18 Sopwith 'Pups'.
- *No. 32 Squadron.* (Maj. T. A. E. Cairnes, D.S.O.) LÉALVILLERS. 18 D. H.2's.

Fifth Balloon Wing.
(Lieut.-Col. Hon. A. S. Byng.)
CONTAY.

- *No. 13 Balloon Coy.* (Capt. G. A. N. Mitchell.) 3 & 4 Sections.
- *No. 17 Balloon Coy.* (Maj. A. C. B. Geddes, M.C.) 13 & 18 Sections.
- *No. 18 Balloon Coy.* (Capt. E. B. Cowell.) 1 & 31 Sections.
- *No. 19 Balloon Coy.* (Capt. N. J. A. L. Prinsep.) 11 Section. (19 Section working with Cav. Corps).

Fifth Army Aircraft Park.
(Major M. Spicer.)
PUCHEVILLERS.

[1] Establishment figures. It is impossible, for these squadrons, to give the actual numbers of the aeroplanes on charge.

No. 1 Aircraft Depot. (Lieut.-Col. R. H. Collier): LILLERS.
71 Aeroplanes Reserve—serviceable.

No. 2 Aircraft Depot. (Lieut.-Col. A. Christie): CANDAS.
51 Aeroplanes Reserve—serviceable.

Engine Repair Shops: (Lieut.-Col. G. B. Hynes, D.S.O.): Pont de l'Arche, ROUEN.

R.F.C. Port Depot: (2nd Lieut. J. H. B. Foss): HAVRE.

Total R.F.C. Strength: 50 Squadrons.
903 Aeroplanes.
34 K.B. Sections.

LEONAUR

ALSO FROM LEONAUR

AVAILABLE IN SOFTCOVER OR HARDCOVER WITH DUST JACKET

ESCAPE FROM THE FRENCH *by Edward Boys*—A Young Royal Navy Midshipman's Adventures During the Napoleonic War.

THE VOYAGE OF H.M.S. PANDORA *by Edward Edwards R. N. & George Hamilton, edited by Basil Thomson*—In Pursuit of the Mutineers of the Bounty in the South Seas—1790-1791.

MEDUSA *by J. B. Henry Savigny and Alexander Correard and Charlotte-Adélaïde Dard* —Narrative of a Voyage to Senegal in 1816 & The Sufferings of the Picard Family After the Shipwreck of the Medusa.

THE SEA WAR OF 1812 VOLUME 1 *by A. T. Mahan*—A History of the Maritime Conflict.

THE SEA WAR OF 1812 VOLUME 2 *by A. T. Mahan*—A History of the Maritime Conflict.

WETHERELL OF H. M. S. HUSSAR *by John Wetherell*—The Recollections of an Ordinary Seaman of the Royal Navy During the Napoleonic Wars.

THE NAVAL BRIGADE IN NATAL *by C. R. N. Burne*—With the Guns of H. M. S. Terrible & H. M. S. Tartar during the Boer War 1899-1900.

THE VOYAGE OF H. M. S. BOUNTY *by William Bligh*—The True Story of an 18th Century Voyage of Exploration and Mutiny.

SHIPWRECK! *by William Gilly*—The Royal Navy's Disasters at Sea 1793-1849.

KING'S CUTTERS AND SMUGGLERS: 1700-1855 *by E. Keble Chatterton*—A unique period of maritime history-from the beginning of the eighteenth to the middle of the nineteenth century when British seamen risked all to smuggle valuable goods from wool to tea and spirits from and to the Continent.

CONFEDERATE BLOCKADE RUNNER *by John Wilkinson*—The Personal Recollections of an Officer of the Confederate Navy.

NAVAL BATTLES OF THE NAPOLEONIC WARS *by W. H. Fitchett*—Cape St. Vincent, the Nile, Cadiz, Copenhagen, Trafalgar & Others.

PRISONERS OF THE RED DESERT *by R. S. Gwatkin-Williams*—The Adventures of the Crew of the Tara During the First World War.

U-BOAT WAR 1914-1918 *by James B. Connolly/Karl von Schenk*—Two Contrasting Accounts from Both Sides of the Conflict at Sea D uring the Great War.

AVAILABLE ONLINE AT **www.leonaur.com**
AND FROM ALL GOOD BOOK STORES

07/09

www.ingramcontent.com/pod-product-compliance
Lightning Source LLC
Chambersburg PA
CBHW021956160426
43197CB00007B/153
* 9 7 8 1 7 8 2 8 2 7 8 3 2 *